W9-BZW-756

Augsburg Commentary on the New Testament

LUKE

David L. Tiede

Augsburg Publishing House
Minneapolis, Minnesota

AUGSBURG COMMENTARY ON THE NEW TESTAMENT
Luke

Copyright © 1988 Augsburg Publishing House

All rights reserved. Except for brief quotations in critical articles or reviews, no part of this book may be reproduced in any manner without prior written permission from the publisher. Write to: Permissions, Augsburg Publishing House, 426 S. Fifth St., Box 1209, Minneapolis MN 55440.

Scripture quotations, unless otherwise noted or translated by the author directly from the Hebrew or Greek, are from the Revised Standard Version of the Bible, copyright 1946, 1952, and 1971 by the Division of Christian Education of the National Council of Churches.

Library of Congress Cataloging-in-Publication Data

Tiede, David Lenz.
    Luke / David L. Tiede.
       p.   cm. — (Augsburg commentary on the New Testament)
    Bibliography: p.
    ISBN 0-8066-8858-0
    1. Bible. N.T. Luke—Commentaries. I. Title. II. Series.
BS2595.3.T45 1988
226'.407—dc19   88-22292
                                                        CIP

Manufactured in the U.S.A.   APH 10-9016

     4   5   6   7   8   9   0   1   2   3   4   5   6   7   8   9

To my parents, Vivian and John Tiede,
with thanksgiving and love

CONTENTS

FOREWORD

The AUGSBURG COMMENTARY ON THE NEW TESTA-
MENT is written for laypeople, students, and pastors. Laypeople
will use it as a resource for Bible study at home and at church.
Students and instructors will read it to probe the basic message
of the books of the New Testament. And pastors will find it to
be a valuable aid for sermon and lesson preparation.

The plan for each commentary is designed to enhance its usefulness. The Introduction presents a topical overview of the biblical book to be discussed and provides information on the historical circumstances in which that book was written. It also
contains a summary of the biblical writer's thought. In the body
of the commentary, the interpreter sets forth in brief compass
the meaning of the biblical text. The procedure is to explain the
text section by section. Attempts have been made to avoid scholarly jargon and the heavy use of technical terms. Because the
readers of the commentary will have their Bibles at hand, the
biblical text itself has not been printed out. In general, the editors
recommend the use of the Revised Standard Version of the Bible.

The authors of this commentary series are professors at sem-
inaries and universities and are themselves ordained. They have
been selected both because of their expertise and because they
worship in the same congregations as the people for whom they

are writing. In elucidating the text of Scripture, therefore, they attest to their belief that central to the faith and life of the church of God is the Word of God.

The Editorial Committee
Roy A. Harrisville
Luther Northwestern Theological Seminary
St. Paul, Minnesota

Jack Dean Kingsbury
Union Theological Seminary
Richmond, Virginia

Gerhard A. Krodel
Lutheran Theological Seminary
Gettysburg, Pennsylvania

ACKNOWLEDGMENTS

I acknowledge with gratitude the debt which this volume represents to several sources. The Board of Directors at Luther Northwestern Theological Seminary approved and funded the sabbatical leave which made the final writing possible. The Aid Association for Lutherans awarded the Fredrik Schiotz Fellowship and the Association of Theological Schools granted an Award for Theological Scholarship and Research. These grants made it possible to complete this manuscript while researching an additional writing project. The dean, faculty, and students at Yale Divinity School were my gracious hosts while I was a visiting professor on that 1986–1987 leave. My students and friends who have pored over Luke's narrative with me for the past 15 years have contributed more than I would dare admit, and my family has again endured my preoccupation. Thank you all!

ABBREVIATIONS

ANQ	*Andover Newton Quarterly*
Ant.	Josephus, *Antiquities of the Jews*
BTB	*Biblical Theology Bulletin*
BWANT	Beiträge zur Wissenschaft vom Alten und Neuen Testament
BZNW	Beiheft zur ZNW
CBQ	*Catholic Biblical Quarterly*
ET	*Expository Times*
HTR	*Harvard Theological Review*
Interp.	*Interpretation*
JAAR	*Journal of the American Academy of Religion*
JBL	*Journal of Biblical Literature*
JJS	*Journal of Jewish Studies*
JSNT	*Journal for the Study of the New Testament*
JThS	*Journal of Theological Studies*
KJV	King James Version of the Bible
LXX	Septuagint (the Greek Old Testament)
MT	Masoretic text (Hebrew) of the Old Testament
NovTest	*Novum Testamentum*
NTS	*New Testament Studies*
Q	Non-Markan material common to Matthew and Luke
RB	*Revue Biblique*
RSV	Revised Standard Version of the Bible
RTR	*Reformed Theological Review*
SBL	Society of Biblical Literature
SBLDS	SBL Dissertation Series
SBLMS	SBL Monograph Series

SBT	Studies in Biblical Theology
SJTh	*Scottish Journal of Theology*
SNTS	Society of New Testament Studies
SNTSMS	SNTS Monograph Series
StANT	Studien zum Alten und Neuen Testament
ThSt	*Theological Studies*
ZNW	*Zeitschrift für die neutestamentlichen Wissenschaft*

INTRODUCTION

1. The Problems of "Introductions"

Luke's story of Jesus is a straightforward narrative. It has a beginning, middle, and end, and the book of Acts is its natural sequel. The unlearned reader and the most sophisticated critic both may appreciate the profound simplicity of this story, perhaps even as they read it together. All commentary and introduction should assist this reading. The clarity and depth of the narrative testimony must be enhanced and not obscured by "introductions."

Modern notions of "authorship" and "history" have interfered significantly with the way Luke is read. The traditional questions of introduction require a kind of information which the narrative simply does not supply. "Who?" "What?" "Why?" "Where?" and "When?" are worthy questions. It is possible to pursue such questions by means of historical research, but the results are thoroughly disputed. This narrative remains an anonymous ancient document of uncertain origin. Some general statements about its probable origin may be made with greater confidence (see below), but decisive answers to these introductory questions remain elusive. Modern interpreters often find that situation quite frustrating.

These are questions which are commonly explored in some detail in evaluating the work of a modern author or artist. They are often answered in personal or psychological terms, relating aspects of an author's work with significant experiences. "This book was written shortly after his wife's death." "This fugue displays the confidence of the young Bach." "Picasso's *Guernica* is a protest against the mindless violence of the Spanish civil war!" Modern sensitivity to individual differences have intensified the introductory questions as quests for the author.

This problem is compounded by the disputed reliability of traditional identifications of who wrote "Luke's" narrative, as well as where, when, and why. While the narrative never identifies the author by name or personal history, traditions dated from the late second and early third century (Irenaeus, *Against Heresies* 3.1.13, and Tertullian, *Against Marcion* 4.2) linked this book and Acts with the name of Luke who accompanied Paul on portions of his travels. It is not impossible that this "beloved physician" (Col. 4:14) and Paul's "fellow worker" (Philemon 24, see also 2 Tim. 4:11) was the author of this narrative, but even then almost nothing is known about this person. Instead of our indulging in speculation, it is crucial for us to remember that both "Luke" and "Acts" are anonymous narratives, as are all of the Gospels. They make no claim with regard to their authorship nor do they identify any of the authors. The documents themselves must bear the weight of interpretation, and the author they indirectly reveal is the only author worth discussing.

This implied author poses intriguing historical challenges for those who regard the author's personal identity as central to the meaning of the texts. Do the passages in Acts which speak in the first person plural ("we") reflect historical memories of traveling companions? Does this mean that one of Paul's companions wrote Acts (and Luke), or did the author perhaps have access to travel journals from them? Or does "we came to Rome" at the end of the narrative in Acts (28:16) include the travelers, the author, and the reader who have sojourned together in the story? Then the "us" among whom these "things which have been accomplished" (1:1-4) would be all the Christians whose testimony is borne in the narrative. Perhaps the author is also reminiscing about personal experiences, but nowhere does the author make such direct claims. Instead the "eyewitnesses and servants of the word" (see the commentary on the prolog, 1:1-4, below) appear to be someone other than "us." Interpretations which insist on a strict historical identification of the author as a companion of Paul appear to be intent on deriving something from the narrative which the author did not provide.

Many "introductions" to Luke invest heavily in proving or disproving the author's identity as Paul's companion, the "beloved physician." In Col. 4:10-17, Luke's name is included among several in the closing greetings. There the distinction between Paul's "fellow workers" who are "of the circumcision" and those who are not appears to identify Luke as a Gentile, or non-Jew. In popular interpretation, this approach has led to a romanticized portrait of the "beloved physician" according to which his version of the gospel is filled with the pathos of a caring man of science, and his story freed from the legalism of Judaism. Reports that in the second century Marcion preferred Luke as less Judaistic have enhanced this view. Even those interpretations which find the historical identification of the author as Paul's companion unlikely often indulge in a careless identification of this author as a "Hellenist" whose cultural status and respect for the Roman order set him apart from first-century Jewish "messianic" hopes. The result has often been thoroughly anti-Semitic readings of the narrative on both a popular and academic level.

Thus even if this author was the "Luke" whom Paul called his fellow worker, and even if he was a "physician" or even a "beloved physician," most of what is written about him as a person is mere speculation. Some technical studies were made within the last century about what "physicians" knew or how they were trained in the Greco-Roman world. Those studies neither prove nor disprove the identity of this author, but they challenge all sentimental attempts to project portraits of a beloved health-care professional onto the past. Luke's vocabulary is only that of a "physician" insofar as all educated persons in antiquity were trained in rhetoric. His words, phrases, and literary methods display a kind of skill that reflects education, but it is not particularly that of medical practice.

Even if this author was "of the uncircumcision," and that is far from clear, most of the descriptions of what was or was not "Jewish" have been written from the point of view of later Christianity.

Before long, almost all Christian readers were non-Jews, or Gentiles, and "the Jews" became "them," or someone else. In Luke-Acts, however, the divisions among Jewish groups are such that some believe and others doubt the proclamation of Jesus as the Messiah. The "Jewish" identity of this author is that of someone who claims Jesus to be the fulfillment of God's promises to Israel. Even as the mission to the Gentiles proceeds forward after Acts 10, it is always a mission conducted by Jewish Christians, and in town after town they begin in the Jewish synagogue. Among the Jewish Christians themselves, significant disagreement existed on the continuing necessity of circumcision (see Acts 15:1-2), and Luke is the author who depicts Paul as continuing to observe circumcision for Jews, that is, Jewish Christians (Acts 16:1-3; 21:20-24).

Many interpreters of Paul have argued that Luke's view is still too closely linked with traditional Jewish piety of observance of the Law. They challenge the historical accuracy of the report in Acts 16:1-3 that Paul circumcised Timothy, citing Paul's apparent refusal to circumcise Titus (Gal. 2:3). They suggest that Luke represents the practical compromise between the views of Peter and the views of Paul as they conflict in Galatians 1–2, and some have argued that this is the kind of churchly solution which allows consensus but which largely misses the principles at stake for Paul. The larger point which must not be missed, however, is that Paul, Peter, and the author of Luke-Acts are all caught up in the question of Christian observance of the Law of Moses. Peter and Paul were unquestionably Jewish, although they did not immediately agree on whether Christian Jews or Gentiles should practice circumcision. The author of Luke-Acts is more intent than Paul on Christian observance of the Law while agreeing that Gentile Christians need not be circumcised (Acts 15–16; 21:17-26).

Then was this "Luke" a Jewish Christian or a Gentile who sought continuity with the faith of Israel? Certainly he was not a "Jew" by the standards of some Judean religious leaders, but neither was Paul, who was an apostate in their eyes. Just as certainly, he was not a Gentile who was indifferent to Jewish ritual and practice. Perhaps he was a proselyte, a convert to the faith of Israel, converted either before he was a believer in Jesus or after. He clearly believed that faith in Jesus as the Messiah and Lord was the culmination of Israel's scriptural faith. Perhaps his persistent effort to anchor his Christian testimony in the Scriptures was natural to one who was at home in the scriptural studies of the Hellenistic Jewish synagogues. Or perhaps this was a studied enterprise of a convert who was the more eager to lay claim to Israel's heritage. Perhaps.

Introductions which begin with a firm position on all of these possibilities then turn the interpretation of the text into a sustained historical argument. This is the most critical problem of "introductions." These interpreters may proceed naively, simply assuming that Luke was the Gentile physician and emphasizing Luke's bond with Paul. Such approaches are seldom troubled by the thoroughly Jewish character of the narrative or by the fact that Acts makes no reference to any of Paul's letters or even that he wrote letters. They also are largely innocent of the questions that arise when historical details in Luke are compared with Mark and Matthew, or when Acts' description of Paul is compared with Paul's letters. The more complex questions of Luke's theology, such as his distinctive interpretation of Jesus' death, are absorbed in general Christian piety.

More informed introductions are sharply aware of these problems. They may deliberate the historical uncertainties with care as matters of introduction, but often their conclusions on the introductory issues remain unexamined in the rest of the discussion. No commentary on the text (including this one) can escape reading the narrative in the light of convictions about the character of the narrative and the identity of the author. Yet the commentary must be constantly aware of how tentative the conclusions on introductory issues are. The text itself must be the standard and court of appeal for historical estimations, since no decisive external testimony exists.

The last century of interpretation of Luke and Acts has also been rich in its discussion of the kind of history and theology which Luke's narrative conveys. But these introductions may also mislead the reader to focus on a particular historical or theological problem which preoccupies the modern interpreter. The validity of a commentary must still be measured by its engagement with the text rather than its exposition of the commentator's historical assumptions or theological position.

Since the author wrote his own "prolog" or "introduction" to the narrative, this commentary will engage several of the classic questions of introduction in conversation with the author's words (see Luke 1:1-4). That section will be more extensive than the usual commentary on verses, and it will reveal the commentator's grasp of the introductory historical and theological issues. But those comments will still strive primarily to illumine the author's testimony, so that those stated purposes may control the reading of the narrative as a whole.

2. Luke as Historian and Theologian

This is not the place for an elaborate discussion of the modern history of interpretation of Luke and Acts (see bibliography), but a few remarks on that history may provide some context for the approach that will be taken in this commentary. They may also help explain why caution is being advised against adamant arguments on questions of introduction where the historical uncertainties are high. In brief, the last century and a half of critical studies have reunited Luke and Acts as one narrative which was long rent asunder by the canonical arrangement which set the Gospel of John between them. The problems of the historicity of Acts and of Luke have been closely tied with assessments of the theology of Luke-Acts, and at least three extended phases of that discussion have marked the subsequent interpretation.

The first is associated with the work of F. C. Baur in the 1830s in Germany. This work was actually part of an extended discussion in the 19th century about the character of historiography and history. Acts was the focus of the conversation, in close comparison with Paul's letters, and questions of historical accuracy were debated at length. Yet the focus was on Luke as an interpreter of history, rather than as a recorder. The theological question was opened in the form of the "theological tendency" or even the "tendentious" character of all historical narration. Sharp contrasts were drawn between Acts and Paul in order to heighten the sense of the theological development of early Christianity. Such development was seen to proceed from the tension between the Pauline and the Petrine schools to a resolution in early catholic tradition, perhaps as early as Acts.

But how early was that? Mid-second century? Late first century? And how early were Luke's sources? Could they be isolated and identified? And what was their theological tendency? The problems of the literary complexity of Luke's narrative were projected on the screen of an elaborate hypothesis of stages of theological development. The bias against the "legalism," "nationalism," and "materialism" of "Judaism" also marred this hypothesis, enforcing the view that Christian history was a sequel to or displacement of Jewish history. In the retrospect of current studies, the simplistic depiction of first-century Judaism was both a historical and theological failing. Yet this discussion has had continuing impact on views of Luke and the Jews among both Luke's critics and advocates.

The second phase of the discussion related more directly to the Gospel according to Luke. At first, it was part of the extended discussion of the reliability of the Gospels in reconstructing the teachings and ministry of the historical Jesus. In the late 19th century, scholars who were more disposed to the historical reliability of Acts also turned to Luke as a competent "historical" presentation. Especially in England, this approach moved from W. M. Ramsay's early studies of the correlation of Luke and Acts with Roman history to Vincent Taylor's discussion of the sources of Luke to the present work of C. K. Barrett and I. H. Marshall. This discussion was far from uniform, but it was generally marked with a concern to demonstrate the historical probability of features which others had treated as ideological fictions. It was greatly enriched by the literary and historiographic discussions of H. J. Cadbury and M. Dibelius in the years 1920–1950 in the United States and Germany. Then what kind of literature is Luke's narrative? Is "the truth concerning the things of which you have been informed" (Luke 1:4) a matter of precise correspondence to actual events or is this an "assurance" about God's faithfulness? And what is the connection for Luke between these kinds of "truth"?

After the Second World War, the students of Rudolf Bultmann turned their hands to the Gospel according to Luke and the Acts, inaugurating the third phase of this conversation. Hans Conzelmann's study, *The Theology of St. Luke*, is the most comprehensive summary of this approach, but many others contributed. Ernst Haenchen's commentary on *The Acts of the Apostles* must also be mentioned. Here Luke is described as a theologian of history with more stress again placed on the theological understanding of Christian history than on its verifiability.

According to this school, Luke's view of history may be generally labeled "salvation history." The phases of history move from the time of "the law and the prophets . . . until John," to the time of Jesus' preaching of the kingdom (Luke 16:16), to the time of the Holy Spirit's work in the church. Christian history is a progressive story, dangerously similar to the triumphalism of other imperial histories. The plane of history has become the arena where Judaism is surpassed as the truth of the Christian story is made manifest. In contrast to the theology of the cross in Paul and the Gospel according to Mark, Luke has written a kind of "theology of glory." Even Jesus' death is more explained as a martyrdom of a righteous one than proclaimed as God's judgment and salvation for a sinful world.

This assessment of Luke's project was compelling for its methodological validity and its theological coherence. It did not endear Luke's narrative to any except the most triumphalist Christian traditions. For those who were suspicious of current secular theologies of history of "the thousand years of the Third Reich," "the manifest destiny" of the United States, or "the inevitable rise of the proletariat," Luke's interpretation of history was also under question. Some suggested it be removed from the canon. Clearly, from the time of Eusebius and Constantine Luke had generally been read as just such a story of Christian triumph at the expense of Judaism. But was this reading true to the character of the narrative or was it the result of reading the story in an altered cultural setting?

Subsequent studies of Luke and Acts have been compelled to come to terms with each of these three phases of the modern discussion. Fresh assessments have been made of (a) Luke's literary skill and style, (b) Luke's usage of the Scriptures to verify the truth of the narrative, and (c) the complexity of Luke's picture of the varieties of Jewish groups and their relationships to the followers of Jesus. The discussion of Luke and the Jews has been particularly productive because of the wealth of recent historical, archeological, and literary research on first-century or second-temple Judaism. Whether the author himself was a circumcised Jewish Christian or a Gentile who laid claim to the Law and the Prophets may never be determined, but this narrative must be interpreted from within the struggles of the faithful in Israel. As history and theology, Luke's narrative testifies to Jesus as the fulfillment of God's promises to Israel.

3. An Introduction to This Commentary

This commentary commends a reading of Luke's story of Jesus which highlights at least three aspects of the narrative. Many other features of the text will also require attention in order to explain specific details and to make comparisons with other writings. Yet, as the comments on the prolog (1:1-4) will indicate, these three dimensions of this book appear to be prominent in Luke's own conception of the work.

1. Luke's "Gospel" is a narrative. It is to be assessed and interpreted as a literary project. It has a beginning (Chaps. 1–2), middle (Chaps. 3–21), and end (Chaps. 22–24) as a good story does. It can be outlined into major sections, and it possesses a sense of "plot" or development. This is not the plot of a modern novel in which the central characters undergo psychological development or change, but it is the story of the interaction between God's reign and plan as deployed in Jesus and the determined will of humanity which resists, accepts, and betrays God's Messiah.

As a literary document, Luke's narrative displays characteristics which are common to ancient gospels, histories, biographies, and "testimonies" to the truth. These comparisons will be made to help illumine Luke's use of literary conventions and distinctive emphases. Luke's acknowledgment of other sources for the story of Jesus (1:1) also invites efforts to identify the relationships between this narrative and other early Christian sources.

This commentary will follow the "two source" hypothesis in which Luke is credited with access to a version of Mark's Gospel and to a collection of sayings which it shares with Matthew, generally called "Q." It is probable that Luke had access to other written and oral traditions. Some of them may have been extensive. It is even possible that the narrative of Luke which we now possess was produced from an earlier narrative (often called "proto-Luke") which was later combined with Mark. But efforts to reconstruct such sources and stages of the development of the narrative have not proved convincing or especially helpful. Thus, questions of sources will not be pursued in order to reconstruct the history of the synoptic tradition nor to resolve issues of the historical accuracy of Luke's account of Jesus. Nor will a possible earlier stage of Luke be posited with which our narrative may be compared. Instead, source questions will be discussed as they contribute to assessing Luke's literary methods and purposes. For example, what scriptural or Christian literature was Luke using in a particular section? How did the evangelist adapt it to his purposes? The goal of the source discussion is the interpretation of the text of Luke's narrative itself.

2. Luke's narrative is a scriptural commentary. The Scriptures it interprets are the Scriptures of Israel. The words "midrash" and "hermeneutical project" could also be used if the narrow Rabbinic or modern connotations of those terms are not too precisely observed. But the infancy stories (Chaps. 1–2), the resurrection appearances (Chap. 24), and the speeches in Acts supply much better terms concerning the "fulfillment" of Scriptures in the story of Jesus and the early Christian movement. In large measure, the "truth" or "assurance" of Luke's entire testimony rests upon its scriptural exposition, even when specific texts are not mentioned in particular stories or explicit claims are not being made. Luke declares that in Jesus, the scriptural will, plan, and reign of God is fulfilled in promise and judgment.

This declaration may prove difficult for modern sensibilities, where the "truth" or "assurance" of the testimony rests much

more directly on rational verifiability. This commentary is con-
servative in the sense that it does not assume that "interpreted
history" must be fictional. Luke does take strong initiatives, as
do other early Christian authors, in giving stories scriptural coloring. He even introduces details which are, for example, more
likely derived from the psalms than from a strictly objective version of Jesus' death. Luke does not provide a mere factual account
of an execution as if that were what truly happened in the eyes
of all present. The facts and memories are refracted through the
lens of the Scriptures so that what truly happened in the presence
and plan of God may be illumined.

Yet the data of historical memory is conserved. Ancient historians knew the difference between mere fiction and actual
events. But the meaning and truth of events were never fully
verifiable. Luke's sense is strong that something was happening
which few if any eyewitnesses could understand. In the light of
Easter, the risen Messiah himself initiated a process of recall and
reinterpretation of what truly happened. It would take "all the
scriptures" to interpret "the things concerning himself" (24:27).

3. The truth to which Luke bears witness is ultimately the
truth about God. All theological histories are finally a kind of
"theodicy," justifying the ways of God in human affairs. Modern
nontheistic history may insist that the proper subject of history
is demonstrable facts or the conflicts of ideas or the development
of social and economic forces. Each of these concepts seeks to
render human experience sensible according to prevailing convictions of the substructures of reality. Part of the reason why
Luke's views of truth and history seem alien to the modern reader
lies anchored in the evangelist's profound theological convictions.
God's will and agency are at work in human history. The question
for Luke and for those who read the Scriptures of Israel in that
era was not whether God was a power with which to reckon. The
question was rather, "Where and how does God accomplish judgment and salvation?"

Luke's testimony is to Jesus the Messiah and Lord as God's way
of ruling the world, God's will at work in the world. None of the
promises which God made to Israel of restoration, redemption,
salvation, and kingdom will fail—at least God will not fail in these

promises. But what happens when the Messiah's death and resurrection have become memories in a time when the Gentiles appear to triumph (21:24)? Is a testimony to God's triumph in Jesus a "theology of glory" if it is written at a time when "the kings of the Gentiles lord it over them" (22:25 NIV). What has become of the kingdom of God and God's righteous rule in history when those who are Jesus' followers appear to be called to suffer (see Acts 9:16)? Here is where the urgency and validity of Luke's testimony emerges, probably in the midst of the difficult situation of Luke's Christian community in the last third of the first century (see the comments on Luke 1:1-4). This is not an abstract theodicy, wrought at the expense of others. This is a word of assurance and consolation, declaring the ultimate lordship of Jesus the Messiah in the midst of difficult times.

OUTLINE OF LUKE

THE BEGINNING: SETTING THE STAGE (Chapters 1–2)

I.   The Prolog (1:1-4)

II. The Visitation of the Lord God of Israel (1:5—2:52)

"Blessed be the Lord God of Israel for he has visited and redeemed his people."   (Luke 1:68)

   A. Annunciations (1:5-56)
      1. Of John (1:5-25)
      2. Of Jesus (1:26-38)
      3. The Blessing of Their Mothers (1:39-56)
   B. Births, Circumcisions, and Presentations (1:57—2:52)
      1. Of John (1:57-80)
      2. Of Jesus (2:1-40)
      3. The Child Jesus in the Temple (2:41-52)

THE MIDDLE: TELLING THE STORY (Chapters 3–21)

III. The Inauguration of the Kingdom of Jesus the Messiah (3:1—9:50)

"You know the word which he sent to Israel, preaching good news of peace by Jesus Christ (he is Lord of all), the word which was proclaimed throughout all Judea, beginning from Galilee after the baptism which John preached: how God anointed Jesus of Nazareth with the Holy Spirit and with power; how he went about doing good and healing all that were oppressed by the devil, for God was with him."

(Acts 10:36-38)

A. Preparing the Way of the Lord (3:1—4:13)
 1. The Voice in the Wilderness (3:1-20)
 2. The Anointing of the Holy Spirit (3:21-22)
 3. The Genealogy of the Messiah (3:23-28)
 4. The Testing of the Son of God (4:1-13)
B. Declaring the Kingdom in Word and Deed (4:14—6:49)
 1. The Messiah's Inaugural Announcement (4:14-30)
 2. Proclaiming the Kingdom in Galilee and Judea (4:31-44)
 3. The Call of Simon (5:1-11)
 4. The Cleansing of Leprosy (5:12-16)
 5. Forgiveness of Sins and Healing of Paralysis (5:16-26)
 6. Torah and Kingdom: Conflicts on Authority (5:27—6:11)
 7. The Called: Apostles, Disciples, and People of God (6:12-19)
 8. The Address on the Plain (6:20-49)
C. Identifying the Messiah of God (7:1—9:50)
 1. Jesus, the Prophet of God (7:1-50)
 2. Jesus, Proclaimer of the Word of God (8:1-21)
 3. Jesus, His Commanding Word (8:22-56)
 4. Jesus, The Christ and Chosen of God (9:1-50)

IV. The Way of the Determined Messiah (9:51—19:27)

"When the days drew near for him to be received up, he set his face to go to Jerusalem."

(Luke 9:51)

A. Jesus Faces toward Jerusalem (9:51—13:21)
 1. He Sets His Face (9:51-62)

"Would that even today you knew the things that make for peace! But now they are hid from your eyes."

(Luke 19:42)

THE END: TRANSCENDING THE TRAGEDY (Chapters 22–24)

"He released the man who had been thrown into prison for insurrection and murder, whom they asked for; but Jesus he delivered up to their will."

(Luke 23:25)

    A. The Passover Plot (22:1-65)
        1. The Preparations (22:1-13)
        2. The Meal (22:14-38)
        3. The Arrest (22:39-65)
    B. The Trials of the Messiah (22:66—23:25)
    C. The Execution of the Righteous Christ of God (23:26-56)

VII. The Vindication and Exaltation of the Messiah (24:1-53)

"Thus it is written that the Christ should suffer and on the third day rise from the dead, and that repentance and forgiveness of sins should be preached in his name to all nations, beginning from Jerusalem. You are witnesses of these things."

(Luke 24:46-48)

    A. The Empty Tomb (24:1-12)
    B. On the Road to Emmaus (24:13-35)
    C. The Messiah's Final Appearance, Commission of the Witnesses, and Departure (24:36-53)

COMMENTARY

The Beginning: Setting the Stage
(Chapters 1–2)

■ The Prolog 1:1-4

The first four verses of Luke are perhaps the most elegant sentence in the Greek New Testament. All translations must strive for a formal tone and structure in order to capture its stylized character. The RSV has done this well so that the conditional clause of the first two verses remains balanced against the statement of result in vv. three and four. Within the first two verses (the protasis), the conditional clause also includes an infinitive clause and a subordinate clause, and each of these has a corresponding member in the last two verses (the apodosis). The outline is very precise.

> Inasmuch as many have undertaken
> > to compile a narrative of the things . . .
> > > just as they were delivered to us . . .
> it seemed good to me also . . .
> > to write an orderly account for you . . .
> > > in order that you may know the truth . . . .

The formality and precise structure of this sentence are indications that the author is following a literary convention. This is a proper preface to a "history" according to the handbooks of ancient rhetoric and writing. In Lucian of Samosata's treatise *How to Write History* (§§53-55), that second-century pagan author stressed that whenever the historian uses a preface, "he will make two points only, not three like the orators. He will omit the appeal for a favorable hearing and give his audience what will interest and instruct them. For they will give him their attention if he shows that what he is going to say will be important, essential, personal or useful. He will make what is to come easy to understand and quite clear, if he sets forth causes, and outlines the main events. The best historians have written prefaces of this sort."

Luke's contemporary Josephus also was aware of the established standards of good history writing. He dedicated the first and second sections of his work *Against Apion* (1.1; 2.1) to "most excellent" or "most esteemed Epaphroditus," commenting on the quality of his "witnesses," and he began his lengthy *Antiquities* (1.1) with a comment on the many reasons why people undertake to write history. Such comparisons with other accounts was a standard way to begin a historical narrative.

Josephus is particularly interesting because he was a Jewish author who was well versed in the conventions of Hellenistic historiography. The fact that Luke wrote this elegant Greek prolog and then moved into a scriptural style of history writing in v. 5 ("and it came to pass in the days of . . .") is not so shocking. This narrative was written by someone who was at home in two cultural traditions of narrative history. Furthermore, Josephus's resumption of his two-volume work with dedications to a patron establishes a clear parallel to Luke's references to Theophilus (1:4; Acts 1:1). It is impossible to know for sure whether Theophilus was a financial supporter of the book, a government official who needed to be set straight on the Christians, or a believer who had already been "instructed" in the faith (see 1:4), but the prolog in 1:1-4 is made to introduce both volumes and the theme is picked up again in Acts 1:1.

This conventional character of the prolog makes it more difficult to penetrate for exact meanings. Which aspects of these lines are rather predictable verbiage which the ancient reader would have

simply discounted as standard historian talk? And where did
Luke's distinctive adaptations of the standard rhetoric cause the
reader to take notice? As in the studies of the speeches in Acts,
scholars have labored carefully to identify Luke's emphases in the
midst of this formal, conventional prolog.

Before proceeding with the commentary, it is worth noting
again what is not said. The author is not named, and the manuscripts which attach a name are already collections of the four
"Gospels" in which each is labeled as "According to . . . ." Nor
is this book called a "Gospel" (see Mark 1:1). The author sets his
project next to other "narratives," identifying its genre more with
historical writing and less with Christian preaching. Nothing is
said of the time, place, or specific situation in which the narrative
was written.

1-2—This is the only book in the New Testament to begin with
a concessive clause referring to other documents. "Whereas," or
Inasmuch as many have undertaken to compile a narrative. This
could be a negative comparison, but the point seems to be that
those **many** of **us** who write these narratives have reliable sources.
Since Luke appears to have used at least Mark and the Sayings
Source ("Q") with regularity, this reference to **many** is probably
a congenial comparison. Luke, therefore, claims good sources
and thereby indicates that he belongs to a community of persons
who are gathering and narrating these traditions.

The things **accomplished among us** is probably a reference to
things which are "fulfilled" among us. That is, these are not simply
things that happened, as if the author is claiming to relate all the
events. These are things and events which will prove to have
been scriptural fulfillments (see Luke 24:44, 26-27). Those who
were **eyewitnesses and ministers of the word** are also presented
as bearing witness to just such fulfillments. Ancient historians
were very sensitive to the question of whether their narratives
had a basis in eyewitness accounts, since some Greek historiog-
raphers claimed that history had to be written on the spot to be
trustworthy. This is therefore also a conventional claim in a preface, but it is the **things which have been** fulfilled **among us** to
which these witnesses bear testimony. The "servants of the word"

would seem to be a designation of Christian evangelists or scriptural interpreters (see 4:20 and Acts 13:5, John Mark). The evangelist is affirming the reliability of Christian tradition.

These words also convey a picture of a community of telling and preaching which is further served by those who undertake the task of writing. The dynamics of text and community memory are alive in these phrases, but difficult to analyze precisely. Is there a hint of correction of other attempts to "undertake" the task? Is there an apology for yet one more version of the story of Jesus when some confusion already exists? This is not the work of a naive author simply relating personal experience. This book is a project among others of formulating a written version of the central truth or faith around which a community is gathered.

3-4—These verses are the most explicit words in the narrative about the author and the narrative. He does not claim to be one of the "eyewitnesses and servants of the word," but he does claim to have **followed all things** carefully from the beginning. The adverb **closely** or "carefully" (Gk: *akribōs*) could imply careful research, which would be a conventional claim by a historian. It might mean careful work with the Christian sources or independent knowledge of the beginnings. Perhaps the assertion has differing connotations between the first and second books. It reveals a Christian author who is at least one or two steps or generations removed from the eyewitness or apostolic origins of the story. On the other hand, this author claims intimate acquaintance with the beginnings or reliable accounts of the beginnings. Some time has passed since the events which are narrated, and these stories have been told and retold in the interim.

The dating of Luke's narrative must begin here. Luke's use of Mark provides a second point of reference. Although Mark is also of indefinite origin, that Gospel provides a rare aside to the reader in Mark 13:14, "Let the reader understand." This appears to be a clue that Jesus' prophetic words about the dire fate of Jerusalem and the temple have been or are about to be fulfilled in the reader's time. Other aspects of Mark's story seem to fit a time of telling closely linked with the Roman conquest of Jerusalem in A.D. 67–73, and Luke's account was written later. Luke's accounts of Jesus' oracles concerning Jerusalem (see 19:41-44; 21:20-24) also appear to be aware of their partial fulfillment, but the author is clearly intent on conveying those prophetic words with a minimum of direct commentary (see the discussion of those passages). **The things . . . accomplished among us** probably include the life, death, and resurrection of Jesus, the beginnings of the church in Acts, and may extend to the enduring divisions and calamity in Israel which call for further interpretation. A date at some time in the last third of the first century (A.D. 67–100) appears probable, and the midpoint in the early 80s may be the most likely.

The phrase **it seemed good** is not weak in Luke, since it may be used to claim the guidance of the Holy Spirit (see Acts 15:22, 25, 28). The language is delicate in both Greek and English, but this does not suggest that Luke's task is casually undertaken.

The word **orderly,** on the other hand, must not be pressed too rigorously to suggest that Luke is claiming to correct matters of chronology in Mark or the other sources. In Greek this is an adverb, describing how the author plans to write. Lucian of Samosata described the historian's task as similar to that of the sculptor, to "give a fine arrangement to events and to illuminate them as vividly as possible" (*How to Write History*, 53-55). Thus "orderliness" may be first of all a claim to "coherence" or meaning. When connected with the claim to have **followed things** "carefully," it also identifies the author as one who has excellent credentials to write this narrative. Still the adverb is a formal claim. Luke has not yet indicated what kind of "orderliness" will be most appropriate. The purposes which the book reveals will establish the canons of order.

This is a crucial matter, since many interpretations insist on particular views of history and truth and then find Luke to be a colleague in their cause. If history is a matter of correct chronologies and factual precision, then is not Luke making such claims for this narrative? But then are the rearrangements which the evangelist makes in Mark's sequence attempts to "correct the record?" Such rearrangements occur at 4:16; 5:1; 6:12; and 8:19. Must the reader choose between these accounts for "accuracy," or is this "orderliness" more a question of larger issues of truth and meaning?

The crucial word is probably **the truth** which this author intends to convey to Theophilus. Again, this is a kind of conventional claim which cautions against overinterpretations. Yet the **truth** (Gk: *asphaleia*) of this narrative is an "assurance" or "foundation" concerning things in which this "Theophilus" has already been "instructed" or **informed.** This could even be formal Christian instruction or catechesis (Gk: *katēchēthēs*). At least the prior allusions to the community and its memory suggest that Luke is not striving for detachment or mere empirical verification. In this commentary, this "assurance" will be understood in such larger terms according to the apparent threats to God's promises which the story addresses. But the matter cannot be decided on word studies or exegesis of the prolog alone. The whole narrative of Luke-Acts must be allowed to demonstrate its kind of **truth** or "assurance."

■ The Visitation of the Lord God of Israel (1:5—2:52)

> Blessed be the Lord God of Israel, for he has visited and redeemed his people.
>
> (Luke 1:68)

These stories of the conception, birth, presentation, and childhood of Jesus and of John have always been deeply loved by Bible readers, but only recently have they been appreciated anew as compositions of the third evangelist. Their thoroughly scriptural coloring and profound respect for Jewish rituals and customs seemed out of place to those scholars who were eager to present Luke as a Hellenistic and Gentile author far removed from Jewish tradition. The contrast in language and style with the highly refined Hellenistic prolog (Luke 1:1-4) was also regarded as evidence that these chapters must have been inserted into Luke's narrative from another source which was more primitive and Jewish. According to some interpreters, Luke's project actually began with Luke 3:1, and both the Hellenistic prolog (1:1-4) and the Jewish birth stories were later additions. But the modern elimination of these chapters provides clear evidence of the distorted understanding of Luke which results from hasty decisions concerning Luke's understanding of the faith of Israel.

This is an author who is trained in the conventions of Hellenistic historiography and who is thoroughly at home in the traditions of the scriptural histories. The sharp contrast in vocabulary and style which occurs between the prolog (1:1-4) and the birth narratives (1:5—2:52) demonstrates that distinct traditions of historiography may still be identified, but such combinations are not infrequent in Jewish writings in the Hellenistic era, especially in books written in Greek. The Jewish historian Josephus, for example, has written his *Antiquities* in constant dependence on the Scriptures, but he has not hesitated to dress up his narrative with the devices of Hellenistic historiography, including stock scenes, speeches filled with pathos, and dramatic depictions.

These chapters are programmatic for Luke. The literary coherence of Luke-Acts may be appreciated more thoroughly when it is recognized that these chapters function like an overture to the Gospel, sounding the crucial themes in visions, oracles, and songs, alerting the reader to watch and listen for what is coming. Then the story of Jesus unfolds when the common synoptic traditions are picked up in Chaps. 3–21 until the climax and resolution in Chaps. 22–24. Then the speeches in Acts explicate Luke's distinctive version of the story of Jesus in terms which are highly consistent with the program announced in these opening chapters. If the visions, oracles, and songs of Luke 1:5—2:52 announce in poetry what the narrative is going to tell us, the body of Luke 3–21 then tells the story, and the final Chaps. 22–24 conclude the story, then the speeches in Acts will recapitulate, almost like a commentary, what the narrative has said.

The scriptural integrity of the whole may also be identified clearly in these opening chapters. The scriptural "coloring" of these stories is more than sentimentality or imitation of archaic phrases from the Greek translation of the Old Testament. Careful examination of those passages to which allusion or reference is made will often prove highly fruitful for interpreting the claims and promises of Luke's story. If the speeches in Acts have been recommended as a kind of "commentary" on Luke's gospel narrative, then a reading of identified passages from the Scriptures (especially Isaiah 40–55 and Deuteronomy) could also be suggested as an exercise in the interpretation of Luke. Old Testament interpreters would, of course, cringe at the suggestion that Deutero-Isaiah is a "commentary" on Luke, and even many of Luke's interpretations of those prophetic passages will appear strained to current historical analysis. But the point is that Luke's narrative is filled with scriptural substance, especially in these opening chapters, inviting the reader to join in "examining the scriptures daily to see if these things were so" (Acts 17:11). Luke's story of Jesus is grounded in the Scriptures and constitutes an uncompromising testimony to their fulfillment in Jesus, the Savior, who is Messiah and Lord (Luke 2:11).

These opening chapters also demonstrate that Luke's story of Jesus is a thoroughly theological testimony. In fact, the theocentric character of the narrative is so marked that the common subject matter of these annunciation, birth, circumcision, and childhood stories is actually the visitation of the Lord God of Israel (Luke 1:68). Thus any reading of these chapters which does not recognize their literary unity with the rest of Luke-Acts or their interpretative integrity as scriptural commentary will underestimate their importance for the whole of the Gospel. But neglect of the nature of the will and plan of God which are initially disclosed in these chapters will result in a misunderstanding of Luke's entire testimony.

The thorough narrative structuring in 1:5—2:52 also deserves careful attention (see outline, p. 29). The parallels between the annunciation, birth, and childhood of John and those of Jesus are too remarkable to be casual. In all the glory of his miraculous birth and destiny, John bears witness to the greater one who follows.

Annunciations (1:5-56)

The Annunciation of the Conception of John (1:5-25)

Zecharaiah and **Elizabeth** are introduced in vv. 5-7, and the scene is identified as taking place **in the days of Herod, king of Judea.** Luke is fond of opening the scene against the backdrop of Jewish and Roman political history (see also 2:1-2 and 3:1-3), although no further mention is made of Herod the Great in Luke's account (see the familiar stories of Herod in Matthew 2). In both the scriptural language and in the details of the Jewish temple ritual (**a priest . . . of the division of Abijah . . . a wife of the daughters of Aaron**), the reader is brought inside the world of the second Jewish temple. Luke's story begins in the temple, and it will reach a climax when the Messiah Jesus returns to Jerusalem and the temple (19:41-46). The historical details are fascinating glimpses into distant Jewish piety and temple practices, but the evangelist provides no more data than is necessary to locate and identify these characters.

Their credentials are, however, very carefully delineated. These are the faithful in Israel, **both righteous before God,** much like Simeon and Anna in Luke 2 (vv. 25 ["righteous and devout"], 37) or Joseph of Arimathea who was also "a good and righteous man . . . looking for the kingdom of God" (23:50-51). In particular, their faithful observance of **all the commandments and ordinances of God** marks them as **blameless** (v. 6). Obedience to the commandments and Law of the Lord continues to be highly regarded throughout Luke-Acts (see Luke 2:23, 24, 27, 39; 16:17; 23:56; Acts 6:13; 7:53; 18:13; 21:20, 24, 28; 22:3, 12; 23:3; 24:14; 25:8; but note Acts 13:39 and 15:5), and faithfulness toward the temple accompanies this piety (see Luke 2:27, 37, 46; 19:45, 47; 20:1; 21:37-38; 24:53; Acts 2:46; 3:1—4:1, 5:20-26, 42; 21:26-30; 22:17; 24:6-18; 25:8; but note Luke 21:5). Zechariah and Elizabeth are, therefore, exemplars of faithfulness for the Christian as well as the pre-Christian community. Yet the barrenness of a couple of advanced age is especially reminiscent of a host of Old Testament stories of the birth of a special child to a barren marriage (e.g., Abraham and Sarah, Genesis 18; Isaac and Rebecca, Genesis 25; Rachel and Jacob, Genesis 30; Hannah and Elkanah, 1 Samuel 1–2), and the plight of the woman stands out in all of those stories.

In vv. 8-13, the story moves beyond the introductions into the dramatic appearance of the angel. Recognizing that the story is an angelophany contributes to an appreciation of several details. **The temple** is a favorite setting for crucial revelations in Luke (see also Luke 2; 19:41-47; and Acts 3–4); and it is not by accident, but by lot (v. 9, see Acts 1:26) that Zechariah has been brought to this sacred place. Thus chosen by God through the institutional routines of the priesthood of Israel and accompanied by the prayers of **the whole multitude of the people** (vv. 8-10), Zechariah's service of God is thoroughly validated. When the angel of the Lord appears to him, Zechariah's response of being **troubled** is fully appropriate (see Luke 24:38). So also the **fear** which **fell upon him** is expected in such displays of divine presence and power (see Luke 1:65; 2:9; 5:26; 7:16; 8:37; Acts 2:43; 5:5, 11; 19:17). God has been at work behind the scenes and in this scene, choosing the time and the place to answer the prayers of the faithful in Israel (**the people**, v. 10, **Zechariah** v. 13). Nothing detracts from the glorious promise of the annunciation: **Your wife . . . will bear you a son, and you shall call his name John.**

Verses 14-17 provide a hymnic expansion on the annunciation itself, explicating the significance of this birth in terms of the Scriptures, indicating the child's distinctive mission in Israel, and providing a contrast to the second oracle of Gabriel in the subsequent verses. This angelic canticle is a prophetic word of the the Lord, revealing God's purposes and plans for Israel in the career of this child of promise. The constant refrain in this section of the "filling" presence of the Holy Spirit (v. 15, see also 1:35, 41, 67, 80; 2:25, 26, 27) is another testimony to the immediacy of God's activity. The angel's poetic and prophetic words are structured into the heart of the narrative (see below on vv. 21-23). They are probably fragments of early Christian worship tradition which the evangelist is conserving and explicating in their scriptural content and new literary context.

The scriptural precedents for John's role and mission are fundamental to Luke's testimony concerning God's work in John. The Law and the Prophets reach a culmination in John (see Luke 16:16). John, however, is more than just one of the prophets, for his specific identity will later be announced by Jesus in the eschatological terms of Malachi's promise of "the messenger to prepare the way before me, and the Lord whom you will seek will suddenly come to his temple; the messenger of the covenant in whom you delight" (Luke 7:27, Mal. 3:1; see also Mal. 4:5, "Behold I will send you Elijah the prophet"). So now, the angel announces **joy and gladness** and proclaims that **many will rejoice at his birth** (v. 14), and that **he will go before him in the spirit and power of Elijah,** calling Israel to return to obedience and making **ready for the Lord a people prepared** (v. 17).

The scriptural allusions in this oracle are not limited to Elijah the prophet. The command that John **shall drink no wine nor strong drink** and the promise that **he will be filled with the Holy Spirit** also recall stories of the last of the judges in Israel (Samson, see Judg. 13:14 and Sam. 1:11, LXX; see also the Nazarite vow in Num. 6:1-4). In the larger context, the judge/prophet Samuel who anointed King David will prove to be the most significant prototype for John the Baptizer. Luke will even stop short of identifying John with Elijah (see Matt. 11:14) and will present Jesus as also fulfilling the promise of the coming of Elijah the prophet (see especially Luke 4:25; 7:11-17).

Throughout this thoroughly scriptural oracle, the message of joy and divine promise is constant. This is the same God who spoke through the prophets of old, and God's word abides forever. God is even providing the messenger to bring the children of Israel back into the obedience of the wisdom of the just. The destiny of this child is described in wholly positive terms, giving expression to God's determined purpose to restore Israel in faithfulness, wisdom, and righteousness (vv. 16-17). Even when John's preaching (or Jesus' or Paul's) will become stern or threatening (see Luke 3), God's gracious resolve for Israel must never be obscured.

Verse 18, however, gives the first glimpse of the problem with which God must contend; suddenly the hope and promise of the angel's first oracle is sharply contrasted with the second oracle to Zechariah. Nothing in the story so far would suggest that Zechariah was anything but righteous, blameless, and devout. But now in the presence of the angel of the Lord, Zechariah's disbelief at this wonderous annunciation is also disclosed as unbelief. The diagnosis of this lack of faith and the pronouncement of its consequences are thus the focus of vv. 18-23.

Of course, Zechariah is in good biblical company. When God promised Abram that his descendents would be numbered as the stars, "he believed the Lord; and he reckoned it to him as righteousness" (Gen. 15:6), but when God next promised to give him the land, Abram asked for a sign: "O Lord God, how am I to know that I shall possess it?" (Gen. 15:8). So also, Abraham and Sarah both laughed and asked disbelieving questions when the Lord announced that they who were "advanced in age" (Gen. 18:11, LXX: "advanced in days" = Luke 1:18) would bear a child (Gen. 17:17; 18:12-15). Zechariah's request for a sign (**How shall I know this?**), therefore, does not finally disqualify him.

But in Luke's narrative, even apparently mild questions or comments may be the occasion for severe responses (see below 4:22; 13:31; 19:39). So now, the angel sharpens the point. This is **Gabriel, the one who stands in the presence of God.** What greater sign would God give than to send such an exalted messenger to make this proclamation? The only sign which Zechariah will receive is that he will be struck dumb **because you did not believe my words which will be fulfilled in their time** (vv. 19-20). The severity of Gabriel's second utterance in no way detracts from the graciousness of the first announcement about John. God is not double-minded, nor have God's purposes changed. Luke has begun to enter into the theodicy (justifying the ways of God) which is central to the whole historical project of Luke-Acts. Even the most righteous among the people of God are constantly in danger of being unable to believe the good news which is declared to them (v. 19). So also Luke presented Paul as quoting Habakkuk when addressing the synagogue in Antioch: "Behold, you scoffers, and wonder, and perish; for I do a deed in your days, a deed you will never believe, if one declares it to you" (Acts 13:41).

Verses 21-23 conclude this wondrous angelophany, displaying Luke's masterful touch with narrative. The scene which was set in vv. 5-7 is now rounded off in vv. 21-23. Meanwhile, Zechariah's encounter with the angel has been similarly balanced between two narrative sections, vv. 8-13 and vv. 18-20, with the angel's canticle (vv. 14-17) standing at the heart of the revelation. The reader has been led up to the high point of that hymnic refrain

and back down to the end of the story (see the chart on Luke
1:26-38).

Even the details in these concluding verses are still part and
parcel of this angelophany, complete with the people faithfully
"waiting" and "wondering" outside the temple. Without telling
us specifically how they knew, the evangelist indicates that they
"perceived that he had seen a vision in the temple." By his nodding to them and remaining dumb, Zechariah had already proved
to be a sign to Israel. Then he went home.

Verses 24-25 are a complementary episode, indicating that Gabriel's words have indeed been fulfilled "in their time" after Zechariah went home! But now the story is all about Elizabeth. Brief
as it is (see also Anna in Luke 2:36-38), this episode completes
the previous scene, but only for the reader—since nothing about
Elizabeth's pregnancy is publicly known for five months (v. 24,
see v. 26). Furthermore, Elizabeth's sense that her pregnancy
removes the reproach of barrenness is another clear allusion in
Luke to the circumstances of her scriptural sisters, Sarah and
Hannah (Gen. 16:2, 1 Sam. 1:1-18).

The Annunciation of the Conception of Jesus (1:26-38)

The close parallels in structure and content between the annunciations of the conceptions of John and Jesus provide a key
to their interpretation.

A. Announcing John (1:5-25)

vv. 5-7 Setting the scene: time, place
                         credentials in Israel of Zechariah and
                         Elizabeth,
                         unlikely circumstances for concep-
                         tion
vv. 8-13 The Annunciation: appearance of angel (Gabriel)
                         Zechariah is "troubled"
                         "Do not be afraid . . . for . . ."
                         "your wife will bear you a son, and
                         you shall call his name John."

vv. 14-17 The Angel's Canticle

> John's "greatness" is explicated in terms of being "filled with the Holy Spirit" and "the spirit and power of Elijah"

vv. 18-20 The Sign is given (for unbelief)

> Question: "How shall I know this? For . . ."
>
> "And the angel answered him, 'I am Gabriel . . .
> And behold, you will be silent . . . because you did not believe. . . .' "

vv. 21-23 Concluding the Episode

> "He could not speak."
> "He went to his home."

A. Announcing Jesus (1:26-38)

vv. 26-27 Setting the scene: time, place

> credentials in Israel of Joseph and Mary
> unlikely circumstances for conception

vv. 28-31 The Annunciation: coming of angel Gabriel

> Mary is "greatly troubled"
> "Do not be afraid . . . for . . ."
> "You will conceive in your womb and bear a son, and you shall call his name Jesus."

vv. 32-33 The Angel's Canticle

> Jesus' "greatness" is explicated in terms of being "the Son of the Most High" and "The throne of his father David"

vv. 34-37 The Sign is given

> Question: "How can this be, since . . . ?"
> "And the angel said to her, 'The Holy Spirit will come upon you . . .

And behold, . . . Elizabeth has con-
ceived. For with God nothing is impossible.' "

vv. 38 Concluding the Episode

"And Mary said, 'Behold . . . let it
be.' "

"And the angel departed from her."

Both the similarities and the differences invite close examination and again demonstrate the careful composition and scriptural content of Luke's infancy narratives. Commentary on the
evangelist's telling of the story may therefore proceed with confidence. On the other hand, these same structural and scriptural
observations make attempts to demonstrate the historical verifiability of the story more difficult, and even the question of Luke's
possible sources becomes more complex.

Traditional refrains from early Christian songs, prayers, and
acclamations still stand out like encrusted jewels in the literary
composition (see vv. 32, 33, 35), and readers are often enticed
by the apparent historical realism of the story to speculate on
what Luke's sources could have been for such episodes. The possibility that actual reminiscences of Mary or Elizabeth could have
been preserved or that Luke may have had written accounts from
which to work can not be finally proved or disproved. Immense
efforts have been made in the past to reconstruct such sources
as a "Mary source"and a "shepherds source" and a pre-Lukan
infancy narrative. More technical commentaries may still seek to
establish criteria by which to identify and describe such possible
pre-Lukan documents and traditions. But the narrative itself requires close scrutiny, not as a route to earlier sources or as re-
pository of historical memory, but as a testimony to the enduring
truth of the meaning of "the things which have been accomplished among us" (Luke 1:1-4).

In vv. 26-27, the evangelist's hand is readily evident, shaping
these stories into a declaration of God's involvement in the timing
and action of the episodes. The mention of the **sixth month** immediately links this episode with the story of the annunciation
of the birth of John which concluded with the report of Elizabeth's

secrecy into the "fifth month" of her pregnancy, and this temporal clue will be central to the confirming sign of the "sixth month" of Elizabeth's pregnancy in v. 36 (see also 1:56). The reader is given insight into this thoroughly orchestrated plan of God. So also, the angel Gabriel has again been **sent** (see 1:19) from God (see v. 28-30).

In comparison with the elaborate credentials given to Zechariah and Elizabeth, Mary's qualifications are surprisingly simple. She is engaged to a man of Davidic lineage named **Joseph,** and she is **a virgin.** Nothing is said directly of her ancestry, age, or righteousness, and Joseph appears to be important to the story only for establishing the legitimacy of Davidic descent. Preserving the Christian memory of Mary's virginity, which was understood as a scriptural fulfillment of Isa. 7:14 (LXX: virgin: see Matt. 1:22-23), Luke is clearly not developing an interpretation of the identity of Mary and Joseph. It is enough to recognize that this child will be a legitimate "son of David." Luke does not even find it necessary to pursue the question of whether Joseph might have found the matter difficult or whether the genealogy might therefore be irregular (see Matthew 1).

Instead, Luke's narrative affirms God's initiative and assures the reader that God's election of Mary has met the necessary conditions. In later centuries, elaborate genealogical, metaphysical, and scientific explanations would be developed of "how" Jesus could be both "son of David" and "Son of God." But Luke does not explore such questions. His very economical account is that this virgin from Nazareth named **Mary,** who was already pledged to a Davidic descendent named **Joseph,** was chosen by God to bear the Messiah, Savior, and Lord.

In vv. 28-31, when Mary is greeted by Gabriel as the **favored one** (v. 28), any uncertainty about that use of the passive voice is soon dispelled by the angel's assurance that she has **found favor with God** (v. 30). She is not simply "lucky" or "gifted"; God is the one who extends favor to her. Her reaction of being **troubled** and **considering . . . what sort of greeting this might be** is appropriate for such a wonderous epiphany, anticipating clarification of its significance. Thus v. 30 is a general word of divine favor, assuring Mary and the reader that God's purposes in this embassy are gracious. The specific announcement of this conception and birth of a son and directive regarding the child's name is therefore the heart of the story which all the rest explicates.

The angel's canticle in vv. 32-33 immediately testifies to the "greatness" of this **Son** in terms of his true paternity. Jesus is at once the **Son of the Most High,** and the one to whom the Lord God will give **the throne of his father David.** He is not simply "great before the Lord" as is John (1:15), but his everlasting dominion is a disclosure of the **kingdom** of God and the rule of King David. The focus is not so much on Jesus' paternity with respect to his physical origins. Nor is there any contrast being developed between physical and spiritual paternity. Rather, the focus is on Jesus the Son of God and son of David who is born to exercise the kingship of God in and through Israel.

The scriptural content of the angel's canticle is crucial to its significance. This is the word of God in full concord with God's promises from of old. Isaiah 9:6-7 had announced,

> For to us a child is born,
>   to us a son is given;
> and the government will be upon his shoulder,
>   and his name will be called
> "Wonderful Counselor, Mighty God,
>   Everlasting Father, Prince of Peace."
> Of the increase of his government and of peace
>   there will be no end,
> upon the throne of David, and over his kingdom,
>   to establish it, and to uphold it
> with justice and with righteousness
>   from this time forth and for evermore.

And in 2 Sam. 7:12-14, these words of divine promise came to David:

> I will raise up your offspring after you, who shall come forth from your body, and I will establish his kingdom. He shall build a house for my name, and I will establish the throne of his kingdom for ever. I will be his father, and he shall be my son.

Thus the angel's canticle simply defines Jesus' "greatness" in terms of the scriptural promises of everlasting dominion given to the Son of God who is son of David. It is foolish to seek to separate God's paternity from David's or to suggest that Luke has crudely combined two sources. The canticle speaks primarily of Jesus' great **reign over the house of Jacob for ever,** and its scriptural content makes it clear why **the Son of the Most High** is also son of **his father David.**

Verses 34-37 then move to the question **How shall this be?** Mary's question is specifically tied to her statement, "since I do not know a man." This is not simply to say, **I have no husband** (RSV) or "I am not married," or "I do not know how babies come." This is to say, "How will this come to be, since I have no sexual relationship with a man?" Thus it is an indirect testimony to the wondrous conception of Jesus by divine initiative. This whole episode has emphasized divine agency, and the angel's canticle has interpreted why Jesus is both son of David and Son of God. Now Mary's question as to how this will happen receives a three-part answer.

Verse 35 speaks in rich scriptural images of the hovering, overshadowing presence of **the Holy Spirit** and power of the Most High. The creation of the world with "the Spirit of God moving over the face of the deep" comes to mind along with a host of other images of the cloud of divine presence and protection (see Luke 9:34). The angel's words clearly heighten the contrast with the wondrous birth of John who "will be filled with the Holy Spirit" (1:15), for now this child will be born of the Holy Spirit. Clearly, Jesus' holiness and role as Son of God were understood to surpass all those who had been set apart before or declared **holy** to the Lord, including King David and his royal offspring who were anointed as adopted "sons of God" (see especially Psalm 2 and Luke 3:22). On the other hand, Luke's narrative appears remarkably reserved in its presentation of "how" this could be, especially when compared with a variety of Hellenistic stories of gods mating with women to produce great rulers or generals. In concert with the faith of Israel, our evangelist tells us no more than that this conception took place by means of the awesome presence of God.

Verse 36 provides a second or confirming answer to Mary's question by pointing to the wondrous conception of John by Elizabeth. The disclosure of a virginal conception is astonishing and without precedent in Israel, but that is not to diminish the marvelous sign of divine favor which the pregnancy of the barren one represents. In fact, Elizabeth's pregnancy is a kind of answer to Mary's question which not only ties the stories together but raises the imponderable and delightful question: Which of these conceptions is more impossible?

Verse 37 then provides the third and final "answer" to Mary's question, **For with God nothing will be impossible.** This verse might well be regarded as a summary of Luke's understanding of signs, miracles, and wonders. Furthermore, it is not original with Luke or with Gabriel. It is an echo of a word of the Lord spoken to Abraham and Sarah when she laughed on hearing that she was to bear a child. "Is anything impossible with God?" (Gen. 18:14, LXX), the Lord asked Abraham. No, even the barren may conceive and a virgin may bear! How? By the will of God and through God's Holy Spirit. And how does that happen? No further speculation is indulged.

Mary's response in v. 38 is thus the only appropriate answer for the faithful. Her question, "How can this be?" has now become the word of obedient faith, **Let it be!** Her question has served the reader well in allowing for a series of responses. In fact, aside from this last glimpse of obedience, little disclosure of Mary's character or thoughts has been given. She is not only the handmaid of the Lord in bearing the infant, but she recedes in the narrative as well so that the identity and dominion of the Son of God and son of David may be presented. With Mary's closing testimony to the word of the Lord and the departure of the heavenly messenger, the parallels between the annunciations point forward to the actions which God has commenced.

The Blessings of Their Mothers (1:39-56)

The first two episodes of Luke's well-told story are now brought together as the two expectant mothers meet. The narrative itself is full of anticipation as the significance of these wondrous children is further expressed in the inspired utterances of the women who bear them. The themes in this passage of joy, blessing, the vindication of the oppressed, and the fulfillment of divine promises are consistent throughout Luke's Gospel, and thus the words of blessing sound a keynote for the evangelist. Nevertheless, these blessings are not original with Luke.

The centerpiece of the narrative is again a hymnic refrain which probably was already traditional in Christian worship. Verses 46b-55 have also been readily lifted from their literary context and used throughout Christian history as "the Magnificat" of Mary. This liturgical usage of these words of praise may have partially obscured their powerful social, economic, and political vision; and the assumption that the song originated with the youthful virgin has often contributed to a merely personal or pious interpretation.

It is important, therefore, to observe that the words are also not strictly original with Mary. On the basis of the reference to the removal of the **low estate** or "humiliation" of the speaker, the divine promise associated with progeny (v. 48, **all generations,** v. 55, **to Abraham and to his** seed **forever**), and the possibility that Elizabeth is speaking to Mary (v. 46a with Mary the subject of v. 56), several commentators have suggested that Luke attributed this song to Elizabeth. A few Latin manuscripts also support this possibility directly. The content of the song clearly fits an older childless woman better than a youthful unmarried virgin.

It seems more probable, however, that Luke meant to attribute this hymn to Mary. The alternating John–Jesus, Elizabeth–Mary episodes almost require a prophetic word from Mary. Still, the words are not original with Mary. The scriptural prototype for the song is clearly Hannah's exultant song over the birth of Samuel. The speaker may be best understood to be the Holy Spirit giving utterance through this series of inspired women, all of whom bear witness to the mighty and gracious dominion of God over the haughty, wealthy, and dominant powers of this world.

Verses 39-40 and 56 are, therefore, the narrative wrappers of these oracular testimonies. Matters of geography (Galilee and Judea) and calendars of pregnancy (sixth month plus three months) are not only intriguing historical details, they also tie the sequence of the episodes together (see 1:25, five months). Even more critically, the reader understands that both Mary and Elizabeth learn of the other's pregnancy only through inspired means.

The evangelist has provided privileged access to a portentous moment when the two women who bore the children of promise first met to share and ponder the secret.

Verses 41-42a introduce Elizabeth's greeting of Mary, indicating that the unborn child is already, at Mary's greeting, leaping, and that Elizabeth's utterance is an inspired word, for she **was filled with the Holy Spirit.** The **loud cry,** therefore, is also a mark of inspired speech (see 23:46). There is no mundane reason for Elizabeth already to know what the Lord has done with Mary. Elizabeth is not merely an experienced older relative who shows wisdom and understanding. She is a prophetess bearing a prophet. Now filled with the Holy Spirit, she is the oracle revealing the will of God to herself, to Mary, and to the reader.

Verses 42b-45 thus include four pronouncements which are at least as much words of God as words of Elizabeth. The human interest of this encounter between two kinswomen who are both pregnant under highly unusual circumstances is not lost, and all of the details about "months" and "womb" and "fruit" bring the story down to earth, within women's experience of maternity. Nevertheless, the content of these pronouncements is primarily theological, revealing how all of these matters are regarded by God, while psychological clues are sparse as to how Mary or Elizabeth may have felt or perceived these events.

The first pronouncement (v. 42b) is the declaration of Mary's favored status before God (echoing the angel's word in 1:28). This is not simply Elizabeth's wish for Mary. The language here is highly traditional, reflecting several scriptural stories where the bearing of children constituted the highest blessing of women. Nevertheless, the phrase **Blessed are you among women** is most reminiscent of Judges 5:24 where Jael is declared to be the "most blessed of women" for having been the assassin of the dreaded Sisera, and Luke 11:27 indicates that the blessedness of bearing children is surpassed by the blessedness of faithful obedience (see also v. 45 below).

The second pronouncement (v. 43) presents one of Luke's ponderable questions through which the identification of Jesus as **my Lord** is the central disclosure. Perhaps this is also a clue to Elizabeth's own humility or consternation or deference to Mary, but the question is best perceived as a rhetorical device which is standard in the scriptural histories. In 2 Sam. 24:21, Araunah the Jebusite greets the approach of David with the question, "Why has my lord the king come to his servant?" Thus Elizabeth's question leads primarily into a consideration of Jesus as the **Lord,** and the preceding angelic annunciation has been explicit in interpreting this "Lord" in terms of the "throne" and dominion of King David.

The third pronouncement (v. 44) links these oracles with Elizabeth's bodily experience of the leaping fetus (see v. 40). But even this is more than a personal event. It recalls another momentous pregnancy when the gymnastics of unborn children provoked a significant question and provided an occasion for revelation. In Gen. 25:22-23, when her unborn twins "struggled [LXX: leaped] within her," Rebecca asked, "If it is thus, why do I live?" and the Lord answered in an oracle. But now Elizabeth is inspired to discern that her infant is leaping **for joy,** and her words are already a prophetic testimony to Jesus on behalf of the unborn prophet she bears.

The fourth pronouncement (v. 45) is the ultimate benediction on Mary. Verse 42b had already spoken of the unsurpassable blessing of this pregnancy, but Mary's profound and simple trust of the word of the Lord is the greater mark of her being blessed by God (see 11:27). The Lord's word of promise is far from **fulfillment** or "perfection," yet faithful Mary is an exemplar of trust. And Elizabeth's prophetic acclamation is also a testimony that God will not fail those who trust so implicitly in God's unfulfilled promises.

Verses 46-55 are thus the inspired words of praise of Mary who sees and believes in advance the fulfillment of God's promises. Since these words are again inspired speech, it may not be so important that some of them do not seem to fit young Mary very well. In fact, this hymn of praise is filled with the phrases and hopes of the very ancient war song which Hannah prayed and sang on the birth and presentation of the child Samuel (1 Samuel 2). There also, the birth of the child of promise was acclaimed as a personal vindication and as a triumph of God the Savior over the high and haughty, the mighty and wealthy, long before this reality was evident. That child would judge Israel and eventually anoint King David as Messiah. Now Mary picks up the refrain, or gives voice to the Spirit's word to Israel. Mary may be expressing things which are far beyond her, but she is speaking prophetically. Her testimony to the purposes and power of God is a revelation of the word of the Lord.

Verses 46b-49 are closely paralleled with Hannah's heart exulting in the Lord and rejoicing in the salvation of God. Even the parallelism of Hebrew poetry indicates that the soul **magnifying the Lord** and the spirit **rejoicing in God** point forward to God as **Savior** (see also 1 Sam. 2:1). While Mary speaks of God as **my Savior,** this is not merely a personalistic statement. The entire Magnificat may be read as an exposition of what it means that God is *the* Savior who is also *my* Savior, and the Benedictus of Zechariah (1:68-79) comes back to the term *salvation* three times (see also the Nunc Dimittis of Simeon in 2:30). Furthermore, the angel announces the birth of Jesus to the shepherds in terms of his being "a Savior, who is Christ the Lord" (2:11).

The repetition of the personal pronoun (**my soul,** v. 46; **my spirit . . . my Savior,** v. 47; **will call me blessed,** v. 48; **has done great things for me,** v. 49) also parallels Hannah's song (my heart, my mouth, my enemies, 1 Sam. 2:1). Clearly Mary's own **low estate** or "humbleness" as the servant of God (**handmaiden,** v. 48) is a demonstration of God's **regard** for the lowly of the world. Both Hannah and Mary are presented as recognizing that their own joy and glory and "salvation" are signs or manifestations of the greatness, might, and holiness of God for all.

Verses 50-55, therefore, move naturally into the public, social, and political dimensions of this same salvation. The birth of the child Samuel was not obviously the demonstration that the holiness of God would be exercised to break the bows of the mighty. The feeble did not immediately gird on strength nor was the cause of the hungry, the poor, the humble quickly championed (1 Sam. 2:4-8). Only prophetic insight could know this to be the truth. So also, Mary's conception is already grasped as the **strength** of God's **arm.** This obscure event is the scattering of **the proud,** the humiliation of the high and **mighty,** the exaltation of the humble, the satisfying of **the hungry** and the reversal of the fortunes of the wealthy (vv. 51-53).

The birth of these children of promise is prophetically expected as a revelation of God's distinctive dominion. This birth is not a benediction on the status quo, whether personally, socially, economically, or politically. The advent of the reign of God in the person of God's Messiah, ruler, and Son will involve the judgment as well as the blessing of God (see also 1 Sam. 2:9-10). The vision of the feast God has in store for the hungry is a prophetic word which challenges realities that appear unchangeable (see Isa. 25:6-8; 55:1-2; 65:13-14 and the comments on Luke 13:26-30 below).

These prophetic words are not simply a frontal attack on all persons of social standing or prosperity. Luke is persistently concerned for the poor and warns repeatedly against the dangers of wealth (see especially the discussion of Luke 6:20 below). Clearly no one may take comfort before God in their status, power, privilege, or affluence. But the prophetic diagnosis is quite precise in this passage, indicating the kind of peril which confronts **the proud.** In direct contrast to the mercy which God shows to **those who fear him from generation to generation,** God scatters **the proud in the imagination of their hearts.** God does not deal with appearances, but "knows the heart" of all humanity without respect to status, as does also the Messiah (see Luke 11:17). Thus, as in Gen. 6:5 where God "saw . . . the wickedness of man . . . and that every imagination of the thoughts of his heart was only evil continually" leading to the flood, so now the coming of Jesus will mean, in Simeon's words "that [secret] thoughts out of many hearts will be revealed" (2:35).

The danger of wealth and power and social status lies in the greater peril of "conceit" or "deceit" or "deception." Here greater possibilities and needs clearly exist for maintaining appearances or image or justifying one's position.

The social, economic, and political consequences of this impending birth are profound. No dimension of human life or culture will lie beyond the lordship of this Messiah. All systems, ideologies, and social structures may be judged by this new standard of divine justice and mercy—which does not mean that Jesus' reign will simply displace all the social, political, or economic systems of the world, at least not yet. But their claim to ultimacy or "divine right" and their ability to justify the rights and privileges of all their subjects have been challenged by the prophetic word of Mary's song. Thus Martin Luther commended these verses to "his Serene Highness, Prince John Frederick," as a standard for faithful governance by saying, "in all of Scripture I do not know anything that serves such a purpose so well as this sacred hymn of the most blessed Mother of God, which ought indeed to be learned and kept in mind by all who would rule well and be helpful lords" (*The Magnificat*, trans. A. T. W. Steinhaeuser, in *Luther's Works*, vol. 21 [St. Louis: Concordia, 1956], pp. 297-298).

Verses 54-55 bring this vision of the societal dimension of the kingdom to bear on Israel in particular. Both Israel's calling as "servant" (see Isa. 41:8) and the promise to Abraham (see Gen. 17:7; 18:18; and 22:17) are to be renewed and fulfilled. The audacity of these words is already stunning when the awesome power of the Roman Empire is considered. Next to that, the kingdom of Jesus which Mary and Luke and the early Christian community announced appears insignificant. And what if Israel has already been decimated in the war with Rome and the temple and holy city of Jerusalem lie in ashes when Luke tells the story? Then Mary's assurance that this pregnancy marks God's renewal or restoration of Israel's peculiar election is either preposterous or profound. Even in Luke's story, as Mary returns to her home her song may raise as many questions as it answers (v. 56). But Luke certainly does not accept any suggestion that Israel's hopes have failed to be fulfilled in Jesus (see also 2:25, 38; 19:11; 23:50-51; Acts 1:6).

Births, Circumcisions and Presentations (1:57—2:52)
The Birth of John (1:57-58)

John's birth is told in a bare minimum of detail, yet completing earlier promises in the narrative and anticipating crucial aspects of the birth of Jesus (Luke 2:1-20). Verse 57 again displays Luke's fondness for the language of "fulfillment" or "fulfilling the time" as Elizabeth's pregnancy came to term. In the series of stories, it is clear that the fullness of God's time corresponds directly to the completion of these births. Verse 58 may suggest that Elizabeth's pregnancy was a secret until the birth, or the friends and relatives may just be responding to the news of the birth of this son. The evangelist suggests that they **heard that the Lord had shown great mercy to her** (or, more literally, "that the Lord had magnified his mercy with her"), indicating the correct theological understanding of this birth, yet providing little specific content of what they heard.

But the point is not so much to fill in the details of human interest as to testify that the birth of John was a "magnification" or enlarged disclosure of God's mercy. Even the report that these friends and neighbors **rejoiced with her** is more than a passing glimpse of community life. It is the fulfillment of the angel's promise that "Elizabeth will bear you a son, and you shall call his name John. And you will have joy and gladness, and many will rejoice at his birth" (Luke 1:13-14). With the birth of the child of promise, the broader circle of those in Israel who hope and faithfully expect God's salvation begins to emerge.

The Circumcision and Presentation of John (1:59-80)

In contrast to the strict economy of the story of John's birth, vv. 59-66 seem conspicuously full of lore as the child is given the name which the angel declared before his conception (1:13-14, see also "Jesus" in 2:21).

Verses 59-66 report the circumcision as a matter of course, reflecting Luke's consistent presentation of the faithful in Israel as fully observant of the Torah. The naming of both John and Jesus is reported to have been accomplished along with the circumcision (1:59; 2:21), although some Jewish traditions would suggest that children were named at birth prior to their being marked for the covenant in circumcision. But Luke focuses on the naming of the child as the occasion for considerable discussion leading to the provocative question, **What then will this child be?** (see below, on v. 66).

Both Elizabeth and Zechariah are adamant with the neighbors and kinsfolk that his name shall be **John.** Perhaps the meaning of the name, "Yahweh has shown favor," is implied with the angel's first command (see 1:13), but nothing is made of such a possibility in this episode. The point is simply that both of the child's parents are remarkably emphatic in insisting that "the name given by the angel" (see 2:21) be used. Elizabeth has already been qualified in the story as a prophetess, and Zechariah, who is now dumb (and deaf, v. 62) as a sign of disbelief, is still able to convey the Lord's command with prophetic clarity: **His name is John** (v. 63). Once again having demonstrated that "they were both righteous before God" (1:6), Zechariah's speech is dramatically restored, and he speaks words of **blessing** of God (v. 64). So far, however, the content of his testimony is not given.

The neighbors who have served as the foil for this dramatic disclosure are now filled with **fear,** indicating that they are also aware of standing in the presence of an awesome revelation. With a characteristic reference to the geographic spread of this news **through all the hill country of Judea** (see especially 5:17), the evangelist sets the stage for the reader to join all the others who are watching this drama unfold. Thus vv. 65-66 supply the crucial clues to understanding what follows, with the three decisive clues given in v. 66: (1) **All who heard them laid them up in their hearts** is almost a directive that all who would rightly understand will join in such faithful consideration (see Luke 2:19,51; 3:15). Right understanding is a matter of the heart which may be receptive or alienated from God (see 1:17; 2:35; 5:22). (2) The question, **"What then will this child be?,"** is thus a question of faith and wonder, inviting Zechariah's interpretive canticle (vv. 67-79). (3) Luke's parting remark, **For the hand of the Lord was with him,** does not attribute this verdict to any of the characters in the story. It is an uncharacteristically direct comment by the narrator to supplement and confirm the readiness of the people to receive this child of divine promise.

Verse 67 thus introduces Zechariah's canticle in the most direct terms possible. **Zechariah was filled with the Holy Spirit, and prophesied.** Once again, the words of blessing which follow are oracular. Zechariah gives voice to inspired utterance, phrases rich in scriptural allusions and visions of divine dominion which far exceed human experience. All those in Israel who may have wondered if the promises of God's kingdom would ever become a reality are hereby alerted that God's determination is unswerving to rescue Israel from her oppressors. Even if Roman subjugation has only become more ominous in the intervening years since this prophecy was to have been uttered, none of these oracular words may be dismissed or explained away. According to Luke, Zechariah's words are the Holy Spirit's testimony to God's saving purpose and plan. None of it will fail to be fulfilled.

Verses 68-75 are printed as one sentence in the RSV, indicating the complexity of the "blessing" which Zechariah, inspired by the Spirit, utters to God. The tradition of Jewish prayer of the "blessing of God" deserves attention in these opening chapters (see also 1:64; 2:28). Along with "magnification" (1:46) and "thanksgiving" (2:38), "blessing" God involves a testimony to God's acts of justice and mercy in the world. Although these prophetic songs are inspired by the Spirit so that in one sense God is blessing God, the dignity of human participation is not thereby diminished. When the risen Christ tells his followers that "you shall be my witnesses" (Acts 1:8), the restoration of Israel's vocation to be a "light to the nations, that my salvation may reach to the end of the earth" (Isa. 49:6) has begun. So now when Zechariah "blesses God," he bears faithful witness, and all that he says in vv. 68-75 follows the word **for,** indicating the specific content of God's blessedness in advance (see also **for** in 1:15, 48, 76 and 2:30).

Each of the actions of God has a distinct but similar content. **He has visited and redeemed his people, and has raised up a horn of salvation . . ."** (1:68-69). The "visitation" of God or of an ancient ruler to the provinces could be for benefaction or for judgment, and Luke will again return to the thought that the "visitation of God" will prove to be a testing of Israel (see 7:16; 19:44). But Zechariah's prophetic oracle reveals that God intends only redemption and salvation. Speaking as if this "visitation" and "redemption" were already accomplished, Zechariah's words must be viewed as predictive within the story and as a decisive pronouncement or interpretation for those readers who know how the story of John and Jesus eventually turned out. The raising up of **a horn of salvation** further specifies the "visitation" and "redemption" in terms of the royal Davidic tradition (see 1 Sam. 2:10; Ps. 132:17).

The thoroughly political tone of this hymn has led some interpreters to attribute it to a pre-Christian Jewish nationalism such as that reflected in the hymns of the Maccabees. Yet its social and political significance should not be diminished by being consigned to possible pre-Christian sources. Verse 70 makes it clear that the evangelist is conscious that this proclamation constitutes a fulfillment of ancient prophetic promises which Israel treasured (see also Acts 3:21). Nothing less is at stake than Israel's long-standing messianic hopes. The claim and content of these verses are only more poignant and distinctive when they are read within the larger context of Luke's composition. Many specifics are still unclear, but John's birth is prophetically identified as a sign of God's promised visitation, redemption, and restoration of Davidic kingship in Israel.

Verse 71 announces the salvation **from our enemies and from the hand of all who hate us** which God promised (**spoke,** v. 70). The syntax of this section thus places this "salvation" next to the "horn of salvation" which God raised up from the house of David. Verses 70-71 are a subordinate clause further specifying the salvation which God is determined to pursue. The reign of God and its "salvation" are as this-worldly and historical as they are divinely given and spiritual. Luke will return repeatedly to the presentation of Jesus as the Savior (see especially Luke 2:11 and Acts 5:31; 13:23) and to the "salvation" brought by Jesus. It is even correct to view Luke-Acts as a project in "salvation history," if it is remembered that this work is a testimony to the determination and faithfulness of God who engages, challenges, and finally will surpass all human systems and culture.

God's direct purposes for inaugurating this dramatic activity are identified in the verbs of purpose in vv. 72-74. That is, God **has visited and redeemed his people, and has raised up a horn of salvation** in order (1) **to perform the mercy promised,** . . . (2) **to remember his holy covenant,** . . . **the oath** . . . **to grant us.** . . . The parallelism of the section again imitates the psalms and

prayers of Israel so that these purposes must be seen as interpreting each other. God's several purposes are unified in saving
activity, and God's initiative is strongly attested. "Performing mercy" and "remembering" are highly active verbs with the substance of scriptural precedent (see Ps. 105:8; 106:45), and John's
destiny identifies how God accomplishes such actions.

Such divine initiative, however, is pursued on behalf of humanity so that God's ultimate purposes in this activity must be
indirectly achieved. That is, God's final determination is **to grant**
or "to give," not to coerce or control. Verses 73-74, therefore,
express the purpose and gift of God's saving mission in terms of
the safety and freedom to worship and serve God throughout life
without fear. The blessing of God which began this prophetic
hymn (v. 68) now reaches its fruition in the liberation of humanity
to serve and bless God in holiness and righteousness. Nothing is
indicated here about "salvation" into another world. The this-
worldly social and political dimensions of divine salvation are
understood to be fundamental to the "redemption" (v. 68) which
is being declared to Israel.

This vision of God's rule must be ranked as one of the New
Testament's most hopeful and dramatic pronouncements of divine
dominion in this world. But how is it true? Or how would it have
been understood in a time when the enemies of Israel were clearly
in control? If the temple lies in ruins and the Roman order is
increasingly suspicious of Christian and non-Christian Jews, how
should the reader understand Zechariah's prophesy of this salvation of freedom to worship without fear of enemies? Certainly,
those who read Luke's testimony in times of peril must have
wondered not only **What then will this child be?** (v. 66), but also:
Whatever happened to God's promises made through this child?

Verses 76-79 thus return to the child John, now addressed in
prophetic speech by Zechariah. Like those present in the story
during Zechariah's inspired proclamation, the readers overhear
this word to the infant. None of the hopeful promise for Israel
of vv. 68-74 is compromised, but now it becomes clear that this
child is part of an extended saving process. Worshiping without
fear of enemies is already envisioned in Zechariah's prophetic

oracles, but the words spoken to the child indicate that this salvation is only now being initiated. God's promises still await complete fulfillment.

John's identification as **the prophet of the Most High** stands in close contrast with Jesus' as "the Son of the Most High" (1:32), but Luke is not thereby diminishing the importance of John. This child of promise is a fulfillment of the prophecy of Malachi of the prophetic messenger who prepares the way of the Lord (see Mal. 3:1 and Isa. 40:3, Luke 3:4-6 and 7:26-27). Whether **the Lord** is now to be understood as the Lord God or the Lord Jesus may be less decisive than that John is the herald of the kingdom, preparing the way of the Lord. The Christian reader knows that Jesus has been proved and exalted as the "Messiah and Lord" (see Acts 2:35-36).

The **knowledge of salvation** which is given to the people through **the forgiveness of their sins** is not a different **salvation** from being liberated from fear of enemies to serve God. **The forgiveness of sins** will be the subject of John's baptismal preaching (see Luke 3:3), but this "spiritual" concern should not be separated from the public and social dimensions of salvation. It is in part through their **knowledge of salvation** that the people will be rescued from the fear of their enemies in their worship. Both dimensions of salvation are "given" by God (see vv. 73 and 77).

The visitation of God which this child manifests (see vv. 67 and 78) is thus already a disclosure of divine mercy, and the baptism of forgiveness will prove to be central to the divine strategy of the deliverence of the people. God's **tender mercies** (literally, "viscera" or "bowels of compassion") have been revealed in that this prophet is authorized with a divine word of forgiveness, not vengeance. Still, the word of forgiveness is not so much the end of God's mission as the necessary means, given the human situation. The "dawning day" or the "dayspring" was probably a rich scriptural allusion to the awesome splendor of divine presence, now come to save and restore humanity (see Mal. 4:2). Perhaps even the rising up of the messianic "shoot of David" (Jer. 23:5) was envisioned. The scriptural images are so rich that it is clear that Luke continues to engage contemporary scriptural interpretation. Nevertheless, the promise of the dawning of a new day of light and life and divine compassion is an image of a new beginning of hope and freedom which has begun but is not yet completed.

Verse 79 thus touches upon the plight of those who sit in darkness and in the shadow of death who need light and guidance. This verse is again an exposition of scriptural hope (see Ps. 107:10 and Isa. 42:7), and it offers a clue to the persistence of the divine project without suggesting that the coming of God's kingdom will create immediate utopias. New liberation and direction may be given to the people, as it was to Israel in the exile, even if the full deployment of the **way of peace** and salvation may be slow.

In the hands of the evangelist, these rich traditional phrases and scriptural hopes are gathered in a prophetic oracle of bold social and spiritual proportions. The birth of this child is a veritable epiphany of divine mercy, for God is determined to give freedom from oppression and the liberating knowledge of forgiveness. Even if in Luke's day many in Israel are literally imprisoned in darkness and in the shadow of death, neither the theological self-confidence of the apparent victors nor the guilt that accompanies defeat could be accepted as God's final verdict. Zechariah, who had once been struck dumb for doubt, had then spoken prophetically announcing a word greatly reminiscent of Deutero-Isaiah's promises to Israel in exile. The dominion of God still means mercy and deliverance for those who wait in hope.

Verse 80 rounds off this oracle with a narrative "growth refrain" (see also Luke 2:40 and 2:52). Any question of whether the evangelist was aware of the parallels with the Samuel story or was only using traditions now disappears. Luke's narrative refrains are modeled on those in 1 Sam. 2:21 and 26 ("Now the boy Samuel continued to grow both in stature and in favor with the Lord and with men"). Luke adapts the form to fit John's case specifically with the mention of his being **strong in spirit** and **in the wilderness.** Nevertheless, both John and Jesus are thus presented by the evangelist in terms which recapitulate the story of the child Samuel whose wondrous birth and childhood prepared him as the forerunner, prophet, and anointer of David.

The Birth of Jesus (2:1-20)

This narrative is a masterpiece deserving acclaim and admiration as well as analysis. Popular dramatizations of the story and scholarly studies have agreed in recognizing the literary clarity, scriptural coloring, and sociopolitical illumination of this precious gem. Its immense popularity throughout Christian history has identified it as "the Christmas gospel," often with little reference to the whole of Luke's narrative. Yet, appreciation for its brilliance is only increased by treating the story critically within the larger purposes of Luke's literary, scriptural, and theological project.

Like the rest of the annunciation, birth, and presentation stories which surround it, Luke's account of Jesus' birth is evocative, intimating, and declaring the infant's identity and destiny in rich traditional titles. The scriptural histories of Samuel and David have supplied motifs for Luke's story of Jesus' birth and childhood. Roman traditions of the prodigies which accompanied the birth and childhood of Caesar Augustus may also have had a direct effect on Luke's telling of the birth of this Davidic ruler in the time of Caesar Augustus. The story of the birth of this Messiah, Savior, and Lord (2:11) is told against the backdrop of Roman imperial history. It is thus a testimony to the ultimate regency of the God of Israel with the child Jesus as the sign and agent of that gracious rule.

Luke's literary art is also more evident when the structured parallels to John's annunciation, birth, circumcision, and presentation are highlighted. A larger proportion of Luke 1 was invested in presenting John's role as forerunner, but his birth was recounted in one verse (1:57 [+ 58?]). By contrast, Jesus' birth is the centerpiece surrounded by the clusters of signs, oracles, and wonder of these opening chapters.

Verses 1-7 alert the reader to view Jesus' birth in the context of contemporary political history. Matthew's Gospel also dealt with the political complications of the birth of "the king of the Jews," but the remarkable differences with Matthew's birth story must be observed so that each account may be read on its own terms. The magi, the angelic guidance of Joseph in dreams, the paranoia and rage of King Herod, and the flight into Egypt are all crucial to Matthew's story of the birth of a child destined for Davidic kingship. By relating the intrigue and murderous hostility with which Herod greeted the reported birth (Matthew 2), Matthew emphasized that Jesus was perceived immediately as a threat. The rescue of the child of promise from the ruler's slaughter of infants also recalls the story of Moses' rescue in Egypt (see especially Josephus' expanded version of Exodus 2 in *Ant.* 2:232-237). Ancient oriental rulers never took lightly popular reports of divinely sanctioned leaders or children of destiny.

But Luke offers no comment on the consequences of this birth for the client king Herod (see Luke 1:5). The reference to the census of **all the world** sets the story against the backdrop of at least the entire Roman Empire, and the mention of **Quirinius, governor of Syria,** is as close as Luke comes to local political realities. No direct confrontation is presented, but Jesus' birth has consequences for the whole empire and provides a new standard for what it means to be Savior and Lord. The emperors would even do well to take notice, including **Caesar Augustus** himself, whom many in Luke's era regarded as the exemplary Savior, Lord, and Benefactor. The Pauline speech in Acts before Herod Agrippa II and the Roman governor Festus restates Luke's conviction concerning the whole story beginning from the birth of Jesus: "This was not done in a corner!" (Acts 26:26).

Verses 1-2 provide a wealth of historical details which has long fascinated general readers and frustrated critical historians. Luke's account simply does not fit with other primary sources on several counts. If this is still the time of Herod's dominion (1:5, "in the days of Herod"; 1:39; 2:1; **in those days**), the Roman procurator would not be likely to be administering a census. In nonbiblical sources, **Quirinius** is reported to be **governor of Syria** only after Herod's death, and the census reported during that administration (A.D. 6-9) was met with the revolt of Judas the Galilean (cf. Josephus, 2.118, 433; 7.253; Acts 5:37). Furthermore, while Roman history includes many accounts of a census being taken in various regions, nothing is known of such an edict by Augustus for **all the world.** It is inconceivable that the Roman annals (or Josephus) would have been silent concerning an event of such magnitude.

Perhaps Luke is incorrect about certain historical details, and perhaps Luke's intent has been misunderstood by readers. The temptation to "explain away" all historical difficulties is hard to resist. The English phrase, **the first enrollment, when Quirinius was governor of Syria** (v. 2), could be read in Greek as a much more general reference to an imperial enrollment process which began "before" Quirinius became governor of Syria. Several apparent historical difficulties would then dissolve, and then Jesus' birth would no longer be connected with the specific census of Palestine which provoked the revolt in Galilee.

But such efforts to defend Luke's historical "accuracy" by detaching the birth story from known particulars seems contrary to the evangelist's method of tying the story of Jesus and the apostles to significant public events. Since the census under Quirinius in A.D. 6-9 provoked a Galilean uprising, Luke may rather be seeking to connect the birth of the true Messiah to that event in a way that others may see the contrast between Jesus and a Theudas who gave "himself out to be somebody" or a Judas the Galilean who "drew some of the people after him" (Acts 5:36-37). Or perhaps the reference to the "first census" was Luke's way of dating Jesus' birth before the census of the revolt. Matters of historical accuracy will always be subject to judgment and probability. But whatever the historical basis of Luke's narrative or the evangelist's intention, Jesus' birth has now been unavoidably connected with imperial Roman policies and actions which have profound consequence for Israel.

The mention of **Caesar Augustus** is also significant far beyond its value for establishing a time reference. Luke is the only evangelist to mention **Augustus** (2:1), Tiberius (3:1), and Claudius (Acts 11:28; 18:2). All of these references indicate the common usage of the emperor's dates for establishing chronologies, but they also serve as backdrop for Luke's presentation of the kingdom of God and of the Messiah Jesus. This is Caesar whose name is Octavian but who has been acclaimed by the Senate as "the August One," worthy of divine favor and human adulation. How then shall the dominion of the God of Israel be exercised in the world where the rule of Caesar is proclaimed to be divinely decreed?

In Luke's day, many subjects of the Roman order even looked back to the time of Augustus as the golden age when the emperor did seem to embody the benevolent favor of the gods, but the intervening decades had seen that promise fail. Tyrants such as Caligula and Nero, who had been the most aggressive in claiming divine sanction for their rule or even divine status for themselves, had also been the most severe with the Jews. The questions of whether and how the God of the Scriptures is still the ruler becomes most crucial when systems, bureaucracies, and ideologies claim absolute or divine warrants for oppressive policies and actions.

Verses 3-5 explain why Jesus **of Nazareth** was born in **Bethlehem,** and the connection with David's line is focal. Nothing is said of Joseph's understanding of these events. Neither **Joseph** nor **Mary** even speak in the narrative until the twelve-year-old child Jesus is left behind in the temple (2:48). But Joseph is the paternal link with **the house and lineage of David,** and **his betrothed** and the unborn **child** are legitimated through Joseph. Matthew makes specific reference to the Micah prophecy of Bethlehem as the origin of the ruler of Israel, but Luke simply identifies David's and Jesus' birthplace as **the city of David** (see 1 Sam. 16:1; 17:12, 15, 58).

Verses 6-7 provide the details of the birth of the Messiah in a sheepfold in David's town. This is more than historical reporting and more than the story of the humble origins of a person of future greatness. The Greco-Roman reader might have recalled Virgil's poetic stories about the ideal ruler as shepherd of the people, born among simple shepherds (see *Aeneid* 6. 791ff. and his fourth *Eclogue).* But certainly the Jewish reader who knew the heritage of the psalms would recall the words concerning David: "He chose David his servant, and took him from the sheepfolds; from tending the ewes that had young he brought him to be the shepherd of Jacob his people, of Israel his inheritance" (Ps. 78:70-71). Even as he lay swaddled in cloths in a feed bin in a town away from home, this child Jesus was destined to be the fulfillment of God's promises to David and all of Israel, indeed to all the world.

Verses 8-20 present heavenly explications of the meaning of this birth. The **shepherds** are the only immediate audience for this angelic revelation, and they tell Mary and Joseph. But Luke's readers are privileged to observe the entire scene and hear the angel's words. The scene is yet one more direct glimpse into the graciousness of God's will and plan in this child, and the relevance of God's purposes for Israel's situation is expressed most forcefully in the announcement, **to you is born this day in the city of David a Savior, who is Christ the Lord** (v. 11).

To appreciate the impact of these words, it must be remembered that by the time Luke's Gospel was written, Israel had experienced more than 400 years of Greek and Roman hegemony. Before Alexander the Great, who conquered Palestine in 332 B.C., the Persians had allowed many Jews to return from the exile. And before the Persians, the neo-Babylonian Empire had conquered the last of the Davidic kings and destroyed the temple in Jerusalem in 587 B.C.. The Scriptures of Israel were written, transmitted, translated, and treasured in these many centuries, and Israel's faith was transformed in vital interaction with the challenges and crises of the times. One persistent challenge was the theocratic claims of all of these oriental empires. Their rulers were regularly ornamented with divine titles and glorious epithets (see the comments on 22:25-28 below).

Ptolemy I, the founder of the the dynasty in Egypt and ruler of Palestine (323–283 B.C.), was called "Savior" (*Sotēr*). Ptolemy III (245–221) bore the epithet "Benefactor" (*Euergetēs*). Antiochus II was surnamed "God" (*Theos*), which made his claim to self-importance clear, although he was known to be arbitrary and immoral. And Antiochus IV (175–164 B.C.), who desecrated the temple in Jerusalem and provoked the Maccabean revolt, was called "the Manifest God" (*Epiphanēs*) in public and "the Maniac" (*Epimanēs*) behind his back. Even the Romans, who were much more reticent to heap up divine claims for their rulers, found it politically expedient to encourage the continuation of this rhetoric of praise in the eastern provinces. Thus a famous public inscription from Priene from about 7 B.C. lauds "Augustus" as filled with a "hero's soul," and making wars to cease so that "the Epiphany of Caesar has brought into fulfillment vast hopes and dreams."

He is declared to be so unsurpassed that "the birthday of this God is for the world the beginning of the Gospel-festivals celebrated in his honor"(trans. Frederick W. Danker, *Jesus and the New Age* [St. Louis: Clayton, 1972], p. 24).

The Scriptures of Israel would not permit the uncritical acceptance of such claims. A passage such as Isaiah 43 must have read like a literature of protest with regard to all the divine claims which were ascribed to these mighty rulers: "I am the LORD your God, the Holy One of Israel, your Savior. . . . I, I am the LORD, and besides me there is no savior. I declared and saved and proclaimed when there was no strange god among you; and you are my witnesses, . . . I am God" (Isa. 43:3, 11-13; see also Isa. 45:21). For hundreds of years, the people of Israel had lived with the theopolitical rhetoric of their overlords. Still they continued to read the Scriptures which spoke of the Lord and Savior who surpassed the kings and rulers of this world. Even after the successors of **Augustus** had destroyed Jerusalem and announced divine sanction of their triumph, Luke's story of Jesus attested him as the *Savior* and *Lord* and Messiah of God's choosing.

Verses 8-9 introduce the angelophany, emphasizing the dramatic disruption of the shepherd's world. **An angel of the Lord, the glory of the Lord,** and **the shepherds** being **filled with fear** are all characteristic elements of an epiphany story. The awesome presence of the messenger from the court of the Most High Lord of heaven and earth evokes fear from all mortals because of the purity, power, and dazzling splendor of such an appearance. In Isaiah 6 the prophet was suddenly transported to the court of the Lord and soon cried, "Woe is me! For I am lost; for I am a man of unclean lips, and I dwell in the midst of a people of unclean lips; for my eyes have seen the King, the Lord of hosts!" (see also Luke 5:8). Now mere shepherds are confronted with this vision of might and radiance, and "they were afraid with a great fear."

Verses 10-13 present the angel's entire message. **Be not afraid!** is almost a standard element of Luke's angelophanies (see 1:13, 30; Acts 18:9; 27:24), but the message which follows indicates why mere mortals need not live in fear. Once again, the reader shares the privileged knowledge of the shepherds, as the meaning of this birth in the very court of the Lord God is disclosed, if only for a moment. While "many" were to rejoice at John's birth (1:14), the angel's official declaration of the **good news** of this birth identifies it as a **joy . . . to all the people.**

This announcement is given with even higher authority than the public inscriptions which declared Caesar's birth to be good news for all humanity (see above). Although later conflict and rejection of Jesus will evoke divine wrath and judgment, God had no ulterior motive in the birth of this Savior, Lord, and Messiah. God's purposes and determination in Jesus' birth are simply to bless and restore humanity.

The titles in v. 11 provide a compound identification of Jesus in his role and work. No real question about Jesus' royal and Davidic status had existed since Gabriel's word to Mary (1:32-33), but now this "Messiah" (RSV: **Christ**) and "Son of the Most High" (1:32) who will be born in the "city of David" (see also 2:4) is also named **Savior** and **Lord.** Luke is certainly not keeping any secrets concerning Jesus' messiahship. Jesus has as many epithets and surnames and titles as any of the Hellenistic rulers (see above).

Savior and **Lord** are especially popular titles among those contemporary rulers, and Luke is the only synoptic evangelist to use the term **Savior** for Jesus (see also Acts 5:31, 13:23; see John 4:42 and several usages in 1 and 2 Timothy and Titus). Luke appears eager to prompt comparisons between God's dominion exercised by Jesus and the lordship of the kings, saviors, and benefactors of the world (see discussion on Luke 22:25). Nevertheless, even the terms **Savior** and **Lord** have long been part of Israel's theocratic language (see the Isaiah reference above). Acts 13:23 also refers to Jesus as the "Savior" promised by God to Israel, indicating Luke's awareness of the scriptural content of the title. Similarly, the terms **Lord** and "Messiah" (RSV: **Christ**) are coupled again in Peter's Pentecost declaration as summarizing the roles which God assigned to the exalted Jesus (Acts 2:36).

Thus the angel's words to the shepherds are an announcement to the whole world of the Hellenistic empires spoken from within Israel's theocratic heritage. This is the disclosure of the true ruler, benefactor, and anointed king according to the design of the Lord God of Israel (see also "Son of God" in 3:22; 4:1-13, 41).

In v. 12, the **sign** of this momentous revelation is only an infant wrapped in shreds of **cloth** in a feed trough. The grand scale of the angel's declaration stands in apparant contrast with the simplicity and commonness of the **sign**. Matthew at least provided the connection that this **sign** was the fulfillment of the prophecy in Isa. 7:14 of an infant as a sign (Matt. 1:22-23). Certainly, the early Christians were familiar with that "sign" prophecy, but Luke lets the contrast stand between the glorious announcement and the humble sign. This again emphasizes that God's ways of ruling and bringing about the kingdom are not overt and coercive (see also the pre-Pauline hymn in Philippians 2). Jesus' identity and role are no secret in this story, but the participants in the story and the readers will be surprised and often perplexed by how Jesus will accomplish his mission.

Verses 13-14 conclude the angelophany with an appearance of the heavenly army chorus. The word **host** is a military term, indicating that from the vantage point of the government of heaven the whole story is filled with divine glory and power and splendor. The "theology of glory" of this story is expressed in the angels' doxology as well as in the shepherds' glorifying and praising God (v. 20). The Lord God is worthy of praise and honor for the fulfillment of prophetic promises which Jesus' birth represents. Furthermore, Jesus' birth confirms that God's "good pleasure" for humanity is **peace**. The phrasing of v. 14 has been complicated by divergent readings in the Greek manuscripts (compare KJV, "on earth Peace, good will toward men"), but God's gracious rule which is exercised directly in heaven is also being inaugurated on earth by means of this humble birth.

In vv. 15-20, the sign of which the angel has spoken is confirmed. Surprisingly little information is new, but that is exactly the point. In v. 15 the angels depart **into heaven,** and the shepherds decide to **go over to Bethlehem and see this thing that has happened. This thing** was previously identified as **a sign for you** (v. 12). **When they see** the sign, they announce that **the saying** of the angel has been confirmed (v. 17).

These concluding verses are a Lukan refrain on "seeing and hearing." This theme will be taken up repeatedly (see the discussion of 8:4-18; 10:21-24), and the tragedy of those who see but do not perceive and hear but do not understand will be explored in detail (see especially 23:32-49). Here when the faithful shepherds **saw** the sign, **they made known the saying which had been told them.** Mary's wonder at these things increases the sense of awe (v. 19, see also 2:51), but the shepherds simply continue **glorifying God for all they had heard and seen** (v. 20). There is no hint of doubt or disbelief. The faith of these shepherds is a blessed state of seeing and hearing, and it produces straightforward witness to the glory and praise of God.

The people will not always be so simple nor so faithful. Mary will soon have more complex matters of the heart to ponder (see 2:34-35, 51) because God and the Messiah will be contending with willful unbelief. But this story is a revelation of the salvation and blessing God intends with the birth of the **Savior who is Christ the Lord** (v. 11), and the angelic hosts join their voices with the faithful of Israel in the praise and glory of God (vv. 13-14; 20).

The Circumcision and Presentation of Jesus (2:21-40)

Zechariah's prophetic canticle concerning John is now paralleled and excelled with **Simeon** and **Anna's** oracles of Jesus. Close analysis of the details of both stories proves fruitful for understanding Luke's precise answer in each case to the question, "What then will this child be?" (Luke 1:66). Both stories are best understood as conveying the visions of aged seers, disclosing the will of God and the destiny of the child of promise in the illuminating ambiguity of prophetic speech. Everyone who has held an infant and pondered what would become of the child knows something of the vision these oracles disclose, but this is a story from the ancient world where signs, portents, and prophecies were of particular interest to historians, poets, and interpreters of the careers and destinies of notable people.

Above all, the births of John and Jesus are announced as signs that God has "visited and redeemed his people," fulfilling the promise made to David (1:68-69). Those who look for **the consolation of Israel** (2:25) and **the redemption of Jerusalem** (2:38) will not be disappointed. As Zechariah's canticle already made clear (see comments above), God's promises to Israel are still full of social and political reality even when it would have appeared to many that the kingdom of this Messiah had failed.

Simeon's oracles, however, with support from Anna, divulge God's unexpected way of fulfilling those promises and disclose the tragic reality of human rejection of God's purposes and means. Surrounded by rich narrative details, the heart of the episode lies in the tension between God's purposes and human willfulness, revealed respectively in the blessing of God (vv. 28-32) and in the blessing of Jesus' human father and mother (vv. 33-35).

Verse 21 again (see 1:59) reports the child's circumcision routinely in connection with his receiving the name given by the divine messenger (see 1:31). In this context, however, Jesus' **name** is not the occasion for profound comment. Considering how much debate surrounded the question of circumcision of Gentile converts (see especially Acts 15 and Galatians 2), it is worth noting that the evangelist simply assumes that the Messiah was fully observant of the Law.

Verses 22-24 make this assumption more explicit with direct allusions to scriptural commands concerning the consecration of the firstborn (Exod. 13:2) and the purification of the mother (Lev. 12:8; note that Luke speaks of "their purification," implying both Mary and Joseph). Luke is interested in temple practices and settings, and intent on demonstrating the faithfulness of Jesus and his followers to true temple worship (see 1:5-12; 2:41-49; 13:35; 18:10; 19:45—20:1; 21:1-38; 23:45; 24:53; Acts 2:46; 3:1—4:22; 5:20-42; 7:43-50(!); 21:26—22:17; 24:6-18; 25:8; 26:21). By mentioning **the law** in each of these three verses, he also stresses that proper temple observance is obedience to the will of God. The word **law** here means the text of Scripture, and it may also be understood to refer to God's theocratic rule. The term is unequivocally positive in this context.

Simeon's credentials presented in vv. 25-28 could not be more impressive. The term **righteous** is explicated more fully for Zechariah and Elizabeth as "walking in all the commandments and ordinances of the Lord blameless" (1:6, see also the discussion at 5:32). His expectation of **the consolation of Israel** is grounded in the scriptural promises of the restoration of the kingdom to Israel (see Isa. 40:1; 49:6!; 61:2), which is preeminently the work of the Holy Spirit. This is, therefore, a spiritual hope in that it is the work of the Spirit of God, but it is also the confidence in God's triumph over the nations and their gods which oppress Israel.

The consolation of Israel (v. 25) for which Simeon waits and **the redemption of Jerusalem** (v. 38) looked for by Anna and others in the temple are clearly technical terms which interpret each other. These terms gather up the hope of faithful Israel which has been expressed in many ways in the Scriptures. The salvation which Jesus brings has also been heralded in very concrete terms in the Magnificat (1:46-55) and in Zechariah's oracle concerning God's visitation and redemption of God's people (1:68-79). The reader quickly senses how freighted with meaning these terms are, and Luke will continue to bring forward named witnesses in the narrative, keeping the concern alive: see Joseph of Arimathea, "a good and righteous man . . . looking for the kingdom of God" (23:50-51), Cleopas and an unnamed disciple hoping "that he was the one to redeem Israel," the disciples asking, "Lord, will you now restore the kingdom to Israel?" (Acts 1:6), and Paul "on trial for the hope in the promise made by God to our fathers, to which our twelve tribes hope to attain, as they earnestly worship night and day" (Acts 26:6-7).

The Holy Spirit rests on Simeon (v. 25), has revealed to him that he would not **see death** until he had **seen the Lord's** Messiah (v. 26), and now inspires him to go to the temple (v. 27). Whatever Simeon "sees" in the temple will clearly be God's revelation to him and to the reader of Luke's narrative with him. "To see the Lord's Messiah" is to discern the fulfillment of God's promises to console, redeem, and save Israel.

Verses 29-32 contain Simeon's first oracle which has been preserved in the Nunc Dimittis of the church's worship. It is his blessing of God, an inspired human testimony to God's salvation as a promise fulfilled in Jesus. This oracle reveals what God's purposes and plans are with respect to this child, i.e., what does this child Jesus mean to God? The entire message is positive, attesting God's saving faithfulness to Simeon, Israel, and all the nations.

Simeon requests to **depart in peace,** as from the court of a great ruler, but in this context these words speak of Simeon's approaching death since he now **has seen the Lord's** Messiah (v. 26) who is also **thy salvation . . . prepared in the presence of all peoples** (v. 31). The aged seer who discerns divine favor in an infant is a common theme in ancient stories, and some thought that prophetic utterances of those about to depart from life were especially important. As Josephus says of Moses' last words, "souls when on the verge of the end deliver themselves with perfect integrity" (*Ant.* 4.179).

The public character of God's revelation is attested in Simeon's affirmation that God's salvation has been prepared **in the presence of** (before the face of) **all peoples.** As in Isa. 52:10 and and 40:3-5 (see Luke 3:6), the point is that God's salvation of Israel confronts all the nations of the world with a new reality, like it or not. These are mighty words of comfort to a people who have suffered public humiliation, with the Babylonian or Roman conquerors demeaning their religious traditions and their God. Now God will be publicly revealed bringing salvation on their behalf. The birth of the Messiah is a vindication of God and of the people of God.

Nevertheless, this does not mean that Israel's inferiority is now simply replaced with superiority. What God had in mind all along was the blessing of the people of God to be a blessing among the nations (Gen. 22:18). So also the great prophetic promises of Israel's consolation in the Babylonian exile made it clear that God was not content merely "to raise up the tribes of Jacob and to restore the preserved of Israel; I will give you as a light to the nations that my salvation may reach to the ends of the earth" (Isa. 49:6, see also 43:9-10). This broader grasp of the salvation God is bringing to Israel in Jesus is further explicated in Acts 1:6-8 when the disciples ask about the restoration and are commissioned to be witnesses to the end of the earth. God does intend to bring liberation from oppression, but this "light for revelation to the Gentiles," the non-Jewish nations, is more than they seem to realize.

The content of this oracle is not original with either Luke or Simeon. The point is exactly that Jesus fulfills what God declared from of old. So also, the mission to the Gentiles which will occupy so much of Luke's narrative in Acts is not the displacement of Israel. The mission is Israel's fulfillment. This has been Israel's calling all along. It is the glory of God's people Israel to be **a light for revelation to the Gentiles.**

Verse 33 displays the proper response to this prophetic disclosure as Jesus' **father and . . . mother** marvel or wonder in faith at what they have heard. Some Christian scribes were troubled to see Joseph called Jesus' father; the KJV followed some manuscripts that read, "Joseph and his mother marveled." Certainly Luke has emphasized divine initiative and the "overshadowing of the Holy Spirit" in the conception of this "son of David and Son of God" (see 1:32, 35), but the best ancient manuscripts suggest that the evangelist was content to speak of Joseph as Jesus' **father** or "parent" (see also 2:41). In this setting, Joseph and Mary are introduced primarily as the audience of the oracles, not in a carefully defined statement of the mystery of Jesus as divine and human.

Verses 34-35 convey Simeon's second oracle, which is also a "blessing," but now directed to Mary and Joseph instead of blessing God. If the first blessing declared what this child means to God, the second announces what Jesus portends for humanity; and the message is ominous. This dire prediction is equally the word of the Holy Spirit, indicating that God's determined will to bring salvation will meet with determined human opposition. The Holy Spirit knows this peril.

The God who is at work in human history is also contending with forces and structures that are entrenched in self-preservation. Thus the servant in Isaiah 40–55 and the Messiah in Luke are God's ways of bringing salvation to the ends of the earth, but no one should assume that their mission, God's mission, will be without suffering. *Suffering fashioned.*

If this child is set for the fall and rising of many in Israel, is it God who has set the stone of stumbling to bring a proud people low or is it human willfulness which causes Jesus to be an obstacle? The passive voice of the verb **is set** allows the question of agency to remain complex. More than one agency must be involved if the real contention and plot of this story is to be recognized. The story of Jesus is permeated with human tragedy as well as God's salvation so that neither becomes a platitude. Nevertheless, this oracle discloses that Jesus is not simply the cause of the decline and fall of Israel. Even the sequence is important, since **the fall and the rise of many in Israel** testifies again to the ultimacy of God's *saving* purpose.

The deeply cryptic message to Mary about the **sword piercing** her **own soul** has been subject to much Christian commentary, especially in circles of Marian piety. It is important that the pain of this mother's soul not be neglected in understandings of the "passion narrative" of the whole Gospel. God's initiative to bring in the Messiah and the kingdom did not take place at a distance from human affairs, and those at hand are quickly caught up in the struggle and the suffering.

Is it God's intention to divulge the (secret) **thoughts out of many hearts** or will this simply be an inevitable consequence of the coming of the light? In either case, the consequences are again ominous, and many episodes in the narrative will demonstrate that Jesus provoked anger, violence, and plots on his life when he refused to allow deceits, denials, and hostilities to remain covered. The entire narrative of Luke-Acts will revolve around the poles of the saving reign of God as inaugurated by Jesus and the defiance to that dominion practiced by human (and some larger than human) antagonists.

Verses 36-39 furnish a reprise to the crucial revelations of the Simeon story. Luke often has stories in pairs, and women figure prominently in the narrative. Here **Anna's** credentials as **a prophetess** help the reader be sure that Simeon was also a prophet. More detail is given with respect to her age, practice of worship, and tribal heritage. The patriarchal culture of Israel is evident in the way she is identified with reference to her father and her dead **husband,** and unfortunately no oracle is reported from this prophetess. Nevertheless, her integrity is assured. Her word to all those looking for **the redemption of Jerusalem** is one of thanksgiving, and she stands with Simeon at the culmination of the prophetic heritage of Israel (see 16:16), drawing words from the prophets of old and bearing witness to their fulfillment in Jesus.

In vv. 39-40, the evangelist provides a concluding refrain or summary. These few words do explain how Mary, Joseph, and Jesus got back to **Nazareth.** Since in vv. 21-22 the circumcision and presentation appear to be closely connected, the reader has the impression that the encounters with Simeon and Anna and the return to Nazareth took place just after the eight days were concluded. In Matthew, the trip to Egypt intervenes between Jesus' birth and the return to Nazareth. But neither Matthew nor Luke is attempting to give a daily account of events. Valiant efforts to prove the historical accuracy of either may distract from the evangelists' purposes and introduce unsolvable historical problems. Like the concluding growth refrain (see the comment on 1:80), the details of the return to Nazareth are related simply to conclude the whole episode, providing a setting for subsequent stories.

The Child Jesus in the Temple (2:41-52)

Luke is the only canonical evangelist to relate a story from Jesus' childhood, and this is the one story told. The apocryphal infancy Gospels tell several tales of Jesus as a powerful and precocious child, and such scenes have always held popular fascination. Some of those stories of Jesus confounding his teachers and being difficult for Mary and Joseph to handle may originate from imaginative readings of Luke. Luke's depiction of Jesus is itself stylized according to conventional scenes from the biographical lore of other famous figures such as Moses (see Philo, *Life of Moses* 1:20-24; Josephus, *Ant.* 2.228-238; *Life* 8–9). The image of the independence of the boy Jesus which this story depicts may be shocking. But Luke's depiction shows remarkable restraint when compared with the biographical lore which other authors have assembled to show how the greatness of their subject was already manifest in the wisdom and power of youth.

This story is again conspicuously full of detail concerning Jewish religious practice, with particular interest in **the Passover** pilgrimage to **the temple.** Jesus will not enter **Jerusalem** again in

Luke's version until the Passover season of his royal entry into the city, cleansing of the temple, teaching in it, and his death (see 19:28-48). This scene serves as a transition from Simeon and Anna's oracular announcements in the temple concerning the child to the body of the narrative where Jesus' role and mission commence as directly commissioned by God. It also foreshadows the controversy and conflict which the wisdom of the Messiah and son of God will provoke.

The heart of this episode, therefore, lies in the exchange between Mary and Jesus over obedience to his **father** and mother. This is a story about the child who is growing in **wisdom** (2:40, 52) and who, as the truly wise, is God's son. Whose child is Jesus, and who are his true parents (vv. 41-42)? In this passage, the question is focused on the identity of Jesus' true Father (vv. 48-49; see the comments on 3:23 and 8:19-21).

This depiction identifies Jesus for the knowing reader, long before the story unfolds. This picture fits with the way the *Wisdom of Solomon* had stated the scriptural identity of the righteous one, "He professes to have knowledge of God, and calls himself a child of the Lord" (see Wis. 2:13, 17). Luke's story provides a glimpse of the Christological identity and messianic authority which Jesus will exercise. This precocious child may already cause the pain of worry to Mary and Joseph. But still greater tensions lie ahead. He will also be perceived as a threat to the religious leaders in Israel when he returns to the temple with messianic rule.

Verses 41-45 provide a lengthy description of the circumstances in which Jesus was separated from Mary and Joseph. The details concerning the customary Passover pilgrimage from Galilee are adequate to allow the reader to form a clear impression. Like the story of Jesus' birth, this scene has been easily adapted for religious dramatization. The improbability of leaving a twelve-year-old **behind in Jerusalem** is addressed by the supposition that Jesus was somewhere in the large company of **kinsfolk and acquaintances.** Neither **his parents** nor the reader yet knows where Jesus is to be found, and it becomes clear that all the interest in the feast has distracted their and our attention.

A lost child (or, as they say on the loudspeakers, "lost parents") is always a cause of grave concern. For these village people from the north, the trip itself was sufficient hazard so that they banded together in groups, and Jerusalem was an imposing and often dangerous place. Now they had traveled **a day's journey** toward home. They had to retrace those steps and apparently search for **three** more **days** (v. 46) to find the child. The reader's vantage point on this story is that of the desperate parents, fearing the worst for their child of promise.

Verses 46-50 present the scene of the less than joyful reunion. The worry, distraction, and anger of the parents stand in marked contrast to the composure and control which the child Jesus is displaying. Before Mary and Joseph even begin to speak to confront the child, they (and we) observe him just long enough to realize that he is holding court with **the teachers** of Israel, both **listening to them and asking them questions.**

The brief interlude of vv. 46-47, therefore, is vital to Luke's prophetic presentation of Jesus in the temple. This is not simply a story of the courage and composure of a lost boy. This is a glimpse of the astonishment of those **who heard him** at his **understanding and his answers.** Like Mary and Joseph, the reader is caught off guard by another perspective which is not preoccupied with worry. The wisdom of this child of God captures the attention of those who have the eyes to see and the ears to hear. It is at least interesting to note that Josephus dated the beginning of Samuel's prophetic activity to his 12th year and his call in the temple (*Ant.* 5.348).

But Mary and Joseph are not able to take all of this in, at least not in the intensity of the moment, and the reader is swept along with their concern. Verse 48, therefore, reports that when they had seen him, "they were stunned," or "struck" or "overwhelmed" (see 4:32; 9:43; Acts 13:12). Their response is a classic parent reaction of relief, anger, and embarrassment: **Son, why have you treated us so?** What did he do to them? And then comes the standard parental scold, which is true enough in its feeling and content: "Your father and I have been hurt with worry seeking you." Quite apart from the doctrinal problems associated with calling Joseph **your father** (see the comment on v. 33 above), the

phrase **your father and I** is an appeal to authority, to filial bonds
and responsibilities.

Jesus' answer (v. 49) addresses both (**you** in plural) with two
more questions which are incomprehensible to them (v. 50). **How
is it that you sought me?** That is to say, no worried search should
have been required. **Did you not know that I must be in my
Father's house?** Translating such cryptic questions cannot avoid
interpretation. The word **house** is not present in Greek, and
perhaps Jesus was merely speaking of his calling to be about his
"Father's business" or "affairs." But the issue is at what *place* he
could be expected to be found, and it is consistent with Luke's
other usage to refer to the temple as God's "house" (see 19:46,
and indirectly 13:35).

The more difficult and crucial question is hidden in the phrase
"it is necessary" (RSV: **I must**) which translates one impersonal
Greek verb, *dei*. Several different kinds of "necessity" will be
discussed throughout this commentary on Luke, but the general
usage of this passage already indicates that Jesus is speaking of
divine will, of necessity which arises from obedience to his heavenly Father. The apparent passive of the term must not obscure
the conviction which Luke shares with many other scriptural
historians that God is an actor in the story. This is not the necessity
of fate, nor would the determinism of Greek and Roman historiography be able to cope with this "necessity" which arises from
the exercise of the will of the living God. Jesus was not simply
destined to be in the temple so that his parents should merely
resign themselves to it. It is because of the initiative of the Holy
Spirit that Jesus is set apart as holy and recognized as the Son of
God (1:35; 2:23), and he will be found at the temple, the house
of God, in obedience to his Father's will.

The conflict with the will of his earthly father and mother is,
therefore, unavoidable. Luke's narrative juxtaposes the anxious
appeal to authority of **your father and I** with Jesus' obligation to
obey **my Father,** and the evangelist emphasizes that neither Mary
nor Joseph was able to understand, no matter what they had heard
years before in Jesus' infancy.

In v. 51, however, Luke reports that Jesus returned with them,
was obedient to them; and his mother kept all these things in

her heart. Thus, for a time, Mary and the reader observe Jesus' prophetic vocation and role as royal Son of God recede from view. No higher authority than Jesus' earthly parents claims his obedience, for now. But Mary and we have been given something to think about, a glimpse of Jesus' teaching and wisdom and a foreshadowing of his calling as prophet and Son of God (see also 2:19).

Verse 52 is then the concluding growth refrain, repeated once again (see the comment on 1:80; 2;40). The annunciations and births of John and Jesus have been depicted as parallel to one another and as recapitulating and fulfilling the annunciations and births of the prophets and kings of the Scriptures. This one episode from Jesus' childhood has supplemented those infancy accounts, gathering up scriptural images once again and anticipating Jesus' vocation as prophet and Son of God who announces and inaugurates the kingdom of God. The gospel of the visitation of God (1:68) has begun, and the Messiah designate has already been to the temple. His next appearance as king will be the time of Israel's visitation (19:38, 44).

The Middle: Telling the Story
(Chapters 3–21)

■ The Inauguration of the Kingdom of Jesus the Messiah (3:1—9:50)

> You know the word which he sent to Israel, preaching good news of peace by Jesus Christ (he is Lord of all), the word which was proclaimed throughout all Judea, beginning from Galilee after the baptism which John preached: how God anointed Jesus of Nazareth with the Holy Spirit and with power; how he went about doing good and healing all that were oppressed by the devil, for God was with him.
>
> (Acts 10:36-38)

Preparing the Way of the Lord (3:1—4:13)
The Voice in the Wilderness (3:1-20)

John's Prophetic Call (3:1-6).　　　If Luke 1–2 served as an overture to the whole, the body of the narrative commences with the famous historical synchronism of 3:1-2. Once again, Luke stands back from the story to view it in the perspective of **the fifteenth year of . . . Tiberius Caesar,** the prefecture in Judea of Pontius Pilate, the tetrarchies of **Herod** Antipas, **Philip,** and **Lysanias** and **the high priesthood of Annas and Caiaphas.** Such chronological references were a convention of Greek historiography, and the significance of Luke's usage of the synchronism could thus be discounted as mere traditionalism. But the Christian sources which the evangelist used apparently had no such materials, and the specific names mentioned suggest that Luke was indeed quite conscious of projecting the story of Jesus against the backdrop of the political and religious history of Israel.

The apparently precise reference to **the fifteenth year of the reign of Tiberius Caesar** is less helpful for fixing dates than it would seem, since Roman sources note several points which could be called the beginning of his reign. Taken together with 3:23 where Jesus' age at the beginning of his ministry is noted, most interpreters prefer a date around A.D. 28 as the year Luke has in mind. But the greater significance of this reference is seen in Luke's pattern of references to the Caesars (see the comment on 2:1) and attention to the network of Roman administration. The politics of the Roman order were filled with claims and consequences for the faith of vassal Israel, and any Jewish group that believed that God's promises of the kingdom would yet be fulfilled had to contend with the political realities of the empire.

After the Romans removed Herod the Great's son Archelaus from being a client king in Judea because of his incompetence and cruelty, they established direct administrative control of Judea through the Roman governors. They allowed Herod's other sons, **Herod** Antipas and **Philip,** to continue as petty **tetrarchs,** but the facade of local rule was transparent. Antipas, who married Philip's wife (see 3:19), was eventually deposed by Caligula after making an attempt to regain the title of "king." **Pilate, Antipas, Philip,** and **Lysanias** (about whom almost nothing is known) are thus all agents of the Roman system, frequently caught up in intrigue and hostility toward each other (see 23:12).

The high priesthood is also largely under Roman control in this period, at least with regard to the appointment of persons to the office. Throughout the centuries of the Hellenistic kingdoms, the high priesthood had persisted as the most legitimate institution of Israel's religious and political identity so that even Herod the Great had found it necessary to control the high priesthood in order to rule as king. After he had systematically killed the last of the Hasmonean high priestly family, the Romans also found it easier to appoint cooperative high priests. Many of them still should be credited with commitment to the sanctity of the faith of Israel. The family of **Annas,** including his son-in-law **Caiaphas,** was continued in the high priesthood for several years. It would now be impossible to render an objective verdict on the integrity with which particular high priests exercised the office under those conditions, but clearly the Pharisees, the Christians, and others who were intensely zealous for the Law of Moses often found fault with the high priesthood.

John the Baptist is presented as receiving his prophetic call in the midst of such religious and political circumstances. The synchronism and the phrase **the word of God came** upon **John the**

son of Zechariah in the wilderness offer almost a paraphrase of the prophetic call of Jeremiah in the LXX: "The word of God which came upon Jeremiah the son of Hilkiah . . . in the days of Josiah the son of Amon, king of Judah, in the thirteenth year of his reign" (Jer. 1:1-2). The reference to **the wilderness** also links the passage back to the last mention of John in 1:80 and provides as well the first direct parallel in the narrative to Mark's Gospel (Mark 1:4). Once again, Luke has carefully introduced John in the terms and mode of the scriptural prophets.

In v. 3, Luke begins to draw in earnest upon clearly identifiable Christian sources, namely the Gospel of Mark and the collection of sayings shared with Matthew which is generally called "Q." As will be noted later (see the comment on 6:20), Luke generally follows one of these sources for an extended portion of the narrative so that the coherence and even the sequence of the source may be identified with some confidence, and Luke's alterations of the source may be explained (see the comment on 4:16-30). In this section, however, the Markan material used in vv. 3-4 stands in close proximity to the "Q" material in vv. 7-9, and vv. 16-18 appear to be constructed out of both sources. The commonality of traditions concerning John may already have produced more agreement than usual between Mark and Q, and the evangelist's efforts to pull the sources together for a section on John may have affected the way the sources are used. In any case, this section already demonstrates that Luke is actively composing a narrative in which sources have been used, but not simply rehearsing the sources while making occasional modifications to score specific points.

John's proclamation of the **baptism of repentance for the forgiveness of sins** is clearly attested in pre-Lukan tradition (see Mark 1:4), but the phrase is a crucial keynote for Luke's treatment of John as well. The preaching of repentance and forgiveness of sins will be focal to the ministry of Jesus (see especially 5:32; 10:13; 11:32; 13:3, 5; 15:7, 10; 16:30-31) and fundamental to the commission of the Christians after Easter (24:46-47; Acts 2:38; 3:19; 5:31; 8:22; 11:18; 17:30; 20:21; 26:20). Furthermore, the washing rituals of the sectarians at Qumran and others in the Jordan valley suggest that John and the early Christians should be understood alongside other movements of repentance and renewal which hoped for the restoration of Israel by God. Luke also presents a very positive assessment of the significance of the "baptism which John preached," emphasizing its efficacy as a divinely instituted means to prepare Israel for the messianic age (see 7:29; 20:4-8; Acts 13:24).

In Luke's presentation of later Christian repentance and baptism, John's baptism will be found lacking the agency of the Holy Spirit, and repentance will be focused much more sharply upon the turn to faith in Jesus (3:16; Acts 18:25-19:6). Still it is difficult to conceive of a higher commendation for John than Jesus' words that he was "more than a prophet. This is he of whom it is written, 'Behold, I send my messenger before thy face, who shall prepare thy way before thee.' I tell you, among those born of women none is greater than John" (Luke 7:26-28).

The absence in Luke's narrative of several interesting details in Mark's presentation invites speculation: i.e., the hair shirt, the leather girdle, the diet of locusts and wild honey, and the crowds from Judea and Jerusalem (see Mark 1:5-6). Luke's account of John's preaching (see the Q material in vv. 7-9 and 17) certainly demonstrates that the portrait has not been softened. On the other hand, the expansion of the quotation from Isaiah so that vv. 5-6 include prophetic material lacking in Mark presents a strong impression of John's preaching of repentance pointing beyond itself to **the salvation of God** which **all flesh shall see** (v. 6; Isa. 40:5; see comment on **all flesh** below at v. 7).

The scriptural quotation now directly explicates John's preaching of a baptism of repentance unto forgiveness of sins. Neither the concept nor the passage is original with Luke, but the evangelist has laid more direct claim to the promise of salvation and restoration which Isaiah 40 offered. This is less a proof text for identifying John as **the voice of one crying in the wilderness** and more a declaration of the coming fulfillment of the promise of God's restored reign. Luke's summary of John's preaching at the end of the section will sound the same note (v. 18).

John's Message for Israel (3:7-20).   Gabriel's first words to Zechariah had revealed John's mission clearly as summarized in the last line, "to make ready for the Lord a people prepared" (1:14-17). Now John has come preaching a baptism of repentance for the forgiveness of sins in fulfillment of the Isaiah prophecy of the voice in the wilderness heralding restoration. This prophetic messenger bears a word of reproof and hope to the people in preparation for Israel's salvation which shall be accomplished in full view of all the other nations ("all flesh," v. 6). John does not yet announce the kingdom of God, nor does he yet bear a message for the Gentiles. Nevertheless, John is a harbinger of the messianic reign, and his message of repentance discloses the judgment and the purification which Israel shall experience in the coming of the Messiah.

Luke has gathered a variety of Christian traditions about John into a narrative unit so this cycle of stories further explicates the repentance which John preached and anticipates Jesus' declaration of the inauguration of the kingdom. Each of the traditional units is distinctive in form and content, but Luke has depicted the whole section as John's message to the people of Israel. The theological, social, and political consequences of such a message are also conspicuous in Luke's account.

Verses 7-9 present a fearsome oracle of judgment in which John's words are virtually identical to their recounting in Matt. 3:7-10. Luke and Matthew have conserved their source ("Q") with care in its sharp warning against self-satisfaction or confidence which is based upon ancestry from Abraham. Other early Christian sources sound a similar warning and insist that the promises made to **Abraham** are intended for his true children, but that mere physical descent is not sufficient (see Galatians 3; Romans 4; John 8:33-39). As a pre-Christian preacher of repentance, John was calling for faithful observance of the will of God including appropriate ethical action (the **fruits that befit repentance**) as marks of being true children of Abraham. Luke has not added anything of the distinctive Christian sense of faith in Jesus the Messiah as the content of repentance or the sign of true kindred with Abraham.

But Luke does not rehearse these traditions unsympathetically nor simply preserve an artifact of pre-Christian preaching of repentance. The commands of God are also intact for Christians, and the evangelist may bring forward John's prophetic voice with integrity to address the reader. In Acts 26:20, Luke presents Paul describing his ministry to King Agrippa as directed by the heavenly vision to declare "first to those at Damascus, then at Jerusalem and throughout all the country of Judea, and also to the Gentiles, that they should repent and turn to God and perform deeds worthy of their repentance." Even after "turning to God" has been understood much more specifically as repentance and baptism in the name of Jesus the Messiah (Acts 2:38-39), good fruit is to be expected (see 6:43-45; 13:1-9).

The mention of **fire** in v. 9 has added signficance in the context of Luke's narrative because of the references to the **baptism of the Holy Spirit and fire** in v. 16 and to the **unquenchable fire** in v. 17. These three uses of the word appear to have already linked the sayings of John in "Q," and their emphasis on judgment, on purification and destruction, indicates that Luke sees the coming of John and then Jesus as a divinely provoked crisis in Israel. An event of eschatological proportions is about to occur. **The wrath** which is **to come** is closely connected with the baptism **of the Holy Spirit and fire,** and the people of God are confronted with impending doom and salvation.

"What then shall we do?" is the critical question, repeated three times in vv. 10, 12, and 14. It is almost identical to the people's response to Peter's preaching in the midst of the Holy Spirit and fire of Pentecost: "Brothers, what shall we do?" (Acts 2:37, see also Luke 10:25; 18:18; Acts 16:30; 22:10). In the wake of John's warning of **wrath** and **fire,** this question unites these diverse groups of the people of Israel in their concern for salvation, for safety in the peril. Luke's literary hand is evident in the question and answer format as well as in the identification of the various groups among the people, the multitudes (v. 10), the tax collectors (v. 12), and the soldiers (v. 14). The ethical content of John's preaching is focal to Luke's interest, defining **fruits that befit repentance** in terms that are specific to each group.

For all the multitudes of the people, the sharing of clothing and food is identified as the crucial mark of repentance. Later in the narrative, Jesus and the apostles will also advocate the cause of the poor with clear support from the Scriptures, and John's counsel already makes it evident that genuine economic need is the issue. This stern preacher advocates an uncompromising but possible practice of **sharing** with those who have need. He does not require an asceticism of alienation from worldly goods.

The **tax collectors** and **soldiers** clearly represent two groups of Jewish people who are cooperative with the Roman order and are often resented by other Jews or thought to be disloyal to Israel. The **tax collectors** had been an institution in Israel throughout several empires, and the use of natives to collect revenue was a standard procedure because it was less offensive and more effective than attempts at direct collection by occupying forces. In some eras and circumstances, the high priests or the local "king" was charged with collections which could be delegated; and at other times or for different levies, the tax collectors reported to foreign administrators. So also, the **soldiers** in the text are most likely Jewish nationals, perhaps in service to the high priest or one of the Herodian tetrarchs.

John's commands to each indicate the abuses associated with their roles. Every system of taxes, tolls, and tariffs is vulnerable to abuse, perhaps especially in the ancient world when the collector often worked on a quota without much accountability except for submitting the assigned total. Unfair collection, quiet graft, and extortion were commonly suspected, perhaps correctly (see 19:8). It is not surprising that "the tax collectors" are often mentioned in the same breath with "the sinners" (see 7:29,34; 15:1; 18:9-14), that is, those who are not faithful to the Law, but the ministry of John and Jesus among this despised and affluent class is surprising.

The abuse of military power to intimidate and "shake down" innocent people has been a problem in every army, and discontent with army rations and pay is commonplace and often dangerous. The question of how much is "enough" for the military and for the soldier will always be a social problem, because it requires taxation, and the corruption of power and greed of the military will continue to be public concerns. But these problems are particularly severe when the might of the army is perceived as an extension of alien domination, as in first-century Israel.

Luke's presentation of John's counsel is again forthright, but not extreme. Neither the tax collectors nor the soldiers are commanded to abandon their tasks. The **fruits that befit repentance** are appropriate to their situations in life. The call of the Messiah and his baptism of fire will be much more radical in its claim and eschatological urgency. For now, the Baptist's message is a clarion call that the time for repentance, for returning to God in faithfulness, has come. And these ethical **fruits that befit repentance** are signs of Israel's eschatological preparedness.

Verses 15-18 enclose a core of traditional sayings from Mark and "Q" that transmit John's highly charged eschatological declarations about the Messiah as the **mightier** one whose laces John is not **worthy to untie,** who will **baptize with the Holy Spirit and with fire,** and whose winnowing shovel will sweep the grain clear of **the chaff.** The images are powerful and filled with prophetic allusions (see Mal. 3:1-3, the coming one, the refiner's fire; Isa. 4:4-5, purifying with water and fire; Isa. 41:15, threshing as judgment, but of the nations!). The intensity of the pre-Lukan memory of John's preaching is intact, but Luke's usage of these traditions also scores crucial points.

In v. 15, Luke introduces John's mighty words as a response to the question of whether he might be the Messiah. Each Gospel deals with the problem of John and Jesus' identities differently. As in the Fourth Gospel (John 1:25), Luke's John addresses the question immediately and directly. These strong traditional words with overtones to Malachi further distinguish the messenger who prepares the way from "the Lord whom you seek" who "will suddenly come to his temple" (Mal. 3:1).

Within the context of Luke's larger narrative, the Messiah's baptism of **Holy Spirit and fire** also has new meaning. The descent of the Holy Spirit and the tongues of fire of Pentecost are more than images of purification (Acts 2:1-4). They are signs of the restoration of true Israel to its prophetic calling and witness in the world. Luke also knows that the Messiah has come "to cast fire on the earth" in judgment in close connection with his baptism (see 12:49-50), but judgment and destruction are not the goal of the Messiah's **fire.** Thus Luke's summary of the whole of John's message is that John's declarations were positive entreaties to **the people** (v. 18), perhaps even words of encouragement or consolation (see 7:18-30; 16:16; Acts 2:40; 11:23; 14:22; 15:32; 16:40).

John the Baptist is a bearer of the word of God, calling Israel to turn around, to return to God for salvation from coming wrath and judgment, but he is not simply a grim prophet of doom. He is himself the fulfillment of prophetic promises, pointing beyond himself to the coming one (see the discussion of 7:18-30). God's messianic ruler is about to appear, and this prospect presents a peril to those in Israel whose lives and deeds are disobedient. But even John bears a word which is ultimately full of promise. Now John must exit for the divine drama to continue.

Verses 19-20 demonstrate that Luke is intent on removing John from the stage before introducing Jesus. The episode of the arrest of John is reported in Mark 6 (but see Mark 1:14!) and Matthew 14—after Jesus' ministry has been under way for some time—but Luke has rearranged his source and used this episode to conclude his account of John's ministry. John will not even be mentioned in the story of Jesus' baptism which follows.

The book of Acts indicates that some clarification continued to be necessary to distinguish between John's baptism and Christian baptism, and the disciples of Jesus and the disciples of John felt some competition and comparison (see Luke 11:1; Acts 11:16; 13:25; 18:25—19:5; and John 1:20). Only a few fascinating traces remain of the first-century community of followers of John the Baptist, but the followers of Jesus clearly found it necessary to emphasize that John himself made no claim to be the Messiah. Both of the later evangelists, Luke and John, quote the Baptist as responding negatively to the explicit question of whether he might not be the Messiah (Luke 3:15, John 1:20, 25).

Verses 19-20, however, are more than a literary device to remove John from the scene. Here Luke interprets John's confrontation with the client ruler and offers a direct comment on the imprisonment of John as an additional **evil thing** of Herod the Tetrarch (v. 20). This preacher of repentance and herald of the Messiah soon ran afoul of the political authorities.

Herod Antipas's marriage to **Herodias,** the **wife** of his half-brother, was a political scandal which Josephus also recalled in some detail, and Josephus included an account of John's imprisonment and death in that context. Luke does not name Herodias's first husband, although Mark and Matthew identify him as Philip. According to Josephus, her husband was another half-brother and son of Herod the Great named Herod. But Antipas's first marriage had been part of a political arrangement with King Aretas IV of Nabatea, and war broke out when he repudiated marriage to Aretas's daughter. Antipas lost much of his army in that war and gained a politically ambitious wife who eventually led to his downfall with the Roman emperor Caligula. The intrigue of these marriages again demonstrates the political complexity of the situation. Josephus does not mention John's denunciation of the divorce and marriage, but he observes that Antipas put John to death out of fear that sedition could arise from the effect on the people of such eloquent preaching of repentance: "he had exhorted the Jews to lead righteous lives, to practise justice towards their fellows and piety towards God, and so doing to join in baptism" (*Ant.* 18.116-119).

Luke maintains that John not only criticized Antipas's marriage to his brother's wife, but he also **reproved** him for **all the other evil things he did.** This herald of the Messiah is not removing himself from the political arena by remaining in the wilderness. Herod and Pilate had to deal with more than one wilderness prophet or leader who rallied public opinion or even armies against their dominion. So also Luke leaves no doubt that John was an active critic of the Tetrarch, even on an issue which was so politically volatile.

Furthermore, Luke's own verdict on John's arrest is that it was one more **evil thing** which Herod did. Since Herod is a figure who will appear at several strategic moments in the narrative, it is important to observe that the evangelist has indicated both John's and his own disapproval. Herod Antipas is a murderer, a "fox," a sadist, and an adversary of the Messiah (see 9:7-9; 13:31-32; 23:7-12; Acts 4:27).

The Anointing of the Holy Spirit (3:21-22)

The New Testament and the Christian tradition testify to Jesus as the Christ and the Son of God. Both of these titles have been used so constantly in Christian worship and piety that many battle lines must be crossed if an understanding of their meaning in first-century sources is to be attempted. *Jesus Christ* could never have been merely a proper name among early Christians, especially among Jewish Christians, for whom Jesus' identity as Messiah was subject to such dispute, and those early believers would have found the later metaphysical debates about the "two natures of Christ" most perplexing. Similarly, *Son of God* was less a title denoting "divinity" or even divine status than it was an identification of Jesus as the true king of Israel who fulfilled the scriptural promises of a ruler of God's own anointing. Neither of these titles is used directly in this brief passage, but Luke's account of Jesus' baptism is a testimony to him as the anointed Son of God.

The absence of John the Baptist from the story is important, but it ought not be overestimated in significance. The phrasing of v. 21 seems to suggest that Jesus had already been baptized along with **all the people,** so that the descent of **the Spirit** occurred during his prayer. The traditional story of John's baptism of Jesus also required comment for Matthew, who quoted Jesus as insisting that he must submit to John's baptism "in order to fulfill all righteousness" (Matt. 3:15). For Luke, the baptism of Jesus (by John) is another demonstration of the Messiah's full observance of every aspect of Jewish ritual and worship (see notes on 2:21-24). Thus even the Messiah is in solidarity with *all* of repentant and prepared Israel.

The traditional story of the baptism, however, has now become the account of God's acclamation and anointing of the true king of Israel. Luke's account of Peter's speech before Cornelius offers the best commentary: "beginning from Galilee after the baptism which John preached: how God anointed Jesus of Nazareth with the Holy Spirit and with power" (Acts 10:37-38; see also the comment on 4:18). For Luke, the mention of Jesus at prayer is not simply a pious touch. Prayer is repeatedly a crucial occasion for divine instruction of the Messiah and his apostles and for the reception of the Holy Spirit throughout the narrative (see 1:10; 5:16; 6:12; 9:18, 28-29; 11:1; 22:41-45; 23:34, 46; Acts 1:14, 24; 2:42; 4:31; 6:4-6; 7:59; 8:15-17; 9:9-19; 10:1-5, 9, 30-31; 11:5; 12:5, 12; 13:1-3; 14:23; 16:25; 20:36; 21:5; 22:17; 28:8; see especially Luke 11:1-13).

The presence of **the Holy Spirit** is best understood as the authorization of divine kingship. Stories from 1 Samuel again furnish the prototypes (see the comments on 1:36-55), but now the scene has moved on to the anointing of Saul and David by Samuel. First Samuel 8 introduced the choosing of Saul with the protest that only God was truly king of Israel, but that God would concede to Israel's request. After Saul was anointed by Samuel, "God gave him another heart . . . and the spirit of God came mightily upon him and he prophesied" (1 Sam. 10:1, 9-10; see also 1 Sam. 11:5-15). And when the Spirit of the Lord departed from Saul, David was chosen: "Then Samuel took the horn of oil, and anointed him in the midst of his brothers; and the Spirit of the Lord came mightily upon David from that day forward" (1 Sam. 16:13). The descent of the Holy Spirit **in bodily form** has thus become a visible sign confirming Jesus' identity and role as fulfilling and surpassing God's rule in Davidic kingship.

The citation of Psalm 2 is unquestionably royal and messianic in Luke's account. Luke adds nothing to the tradition here, but the tradition itself is very complex in its interpretive enrichment of Psalm 2. Some of this intrascriptural discussion was already part of Jewish commentary on this psalm about the Lord's "anointed" king, and the apparent adoptionism of the psalm ("today I have begotten you") was displaced in pre-Lukan Christian traditions by allusions to Isa. 42:1 ("my servant, my chosen in whom my soul delights") or possibly 2 Sam. 22:20 (of David: "he delivered me because he delighted in me"). Luke also cited this psalm in Peter and John's words in Acts concerning opposition to God's "holy servant Jesus, whom thou didst anoint" (Acts 4:27).

The voice from heaven addresses the newly anointed king of Israel, Jesus. This king is not merely the adopted son of God as David and his line had been. Jesus is the true **Son** of God in terms of his begetting, as these early chapters attest, but also in terms of his complete concurrence with God's will, as will soon be proved (4:1-13). Nevertheless, the voice from heaven speaks in scriptural phrases to identify the beginning of Jesus' reign which was announced by angels before and at his birth. God's word to Jesus confirms the promise of divine dominion in Israel made to David and his heirs. Jesus is the one of whom God had spoken to David: "I will raise up your offspring after you . . . and I will establish the throne of his kingdom forever. I will be his father and he shall be my son" (2 Sam. 7:12-16). Now the narrative will display how this anointed son of David and Son of God will exercise God's dominion in Israel.

The Genealogy of the Messiah (3:23-38)

Modern readers are likely to be uninterested in the very details which were so fascinating to ancient historians and interpreters. Even very technical assessments of these verses may claim little success in "cracking the code" concerning their structure and meaning. Studies of Matthew's genealogy have made more progress in grasping how the details fit within the evangelist's purposes, but the discrepancies with Luke's list remain as baffling as they were to older interpretations which attempted to demonstrate how both genealogies could be justified historically.

Scholars have offered several intriguing suggestions which may have merit. Eleven cycles of 7 generations each add up to the 77 named. Jesus may be counted as the 1st of the 7th cycle of 7 generations since David and the 1st of the 12th cycle since Adam. Perhaps the apocalyptic scheme that history would last through 12 "parts" is implied (see 4 Ezra 14:11). It is not impossible that Luke has drawn upon another Christian source which developed such ideas in greater detail. But Luke's own interests in the list would seem to be more modest.

The genealogy serves in Luke's narrative to offer another demonstration of Jesus' legitimate paternity from **David** and finally from **God**. The Messiah's Davidic heritage (bypassing Solomon: see Jer. 22:28-30; 36:30-31) is reckoned through **Joseph** (*as was supposed*). Luke is aware that Joseph is the adoptive father. Perhaps he would agree that **God** was the true, not adoptive, father. The point, of course, is to emphasize Jesus' legitimacy as son of David and Son of God. Jesus' paternity can be traced directly to God and indirectly to God through the Davidic line.

The patriarchal character of this list reflects a more culturally acceptable view of legitimacy according to first-century standards than Matthew's genealogy. Matthew includes notable exceptions in a line traced through women (and what women!). Luke's tracing his ancestry all the way back to Adam, beyond Abraham (see Matt. 1:1-2) may identify Jesus with all of humanity including the Gentiles, but Luke does not develop the idea. It is also possible that the identification of Adam as "the son of God" fits with early Christian discussion of Jesus as the "second Adam" (see Romans 5), but Luke never touches on this theme in his narrative.

This list is an elaboration on Luke's presentation of Jesus as born into the family of Abraham, Isaac, and Israel, identified with his earthly "parents" (see 2:33, 41, 43), but truly the Son of God and son of David who will exercise God's reign in Israel. Jesus has now attained the respectable age of maturity (**about thirty**) to commence his rule. To say that he is beginning **his minstry** (RSV, v. 23) is only adequate if it is remembered that such "ministry" is an activity of consequence to the Messiah. The task he is undertaking would yet be viewed by his accusers as the beginning of his "stirring up of the people" (23:5; Gk: "beginning from Galilee"). It would be interpreted by the apostles as the beginning of his reign as the anointed one after John's baptism (Acts 1:22; 10:37-38).

The Testing of the Son of God (4:1-13)

Jesus has been announced by Gabriel as the Son of God (1:32, 35). He has demonstrated the complexity of his obedience to his "Father" in the temple (2:41-52). He has been acclaimed as "my beloved Son" by the voice from heaven (3:22), and his genealogy has been traced through his earthly father and forefather David to Adam, the son of God (3:23-38). Now the newly anointed **Son of God** completes his last act of preparation for public activity. His obedience to the will and reign of God is proved by the devil's tests in the wilderness.

Preachers and other interpreters must exercise particular caution to avoid being drawn into historical and psychological speculation about this episode. Modern preoccupation with "what really happened" has threatened to reduce the narrative to an account of hallucinations due to sensory deprivation and hunger, while guesswork about Jesus' own psychological (or psychic!)

health has distracted attention from the evangelist's carefully drawn account. As a transmitter of a traditional Christian story and as a narrator, the evangelist has interpreted this encounter as a test which displays Jesus' full obedience to God's rule and law as the basis of the ministry which will follow.

The story came to Luke and Matthew from Q. Mark had reported only that Jesus "was in the wilderness for forty days, tested by Satan, and he was with the wild beasts" (1:13). Although Luke is generally following Mark's outline in these chapters, his narrative is thoroughly recomposed, with alterations (Luke 3:21-22//Mark 1:9-11), additions (Luke 3:23-38), and changes in sequence (see Luke 4:14-30//Mark 1:14b, 6:1-6a). The close parallels with Matthew in this passage indicate that both evangelists followed their source closely. Luke has rewritten his introduction and conclusion (vv. 1-2, 13), has expanded the devil's claim to be the world ruler (v. 6), and has apparently rearranged the last two "tests" so that the episode concludes once again at the temple in Jerusalem. The traditional heart of the story, however, is a scriptural deliberation about the obedience of Jesus as the true ruler and Son of God.

This is not a "temptation" story in the sense of mere personal enticement. This scene depicts Jesus' obedience to God's rule against a rich backdrop of Israel's history. In Luke's context, the reader might think of another newly anointed son of David, Solomon, praying to rule with understanding and discernment between good and evil in obedience to God's will (see 1 Kings 3:1-14). Or perhaps the precedent of Moses and Elijah's 40 days of fasting before the Lord would have been suggestive of Jesus' prophetic role (Exod. 34:28; Deut. 9:9,18; 1 Kings 19:8). The symbolic significance of this story is not exhausted by one set of associations.

Jesus' three citations from Deuteronomy, however, make the precedent of Israel's testing in the 40 years in the wilderness most compelling. Each of the tests "proves" Jesus to be the true and faithful Son of God even as Israel was "proved" to be unfaithful during the 40 years in the wilderness (see Ps. 95:10, Deut. 8:2-5 [MT], of Israel; "the Lord your God has led you these forty years in the wilderness . . . testing you to know what was in your heart, whether you would keep his commandments, or not . . . know then in your heart that, as a man disciplines his son, the Lord your God disciplines you"). That was all Israel, God's son in a general sense (see Hos. 11:1; Exod. 4:22; Matt. 2:15), being tested and found wanting by God. This is the ruler of Israel, God's son in the particular senses of divine paternity at conception and authorization as king. Now **the devil** is the "tester," although Luke emphasizes the directing activity of the Holy **Spirit** (v. 1).

Luke uses this traditional story of scriptural interpretation of Jesus with literary and theological sensitivity. He conserves the scriptural citations so that the reader may still find the larger context of Deuteronomy 6–8 and Psalm 91 instructive for understanding the debate between **the Son of God** and **the devil.** In short, Jesus alludes to relevant passages while the devil quotes the verse out of context, doing violence to the sense of the psalm. But Luke also puts the story to work within his narrative.

Verses 1-2 link the episode back to the Jordan location of the Baptist and, by inference, to Jesus' anointing (see 3:3). Luke is interested in geographical details, and he is even more intent on stressing the agency of the Holy Spirit. In Simeon's introduction, the Spirit is mentioned three times in three verses (2:25-27). In Jesus' anointing, the Spirit, which has descended on him just prior to the interlude of his genealogy (3:22), is mentioned twice more in one verse. To say that Jesus is **full of the Holy Spirit** and is **led by the Spirit** is more an affirmation of the objective agency of God's Spirit than an assessment of Jesus' spirituality. The same Spirit which directed Simeon to identify the Lord's Messiah now has anointed Jesus and is leading him in the wilderness. Mark and Matthew's statement that the Spirit "drove" or "led" Jesus *into* the wilderness is also strong, but Luke's statement that Jesus was led in the wilderness is more reminiscent of Israel's being led by the pillar and cloud of divine presence throughout 40 years *in* the wilderness. Luke's introduction of the story also concludes with the implication that it was at the end of his 40 days of not eating that the devil approached him in his hunger with these specific tests (so also Matt. 4:2, in different words).

In the first trial (vv. 3-4), the devil addresses a genuine human need with a phrase emphasizing a real condition: "since" **you are the Son of God.** Neither Jesus' identity nor his powers is doubted. The question is how he will use his authority and power. The people of Israel cried for **bread,** and God supplied manna. Even King David took extraordinary (messianic?) privileges, seizing holy bread when he and his troops were hungry (1 Samuel 21). Jesus' answer (from Deut. 8:3a) indicates that this ruler and Son of God will not seize authority even out of genuine human need, but will listen to the word of God and live by "everything that proceeds out of the mouth of the Lord" (Deut. 8:3b). Jesus is not contending merely with human forces, but neither is the devil. The reader may observe that the Son of God, Jesus, is directed by the Holy Spirit and instructed by the word of God when tested so that he will not use his authority for personal advantage no matter how compelling the need.

The second test in Luke's sequence (vv. 5-8) escalates the question of authority, and Luke appears to have elaborated the devil's speech in a few details. Now **in a moment of time,** the devil shows Jesus all the kingdoms **of the world** (see "Caesar" in 2:1) and promises to bestow **all this authority and their glory; for it has been delivered to me and I give it to whom I will.** This verse has often been cited as proof that the kingdoms of the world are in the hands of the devil, but when did the devil's words become so credible? The issue precisely is this: who has the authority to establish Jesus as Lord of earth (and of heaven), and from whom is this authority derived? The **worship** which the devil requires is merely the obeisance before authority which oriental rulers expected as acknowledgment of their divinely bestowed authority.

Jesus does not accept the truth or validity of the devil's claims, let alone allow himself to be "tempted" by such enticement. Only the dominion of the God who brought Israel out of Egypt can be recognized. The Scriptures had long revealed that all other "gods" and "powers" are subordinate or idols, although Israel was slow to learn. Thus Jesus' recitation of Deut. 6:13 is basic to Israel's catechism, and it is also the crucial confession of the theocratic convictions of Israel's monotheism. God's claim to dominion "on earth as in heaven" (Matt. 6:10) remains a challenge to the claims of the principalities and powers.

The third "test" has probably been moved to this sequence by Luke (compare the second "test" in Matt. 4:5-7). Luke specifically mentions **Jerusalem,** and the conclusion of this episode at the temple foreshadows Jesus' climactic return to the temple in 19:45—21:38. The devil's misuse of Scripture (see the comment above) may seem amusing, and certainly it was a warning against unfaithful citations of Scripture. Again granting that Jesus truly is the Son of God, the devil is suggesting a course of action which would "prove" Jesus' authority over against God. But the psalm speaks this word of promise specifically to the faithful one who trusts in God and cleaves to God in love (Ps. 91:1, 14). Jesus is the one who is being tested as Israel—not God—has been, and Jesus refuses to put God on trial.

The question of God's justice will in time become much more complex when this Son of God is executed "at the hands of lawless men" (Acts 2:23) on the charge of being "the king of the Jews" and "the Messiah" (22:68; 23:2, 35-38). But even then Jesus does not put God to the test or try to force God's hand, as some modern interpreters have suggested. The unholy alliance of the devil, the religious leaders, Judas, Pilate, and Herod are the ones who will put God's justice to the test by killing the righteous one (see 22:3-6; Acts 4:23-31). Thus Luke ends this story with a note which will haunt the narrative until Jesus has completed his messianic teaching of Israel in the temple (21:38): **The devil . . . departed from him until *an opportune time*** . . . "then Satan entered into Judas . . . he agreed and sought an *opportunity* to betray him" (4:13; 22:3-6).

Declaring the Kingdom in Word and Deed (4:14—6:49)
The Messiah's Inaugural Announcement (4:14-30)

Jesus' appearance in **the synagogue** at **Nazareth** is an event of programmatic importance in Luke's Gospel, and the structure of the entire section illumines its significance (see the outline on p. 137). The complexity of the Nazareth episode itself invites attempts to divide it. The devastating turn from the glorious proclamation at the beginning to the harsh oracles and near murder at the conclusion has caused many interpreters to stop with v. 21 or 22a. But the literary, scriptural, and theological integrity of the entire episode is fundamental to understanding "what went wrong in Nazareth" as well as why this story is so crucial to the whole project of Luke-Acts.

Luke's hand is more thoroughly evident in the construction of this speech narrative than it will be again until the beginning of the next major section at 9:51. Traces of Mark's account of Jesus in Nazareth confirm Luke's awareness of that version, and thus Luke's omission of this Markan material (Mark 6:1-6; see Luke 8:40-56//Mark 5:21-43; and Luke 9:1-6//Mark 6:6b-13) also provides indirect evidence of Luke's intentional departure from Mark. Yet more importantly, Luke's story of Jesus now includes a scriptural "speech" or declaration of the newly inaugurated Messiah. This address anticipates the scriptural "speeches" which the apostles of this Messiah and Lord will give to proclaim repentance unto forgiveness and restoration in Acts. Luke has not created such speech narratives out of nothing, since traditions of preaching on the Scriptures in the synagogues had existed for generations and Jesus and his disciples surely did engage in such practices. But Luke has made these scenes focal to his narrative, and his accounts of synagogue proclamations are so full of interest and detail that they remain the most complete sources for information concerning synagogue practice which can be dated to the first century.

The angels, those inspired by the Holy Spirit, and the evangelist have carried the narrative to this point. God has been the protagonist so far in the story, with assistance especially from John the Baptist who has been the most thoroughly developed character. Prophetic disclosures of human resistance have been given (1:20, 2:34-35), and Herod and the devil have already emerged as antagonists to God's reign through this Messiah. But the Messiah himself has indicated his obedience to his Father as a child (2:49), and he has recited phrases from Deuteronomy demonstrating his complete faithfulness to God's will and word (4:1-13). The human response in the story has displayed the expectation and faith of many in Israel with no major opposition from among the people, beyond some disbelief or perplexity (1:12, 18-20). This episode will be the long-awaited first depiction of the active agency of the anointed Son of God and of the reaction of the people he has been sent to rule.

The literary structure of the episode displays the dynamic of the narrative. Within the envelope of Luke's introduction and conclusion, Jesus makes two major declarations and the people give two distinct, but increasingly negative, responses:

> 14-15 Luke introduces the scene with a "summary"
>> 16-21 The anointed one declares an oracle of promise
>> 22 The people respond in disbelief
>> 23-27 The prophet declares oracles of judgment
>> 28-29 The people respond in violent rejection
> 30 Luke "concludes" the scene

Each of the sections of the Messiah-prophet's speech (16-21, 23-27) may be outlined in much greater detail to demonstrate the ways the evangelist has placed the scriptural resources at the heart of Jesus' declaration:

A. And he came to Nazareth, where he had been brought up . . . And he entered as his custom was on the sabbath day into the *synagogue*
> B. *And stood up* to read
>> C. *And there was given to him* the book of the prophet
>>> D. *And* when he *opened the book* he found the place where it was written
>>>> E. "The Spirit of *the Lord* is upon me, because he has anointed me to *preach good news*
>>>>> F. He has sent me to proclaim *release to captives*
>>>>>> G. And recovering of sight to the blind.
>>>>> F.ʹ (To send for the *oppressed in release*)
>>>> E.ʹ To *proclaim the acceptable year of the Lord*
>>> D.ʹ *And* when he had *closed the book*
>> C.ʹ Having *given it back* to the attendant
> B.ʹ He *sat down*
A.ʹ *And* the eyes of all in the *synagogue* were fixed on him.

The larger structure also conveys Luke's emphasis: the Messiah-prophet has come declaring the inauguration of God's reign of justice and mercy. This announcement has had the effect of divulging the tragic rejection of God's rule in the "secret thoughts of the hearts of many" (2:35). For them Jesus thus portends destruction rather than restoration.

The scriptural citations and allusions are again central to the meaning of the scene. There can be nothing ornamental about this usage of the Scriptures, since the scriptural word of God is definitive of the Messiah's mission. But which passages are so programmatic? And how does the way they are heard affect their significance? False prophets and the devil himself could also quote the scriptures. Careful study of pre-Christian and earliest Christian usage of the Scriptures holds promise for understanding why certain portions of the Scriptures were crucial, and more modern critical readings of the Old Testament may be less relevant. Nevertheless, it is reassuring to discover that the content and context of the texts used in Luke 4 still appear to be very much to the point for the modern reader.

In Luke's world, the Scriptures of Israel are the word of God which validates Jesus. Only in later centuries would Gentile Christians suggest that Jesus also validated the Scriptures of Israel. Thus the passages to which Luke's Jesus refers establish the framework for his mission and indicate precedents for discerning how the Messiah's reign confronted people in the "now" of Jesus' era, in the context of Luke's story and of his "present times" as well as in "now" of the modern reader. Luke's narrative will not allow the prophetic word to be neutral in any era.

Verses 14-15 present a transition to the narrative of Jesus' ministry in **Galilee** which differs significantly from the more common account in Mark and Matthew, where Jesus announces the nearness of the kingdom and calls for repentance. Luke does not report the content of Jesus' preaching until he actually preaches, but he again emphasizes the agency of the Holy Spirit (**in the power of the Spirit**) as directing and authorizing his entry **into Galilee.** He also alerts the reader that whatever Jesus has been saying in the synagogues of Galilee, he has already gained an impressive reputation. In Luke's story, never is there any hint that the people in Nazareth knew anything of Jesus' spectacular birth or destiny. Did Mary or Joseph or Simeon or Anna spread the word of events in Judea? Did Jesus display remarkable gifts to the people in Nazareth? Nothing is said until now, except that Mary "kept all these things in her heart" (2:51). The reader knows a great deal about Jesus but very little about what the people in Nazareth may or may not know. The reader sits in the congregation in the synagogue of Nazareth and listens with them to this famous Jesus for the first time, whether ready to hear him or not.

Verses 16-17 are packed with pictorial detail and movement. This is a homecoming to the place and faces of growing up and of traditional rituals every **sabbath.** All the quaint and interesting customs are unremarkable and authoritative for the congregation. The visitor stands up to read from the prophet. Because he was a visitor or because of his reputation, he may have been told, "If you have any word of exhortation for the people say it!" (Acts 13:15). When he **found** the text he would read. Was it a regularly appointed passage or did he choose it? Did Jesus himself add the allusion from Isa. 58:6 to the reading from Isaiah 61? Or did this connection arise from some Jewish or early Christian exposition of Isaiah or from Luke's own understanding? Or did the alternative versions of the text of Isaiah which circulated in the first century possibly include such a reading? Did Jesus "unroll" a scroll or "open" and "close" a "book" (vv. 17, 20)? The passing details catch the reader's attention because they are unusual, but the evangelist reports them as thoroughly usual and uses them to rivet attention on the passage itself and Jesus' word on the passage.

The waiting is finally over with vv. 18-19, and the content of the passage from **Isaiah** which is read supplies even more than anticipated. Several studies have suggested that this portion of Isaiah was not understood to be specifically "messianic" (i.e., promising an anointed ruler) in early first century (or earlier) interpretations, but then Luke's use of the passage is even more remarkable. Even memorizing this composite quotation from Isa. 61:1 and 58:6 would be a productive exercise toward understanding Luke's testimony to "the things which have been fulfilled among us" (1:1) in Jesus. Just as Isa. 49:6 is fundamental to the themes and outline of Acts beginning from Acts 1:8 (see the note above on 2:29-32), this portion of Isaiah announces the program of Luke's Messiah Jesus in the most specific terms possible.

The Spirit of the Lord is the Holy Spirit whom Luke has constantly introduced as resting upon and directing the participants in the story, and especially Jesus. **Because he has anointed me** is also to be understood quite literally as a reference to Jesus' baptism (see the comments on 3:21-22; Acts 10:37-38). No sharp distinction between *Messiah* and *Son of God* would make sense for Luke, since Jesus is one and the same (see 4:41). Similarly, the fact that this passage speaks of one being anointed to a prophetic vocation of **proclaiming** only compounds Luke's grasp of Jesus the Messiah as prophet-king. The Holy Spirit is the active presence of God, resting upon, anointing to mission, and exercising God's reign in the world in Jesus.

To proclaim good news to the poor will prove to be one of the most enduring and compelling descriptions of Jesus' work as bringer of the kingdom of God. This traditional phrase still requires explication, and it could be simply a religious metaphor. Some translators suggest that it should be rendered, "to proclaim the gospel to the poor" since the verb has the same root as Mark's noun for "gospel" (*euangelion/euangelizesthai*). Several theories have been offered for Luke's lack of the use of the noun *gospel*, and perhaps quoting the verb out of Isaiah was less confrontive to the "gospel" of Caesar. But in Isaiah and in Luke, **the Spirit of the Lord** comes upon the anointed one to authorize a declaration which makes claims and has consequences for this world as well as for the world to come. Jesus announces and brings "salvation" to the economically disadvantaged, the suppressed, the imprisoned, and the disabled. The rest of his career will demonstrate that the liberation from such bondages which Jesus brings is not simply a word of encouragement or message of spiritual significance (see the comments on 6:20).

The **release to the captives, recovery of sight to the blind,** and **setting at liberty those who are oppressed** are thus quite specific messianic agenda in Luke's presentation of Jesus. Of course, they are spiritual agenda, for it is **the Spirit of the Lord** who has authorized them. But they are not mere platitudes. They are only

meaningful (and dangerous) when the Messiah and his representatives begin to take them literally.

To proclaim the acceptable year of the Lord (v. 19) may be
the most telling phrase of all. Many historical problems remain,
but the allusion to **the acceptable year of the Lord** fits in Isaiah
61 and Luke 4 as a reference to the "year of jubilee" commanded
in Leviticus 25. It was to be a time of restitution and restoration
for all Israel. Debts were to be forgiven, land returned to families
who had leased them or used them as collateral. On the anni-
versary of the 7 x 7th year or the 50th year, this program of land
reform and forgiveness was to be God's way of renewing the
society of Israel. But this program of God's reign remained a hope
rather than a practice. This vision of divine justice requires a
redistribution of resources and assets which challenges private
ownership rights. Small wonder that **the acceptable year of the
Lord** would remain a religious symbol, projected into an uncertain future when God's dominion would be revealed to the whole
world. No one could object to that scenario, and the poor and
oppressed could be reassured that the day of God's justice was
still coming.

In vv. 19-20, the interest of those present is intense, and Jesus'
declaration is inescapable. The details which drew the reader's
attention into the scene, focusing upon the prophetic word, now
hold it in reverse sequence:

> standing to read
>   book is given
>   opening and finding the place
>   (Isaiah's text is read)
>   closing the book
>   returning it to attendant
> sitting to speak.

The ritual is spare, and Luke prolongs the silence surrounding
the reading so that the **eyes of all in the synagogue were *fixed
on*** Jesus' every move. **Fixed on** is the same word which Luke
uses for the intense gaze of the maid who picks Peter out of the
crowd and accuses him in the court of the high priest (22:56),

and for several scenes of sharp scrutiny in Acts (1:10; 3:4, 12; 6:15; 7:55; 10:4; 11:6; 13:9; 14:9; 23:1). The reader watches the eyes of the people watching Jesus, observing their silent fixation, but not yet knowing what they are seeing.

Jesus' exposition of the text is also severe and profound in its brevity, breaking the silence and moving beyond the enigma of what has been "seen" with their eyes to the revelation of what has been "heard" with their ears. Luke will return frequently to old prophetic puns on "seeing and hearing" (7:24-25; 8:10; 9:44-45; 10:23-24; 24:13-35). But for now, Jesus' one-sentence proclamation compels all who "see and hear" to the most literal reading of Isaiah possible. As when Peter lays claim to the prophetic word as being directly fulfilled in the dramatic displays of Pentecost ("this is what was spoken by the prophet Joel," Acts 2:16), Jesus leaves no middle ground (see also 24:44, "everything written about me . . . must be fulfilled"). Everything which has been read from Isaiah is programmatic for Jesus: **Today!** Jesus is the fulfillment of the prophetic word of God. Both the content of the prophecy and the identity of the proclaimer confront those who see and hear.

Verse 22 is the dramatic hinge of the whole episode. The theological content is now uncompromisingly clear, but the response to this revelation is at first noncommital and then disbelieving. All the verbs in this verse are in the imperfect tense in Greek, suggesting a somewhat extended gathering of the response. They were first **speaking well of him** . . . **and wondered at the gracious words which proceeded out of his mouth.** After all, this was one of the great texts of promise, treasured in the worship of Israel. First-century believers loved the prophetic promises of the coming of God's reign as much as any later Christians who sing them in Handel's *Messiah* throughout Advent. But what if God actually inaugurated this kingdom? General approval and even words of praise and wonder are still not acceptance. ". . . and they were saying, 'Isn't this **Joseph's son?**' " (cf. RSV).

The question again discloses disbelief (see note at 1:18). The question is not particularly hostile, since Luke also identifies Joseph as Jesus' father (see 2:27, 41, 43, 48; 3:23). To identify him as "the son of Mary," as in Mark 6:3, would probably be more overtly adversarial since then it would raise the question of his legitimate paternity. Still the question reveals the disbelief of the people, because they are only dealing with the substance of the pronouncement in an ad hominem fashion. They have not accepted the word of this hometown son of Joseph as the word of the anointed Son of God.

In vv. 23-27, therefore, Jesus turns the word of promise into a word of indictment of unbelief, attributing hostile reponses to the people. Verse 23 explicates their question as a challenge to the physician to heal himself. The reader has not yet heard the stories of Jesus' healings in Capernaum (see 4:31ff.), and Jesus' counterchallenge is shocking: "**Doubtless you will quote** . . . **truly, I say to you** . . . **but in truth, I tell you**" (vv. 23, 24, 25). Jesus presses the attack, compounding the conflict.

The one maxim is checked with another. The physician is also the prophet, and **the acceptable year of the Lord** has been rejected by the people in the synagogue because the prophet is not **acceptable in his own country.** Jesus gives voice to both sides of the intense infighting, alerting the people in Nazareth and the reader to the defiance of God's reign which is implicit in their apparently mild response. Is Jesus unfairly putting words in their mouths or is he the true prophet-Messiah who uncovers the secret thoughts of the hearts of many (2:35)? Both the people in Nazareth and the reader must come to terms with this display of authority.

The stories from **Elijah** and **Elisha** in vv. 25-27 supply more prophetic precedents for the word of judgment which Jesus is bringing. The outsiders, the outcast, and even the Gentiles receive the prophet and the benefits of God's reign ahead of the elect. The widow **Zarephath** of **Sidon** and **Naaman the Syrian** leper (1 Kings 17, 2 Kings 5) are figures of reproach to Israel, signs that the salvation which God intends for Israel may first insult those who justify themselves on the basis of their status or identity. Luke refuses to allow the prophetic words of consolation to be read as pastoral reassurance to people who are unready to accept the determination and program of God's reign when inaugurated by the Messiah.

Verses 28-29 demonstrate the tragedy which Jesus, therefore, discerns and provokes among the people. They have said nothing since their first response in v. 22. Now they have **heard** the prophetic-messianic pronouncement uttered against them, and their mild disbelief is displayed as violent rejection. They have indeed rendered a verdict about Jesus and thus also about themselves. It is possible that the scene of taking Jesus **out of the city** to throw him down **the hill** was understood by Luke to suggest a ritual execution of a false prophet in which the victim was pushed over a rise so that crushing stones could be dropped on him. In any case, they have acted out the very rejection which Jesus attributed to them, and they have determined to execute this prophet-Messiah, refusing to accept him as the Son of God or his proclamation of the word of God.

The question of whether Jesus is a true or false prophet and Messiah could not be taken lightly in the first (or in any) century. The testimony of the preceding chapters clearly articulates the evangelist's convictions so that the reader is not in doubt about the question, but even the people in Nazareth in the story are not without resources. They have heard of what Jesus has done (vv. 14-15) and, even more critically, they would know the test for true and false prophets as given by Moses in Deuteronomy 18. The false prophet was to die, but the true prophet was to speak to Israel all the words commanded by God and Israel was to hear. The true prophet would utter only the words of God, and the people were not to fear the false prophet because he would be exposed when his words did not come to pass or come true. Thus Luke's story shows that Jesus spoke only scriptural words of God, indicted Israel for not hearing, and was already proved to be a true prophet by their predicted reaction. And if the people had only waited to see if Jesus' words would come to pass, they would soon have known him to be the true prophet who performed the program he had declared (see the comment on 7:22).

Verse 30 concludes the episode on a most unsettled note. The intent to kill Jesus is as clear as the devil's determination to seek an "opportune time" had been in v. 13. Luke does not explain why they were unable to kill Jesus at that time. Jesus has proved to be more than a match for human and superhuman adversaries. Nevertheless, the early displays of faith in Israel and of reception of Jesus as the Messiah have now been clouded with opposition and attempted assassination. From now on, the struggle between the determined will of God to reign in justice and mercy and the willful human rejection of that dominion will move to its tragic and gracious conclusion.

Proclaiming the Kingdom in Galilee and Judea (4:31-44)

Luke follows the sequence of Mark 1:21-38 closely for the rest of this chapter. No new episodes are added to Mark's narrative and none is omitted. The third evangelist conserves the tradition, confident of its vitality and veracity as testimony to "the things which have been accomplished among us" (1:1). But Luke also uses the Markan material within his narrative structure, adapting the tradition so that it contributes coherence and clarity to his version of the story of Jesus.

Mark's narrative is focused on the "secret revelation" of the identity of Jesus "the Holy One of God" (Mark 1:24). Mark sharpens the reader's awareness that "the gospel of Jesus Christ, the Son of God" (Mark 1:1) is the disclosure of a "messianic secret" which is vulnerable to misinterpretation. That Jesus truly is the Messiah and Son of God is a mystery to be pondered throughout Mark until this Christological enigma is finally unveiled at Jesus' death (Mark 15:32, 39).

Luke also recalls stories of hostile and rash disclosures of Jesus' identity and of Jesus' commands to silence. But Jesus' identity as Messiah and Son of God is less cryptic in Luke. To use a distinction which would be drawn later in Christian theology, the question for Luke is more soteriological than christological. That is, Luke elaborates Mark's complex disclosure of Jesus' identity into further displays of the mission and work of the Son of God and Messiah who was sent to proclaim God's dominion in Israel.

Verses 31-32 present Jesus' ministry in Capernaum as a direct sequel to his proclamation and rejection in Nazareth, while all the remaining episodes in the chapter precede Jesus' coming to Nazareth in Mark. In Luke's context, therefore, the amazement at Jesus' teaching stands out as very positive. The rejection in

Nazareth is now bracketed with summary statements of impressive receptions of Jesus' teaching (see also 4:14-15). The authority of his word in his Sabbath teaching is recognized without any negative comparisons toward the scribes (see Mark 1:22). Luke does not make an explicit claim that these people responded fully in faith or became disciples, but they have been impressed by the content of his message. Luke has returned to his depiction of faithful Israel receiving the Messiah.

In vv. 33-37, Jesus displays his power over demonic powers for the first time in the narrative. The traditional heart of the story lies in the verbal exchange between the possessed man and Jesus, and here Luke agrees with Mark almost verbatim. This is a confrontation between powers which is accented slightly by Luke's report that **he cried out with a** *great shout,* "*Hey!* What's it to us and to you, Jesus of Nazareth?" The wild, fearsome forces of chaos rush out at Jesus, but to their violent destruction, like moths to the flame. The questions are challenges, and the confession of Jesus' identity is a taunt, even if it is true and Jesus has been identified publicly as **the Holy One of God** (see also the devil, "since you are the Son of God," 4:3, 9). But once again, Jesus is more than a match for such attacks, and he is able to discern the true adversary in the midst of all of the wild display. With a word Jesus **rebukes,** "silences," and "expels" him, as Luke adds, "hurling the demon into their midst without harming the man!" (cf. RSV, v. 35b).

The lore of demon possession is fascinating, and many similar stories exist in first-century sources. The ability to overpower such dark forces was understood as a divine gift which provoked the spirits to attack, and people who possessed such spiritual powers could have received them from God, Beelzebul, or other spiritual intermediaries (see 11:14-26). But in this passage, Luke moves the reader's attention beyond preoccupation with the stunning display itself and on to the question, "What kind of word is this?" The act or deed is an exercise of one whose word itself works with authority and power. So far it is a question, but the reader knows that Jesus did not receive this authority from the devil (4:6). This is a display of the power of God's kingdom over the realm of demonic forces. In Nazareth, Jesus announced "release to the captives" and "liberty to the oppressed," and now his deed is as good as his word. This exorcism is a demonstration that he is the true prophet with God's words in his mouth (Deut. 18:18). He is the anointed one who exercises the liberating power of the kingdom of God.

The story of the healing of the **mother-in-law** of Peter (**Simon**) (vv. 38-39) is a bit surprising in Luke's sequence, since Peter is not called until later (Luke 5:1-11, see Peter's call in Mark 1:16-20 where it precedes this story). Luke has also intensified this traditional healing story so that it is now another encounter with powers. The action verbs heighten the drama. Jesus **arose** to go to **Simon's house.** They **besought him for her** because of her **fever,** and he **stood over her and rebuked the fever** so that **immediately she arose and served them.** Each of these new elements escalates this healing into a display of saving power. The word **rebuked** is particularly striking, since it has just been used of the demonic forces. This is another display of the liberation which the Messiah Jesus brings.

In vv. 40-41, Luke identifies all of Jesus' work of exorcism and healing as the exercise of the authority of the anointed Son of God. The content is thoroughly traditional, but Luke has rewritten Mark so that Jesus healed **every one** of **any that were sick with various diseases.** As in Mark, no specific stories are told, but this is a general or summary account of healings and confrontations with screaming demons. The most noteworthy Lukan touch is his report that these demons were crying out to Jesus, **You are the Son of God!** Jesus' rebuke thus prevented them from speaking **because they knew that he was the** Messiah.

The demons know the truth about Jesus, and their declaration of him as **the Son of God** is correctly an identification of him as the Messiah. The reader also knows this truth from the birth, infancy, childhood, baptismal, and inaugural stories which have preceded, but the demons have no concern for the significance or correct understanding of their words. They reveal this Son of God to be the Messiah before he has shown what that will mean. Perhaps they intend to allow any and all prevailing concepts of the reign of God to dictate the terms. The demons are correct

Christologically, but their premature announcement could threaten or distract from the messianic mission that God has given to Jesus. Jesus has already shown that he will not allow the devil to tell him what it means that he is the "Son of God," and he does not intend to allow the demons to mislead the crowds either. Luke's entire narrative may be read as affirming Jesus' way of enacting the roles of Son of God and Messiah. Jesus is exercising the reign of God correctly.

Verses 42-43 thus testify to Jesus' resistance to the will of the crowd and obedience to God's will. Mark's mention of Simon and the others is replaced with reference to the crowds that are seeking him, which makes sense in the sequence of Luke's narrative (see Simon's call, 5:1-11). The silence in Luke about Jesus' prayer (Mark 1:35) is more surprising, since Luke is so interested in Jesus' receiving direction from God through prayer (see 5:16; 6:12). While Luke emphasizes that the crowds wanted to prevent Jesus from **leaving,** he does not indicate what they had in mind beyond keeping this healer and teacher around. Could they have some notion of him as Son of God and Messiah from the demons' words? Jesus' silencing of the demons and his refusal of their plans, however, are grounded in his clear sense of messianic mission from God.

This Jesus who "must be in my Father's house" (2:49) also **must preach the good news of the kingdom of God to the other cities.** The necessity which directs him is not a cold determinism, but it is the will of God: **for I was sent for this purpose.** Clearly God is the sender. God is the one whose determined will obligates his Messiah to declare and deploy God's rule. No one else may determine the Messiah's course or work, whether their purposes are hostile or friendly (see also 13:31-35). Luke will later show great interest in the "sending" (Gk: *apostellein*) of the 12 apostles (see 9:1-6, 10; Acts 1:1-26) who will be the delegates of the Messiah and Lord who is himself **sent** by God. The demons have some clue that the "Holy One of God" is on God's mission in the world, and the crowds may or may not grasp that Jesus is "sent." But in Luke, Jesus communicates his clear understanding of his mission to bring the will and word and reign of God in its liberating power to all the cities of Israel.

The mention of Jesus' preaching in the synagogues of Judea in v. 44 completes this picture in Luke, although it creates significant geographical problems. Does Luke intend to report a journey into the southern territories prior to Jesus' setting his face to go to Jerusalem in 9:51ff.? He is back at the lake of Gennesaret in the next verse (5:1), and the history of Lukan interpretation is filled with creative efforts to explain the problem, including many textual variants in the manuscripts. The reference is probably best understood as a Lukan summary to the effect that Jesus continued preaching in all of the Jewish synagogues (cf "Judea" understood more generally in 1:5; 6:17; 7:17; 23:5; Acts 10:37!).

The mission of the Messiah and Son of God and true prophet has met rejection in his "fatherland" of Nazareth, but it has also continued throughout the synagogues of the rest of the land of Israel. In Jesus, God's dominion confronts the people of God, fulfilling the "utterances of the prophets which are read every sabbath" in the synagogues (see Acts 13:27). Whether or not they will receive him will also be revealed, and Luke depicts tragic rejection as well as faith. Luke tells the story which the prolog to John's Gospel articulates in summary fashion: "He came to his own home, and his own people received him not. But to all who received him . . . he gave power to become children of God" (John 1:11-12), or Luke might say, "to all who received him, his mission was the fulfillment of God's promised kingdom."

The Call of Simon (5:1-11)

This is one of the best-told tales in Luke's narrative, and its story form is crucial to its meaning. It has the ring of a tall tale, a fish story which will leave them buzzing endlessly on the docks in Capernaum. But the stupendous catch of fish is only the opportunity for a greater wonder in the story. Suddenly the nets ripping with fish and the sinking boats fade from view, and the story focuses on Simon Peter's vision of faith and the call to discipleship.

This is an epiphany story in which earthy details are the media for the disclosure of divine presence, and it is an epiphany-call story in which Peter's vision is the occasion for hearing the call of the Lord to discipleship and to the mission of the kingdom. By the end of the episode, the fishermen have apparently walked away. Both boats wallow in the shallows under the burden of the astounding catch which becomes riper by every minute of midday. The miracle of faith has so overwhelmed the astonishing catch that the practical matters of boats, business, family, and fish are simply left behind.

Several elements of the story are found elsewhere in early Christian tradition. Mark's version of the call of the fishermen occurs at the beginning of his Gospel and bears several similarities to the last verses in Luke's story (see Mark 1:16-20 and Matt 4:18-22). The detail of Jesus sitting in a boat and teaching the people on the seashore also appears in Mark (4:1-2) and Matthew (13:1-3) as their introductions to Jesus' parables. The story in the Fourth Gospel of the appearance of the risen Jesus to Simon and the disciples on the shore of the Sea of Tiberius also includes many similar features (John 21:1-11). Yet none of these traditional stories was the direct source for Luke's telling.

Certain Old Testament episodes may actually have had more impact upon Luke's narrative than the specifically Christian traditions. Attention to the details of these precedents illumines the focus of Luke's account, and each of the stories is rich in Israel's experience of the awesome and fearful holiness of God's presence.

In Exodus 3, Moses was tending Jethro's sheep when the angel of the Lord called to him from the burning bush, and God told him to remove his shoes on holy ground. "And Moses hid his face, for he was afraid to look at God" (v. 6). This divine epiphany evoked mortal fear, but it was also the revelation of God's will and the call of the prophet.

In Judges 6, Gideon was beating out wheat in the wine press when the angel of the Lord called him to deliver Israel. He hesitated until the angel caused fire to spring from the rock, consuming his sacrifice, and then he said, "Alas, O Lord God! For now I have seen the angel of the Lord face to face." But the angel said, "Peace be to you; do not fear, you shall not die," and Gideon was obedient to the call.

In Isaiah 6, the prophet Isaiah encounters God's presence in a much grander setting with a vision in the temple of the glory of the reigning Lord, but this epiphany or theophany story is also filled with mortal dread. "Woe is me! For I am lost; for I am a man of unclean lips, and I dwell in the midst of a people of unclean lips; for my eyes have seen the King, the Lord of hosts!" (v. 5). If all the dross of sin were purged away, would there be anything left of this sinner? Yet when his unclean lips are purified with a burning coal from the altar, Isaiah says, "Here am I send me," and he is called to bear a severe message to Israel.

These are all epiphany-call stories, and their structure indicates their meaning. The human person is located quite precisely, often in the midst of mundane tasks. The display of divine presence is quite dramatic or miraculous. In fact, these displays are so impressive that they may take over the stories, as if the burning bush, the fire from the rock, the transformation of the temple, or the boatload of fish were the point. No doubt these wonders will astonish and delight every new generation which hears about them. But these demonstrations of divine power and presence are consistently focused on the call of the prophet, judge, or apostle.

In vv. 1-3, Luke has set the scene of this story by a summary account of Jesus' teaching. The ordinary setting of **fishermen washing their nets** has become slightly unusual as this teacher borrows the boat to teach from offshore. Luke again emphasizes the positive expectation which Jesus' preaching is meeting among the people (see 4:15, 37, 40, 42). The story is surrounded by faith, and the crowds who have come **to hear the word of God** now include these fishermen. Furthermore, in Luke's version Jesus has already been to Simon's house to heal his mother-in-law before this dramatic call occurs. But Luke does not tell us what Jesus taught on this occasion. The picturesque scene of Jesus teaching from the boat is only the introduction to the encounter which follows.

In vv. 4-5, the exchange between Jesus and Peter (Simon) over when or where to fish has long invited allegorical interpretations about Christian evangelism (see also John 21:4-11). Christian storytellers who know how this event comes out (see v. 10) can hardly resist some delight at Peter's protests about how to pursue his trade. This was just the beginning of Jesus telling Peter how to fish! But in the story, Peter's protests merely heighten the subsequent drama without any overtly Christian meaning—yet. Even Peter's address of Jesus as **Master** is respectful, but still expressing only a general sense of Jesus' authority without specifically Christian understanding (see the discussion at 8:24). Peter's obedience **at your** (Jesus') **word,** however, begins to hint at a deeper level of regard which Peter holds for the teacher.

The catch is stupendous (vv. 6-7), a veritable **shoal** or school or mess **of fish** of a magnitude which exceeded even their most optimistic hopes. The fishermen even **beckon** by nodding their heads to **their partners in the other boat** while their hands are full. The nets are breaking and both ships are starting **to sink.** Clearly, Jesus' advice on fishing should be followed. Perhaps he would be available for another trip.

But finally this is not a fish story, and Peter is the first to recognize that. Up to his armpits in fish, suddenly the magnitude of what is really happening is revealed to him. This is not merely a wonder. Like the burning bush, the fire from the rock, and the transformed temple, this catch of fish is a manifestation of divine presence. The mere mortal of unclean lips has been confronted with the holiness of God.

"Depart from me, for I am a sinful man, O Lord!" is hardly the response that one would expect from a fisherman with a full boat. But then neither would it seem likely that the story would conclude with all of these fishermen leaving their boats and the catch and **everything** when they had just made such a stupendous catch. But this plea that the Lord depart does fit with the scriptural precedents. Interrupted in their daily lives, the prophets, judges, and apostles of God are sharply aware of God's purging and awesome presence, and they are called out to be representatives of God's will and rule on this earth. Peter is not presented as uncommonly guilt ridden, but he has suddenly seen the overwhelming disparity between the power and purity of God's reign in Jesus and his own mortal, compromised life.

The others join in Peter's response. Their **astonishment** (v. 9) at the catch of fish has also apparently escalated into profound insight and readiness to obey. This account of their call is remarkably different from the account given in Mark 1:16-20 and

Matt. 4:18-22. But the effect of all of these stories is the same. **They left everything** on the spot **and followed Jesus.**

Jesus' word to Simon **"Do not be afraid!"** thus includes all the disciples who have now joined in on the epiphany. But Simon's experience is the central event, and Jesus first gives him the word of assurance which the angel of the Lord spoke to Moses, Gideon, and Isaiah. God's presence is certainly awesome, but this revelation is not intended to destroy or condemn. This epiphany is rather a call. **"Henceforth you will be** fishing for people."

The Messiah and his apostles are seeking the lost. This is the mission of God, the mission of the kingdom of God, and the followers of Jesus are called and conscripted into the service of this mission. To this point, Jesus has been conducting his mission of word and deed alone. Again compared to Mark and Matthew, Jesus' call of his disciples occurs rather late in the sequence, but in Luke it is very clear that the apostles and disciples of Jesus are brought into his mission which is well under way. Now they, and we, will need to hear a great deal more about how this reign of God is going to be deployed.

The Cleansing of Leprosy (5:12-16)

In this episode, the Lord Jesus again exercises his sovereign will by means of his authoritative word. In a highly symbolic act, Jesus heals a victim of **leprosy** and evokes nothing but praise and faith from the crowds. The impact of what Jesus is doing is not wasted on these multitudes who then press in **to hear and to be healed** (v. 15). Objections and hostility will soon follow, but this story is unclouded by suspicion.

The healing itself is very dramatic. The condition which the book of Leviticus (see chaps. 13–14) calls "leprosy" clearly included a complex variety of diseases, according to the diagnosis of modern medicine. But the social effect was always the same— exclusion from the community. People often failed to distinguish the condition from the person. At least Luke saw that this was a person who was afflicted with leprosy. In Mark 1:40 and Matt 8:1 he was a leper. The person was "unclean." The fears of contamination were probably most like those associated with the fears of contagion from AIDS in the modern era. To be healed meant to be restored to friends and family and community as well as to be rid of the disease.

These human consequences of the healing must not be neglected, for the picture of the man falling on his face before Jesus pleading for healing is filled with pathos. His implicit and desperate trust is also transmitted by all of the Gospel accounts: "**If you will, you can make me clean**" (Mark 1:40; Matt. 8:2; Luke 5:12).

Jesus pays close attention to the sacrifices and rituals which are required for the healed person to be restored to the community by **the priest** (see also the 10 lepers in 17:11-19). All of this is in strict accordance with "the law of the leper for the day of his cleansing" (Lev. 14:2). The Messiah is observant of the Law of Moses, respecting the need for **a proof** or "witness" **to the people** (v. 14). The law is not a "burden" or obstacle in this matter. It is a God-given ordinance for the protection of the people but also for the restoration of the healed.

Luke's version of the story contains several distinctive features which heighten the symbolic character of the healing. In Nazareth, Jesus had referred to the time of Elisha when "there were many lepers in Israel" and only Naaman the Syrian was cleansed (Luke 4:27). This was one of Elisha's greatest prophetic healings. Some of the rabbis suggested that healing leprosy was more difficult than raising the dead. And now Jesus was fulfilling this prophetic precedent, but this time he has met faith in Israel where Elisha found none. Jesus was carrying out the prophetic mission he had announced in Nazareth, and he would soon mention the cleansing of people with leprosy as a demonstration to John the Baptizer that he was truly the fulfillment of John's prophetic declarations (Luke 7:22).

The introduction and conclusion of the story weave the episode into the fabric of his narrative. The story stands in Mark's sequence, but now it identifies the location as **one of the cities,** underscoring the Galilean location of this series of episodes. This man who is **full of leprosy** (Luke loves the words *full* and *fulfill*), **when he saw Jesus, fell on his face pleading** (v. 12). At the risk of overstating a minor feature, it should at least be noted that

Luke treats "seeing" and "hearing" as highly significant events. He does not explain how this man knew, but he depicts him as having "seen" with the eyes of faith. So also in the conclusion, when this report spread abroad many **gathered to hear and to be healed** (v. 15). With Jesus **withdrawing** from the crowd to **pray,** the focus of the narrative once again returns to him. But all that has happened in this story is now caught up in the will and plan of God.

The afflicted man was correct: the question upon which his healing depended was whether Jesus willed it. But this is not a question of whim or of personality. Luke even drops Mark's reference to Jesus being "deeply moved" with pity or anger. It is risky to try to estimate why Luke did not preserve such an intriguing feature of the tradition, but the effect of the omission is for the reader to be drawn even more sharply into the revelation of the will of the Lord. And as Jesus prays in the conclusion, the reader is aware that Jesus' will is one with God's.

And is it God's will that people with such dread afflictions be healed and cleansed and restored to the human community? Yes! In fact, such healing is central to the mission of the kingdom which Jesus and his disciples pursue. And why are not all people healed? The text does not say. Clearly the struggle with sin and disease and death itself is far from over, even for God and God's Messiah, Jesus. But like the first rays before the day breaks, this story illumines human suffering with the clear light of hope in God's unswerving will to forgive, restore, and heal. It also directs the apostles and servants of this kingdom of mercy to pursue health for the afflicted with all impatience and urgency.

Forgiveness of Sins and Healing of Paralysis (5:17-26)

This pericope has long been recognized as one of the most complex little stories in the Gospel tradition. The whole narrative revolves around Jesus' tantalizing question, **"Which is easier, to say, 'Your sins are forgiven you,' or to say, 'Rise and walk'?"** Yet the parts of the whole are also easily discerned as a controversy (vv. 20b-24a closely paralleling Mark 2:5b-10a) enclosed by a healing story. Students of the forms of oral storytelling are fascinated with the observation that if the controversy is pulled out of the narrative, the healing story is still intact: "Jesus, seeing their faith, said to the paralytic, "I say to you rise and take up your cot and go home. And immediately he arose and went home." Many have further suggested that the healing story was later augmented with the more complex controversy about forgiveness.

This discussion is not merely an academic dispute, since even the most popular interpretations are usually drawn either into considering this as primarily a miracle story or fundamentally a revelation of Jesus' authority to forgive sins. Then the gap between the parts is often closed by the suggestion that sin was probably the cause of the man's paralysis, or at least that is what people in the first century may have thought. But this easy resolution does not come from the text, and it can be a cruel message for people with physical disabilities. Simply on this narrative level it is important to observe that even after Jesus has pronounced the man's sins to be forgiven, the man still has a physical disability. The healing comes later, and it is seen to prove something about Jesus, not something about the man (see also John 9:2-3).

The tension between the parts of the story is actually central to its power, and neither the healing nor the pronouncement of forgiveness must be allowed to overshadow or absorb the other. Jesus' question, **"Which is easier?"** is also characteristic of several of his other sayings. "It is easier for heaven and earth to pass away, than for one dot of the law to become void" (16:17). "How hard it is for those who have riches to enter the kingdom of God! For it is easier for a camel to go through the eye of a needle than for a rich man to enter the kingdom of God" (18:24-25). Such discussions about "easier and harder" and "lighter and heavier" were well known among Jewish teachers, and frequently they involved impossible comparisons. They were more like riddles to be pondered than questions to be answered. The point was the conundrum itself.

The theologians present in that house may think that the forgiveness of sins is by far the more weighty matter, and the crowds may be more impressed with the healing. But Jesus cuts through any debate about which is easier or harder by using the healing as a demonstration of the truth of his declaration of forgiveness.

Mark, Matthew, and Luke agree in the body of this story, but each evangelist also proclaims a distinct message. For Mark, the tension of the conundrum contributes to the crowd's perplexity at who Jesus may be, because they had never seen anything like this before. Certainly Jesus has now been revealed as possessing messianic authority, but all of this will only be clear when this Son of man has given his life as a ransom for many (Mark 10:45). In Matthew, the introduction to the wonder story is reduced signficantly so that there is no dramatic entrance through the roof, and the conclusion of the whole is focused in the confirmation that the forgiveness of sins was an authority which God had given to humans (Matt. 9:8, see also Matt. 16:18-19; 18:18-20).

Luke also keeps the conundrum alive, but Luke's telling of this traditional and complex story heightens the drama and proof of the healing. This is the first occasion since Nazareth where Jesus' public ministry of word and deed again meets objection, and the first encounter with the religious leadership of Israel. Now, as the healing is presented as a clear corroboration of the authority of Jesus' word, the antagonism of the teachers of Israel also stands out more sharply.

The introduction (v. 17) is Luke's, with much more pictorial detail about when all this happened, who was there, and the places from which they came. This narrative detail fits with Luke's style of imitating scriptural histories, and it also contributes human interest. In a few words, the evangelist has set the scene with Jesus seated as the teacher, surrounded by the teachers of Israel from every direction as far away as Jerusalem. **And,** Luke marks the moment, **the power of the Lord was with him to heal.** This is virtually the same as saying that "Jesus returned in the power of the Spirit into Galilee" and "the Spirit of the Lord is upon me" (Luke 4:14, 18; see also 4:36), but now the reader is aware that the healing which is about to take place is the work of the Lord God (see "the Lord" in Luke 1–2). Any conflict with Jesus will also be contending with God.

Since this is the first appearance of the **Pharisees** along with the **teachers of the law,** it is worth noting that Luke's presentation of them will prove to be very complex throughout the story. They are not simply evil. In fact, Luke treats them with far more respect than most interpreters, although they are frequent adversaries of Jesus and of the apostles in Acts. In Acts he also reports that Gamaliel rose up to prevent an attack on the disciples lest the group "be found opposing God!" (Acts 5:34-39), and he mentions "believers who belong to the party of the Pharisees" (Acts 15:5). The **Pharisees** are not simply rigid legalists, nor do they represent all of Israel. Thus the intense stress of charges and countercharges between the Pharisees and the Messianists are over who is blaspheming or apostate and who is faithful. This conflict must be regarded as a struggle within Israel. The question being debated is which group is true Israel and which has proved unfaithful. Both the Pharisees and the followers of Jesus are making their appeals to all of Israel, but for the Messianists, repentance and faith in God can only lead to hope in the kingdom of God which the Messiah Jesus has inaugurated.

In vv. 18-19, Luke follows Mark's story line, but the phrasing and words are Luke's. Now the roof is **tiled** and not merely dirt but, more significantly, in Luke the man is someone who is **paralyzed** rather than being "the paralytic." Luke is generally more able to write a careful Greek sentence, and this touch for distinguishing "people with disabilities" from "disabled people" is again noteworthy (see Luke 5:12).

In v. 20, the phrase **When he saw their faith** does not require unique spiritual discernment. After all, they have torn a house apart. They must believe that Jesus will be able to help this man. None of the evangelists tries to distinguish the faith of the bearers from that of the disabled man. They are all expecting healing, and instead Jesus pronounces forgiveness. The perfect passive form of the verb "have been forgiven" in Luke indicates that his sins have been forgiven by God.

Now the tension mounts as the controversy (vv. 21-24) begins. The poor man lies there as the theologians grumble to themselves over who Jesus thinks he is, since **only God can forgive sins.** And Jesus adds to the tension. He does not immediately deal with the paralyzed man, but he moves in on their discussion. Perhaps Luke intends to suggest that they were speaking under their breaths as they accused him of blasphemy. Certainly if they had said that publicly, Jesus would not need to speak about them **questioning in your hearts** (v. 22). In fact, the word which the RSV translates as **question** is the same word which Simeon had used in Luke 2:35 to speak of the "secret thoughts" or "questionings" of the heart which the child Jesus was destined to disclose (see also 6:8; 9:46-47; 24:38). Now the Messiah is exercising a kind of spiritual discernment which threatens those who would choose to keep their objections to themselves.

They have raised the gravely serious charge of blasphemy against Jesus. He is claiming divine prerogatives. Who does he think he is? And Jesus has pulled all of this into the open, pressing the point. Neutrality is impossible. Now Jesus has a question for them about matters of what is easier or more difficult, lighter or heavier. It is a scholastic question which could invite endless debate. "Some say that forgiveness is more difficult. Only God could do it. But others say that only God could heal a paralyzed person." But Jesus is not playing games. Just when they or we are tempted to rush in with an answer to such a conundrum, he cuts through it all by a challenging announcement.

After all, the man is still paralyzed, and now he turns his healing into a demonstration that he has the authority to declare God's forgiveness. In v. 24, he identifies himself as the Son of man and thus lays claim to the authority which God gives to this angelic figure in Daniel 7:13-14. But even then the stakes have risen, because the dominion which the Ancient of Days would give that Son of man was being claimed here and now **on earth** by Jesus. Jesus is not backing away from their charges. He is rather escalating this encounter so that the healing would be a clear revelation that they are not merely contending with another teacher or even a healer. They are up against the authorized agent of God's kingdom. Jesus speaks for God. He does indeed have God's authority to forgive sins, and they are about to witness a demonstration.

Now back to the paralyzed man. Jesus' words to him are simple and immediately effective. He tells him to pick up his cot and go to his house, and he does so, **glorifying God.** His joy at the healing may well have been compounded by the relief at getting out of the midst of this intense dispute between Jesus and the religious leaders. And he knew that God was the one to be praised. Jesus had made the point very clearly. This was a revelation of the healing power of the Spirit of the Lord and of the authority of the kingdom.

In v. 26, Luke wraps up the story with the astonishment and awe of the whole assembly. He says—literally—"Ecstasy seized them all, and they all glorified God, and they were all filled with fear saying, 'We have seen amazing things today.' " All of them? Even the religious leaders? Apparently yes. At least they were stunned into joining the praise of God and overwhelmed with the jolt of this conclusion. Debate about "which is easier" would be out of the question. Even discussion of just "who" Jesus thinks he is has been silenced by his revealing and confronting declaration. And the "amazing things" or **strange things** which they have seen are simply unexplainable. This word is used for bizarre and wondrous things in the Hellenistic world, "believe it or not" kinds of things.

In the end this story has turned into another divine epiphany, a revelation of the power, presence, and authority of God at work in Jesus' words and acts. Whether those who objected and grumbled about "blasphemy" will continue to be persuaded after leaving is still unclear. But for the present, all the theological conversation is silenced, all the scholastic debate stunned by a tour de force of Jesus' mighty deed. The awesome and fearsome glory of God has been glimpsed, as by Peter on the boat (5:1-11). Not even those who so eagerly tore the house apart to bring the man to the healer could have expected such a conclusion.

Torah and Kingdom: Conflicts on Authority (5:27—6:1)

The Call of Levi: Tax Collectors and Sinners (5:27-32). Luke is now following Mark's narrative sequence of a story of conflicts with the religious leaders over who can pronounce forgiveness (5:17-26; Mark 2:1-12), eating with tax collectors and sinners (5:27-32; Mark 2:13-17), fasting (5:33-39; Mark 2:18-22), plucking grain on the Sabbath (6:1-5; Mark 2:23-28) and healing on the Sabbath (6:6-11; Mark 3:1-6). Mark's account already appears to have used the traditional story of the call of Levi the tax collector as the occasion for recording the Pharisees' complaint against the disciples about their questionable associations. In all three Gospel accounts, Jesus and his disciples go to Levi's house for the banquet, but the Pharisees make their complaint about the disciples. This may well reflect the later era when the church was accused of apostasy.

As a result, this episode combines the story of the "call" of a disciple with the "invitation" of sinners to meal fellowship and concludes with justification of a "call" to sinners to repentence. Taken together, these verses explore several dimensions of God's call. Jesus' messianic authority to "choose" or "elect" his own disciples is revealed along with his mission to reach out to the lost. And at the same time, the early church's ministry among the sinners and unrighteous was also defended.

The scandal of the mission of Jesus and his early followers must not be diminshed. Ridicule of the Pharisees as mere "legalists" is unfair and minimizes the power of the account. Their concern for "separation" and "holiness" was anchored in the scriptural commands to Israel (see Lev. 10:10; Neh. 10:28), and Israel had learned the bitter lesson of the sin of going after the ways of the nations. **The Pharisees and their scribes** were serious students of the Scriptures pursuing a reform of Israel. They were also calling Israel to repentance, but for them it was a call to strict observance of the commands of God given by Moses.

Luke's version of the story seems to be especially aware of the depth of the conflict, since it concludes with the specific mention of the call of sinners **to repentance** (v. 32). What is most shocking about Jesus is that neither he nor his disciples made repentance a prior condition to the call to discipleship or to table fellowship. The Pharisees were also eager to gather the lost of Israel, but repentance and purification and observance of the scriptural commands would need to precede table fellowship, let alone discipleship. And **sinners** and dishonest **tax collectors** were still further away from holiness. How could they keep the commands concerning ritual purity if they ate with the unobservant? Soon there would be no one left in Israel keeping the faith. In this light, it is also much easier to see why these issues continued to be very difficult for Jewish Christians as soon more and more Gentiles were included as heirs of the promises.

Jesus called a **tax collector** to be a disciple. Not all tax collectors were regarded as quislings or collaborators merely because they worked within the religious and economic system which the Romans allowed. But their reputation was probably about like that of a "loan shark." They were socially necessary, but hardly exemplars of holiness. No teacher would solicit disciples from among their kind. And when Levi commits himself by "leaving all" to follow Jesus, he still throws a **great feast** for his "colleagues," and Jesus joins the party. Outrageous! Where is the penance?

In v. 30 the scene shifts to the objections of **the Pharisees and their scribes** against Jesus' disciples. It seems unlikely that we are to think that the Pharisees were also present at the party. This must be another occasion, but all the evangelists set these scenes next to each other.

Then in v. 31, Jesus is speaking, apparently in response to the criticism of his disciples. Or is this still another scene? Whether all this happened at once or over several occasions, the evangelists hold these disparities together by means of the dialog. Jesus' word thus stands as a summation and an answer to such complaints. It is a declaration of God's mission or sovereignty of mercy, first in the form of an old proverb, **"Those who are well have no need of a physician, but those who are sick."** Verse 32 is then a summary of the Messiah's entire progam: **"I have not come to call the righteous, but sinners to repentance."**

Neither the proverb nor Jesus' application of it to himself is cynical. There is no suggestion that the Pharisees are really sick or unrighteous. But they may not criticize Messiah's freedom to reach out to sinners or his way of calling them to repentance (see also Luke 15:1, 25-32). On later occasions Luke's Jesus will also criticize the "righteousness" of the Pharisees as "self-righteousness" (Luke 11:39-44; 12:1; 16:15; 18:9-14), and Luke will further question their sincerity (Luke 11:53-54; 13:31; 14:1-4; 16:14). But in this episode, Jesus' words are a declaration of Christian liberty in mission to sinners and disreputable people. Jesus' followers would henceforth reach out to such people in the name and authority of the Messiah Jesus. This is the strategy of the kingdom of God, and the righteous must simply be advised not to object, not even on the grounds of the preservation of God's law. Something greater than the law is here: the Messiah and his gracious reign.

Concerning Fasting and Festivity (5:33-39).   This passage combines a traditional conflict story (vv. 33-35) with two complex parabolic sayings about "old and new" (vv. 36-38) and a final aphorism which commends vintage wine (v. 39). Only the last element is completely new to Luke, and the diversity of the pieces cautions against too hasty assessments of the whole. The evangelists were also collectors of tradition, and each of these memory pieces contains intriguing contours which are open to many new meanings. On the other hand, Mark 2:18-22 has already gathered the parabolic sayings as commentaries on the conflict about fasting, and Luke has both remodeled elements of the sayings and added the statement about preference for old wine. This conclusion seems quite enigmatic or even ironic in this context. Finally it is Luke's rendition of the Jesus traditions which commands our attention, and the issue is not precisely what Jesus said or what all he could have meant. Rather, the question is how Luke's telling of the Jesus story constitutes his testimony to the new order which Jesus inaugurated.

In Luke's version, the unnamed questioners who ask Jesus about fasting could be "the Pharisees and their scribes" from the preceding story (5:30), but then the comparison with **the disciples of John . . .** and **of the Pharisees** seems to imply non-Pharisaic questioners. Given the importance of fasting in first-century Jewish practice, these questioners need not be from the most ascetic or scrupulous schools (i.e., John or the Pharisees) to be concerned about this matter. Luke certainly takes the question seriously even adding that these others **fast often and offer prayers** while Jesus' disciples **eat and drink.** This same contrast about fasting and feasting arises again in Luke 7:33-34, and there both John and Jesus are criticized. The question for Luke is not *whether* fasting is appropriate, but *when.*

Luke duly records the stories which tell that Jesus "ate and drank" and generally took liberties with established religious practice. But in this case Luke does not accept this criticism as still applying to the Christians of his day. Of course Luke knew that fasting could be self-righteous (see 18:12). Still, the old ways are not ridiculed. Now they are generally savored over the **new wine.** Consider the positive picture of Anna as one who was constantly worshiping with "fasting and prayer night and day" (2:37). Of course she preceded the time of the Messiah's presence, but the prophets, teachers, disciples, and elders in Acts again worship the Lord with fasting and praying (Acts 13:2-3; 14:23). Those **days** in which the bridegroom will be **taken** up have happened (see Acts 1:11). Thus the radical newness and freedom which characterized the practice of Jesus and his disciples while he was still with them no longer characterized Luke's own times.

Fasting was and is a form of preparation, specifically a preparation of repentance. Of course preparations must not be allowed to ruin the festive occasion, and the disciples of Jesus in Luke were aware that festivity was in order while Jesus was with them. But Luke's retrospective view also emphasized that God had again "given" repentance to Israel and to the Gentiles (see Acts 5:31; 11:18). Jesus' "departure" (9:31; Acts 1:1-11) inaugurated that new phase of repentance. Thus the present time was invested in proclaiming "repentance and forgiveness of sins . . . to all nations, beginning from Jerusalem (24:47; Acts 2:38; 17:30).

Christian readers have been given a glimpse of the holy hilarity of the kingdom. Fasting and the sackcloth of repentance were too dour while Jesus was with his disciples, and they will not fit with the newness which is to come. Even now as Christians return to fasting along with prayer awaiting the full disclosure of the kingdom they know that endless repentance does not lie ahead. Even if they might want to continue with the old ways, since **the old is good,** they know the new wine of the freedom of the kingdom is the will of the bridegroom. As when the Messiah was present, so again at the full disclosure of his reign, feasting will replace fasting. Thus Christian prayer and fasting which prepares for the full disclosure of the departed Messiah is already full of the hope of the feast to come.

The Lord of the Sabbath (6:1-5).   Luke includes many stories of Jesus' challenges to Sabbath observance where his offense
was either implied (4:31-37) or directly stated (6:1-5, 6-11; 13:10-
19; 14:1-6). Christian readers often take these stories lightly as
encounters with "legalism," frequently using caricatures of religious rigidity as foils for their own "enlightened freedom." But
Luke's story underscores the gravity of Sabbath observance and
thus Jesus' messianic license is even more compelling. Jesus is
not merely a sophisticated or liberal interpreter of the Law. He
is the embodiment of the reign of God, and his authority su-
percedes the Law itself.

In the era of the second temple, the debate was intense over
how the Law was to be faithfully observed. First Maccabees 2:29-
50 tells of a dispute among those who "were seeking righteousness
and justice" in the revolt against Antiochus IV "Epiphanes." Some
chose to "die in our innocence" rather than fight on the Sabbath,
while others concluded that it was necessary to fight the Gentiles
on the Sabbath "for our lives and our ordinances." In Jesus' era,
among the Pharisees the "strict constructionists" are associated
with the school of Shammai, and the school of Hillel is generally
open to more human considerations in Sabbath interpretation.
Yet all agreed that the observance of the Sabbath was fundamental
to Israel's witness to God's rule in the world.

Luke also depicts Jesus and the disciples as regular in Sabbath
observance, especially as connected with synagogue teaching and
prayer (4:16, 31; 6:6; 13:10, Acts 13:14, 42, 44; 16:13; 17:2; 18:4;
20:7). In spite of the several stories of scandalous Sabbath practice
during Jesus' ministry, no such stories are told of the disciples in
Acts. Yet the conflicts with the high priest over the apostles'
healing and preaching in the temple (Acts 4–5) again demonstrate
that the stakes are very high: "We must obey God rather than
men!" . . . "You might even be found opposing God!" (5:29, 39)

Here the issue is that plucking and husking grain was a form
of "harvesting" and was defined by some as "labor" which was
not to be done on the Sabbath. But Jesus does not take up that
question, which could have been debated among various views.
Nor does he suggest a generally more humane interpretation of
the Law as in Mark, where he says, "The Sabbath was made for

people, not people for the sabbath" (Mark 2:27). Instead, he escalates the challenge to his disciples into a confrontation with his authority as the agent of God's heavenly rule, **The Son of man is lord of the sabbath!**

King David set a precedent when he and his troops ate **the bread of the Presence** when he was hungry. The point of the precedent, however, is not that it was such a dire circumstance. Perhaps Jesus' disciples could have been defended on the specifics of their need, since such cases were debatable in Israel. But Jesus has emphasized the prerogatives of the ruler. As David had royal privileges and authority, so much more does the authority of the Son of man supercede the commands of Sabbath observance (see also 5:24 above).

A Sabbath Confrontation (6:6-11).   This episode concludes the series of conflict stories which Luke has taken over in their Markan sequence. Once again, the healing story in the midst of the episode receives little attention since it is presented primarily as the occasion for an intense confrontation between Jesus and the religious leaders. The healing is a miraculous restoration of a "paralyzed" or **withered** right hand, and Jesus brings the man into the midst of the assembly as an object lesson on the issue of what is **lawful** or "authorized" on the Sabbath. He even extends the range of the discussion by asking whether it is **lawful . . . to do good or to do evil, to save life or to destroy it.**

The negative possibilities sound blasphemous. No one would suggest that it is **lawful to do evil** or **to destroy** life, not even if one were trying to defend the necessity of battle on the Sabbath. Jesus' question has an edge of anger, already implying that neither he nor his adversaries are engaging in a sincere debate about Sabbath observance. Something else is at stake. While he is about to save a life, they are spending their Sabbath in destroying one.

Even as the heat of conflict increases in the narrative, Luke is very careful to identify its agents and nature. In v. 2 above, Luke speaks of "some" or "certain Pharisees" who object, while Mark simply says "the Pharisees," and Luke's distinction among Pharisees will appear repeatedly in the story (see also 13:31; 19:39; Acts 15:5). In this confrontation over Sabbath healing, Luke specifies the adversaries even more immediately than Mark as **the**

scribes and the Pharisees. Mark merely suggests that "they were watching him," and it is only at the end that it is clear that "they" are "the Pharisees" (Mark 3:2, 6). Yet Mark suggests that they were not simply looking for a reason to "accuse him," because in the end the Pharisees were taking counsel with the Herodians on "how to destroy him." In Luke the episode still concludes with mad rage against Jesus, but they are discussing **what they might do to Jesus.** They are not consciously planning his murder.

The conflict is still intense in Luke, and Jesus presses the point. Both Mark and Luke agree that these adversaries were seeking to test Jesus, as Luke says, "in order to find a way to accuse him." Then Luke adds that since Jesus **knew their thoughts** (see the same term in 2:35; 5:22; 9:46-47; 24:38), he brought the man into their midst and exposed their scheme by taking the initiative. The struggle of wills and plans will increase step by step in Luke's narrative, and the Pharisees will often be central to the story (see 11:53-54; 15:1-2). Those who contrive an intentional plot on his life will emerge much later as "the chief priests and the scribes and the principal men of the people" (19:47; 20:19; 22:1-6). Often the Pharisees seem to be concerned to prevent Herod or the Romans from killing Jesus (see 13:31; 19:39).

These Pharisees are not apparently murderous schemers, but they are seeking to discredit and accuse Jesus. They are not innocent. Jesus exposes and denounces their little ruse to catch him in violation of the Sabbath. He labels it as an effort to **destroy** a life, while his healing is a messianic fulfillment of the Sabbath. The life he sees them seeking to destroy is probably his. Those who set the trap have been caught in their own casuistry, and these rationalists are filled with insane rage, talking with themselves about whatever they might do with Jesus.

The resistance which the reign of God and of God's Messiah exposes may be subtle and clever. It may seem quite rational and politically astute. But the Messiah will expose its irrational and enslaving methods, and the adversaries will be shown to be contending with God.

The Called: Apostles, Disciples, and People of God (6:12-19)

Luke has now rearranged two episodes in Mark, the healings by the sea and the call of the Twelve (Mark 3:7-12 and 3:13-19) and forged them into a single story which serves as a transition from the controversies (5:27—6:11) to the sermon on the plain (6:20-49). Now the apostles, disciples, and people are carefully distinguished, standing about Jesus in widening circles, but all ready to hear his words. With all of the controversy and conflict which Jesus has met, the stage is set for a positive reception of Jesus' most extensive and definitive speech in the whole Gospel.

Verse 12 opens with a Lukan transition, **in those days,** or "and it came to pass in those days" (see 1:5; 2:1; etc.) and continues with the emphasis that Jesus went up to the mountain **to pray . . . and all night he continued in prayer to God.** Even on a narrative level, it is already clear that the moment is marked with gravity, and the mention of prayer strengthens this impression. Jesus' authority has been challenged as he has repeatedly asserted his program of the kingdom. Now as he moves into structuring the leadership of his movement and giving specific counsel on the kingdom to his followers, he first communes with God in prayer. The community and policy which he is about to establish will truly be instruments of the reign of God. Jesus at prayer is confirming the will of God (see also the discussion of prayer in Luke 11:1-13).

Verses 13-16 present the "choosing" of the **twelve, whom he named apostles** as a divinely guided election (see also Simon, James, and John in 5:1-11 and Levi in 5:27-32, and note the structural outline on p. 137 below). In Acts 13:17, Paul refers to God as "choosing our fathers" (see also Deut. 4:37 and 10:15). Before Luke, the tradition of "the Twelve" could already be understood as a link to "the twelve tribes of Israel" (see Luke 22:30//Matt. 19:28; see also Acts 7:8 and 26:7), although "the Twelve" does not always require this symbolic association (see 1 Cor. 15:5; Acts 6:2). Yet in the light of 22:29-30 ("as my Father appointed a kingdom for me, so do I appoint for you that you may eat and drink at my table in my kingdom, and sit on thrones judging the twelve tribes of Israel"), it is clear that Luke understood Jesus' "choosing" of the Twelve as definitive of God's mission to Israel. The sending out of the Twelve in Luke 9:1 as contrasted to the sending of the seventy in Luke 10:1, 17 will heighten the symbolic character of the number. The full import of the Twelve is most clear in the Spirit-guided "election" of the replacement of Judas "who was numbered among us" (see Acts 1:17-26). Jesus is reconstituting the community of Israel around "the Twelve." This is God's design for the restoration of true Israel in the mission of witness for which God has set apart a chosen people.

"The Twelve," however, are not "patriarchs" or "judges" of Israel so much as they are **named apostles** of the kingdom of God and of God's Messiah (see Acts 1:2, "apostles . . . chosen through the Holy Spirit"). This identification is very strong in Luke to the point that only Luke explicitly says that the Twelve were named the apostles (assuming that the variant reading of Mark 3:14 is derived from Luke). Apart from two traditional allusions in Acts (14:4, 14) where Paul and Barnabas are mentioned as "apostles," none but the original or restored "Twelve" could qualify for this office (see Acts 1:21-22). It is not difficult to see why Paul found it necessary to fight for the legitimacy of his being an "apostle" (see Gal. 1:1) when he was so clearly not one of "the Twelve."

Luke is again underscoring the call of Israel to mission. The Twelve are not merely patriarchs, but they are authorized ambassadors of the Messiah and his kingdom (see Luke 22:30; Acts 1:22-25). From the beginning Jesus was not merely restoring Israel's heritage of tribal leadership. He was reestablishing the vocation of bearing witness to God's reign (Luke 9:1-6; Acts 1:6-8).

Complex issues of early Christian spiritual authority and ecclesiastical office are clearly at stake in these identifications, and Luke is contributing to the validation of the "twelve apostles." Luke knows that Paul was also the Lord's "chosen instrument . . . to carry my name before the Gentiles and kings and the sons of Israel" (Acts 9:15). Jesus' reconstitution of "the Twelve" does not prevent his later extraordinary appointment of Paul. The boundaries of institutional office will not prevent God from raising up charismatic leaders.

The list of names of the twelve apostles is fundamentally consistent among the sources (see also Mark 3:16-19; Matt. 10:2-4; and Acts 1:13), except that the name "Thaddaeus" in Mark and

Matthew appears in Luke's lists as **Judas the son of James,** and some variety exists in the sequence of the names within the list. **Simon who was called the Zealot** (see also Acts 1:13, "Simon the Zealot") is identified as "Simon the Cananaean" in Mark and Matthew. Interpreters have struggled to discern whether Simon was a member of the "Zealot" group whom Josephus identifies as the leaders in the revolt against Rome of A.D.. 67–73. Probably the origins of the party of the Zealots lie between the time of Jesus and the writing of the Gospels. The word could simply mean one who was known to be zealous for the faith, like Phineas (see Num. 25:6-15; 1 Macc. 2:26,54), but even Phineas was associated with bloody religious warfare. It is now impossible to know enough about Simon to estimate whether this label fit his prior history or the Christians also regarded him as some kind of "zealot." But it is clear that "the Twelve" and the larger group of **disciples** were a disparate group: fishermen, a tax collector, a "zealot," and the "betrayer," among a broader group of disciples and followers, of women, soldiers, Pharisees, rich and poor.

Verses 17-19 underscore this diversity as the context of Jesus' major address to his followers. He **came down** the mountain with the Twelve whom he had taken apart from the larger group of disciples, and then he was surrounded by the **great crowd of his disciples** and an even larger **multitude of people.** And this multitude has come from vast distances of geography and culture. Jerusalem and Judea in the south are also religiously and ethnically far removed from the coastal cities north in Syria. Are some of these people Gentiles? Not necessarily, although they are clearly not all "Judeans." In fact, the use of the term the **people** suggests that Luke probably envisions people of Israel who have come from the extent of Palestine.

And they have come **to hear him and to be healed,** including those troubled with unclean spirits. And the Messiah who is about to speak to these eager "hearers" is also possessed of the **power** to heal. In deed and word, Jesus is authorized by the Spirit of God. In fact, Luke says, he **healed them all**!" Without telling any specific healing story, the evangelist has set a dramatic stage for the address which is to follow. Jesus, his apostles, the larger group of disciples, and the far-flung multitudes are all gathered in a panoramic scene, filled with a vast range of human experience and need which Jesus has met. The expectation of faith is high, and the mix of humanity is rich. This is the human face of the kingdom of God.

The Address on the Plain (6:20-49)

Luke wraps up this section of his Gospel by rehearsing Jesus' second major address, just as he began the section with the Messiah's inaugural declaration in Nazareth (4:14-30). By now Jesus has established the inner core of his apostles by calling Simon, James, and John (5:1-11), and has filled out "the Twelve" before this last declaration of the policies of his reign (Levi, 5:27-32; the Twelve, 6:12-16). And, in the midst of the section, his acts and words have underscored his authority. A schematic outline underscores the "bracketed" structure of this section:

Declaring the Kingdom in Word and Deed (4:14—6:49)
1. The Messiah's Inaugural Announcement (4:14-30)
2. Proclaiming the Kingdom in Galilee and Judea (4:31-44)
   3. The Call of Simon (5:1-11)
      4. The Cleansing of Leprosy (5:12-16)
      5. Forgiveness of Sins and Healing of Paralysis (5:16-26)
      6. Torah and Kingdom: Conflicts on Authority (5:27—6:11)
   7. The Called Apostles, Disciples, and People of God (6:12-19)
8. The Address on the Plain (6:20-49)

Jesus' famous "Sermon on the Plain" (6:20-49) is a major policy statement of the kingdom. This address explicates the "good news to the poor" which was announced in Nazareth and further demonstrated in the messianic acts of Jesus throughout Galilee. Of course it is a "spiritual" statement, quite properly regarded throughout the centuries as a Jesus' "sermon" to his disciples. This is, after all, the one on whom "the Spirit of the Lord" rested "because he has anointed me to declare good news to the poor" (4:18; Isa. 61:1). But Luke's version of the "sermon" mightily resists the kind of "spiritualizing" of Jesus' address which would deny or diminish its claim on the here and now.

Matthew's version, the "Sermon on the Mount," has been better known and loved by far, perhaps in part because its "spirituality" seems more congenial to many Christian traditions. To speak a benediction on the poor "in spirit" with the assurance of the kingdom "of heaven" (Matt. 5:3) certainly sounds less like a critique of present realities, and those who "hunger for righteousness" (Matt. 5:5) could include all religious people, while the blessing of those who "are hungry now" (Luke 6:21) threatens many people who are accustomed to "counting their blessings" of health, prosperity, and happiness. Furthermore, Matthew's version, which contains more than three times as many verses, still does not include those ominous woes of Luke 6:24-26. Sentimentalizing Matthew's "sermon" is certainly a misinterpretation, but such a reading of Luke's version of Jesus' address is almost impossible.

These verses are also the beginning of an extended section where Luke is no longer following Mark's content or sequence. Luke 6:20—8:3 has been called the "small interpolation" by scholars who have maintained that Luke's narrative is fundamentally an expanded version of Mark's structure (see also 9:51—18:14, the "large interpolation"). It is important to observe that Luke has taken up his second major source without breaking stride in the narrative. A new section does not begin until 7:1. Although a major division will occur the next time Luke moves away from the Markan sequence at 9:51, Mark's structure does not dictate the organization of Luke's story.

As noted in the introduction, this second major source for Luke is commonly called "Q," and the similarities between Matthew and Luke's versions of the sermon are so compelling that it appears secure that this is one of the major places where both evangelists are drawing on such a written source with materials that Mark did not have. Since such a document no longer exists, as far as anyone knows, it is impossible to determine with great precision exactly where Luke and Matthew have restated this source in their own versions of the story. In general, it is argued that Matthew appears to have elaborated this material, while

Luke's briefer version may be closer to the source ("Q"). Certainly the differences between Matthew and Luke's account are fascinating and provocative, and it is very helpful to recognize that both evangelists are probably working with a document ("Q") before them or with (oral or memorized?) versions of that document. But elaborate arguments concerning who may have restated this source which no longer exists lead to increasingly uncertain interpretation. The effort to interpret each version within its own narrative context is much more rewarding.

Luke's setting of the context thus provides a distinctive "staging" of this extended speech. The larger structure (see outline above) identifies this as a major policy address, stating the particulars of the dominion of this Messiah for his followers. Furthermore, the preceding delineation of the ranks of the called as "the twelve apostles," "the disciples," and "the people" indicates a discriminating assessment of all these "hearers" of the address (see 6:12-19; v. 17: "they came to hear him and to be healed"). It already seems likely that they will not all "hear" the address in the same way, and the reader "overhears" the several messages of the address as they speak to this diverse audience, all of whom are highly positive "hearers."

The first section (vv. 20-26) is explictly addressed to the **disciples,** with perhaps some distinction even made among them (see below). The second section (vv. 27-36) differs in form and content from the blessings and woes and seems to be addressed to a broader audience of **you that hear** (v. 27). The third section (vv. 37-49) may envision yet another audience, perhaps the church of Luke's own day or the reader. It brings this address into the realm of long-term consequences for the community of followers of this "Lord." To be sure, the integrity of the whole address must not be fractured into too specific audiences, especially since all of these groups are clearly envisioned as hearing all of the address. Nevertheless, Luke's narrative draws the reader into contemplating a complex scene where the differing aspects of the address "speak to" the variety of "hearers." Finally, the reader's place within the audience will also be affected by how "you hear."

Promises and Warnings (6:20-26).   After the lengthy build-up of vv. 12-20, Jesus **lifted up his eyes on his disciples and said** . . . This is the crowd within the crowd, as Luke has set the scene (v. 17). They have all come "to hear," but Jesus is beginning with a more select audience while the crowds of people overhear. The direct address of vv. 20b-23 is so meticulously paralleled with the direct address of vv. 24-26 that the contrast between the "blessings" and the "woes" is inescapable. Every disciple is confronted with both. Jesus is not saying two things, but one; yet this address of the Messiah is a two-edged sword. Even the disciples are divided.

Blessed are you poor . . . for . . .
      hungry now . . . for . . .
      grieving now . . . for . . .
      whenever people hate you . . .
       for . . .
Woe to you . . . rich . . . for . . .
      full now . . . for . . .
      laughing now . . . for . . .
      whenever all people speak well . . .
       for . . .

Does Jesus have two groups in view among his disciples? Perhaps the apostles who have "left everything" (5:11, 28; 18:28-30; see also 9:57-62; 10:23-24) stand in the center circle of blessing, while beyond the line are those followers who still cling to their resources, plenty, good times, and reputations as blessings (**But woe to you who . . .**). Or are all of the disciples of Jesus confronted with the promises and warnings of Jesus' rule so that the uncompromising authority of the Messiah redefines the very basis on which each person's standing before God is established? Then the disciples and all **you that hear** (v. 27) and the reader who overhears this address discover that no matter whom Jesus is directly addressing, the policy of his reign is inescapable.

The persons identified as "blessed" or "fortunate" in vv. 20b-23 are certainly contrary to any usual expectation or standard "theology" of being lucky or happy. If this were not part of Jesus' mission of the kingdom to the poor and outcast, it could be merely

Those who have need are the priority (handwritten note)

a perverse glorification of suffering. It is not a glorification of the nobility of poverty, hunger, grief, or dishonor. But it is a declaration of the priority of those in need in the policy of this reign. Those who have "left all" to follow Jesus are not superior because of their ascetic virtue, but they have entered into Jesus' campaign (**yours is the kingdom of God**) to bring good news to the poor. The poor, hungry, and grieving may already be said to be **blessed** because the promises of God are being conferred upon them now with the authority of the Messiah. The future reality of God's kingdom is crucial to its present authority. The future of those who appear to have no future is already assured, and the rest of the world would be advised to discern that this is the way the reign of God works.

No doubt these words of Jesus had also been specifically attached to Christian experience in a variety of ways. They too had known poverty, hunger, and grief. Verses 22-23 are particularly transparent to the experience of Jesus' followers, including the time of the writing of this Gospel. Their confidence that Jesus truly was the Messiah and God's way of ruling in the world had clearly been tried, not least by their being regarded as heretics from the faith of Israel and excluded from the synagogues (see Acts 21:21, for example). Now they could know that not only were the poor, hungry, and outcast of Israel given priority in the mission of the Messiah and his reign, but those who suffered exclusion and humiliation for the sake of this **Son of man** could be reassured that this was a mark of blessing. It was not a sign of being cut off from the promises of God.

Verses 24-26 are thus the converse, still speaking a word of assurance to those with ears to hear. While those who are wealthy, full, laughing, and adulated seem to have everything going for them, they are actually in the greater peril. They may well be tempted to take security in their apparent "blessings" and unable to let go of such securities to get in on the dynamic mission of the kingdom.

Luke will pick up this theme repeatedly in the story (see especially 12:13-34; 14:33; 18:18-30). When Luke presents Jesus' policy on "the poor" or "the rich," the issue will certainly be "spiritual," but not in the sense of superior moralities. The issue is that of true and false security before God in this world and in the world to come and the danger of a security based in goods, wealth, or reputation. How much good can "unrighteous mammon" do you in the eternal habitations compared to the true righteousness of the kingdom (see 16:1-15)? Only the promises of God will prove truly promising. The authority of God's Messiah Jesus is grounded in his exercise of God's peculiar and saving reign. The **false prophets** will tell people what they want to hear and give them assurances based on their own idols of security, and people will praise the false prophets. But all who are "hearing" or "overhearing" this major policy address would be well advised to listen to both the warnings and the promises.

The Ethics of the Kingdom (6:27-38).   Commentators generally divide the rest of the "sermon" into three parts, vv. 27-36 on the command to love, vv. 37-42 on not judging, and vv. 43-49 on fruits and foundations. This collection of sayings materials does not have any obvious structure, and the customary division preserves the close connection which Matthew makes between the commands against judging (Matt. 7:1-2) and the words about the speck in the brother's eye (Matt. 7:3-4). But it may obscure Luke's literary restatement of the tradition.

Verses 27-38 are marked as a unit in Luke by his introduction which resumes Jesus' address and broadens the audience which is envisioned: **But I say to you who hear** (v. 27), while the next section opens with Luke's introduction, **He also told them a parable** (v. 39). Verses 27-38 thus offer a remarkable exposition on the ethics of love as the ethics of the kingdom. Jesus speaks throughout the section, always in direct address to the hearers, with no asides or notes from the evangelist, and Jesus' theme is love and judgment. Only the larger Lukan account of the "address" makes it clear that this is a "kingdom" speech.

This section is an ethical exposition of the Beatitudes, and the church's situation which began to be evident in vv. 22-23 makes the extravagance of this loving all the more impressive. As ethics, this counsel is in the realm of law. The brilliant usage of these commands by Tolstoy, Ghandi, and Martin Luther King in developing the philosophy of nonviolence have demonstrated the power of the address as a strategy for social change. It offers an alternative vision, especially in Luke where the particularities of poverty, reprisal, extortion, and loan policy are so prominent. This address has provided centuries of believers with a mode of action quite contrary to the oppressive systems which needed to be changed.

Yet, even the commands to love are still commands and must not be disguised as the "gospel." Glorious as these commands are, the "ethics of the kingdom" will also prove impossible to practice perfectly. But this is not a counsel of perfection. Even as Jesus is emphasizing that his followers must attain a standard which far excels all that the "sinners" do, Luke offers no hint of despair. Rather, the whole address is grounded in the confidence that Jesus is going beyond a moral appeal. He is also revealing something else, that is, God's reign and the incredible measure of God's grace in the world. "What is impossible for human beings is possible for God!" (18:27). Through Jesus' reign, even the formerly impossible begins to be possible. Jesus' entire ministry, ending in his death, will be a demonstration of this radical self-giving, and then God will vindicate Jesus' obedience in his resurrection and exalt him in glory. These imperatives to his disciples will soon be grounded in his enactment of God's reign. The Messiah is announcing the law which he will fulfill. The call to obedience is much more profound for the Christian than mere idealism.

Verses 27-31 are thus quite literal commands for all who "hear," and specific counsel for those who have experienced the abuse, exclusion, and defamation of v. 22. The golden rule is not original with Jesus or the evangelists, but it sounds quite shocking when applied to enemies, abusers, thieves, and beggars. Yet this is not a counsel of masochism, as if Christians are simply doormats. Nor should such a command, which is grounded in the promise of the kingdom, ever be used to give God's sanction to violence. This is a vision of courage and integrity and of worth from outside the immediate exchange.

Verses 32-36 press the implications of this command to love. In vv. 32-34, three conditional sentences draw a sharp contrast between the standards which even **the sinners** regard as good behavior and the kind of self-giving which Jesus commands. The contrast with **the sinners** is a reminder that the Law of God had long called Israel to kindness and goodness to the outsider, the widow, and the orphan. It had also forbidden lending at interest. Israel was set apart from the "Gentiles" and "sinners" in observing God's Law.

Yet Jesus is making a distinction which goes beyond usual interpretations. In each case the argument turns on the suggestion that if you only live like the sinners, "what kind of grace is that for you?" When the RSV translates this as **what credit is that to you?** it has captured the sense of "why could you claim to have done anything special?" But the question, "What kind of grace is that for you?" indicates that the issue is not merely *how much* one has done, but the *kind* of "grace" which is at work. The grace of the kingdom is qualitatively different.

The summary in v. 35, therefore, is a restatement of the command to **love your enemies** (see also v. 27), now filled with the further specifics of **doing good** and **lending, expecting nothing else in return,** and the reason is not that "this will prove to be a smart business practice anyway." Yes, there is a promise of great reward, but such practices really prove that **you will be** children **of the Most High.** This is the economy of the kingdom of God, the peculiar logic of the kind of grace which only God and those in God's family would think to practice. Other moral philosophers of this era would also speak of those who practice virtue as God's "friends" or "spies" in the world—or even children—but none would counsel such extreme measures. The standard of love, doing good, and even generosity in lending is finally a distinctive divine standard of the mercy which Jesus' whole ministry revealed (v. 36). This mercy is the kind of grace which the Messiah is now declaring to be definitive of his reign.

Verses 37-38 are then a kind of reprise on not judging, and they belong to the logic of this section (see discussion above on the outline). These statements anticipate the "parables" which follow, but they need to be kept in close connection with what precedes lest the conclusion be merely a return to moralism, as in the RSV: **For the measure you give will be the measure you get back** (v. 38). This may be more adequate than Matthew's

version of this saying. But Luke's text is much more discriminating: "By the measure you measure, it shall be measured out
to you." This **measure** is not mere quantity, but the standard or
quality of measurement. As Luke emphasizes by the second line,
the issue in **not judging** is that the Christian can not be condemning because God's standard of mercy (v. 36) is the only **measure** which may be used. And only Luke describes the incredible
extravagance of this **good measure, pressed down, shaken together, running over** (v. 38). Once again, the "gospel" in the text
shines through the disclosure of the extravagantly gracious measure of God's mercy.

The ethical concerns of this entire section are remarkably this-
worldly, demonstrating that the Messiah is bringing the reign of
God into the contested arena of human life. People who even
start to live this way may seem odd or deluded, and the "righteousness" of this kingdom will be "alien" in the world. Perhaps
it will even be threatening. But it is God's saving way as enacted
by Jesus who now had declared this divine standard and method
of mercy to be definitive for the behavior of his followers.

The Peril of Hypocrisy (6:39-49).   Luke marks the beginning of this section with a brief sentence of his own which resumes
the narrative: **he also told them a parable.** The audience is still
"you that hear" (v. 27) and the "disciples" upon whom he "lifted
his eyes to speak" (v. 20). Apart from these few explanatory notes,
the evangelist is intensively compiling Jesus' sayings. It is not
even clear exactly which of the items that follow is the "parable"
Luke had in mind, but the kind of sayings material has definitely
changed. Now there are no more direct ethical instructions. Instead the "address" concludes with a diverse collection of warnings about the consequences of "hearing" and "not doing."

To catch the drift of these enigmatic or epigrammatic utterances, v. 39 must be read in close connection with v. 40. These
proverbs could mean many things in other contexts, but here the
point seems clear that Jesus is the authoritative teacher who will
not lead into a pit; in time Jesus' hearers may hope fully to comprehend and represent his teaching. This is not a gnostic assurance that all of the followers of Jesus are now spiritually superior

to their brothers and sisters. It is rather a warning against assuming too quickly that the "hearers" have attained any such
enlightenment.

Verses 41-42 thus serve as an explication of this warning. It is
a traditional saying of Jesus which was probably already proverbial
before him. The point is still well taken. The humorous image
of someone with a **log** in an **eye** offering to play doctor for someone
with a **speck** in another's eye must not be missed. It is impossible
to tell this without allegorizing it, since specific applications immediately spring into the mind of every hearer.

Verses 43-45 are also full of allegorical possibilities to be explored. In fact, v. 45 is already an allegory expositing the image
of the good tree. Since this image has positive implications as
well as warnings, it is worth noting that the concept of **good fruit**
has long been one of the best for speaking of the Christian life
without creating a new legalism. Luke will pick up the theme in
greater detail later in the story (see 8:5-15; 13:6-9). Once again,
this is not merely a moral appeal so much as it is a prophetic
diagnosis. The **fruit** will disclose the **tree,** and the utterance of
the **mouth** will reveal the **heart.** Even in the repetition of the
sayings traditions, Luke's Gospel discerns the complex connection
between what the heart believes and the mouth says. The words
may disclose the state of the will, but words may also be used to
disguise the convictions of the heart.

Verses 46-49, therefore, conclude the section with a sharp
warning against hypocrisy in confessing faithfulness to the lordship of Jesus. The first line is particularly shocking because it is
suddenly a word of direct address (note this also, less abruptly,
in vv. 41-42). The hearers of the address are not merely being
instructed, but they, Luke's church, and the modern disciple are
confronted with the Messiah's authority. Jesus has been expound-
ing the ethics of the kingdom and revealing the extravagance of
God's mercy. But he has also been addressing the "hearers" with
the agenda of the kingdom of God which are directives for him
and **you.**

The contrast between the **house** founded on the **rock** and the
house **built on the ground** has been subject to so many further

allegorical applications that its basic point of comparison has become forgettable. But both Matthew (7:21-27) and Luke concur
that Jesus was speaking about "hearing and doing" Jesus' command as the sure foundation. Anything less is perilous hypocrisy.
Luke's phrase about **every one who comes to me and hears my
words and does them** underscores the nature of faithful discipleship, while one who **hears and does not do them** is in danger
of destruction. The issue is "doing" what Jesus commands.

This is hardly a word of "gospel." The Messiah is laying down
the law, and the uncompromsing law of the kingdom he is inaugurating is certainly no easier than the Law of Moses or any
other form of God's command. The address has conveyed several
glimpses of the gospel of God's extravagant grace, but it ends on
the note that the law also is radical. It will not work to domesticate
the gospel into a moralism, nor is it possible to diminish the
commands of the Messiah into precepts to be observed when
convenient. The authority of this Messiah and of the reign of God
have been declared to all who have heard. Now "you who hear"
are confronted with the will of God.

Identifying the Messiah of God (7:1—9:50)

Luke 7:1 marks a transition in the narrative. Jesus has now
concluded **all his sayings in the hearing of the people,** and the
focus of attention shifts to a more intense scrutiny of who this
Jesus is proving to be. The mention of the place (**Capernaum**) is
quite inconsequential, except as it suggests movement to another
stage. But Luke has pulled together the following stories into a
"Christological drama" in which the authority of Jesus' messiahship will be revealed, while still hidden in the mystery of the
necessity of his rejection and death. "Who Jesus is" will be made
evident in a variety of displays, but "why he must die" becomes
the motive power of the plot of the narrative.

Calling this section a "Christological drama" could also invite
misunderstanding. Often interpreters have moved into the Gospel narratives laden with the equipment of the Christological
debates of later centuries of the church when the questions were
about Jesus' divine and human "natures," and then Christology

was fundamentally a discussion of metaphysics. Important as that kind of Christological analysis is, it may obscure the evangelist's testimony to Jesus' role, authority, and identity as the agent of God's reign. Luke's "Christology" is not generally invested in issues of Jesus' nature or even of exploring his unity with God (see 10:21-22 for an exception), but it is a persistent demonstration that Jesus is truly the anointed one of God, the fulfillment of God's promises and the faithful revelation of God's will and rule. This "Christological drama" is, therefore, not an abstract discussion of God's being or essence. It is a dynamic demonstration of God's will and greatness, driving finally to the mystery of the necessity of the death of the Messiah.

Jesus the Prophet of God (7:1-50)

The first series of stories appears to be collected around the identification of Jesus as the prophet. This is not a strict topical structure, since Luke appears to have continued to follow the "Q" traditions, moving from the "sermon" into the episodes of the healing of the centurion's servant (7:1-10) and the encounters with the messengers of John (7:18-35). But the note about the **prophet** which arises in the exchanges with John's disciples (7:26) has now been supplemented with stories unique to Luke which highlight Jesus' identity as "prophet" (7:11-17, 36-50).

Once again it is important to observe that Luke is not suggesting that Jesus was "merely a prophet," as if the designation as "prophet" were to diminish his authority or distinctive relation to God. Acts 3:22-26 demonstrates that Luke's concept of "prophet" extended to Jesus' fulfillment of the scriptural promise of "the prophet like Moses" (Deuteronomy 18). This was a role of high authority, since the very fate of the people of God hung in the balance of whether or not they would "hear" or "listen to him in whatever he tells you" (Acts 3:22-23). Thus Luke is confronting the reader with a strong word of testimony by beginning this "Christological drama" with an expanded demonstration of Jesus as the "prophet."

The Centurion: Foreign Recognition of Genuine Authority (7:1-10).   This first story in the section does not yet introduce the identification of Jesus as prophet, but it deals with the larger issue of authority. Following Q, both Matthew and Luke relate an episode of the healing of a Gentile centurion's servant, and it is a miraculous healing, especially since Jesus does it from a distance. But the wonder of the story is focused on the centurion's implicit faith in Jesus. Even Jesus **marveled at him** (v. 9, Matt. 8:10). Thus the healing recedes into the background while Jesus discerns the significance of such trust and pronounces it to be exemplary.

1-3—Luke builds contrasts from the beginning. Since the term which is translated here as **the people** is consistently reserved by Luke for Israel, both the audiences and their **hearing** are distinguished. This foreigner had only **heard of Jesus** while **the people** (of Israel) had heard him and his words. Still it is not so significant that he would send an embassy to a healer of some fame if a **valuable** (RSV, note) servant were sick. In contrast to Matthew's story, the centurion himself does not come, nor does Luke mention this officer's concern for the servant's suffering. Everything is done at a distance. It could be that he merely does not want to lose a slave.

The human interest in the story emerges with the pleading of the Jewish elders who are willing emissaries of this centurion (vv. 4-5, only in Luke). There is no hint that these elders find it degrading to be bearers of such a request, and Jesus promptly heads off with no commentary. As with the Roman centurion Cornelius who is "a devout man who feared God with all his household, gave alms liberally to the people, and prayed constantly to God" (Acts 10:2), Luke depicts this officer as a genuine friend of Israel. These elders who **sought** Jesus **earnestly** were correct in regarding the centurion as **worthy** . . . **for he loves our nation, and he built us our synagogue.** And Jesus does not hesitate, which probably indicates that Luke sees the whole encounter as authentic, reasonable, and honorable.

6-8—The surprise comes when the centurion sends another embassy of his **friends.** It is not the Jews or the Jewish Messiah who have hesitated to come into the house of this Gentile (see Peter in Acts 10:28). But now the centurion, speaking through his friends, addresses Jesus as **Lord** or "Sir," and he insists that

he is **not worthy to have** Jesus **come under his roof.** The deference to Jesus is amazing, as well as the sensitivity to Jewish
customs. He simply will not ask Jesus for extraordinary considerations, although Jesus and the elders are already on their way.
None of them is prepared for the depth of faith which he displays.

The cultural dimensions of the encounter are penetrated still
further when the centurion observes that because of Jesus' extraordinary **authority,** he need not come anyway. The episode
now escalates into a story of the ability of someone who deals in
authority all the time to discern real authority when he sees it,
even if he has only heard about Jesus from afar. "Just **say the
word,**" he says, and it will be as good as done! That is how
authority works when it is real.

Even Jesus is impressed (v. 9). His words to **the multitude that
followed him,** probably including the elders and his disciples,
are simple praise. In Matthew's version these same words reflect
negatively on Israel because they are connected with an oracle
of judgment on those "sons of the kingdom" who will be thrown
into utter darkness at the judgment (Matt. 8:10-12; see Luke
13:28-29). But in Luke where Jesus has been addressing his own
apostles, disciples, and people—the faithful—his comment is a
straightforward commendation: "**Not even in Israel have I found
such faith!**" And of course, the servant was healed (v. 10).

The **faith** of the centurion is a discernment of Jesus' authority
and an implicit trust in it. Other stories will struggle with problems of the rejection of Jesus by his own people, but this story
is an object lesson for all—Jesus, the Jewish elders who come to
him expecting that he will be able to heal the servant, the disciples in the entourage, and even the reader. The centurion never
makes it to the stage of the drama. He only speaks through messengers, the Jewish elders, and his friends. But even from a
distance, he can recognize authority, and his insight is instructive.

The Great Prophet and God's Visitation (7:11-17).   This is
one of Luke's well-told tales, where the evangelist's literary art-
istry both enhances the human pathos and underscores the theological point of the story. Like the birth narrative (2:1-20) or the
call of Simon (5:1-11), this Christian favorite is found only in Luke,

and it is filled with scriptural precedents as well as arresting narrative details.

It is a wonder story with all of the usual structure of a miracle: human interest in setting the scene (vv. 11-12a), detailed account of the plight of the afflicted (vv. 12b-13a), a dramatic encounter with the healer (vv. 13b-14), a clear display of the effectiveness of the miracle (v. 15), and a chorus of wonder or acclaim which provides a clue to the meaning of the event (vv. 16-17). The details of the story capture great feeling and interest: the widow's plight at the loss of her "only-begotten" (see also 8:42, 9:38), Jesus' being moved with pity, his touching the litter and stopping the funeral procession, his raising the dead man with only a word, and the statement **he gave him to his mother.** It is almost impossible to speak about this story without retelling all of the details. The pathos and glorious scandal of Jesus' violation of taboo in order to bring life are filled with confidence (see Acts 3:15; Jesus, "the Author of life").

This is one of three Lukan stories of the resuscitation of a dead person (see also 8:40-42, 49-56, Jairus's daughter; Acts 9:36-43, Tabitha). The story of the reviving of Eutychus in Acts 20:7-12 differs in form as well as in the stress that the boy was not dead. The story of the resurrection of Jesus is of a very different order, since it is much more than a resuscitation and Jesus' bodily form is altered (see the discussion of Luke 24, and see 1 Cor. 15:35-50). Close comparison of these stories will indicate the evangelist's conviction that these resuscitations are displays of the authority and power of the kingdom over death itself (see 12:5).

The scriptural precedents to Jesus' action are fundamental to the significance of this event. This is a display of Jesus' **compassion** for the **widow** and those who suffer, but it is also a revelation of Jesus' identity as "the prophet." The stories of Elijah and Elisha's raising of children were revelations of their being prophetic "men of God," "and the word of the Lord in your mouth is truth" (1 Kings 17:17-24, 2 Kings 4:18-37). The Elijah story is particularly similar, since the woman is a poor widow with only one son; and when Elijah raised him, "he gave him to his mother" (1 Kings 17:23, Luke 7:15). In Nazareth, Jesus has also referred to Elijah and Elisha's precedents with an explicit mention of the widow to

151

whom Elijah was sent (4:26-27). Jesus is clearly fulfilling and surpassing the scriptural prophets. Luke even refers to Jesus as **the Lord** (v. 13), reflecting the confessional language of the early Christians (see 22:61; 24:3).

Is Jesus Elijah returned? The book of Malachi (4:5-6) promised, "Behold, I will send you Elijah the prophet before the great and terrible day of the Lord comes." The task of the returning Elijah was to be to "turn the hearts of the fathers to their children and the hearts of the children to their fathers," and this task was specifically assigned to John the Baptist by the angel of the Lord (Luke 1:17).

Nevertheless, while the angel speaks of John going before Jesus "in the spirit and power of Elijah," Luke stops short of a specific identification of John as Elijah returned. By contrast, Matthew says of John, "and if you are willing to accept it, he is Elijah who is to come" (Matt. 11:14). Clearly there was continuing debate among the early Christians and perhaps among the disciples of John whether "to accept" that John or Jesus was Elijah returned, and the next stories in Luke will sort out John and Jesus' roles very carefully (7:18-35, especially v. 28). Elijah will also appear with Moses to speak with Jesus concerning his "departure" on the mountain of transfiguration (9:28-36), so clearly neither Jesus nor John is merely the "returned Elijah."

On the other hand, Luke's Jesus, who is truly "a prophet mighty in deed and word before God and all the people," not only fulfills the promise of the "prophet like Moses" (Acts 3:22), but he also surpasses John in fulfilling the prophetic role of Elijah. Even his raising the dead by his word alone outdoes Elijah's or Elisha's stretching themselves out on the corpse. It is at least interesting to note that the Elisha stories were already a kind of fulfillment of Elijah's prophetic office, but neither in Malachi nor in the Gospels is it thought that the role had yet truly been fulfilled. Luke's high regard for John also does not obscure his conviction that only Jesus fully completes the promise of Elijah returned.

The conclusion (v. 16) of this episode announces the meaning of the story in the words of the acclamation of the crowd. The two statements interpret each other and should be treated as a parallelism interpreting the people's "glorification" of God: "A great prophet has been raised up!" "**God has visited** God's **people.**" The RSV's use of the active voice ("**A great prophet has arisen!**") misses the point that God is the actor in both sentences. The "divine passive" could be debated in many texts where it might not be clear just who the actor may be, but here the second sentence makes it obvious that this great prophet has been "raised up" by God, because this is God's visitation.

The people's glorification of God is their testimony to what is truly happening in the scene, and Luke concurs. Jesus has been identified and validated as an Elijah prophet, fitting, fulfilling, and surpassing Elijah. This is the work of God, and it is a divine "visitation." This concept of "visitation" was also part of the promise associated with the birth of John, linking God's "visitation" and the "redemption" of God's people (1:68). God's visitation may also portend destruction if it is not discerned (see 19:44). But for those with the eyes to see and ears to hear, this mighty act of Jesus is a manifestation of the saving "visitation" of God's reign, and Jesus is "the prophet" who speaks for God and enacts God's will.

"The One Who Is to Come" Has Come! (7:18-23).   Luke's mastery in the faithful and creative use of the tradition is evident in this section. In vv. 18-35 "Q" is clearly the source, and the verbal correspondence with Matthew's version is frequently very high. Still, the evangelist's hand and purpose are consistently evident as these pronouncement stories are woven into the fabric of Luke's narrative. Now the tradition expresses a clear word of testimony to the surpassing greatness of Jesus and the righteousness of the kingdom of God which he inaugurates.

The transition in v. 18 ties this episode directly into the preceding stories so that now the reader knows that **John** is well aware of all that has been taking place, perhaps even Jesus' recent acclamation as the "great prophet" and "divine visitation" (7:16). Now John and **his disciples** raise the question of Jesus' identity in much more specific terms. The specificity comes from the fact that John had already announced the coming of the "mightier one" in dramatic terms. In response to the question of whether he might be the Messiah, the Baptizer had declared that they had not yet seen anything to compare with the power and judgment which this mightier one would bring at his coming (3:15-17). Even the word describing the people's "expectation" concerning John in 3:15 is repeated in the question of whether "we should 'expect' another' " (7:19, 20).

It is difficult to know what this question might have meant to John himself or his disciples back in the time of Jesus' ministry. Were they simply seeking confirmation? Did they have serious misgivings about where the judgment and fire had gone? Or was John giving his last indirect witness to Jesus by letting him declare his identity to his disciples? The scene is poignant, especially when Jesus bears his testimony concerning John, but he does so only after John's disciples have departed (v. 24). Did John ever hear how highly Jesus thought of him? Or did John's disciples ever get the picture of Jesus' surpassing of John?

It may be impossible to decide those historical questions, but interpreters have been fascinated with the possibility of at least reconstructing an ongoing dispute between the disciples of Jesus and the disciples of John in the early years of the church. As noted above (see the discussions at 3:18-20; 7:11-17), Luke-Acts takes great pains to sort out the connections between John and Jesus. Apparently the "baptism of John" continued to be practiced. Part of the value of the John–Jesus stories, therefore, was their demonstration that the disciples of Jesus had instruction which went beyond that of John's disciples. The early departure of John's disciples in this story fits that picture.

In Luke's story, however, the question from John's disciples is tied in with Luke's presentation of Jesus as the prophet par excellence. Only Luke repeats the pointed question, first on John's lips, then as recited by the **two** chosen disciples (vv. 19-20). The testimony of **two** witnesses will be borne back to him. But before Jesus answers, they are also going to see something.

Verse 21 is Luke's insertion which augments the "Q" story and ties it into Luke's narrative. It is almost as if the evangelist suggests that Jesus first answered them in action and then his words had new impact (v. 22). Luke does not actually tell the stories of these wondrous healings. Only the summary statement is provided (see also 4:40-41; 6:19).

It may be important that Luke had not yet told any stories of Jesus' healing of the blind (see 18:35-43). Of course no evangelist claims to have told everything that Jesus did, but Luke's summary assures the reader that John's disciples would have **seen and heard** almost the whole list recited by Jesus in v. 22 because of what has happened in the story since 4:14-30: blind have received their sight (7:21), the lame (i.e., paralyzed) have walked (5:17-26), those with leprosy have been cleansed (5:12-16), the dead have been raised (7:11-17), and the poor have heard the good news (6:20-23). Only a specific story of the deaf hearing seems to be lacking, unless 6:17-20 may be counted where Luke speaks of the multitudes "who came to hear him and be healed of their diseases . . . and he healed them all." The picture is more than adequately clear without insisting on too rigid a framework. Luke's own summary in 7:21 also refers to curing evil spirits (4:31-37, 40-41), an aspect not mentioned in Jesus' declaration.

Jesus' words to John's disciples are filled with the phrases of Isaiah (see Isa. 29:18; 35:5-6; 61:1). Jesus is declaring to John's disciples that they have **seen and heard** the fulfillment of the scriptural promises of the restoration. What more could they expect of the one **who is to come**? This is the kind of "seeing and hearing" which only the most "blessed" will experience (see 10:23-24, contrast 4:20-21, see discussion). The leaping lame man in Acts 3 will be a further sign that the restoration continues in the early church. The age of the kingdom has clearly been inaugurated.

Yet Jesus' words also mark the fulfillment of his own declaration of his vocation at Nazareth (4:18-19) in the words of Isaiah 61. The program of the kingdom which the newly anointed Messiah announced has set the agenda for Jesus' words and deeds: good news to the poor, release to the captives, recovery of sight to the blind, liberty for the oppressed, and the year of jubilee. The problem in Nazareth is that they did not wait to see whether Jesus would deliver on the program he announced. Now he has done so, and the reader of Luke's Gospel can "see and hear" right along with John's disciples exactly how Jesus is fulfilling the role of "the one who is to come."

The reign of God which Jesus inaugurates is not so filled with judgment and vengeance as John's preaching predicted, at least not yet. The contrast between Jesus and John which follows in the text further highlights that Jesus' preaching is not simply an intensification of John's warnings of impending wrath. Not even John can set the terms for the kingdom which God has brought in Jesus. It is not possible to know whether John or his disciples ever understood that the gracious fulfillment far surpassed John's ominous alert. But, as vv. 24-35 will show, the validity of John's ministry as God's messenger is affirmed right along with Jesus' identity, causing the mystery of the rejection of both to stand out more sharply. Thus Jesus' final word to the messengers of "blessing" on the one who is not scandalized at him (v. 23) is not merely counsel to John to accept him as God's promised agent. It is also an alert to the "hearer" of the story of the blessing of faith and the peril of rejection of Jesus.

The Greatest Prophet Is Surpassed (7:24-35).   These verses are almost verbatim in Matthew and in Luke, and they are filled with the fascinating details of Near Eastern give and take. The rhetorical questions are all absurd, revealing the character of John by contrast. Of course, no one went into **the wilderness** to see a flimsy reed blown this way and that by the wind. John was a force, challenging those who came to be baptized as a "brood of vipers" (3:7-14). He did not wait to see which way the wind was blowing! And as for **soft raiment,** he was famous for his hair shirt and leather girdle (Mark 1:6//Matt. 3:4, not mentioned in Luke). John had none of the signs of successful people pleasers. His call was from God, and it was a specific prophetic vocation.

John is not just any prophet. Jesus testifies to John as the fulfillment of the prophecy in Mal. 3:1 of the "messenger before my face who shall prepare the way before me." Matthew 11:14 follows this logic as far as identifying John as "Elijah" the prophet as promised in Mal. 4:5. Perhaps this identification was already present in this context in "Q," but then Luke's silence on Elijah is all the more significant. But as discussed above (7:11-17), Jesus has just been identified as "the great prophet" in the resuscitation which fulfilled and surpassed Elijah's role. Thus both John and

Jesus are "great prophets," but the distinction between them is as crucial as their commonality.

Both Matthew and Luke follow the tradition ("Q") in acclaiming John as the greatest human being ever born, which could include Jesus, since he was also **born of woman**. Certainly it would include all of the great prophets and servants of God of Israel's history. And this is not merely a statement about John personally, but about John's role in God's design. As will become more clear in 16:16, John marks the culmination of God's dealing with Israel through the Law and the Prophets. Although Luke does not say that "Christ is the end of the law" (Rom. 10:4), his version of these sayings leads to a similar conclusion. The **greatness** of John lies in his being the last and greatest of the prophets before the time of the kingdom which Jesus inaugurated. It is thus quite important to Luke that the Holy Spirit anointed Jesus to mark the inception of the age of the kingdom and that John was off the scene (see the discussion of 3:20, 21-22). Now even the **least**, or the first in the kingdom is greater than John because God has begun a new regime or dispensation.

Verses 29-30 present another remarkable Lukan interpolation in the "Q" sequence making particular sense of these traditional stories. All the people and tax collectors "having heard" Jesus' words concerning John now "justify God" because they had been baptized with John's baptism. Since this section also concludes with the note of **wisdom** being **justified by all her children** (v. 35), Luke's version of the entire exchange has become an exposition on the "justification" of God and of God's wisdom by all the faithful in Israel.

And who are the faithful? In this passage clearly not the religious leaders who have "rejected" God's purpose or plan or will as it relates to them. The mark of this rejection is that they have not submitted to the baptism of repentance which John preached. Once again, John's baptism is a crucial dimension of God's unfolding plan. Luke regards the whole story of Jesus and the apostles as a confrontation between the "will and plan of God" and the "wills and plans of sinful people" (see also 23:51; Acts 2:23; 4:24-28; 5:38-39). Those who repented when repentance was offered by God are now ready to bear witness to the righteousness of God. These "people" and **tax collectors** (see 3:7, 10, 12) were once the "brood of vipers," but they have become the true children of Abraham, not by their birthright but by their repentance. This is true Israel testifying to the faithfulness and righteousness of God and of God's reign. They are the "people prepared" (1:17) which John raised up.

The word of judgment, however, falls on the religious leaders. They are burdened with the label of those of **this generation,** which is traditionally negative (see 11:29-32, 50-51; 17:25; Acts 2:40; Deut. 32:5, 20). As Jesus' statement in 10:16 demonstrates, the "refusal" which they have practiced is that of not "hearing" the word of God. They have not merely rejected John's preaching and baptism. They have refused God and are in peril of being cut out from the faithful of Israel (see Acts 3:22).

The comparison with the petulant children (v. 32) is thus a critique of those religious leaders who neither want to play party games when the other **children** are celebrating nor join in the wailing when they are sad. They insist on setting the "rules" for what to play when, while missing the fact that God is setting the occasions. They have not listened to John or Jesus to "hear" the word of God, and thus they can only object to both of them. Who is John to dare to proclaim a fast of repentance as if the end of the age were upon Israel? Is he possessed by **a demon** (v. 33)? No, it is the Holy Spirit! And who is Jesus to **eat and drink** and celebrate with **tax collectors and sinners** as if the messianic banquet had already started and these riffraff were on the guest list (v. 34, see also 5:29-32 and 14:1—15:2)? How dare Jesus challenge those whose whole lives are invested in preparing a purified Israel to be worthy for the kingdom?

These are not silly issues, although the analogy is insulting. The conflicts between Jesus and **the Pharisees** and between the disciples of both are serious business in which the identity of faithful Israel is at stake. Jesus' legitimacy is on the line. In Deut. 21:20-21, the rebellious son who is "a glutton and a drunkard" is put to death. The rumors about Jesus are as serious as the charges that John **has a demon.**

But the true **children** of **wisdom** justify God in the baptism of John and the ministry of Jesus and now justify the wisdom of

God. They see the "purpose of God" at work in John and Jesus. God's way of gathering faithful Israel has not proved to accord with the plans and purposes of these religious leaders. God's Spirit has been at work in the Baptist and the Messiah. John and Jesus have provoked a crisis in the religious institutions of Israel. Those who reject the Baptist's call to repentance and the Messiah's declaration of the kingdom have resisted and refused God. Those who have responded to the surprising ways of John and Jesus in their times are truly the blessed, the new faithful of Israel who accept God's purposes and means for dominion.

The Prophet Who Forgives Sins (7:36-50).   Luke concludes this chapter of stories concerning Jesus the prophet of God with an episode rich in human interest and filled with tension. In this larger context, the whole encounter with the woman with the ointment becomes another demonstration that Jesus truly is **a prophet** or "the prophet," since he knows better than anyone else **what sort of woman this is** (v. 39). Although **Simon** the **Pharisee** and those who were **at table** with him (vv. 39, 49) may only be able to see the scandal of Jesus' behavior, those who observe and overhear the exchanges between Jesus and Simon with the eyes and ears of faith are given a revelation of the grace and authority of the salvation which Jesus brings.

The power of the story may be largely credited to Luke's ability to gather diverse sources and forms into a coherent narrative, but attempts to reconstruct Luke's written sources for this story are frustrated by that skill. This is the last major episode in the section (6:20—8:3) where Luke does not appear to be using Mark as a source. Similarities in detail suggest that Luke may have provided an alternative version of Mark's (14:3-9) traditional story of the woman who anointed Jesus with **an alabaster flask of ointment.** On the other hand, the contrasts may be more telling. This is not a story of the "anointing" of the "head" of Jesus for burial or a dispute about the expense of the ointment, and the scene is the home of **Simon** the **Pharisee,** not "Simon the leper." It would be closer to see this as the "anointing" of the "beautiful feet" of "the one who brings good news" of salvation (Isa. 52:7). In any case, the interpretation of this story in Luke is not well served by elaborate discussions of what sources Luke might have had or how they corresponded to the historical events.

It is instructive, on the other hand, to observe that Luke's literary skill does not obliterate the distinct devices of a variety of oral forms which have been gathered in the narrative. The allegorical parable of the two debtors (vv. 41-43) heightens the tension in the story which leads to Jesus' pronouncement to **the woman** (vv. 47-48). Jesus calmly elaborates his conversation with Simon while the woman is profusely **wetting** his **feet with her tears,** wiping them **with her hair, kissing** and **anointing** them. As in the theological discussion about forgiveness while the paralyzed man lies in the midst of the group (5:17-26), the human tension is almost unbearable. Clearly the story proceeds at two levels. The word to the woman which relieves the tension (v. 48) must be followed by another which directly confronts the issue which is at controversy with the religious leaders, the forgiveness of sins (vv. 49-50). The parable lies within the "healing" or "salvation" story, and all of this is part of a larger controversy over the prophet who forgives sins.

36—The banquet setting merits special attention. Luke's Jesus not only eats and drinks with "tax collectors and sinners" (5:31; 7:34), but also is received at the table of **the Pharisee** (14:1). It is a mistake to miss the seriousness with which Jesus deals with the Pharisees or to make them into a new class of sinners which may now be scorned (see 5:17-26; 18:9-14). Questions about the people with whom you associate, especially in table fellowship, are important to both Jesus and the Pharisees. As will become even more crucial in 14:1—15:3, the discussions about banquet etiquette are fundamentally about who is acceptable to God. Who are the "elect" on the guest list of the messianic banquet? The tension in the story over the behavior of the woman and Jesus is more than the violation of propriety, as if that were not enough. The separation of the elect from the sinners of the world is challenged by this "prophet" who knows full well what kind of woman is touching him.

37-38—The woman's behavior is stunning. As these men who are teachers of Israel recline around the table in the fellowship of a meal, she appears **weeping** at Jesus' **feet, wiping her tears** with her **hair, kissing his feet,** and **anointing them with** costly **ointment.** Her exact "sin" is never disclosed. The long-standing tradition that she was a prostitute is probably based on interpretations of her actions at Jesus' feet linked with general suspicions that "sinful women" must be harlots (see Matt. 21:31-32). But Jesus gives no hint of a sexual meaning to her actions when he comments on them (vv. 44-46). Instead, these are acts of hospitality, of deep love with no erotic connotation (v. 47). Yes, she is **a sinner.** Luke's introduction of her (v. 37), Simon's judgment (v. 39) and Jesus' declaration (v. 47) agree. Attempts to determine what was the "sin" of the "sinful woman" may reveal more of the interpreter's biases than the woman's past. Jesus' interpretation of her act is all that matters.

39-47—The disapproval and discomfort which Simon and the other men at the table (v. 49) feel are focused in a sharp objection against Jesus as **a prophet.** Talking strictly to himself, Simon, who "invited" Jesus to this feast, now sees this woman's presence as a test of Jesus. But Jesus "answers" aloud and puts Simon and his hospitality to the test. It is Jesus who takes the initiative to bring the controversy into the open, and Simon responds to Jesus as the "teacher" by entering into the dialog (41-42). The allegorical parable requires that the logic of love and forgiveness be accepted as valid on its own terms. The point is that immodest love arises from extravagant forgiveness. The question of whether either debtor was "worthy" or "righteous" has simply been excluded, and thus the issue of **what sort of woman** she is has also been transformed.

All the details of Near Eastern hospitality in vv. 44-46 indicate the intimacies of a loving reception. Such practices vary significantly from culture to culture, and they may seem shocking or erotic out of context. Even hugs, kisses, sharing bed and board, and attending to the visitors' needs will take several forms. Footwashing has certainly been replaced in Western cultures by access to a hot shower before dinner. But Jesus marks the woman's actions as a standard for complete acceptance far surpassing the perfunctory.

Such effusive love as she has displayed, however, may be felt as an implied criticism of less generous displays, and Jesus has the nerve to press the point explicitly. The **sort of woman** she is turns out to set a high standard of love which judges Simon's hospitality or reception of Jesus. Simon has not yet grasped "what sort of prophet" or "Messiah" or "Savior" Jesus is, although Jesus has also accepted him by coming to his dinner.

48-50—Between Jesus' first declaration of forgiveness (**Your sins are forgiven,** v. 48) and his final dismissal of the woman (**Your faith has saved you; go in peace,** v. 50), the issue of Jesus' identity and authority arises again in the form of the question, **"Who is this, who even forgives sins?"** (v. 49, see 5:22). Clearly the question is not original with Luke, but in this context it reveals the reluctance or rejection of those who ask it in contrast to the implicit faith of the woman. They cannot suspend judgment in the face of such an encounter without revealing their lack of faith in this "prophet."

The woman held nothing back. Her faith was implicit. The long debate about whether her forgiveness was a "result" of her faith or her love was a sign of her previous forgiveness is a scholastic confusion of the story. The passive voice of the verb ("have been forgiven") indicates Jesus' declaration of God's action, but the perfect tense ("have been forgiven" . . . "has saved") refuses to yield the exact moment of God's action. Those at the table understand that Jesus is the one who has done the forgiving, and this is God's will and deed. But the "loving" and "forgiving" are all bound up in the kind of trust in Jesus which is truly saving, and this "faith" does not wait for the word of forgiveness (v. 48) before displaying an extravagant love.

Tax collectors and sinners, women and men have "justified God" by discerning Jesus to be the true prophet. Jesus is declaring God's will and enacting God's rule in his word and deed. The principles of grace, love, and forgiveness which characterize this dominion may be offensive to those who are trying to protect the standards of righteousness of the Law and the Prophets. Jesus will be a threat they are finally unable to tolerate. But for those who can see and hear, like this sinful woman who receives him in extravagant love trusting his acceptance, Jesus is the fulfillment of God's promises.

Jesus, Proclaimer of the Word of God (8:1-21)

The Messianic Mission Moves Forward (8:1-3)   These first verses of chap. 8 are a Lukan composition, a summary which provides a perspective on the episodes which follow. Luke 4:40-44 is a similar Lukan summary, but it serves to conclude the previous stories, while 8:1-3 is better connected with the narrative which follows it. Commentators often include 8:1-3 with the preceding narrative largely because it is the last of the non-Markan material which has been described as part of the "small interpolation" (see discussion above at 6:20). Since these verses move the reader smoothly into the Markan material, the debate over whether they belong with what precedes or what follows is evidence of Luke's narrative skill. But their force is best appreciated when they are allowed to set the scene for the immediate and larger contexts of the unfolding mission of the Messiah and his disciples.

The immediate context is 8:1-21, where Jesus and his disciples move on to the first phase of their mission of promulgating the word of the reign of God in Galilee. The debates and conflicts of Luke 7 over Jesus' identity recede as Jesus leads his disciples into the mission of declaring, hearing, and doing the "word of God." Luke's summary description of Jesus' mission (8:1) and detailed account of who his followers were (8:1-3) bring the immediate focus down to this small band of men and women who are also Jesus' true "mother and brothers" (8:21). Although a larger public is present in these scenes (vv. 4, 19), the section holds together in its primary concern with how Jesus' followers are "hearing the word" as they first join in the mission.

In the larger context, Luke has structured the narrative so that the Markan material he uses in 8:3—9:50 is now the substance of the ministry in Galilee. The mention of **the twelve** in 8:1 anticipates their first independent mission in 9:1-6. The sending of "the seventy" in 10:1-20 will then belong within the context of Jesus' movement beyond Galilee on the way to Jerusalem. Thus 8:1-3 alerts the reader that the followers of Jesus are not only hearers of Jesus' proclamation (see 6:20-49). They are also involved in the mission of the word of God.

1—The Lukan phrasing (**soon afterward** or "And it came to pass") marks the transition. The traditional translation language about **preaching and bringing the good news** (RSV; see also 4:43-44, and 9:6, "preaching the gospel") must not be allowed to blunt the edge by sounding like predictable Christian rhetoric. Luke does not even use the noun "gospel" or "good news." What Jesus is doing is "heralding" and "declaring" God's dominion, just as an official legate of Caesar could confront a territory with the authority of the Roman order. And in this scene **the twelve** and **some women** accompany the Messiah.

2-3—This identification of the women highlights a facet of Luke's Gospel which deserves more attention. Only Luke has any of this detail, and it fits with his consistent presentation of women in crucial roles of prophecy, leadership, and witness. These women are distinguised from **the twelve,** who are the apostles, but the other male "disciples" are similarly set apart from them (see the discussion at 6:13). Two of these women, **Mary Magdalene** and **Joanna,** are also specifically mentioned as among the women who were the first witnesses to the resurrection (24:10, 24). In Acts 1:14 "the women" will again be identified in the inner circle of the upper room. In addition to many stories of Jesus' direct dealings with women (see especially 7:11-17, 36-50; 8:43-48; 10:38-42; 13:10-17), Luke has depicted Elizabeth, Mary, and Anna in prophetic roles (chaps. 1-2). Such ministry and leadership will also continue in Acts with women such as Dorcas (9:36-43), Lydia (16:11-15), and Priscilla (18:24-28). Often these stories are closely paralleled with episodes about men. Without his belaboring the point, Luke's narrative simply conveys the confidence that God, the Messiah, and the Holy Spirit called out women and men together to discipleship and testimony to the reign of God.

These women are also interesting for their background. There is no insult involved in the report that they were people **who had been healed of evil spirits and infirmities,** even in the case of Mary Magdalene, **from whom seven demons had gone out** (see the discussion of exorcism as healing in 9:42). The traditional suggestion that she was the "sinful woman" of the preceding episode (7:36-50) is dangerously misleading, especially when connected with the ascetic prejudice that the woman's sin was sexual. Mary and the other women are people who have been **healed**, and exorcism was salvation from an affliction, not a forgivness of personal sins. They have received the benefits of the kingdom. Furthermore these are people of public repute who have **means** and "resources" from which they are endowing or supporting the mission. Nothing more is known of **Susanna** or the **many others**, but **Joanna**, who appears again at the resurrection (24:10), is married to a steward in **Herod's** court. Like Joseph of Arimathea (or even in league with him, 23:50-56) and Lydia, the "seller of purple" (Acts 16:11-15), these "women of means" are featured positively. They are not disparaged either because they are women or because they have means and high station.

Luke's confidence in the significant role of the women in the mission is even more impressive when contemporary Roman suspicions are noted. Several stories are told of women in high places in Rome being deluded by the eastern cults of the Jews and Egyptians. Josephus even attributes the expulsion of the Jews from Rome under Claudius (see Priscilla and Aquila, Acts 18:1-4, 24-28) to the defrauding of a prominent Roman woman by a Jewish "interpreter of the Mosaic law and its wisdom" (see *Ant.* 18.65-84). The prominent role of women in the kingdom of this Messiah could be regarded as a threat to the Roman order, as the Christian movement became one of the oriental religions which it resisted (see Suetonius, *Tiberius* 36; Tacitus, *Annales,* ii.85; v.5). But Luke's Jesus does not back down.

The Sowed Word of God (8:4-15).   Luke now resumes his use of Mark's narrative, but he remodels and restates it in important ways. By moving the story of Jesus' "mother and brothers" to the end of this section (8:19-21) instead of prior to it (Mark 3:31-35), he marks the conclusion with a word about those who "hear the word of God and do it" (v. 21). Furthermore, the crowds of people who gather around to hear his words (v. 4) are identified more specifically with the cities and villages to which he has gone declaring God's reign (8:1).

5-8—The parable itself is transmitted with great fidelity to the tradition of the words of Jesus. It is slightly abbreviated from

Mark at the point of describing the rocky soil, and it only speaks of **a hundredfold** yield instead of Mark's thirty, sixty, and hundredfold (Mark 4:8). Such economy of expression may even better grasp the central point of the "parable proper" apart from more elaborate allegorical elements. Thus the earlier parable of Jesus was probably a very compact point of comparison with a surprising turn. In the face of various and persistent obstacles, the proclamation of the kingdom will yet produce an astonishing yield. It is a word of profound encouragement to Jesus' followers in the time of his ministry and in the post-Easter community. The kingdom is the work of God, and it will not fail. The traditional refrain which concludes the parable is then a direct word of assurance, "Let those who have ears to hear this, do so!"

9-10—The problem of "hearing" and "understanding" or "believing" and "doing," however, proves to be more complex. Mark has pressed the issue with dramatic intensity so that the straightforward revelation (mystery) of the parable has become a confounding riddle for "those outside" (Mark 4:11), and Jesus has chosen to speak in such "riddles" in order to prevent them from understanding the revelation of the kingdom. Of course, Isaiah 6 lies behind Mark and even behind Jesus' words. The burden of a prophet's calling was stated in exactly these terms. Isaiah was given the unhappy task of declaring the word and will of God in full expectation and intention that the people would not grasp it. God's message would judge rather than save, at least for a time (see Isa. 6:9-13). It is not so surprising to see Mark laying this stone of stumbling in the story of Jesus, nor to see Matthew removing it by saying that Jesus taught in parables "because" people lacked understanding (Matt. 13:13).

Although Luke softens the offense of the prophetic reproach, he does not turn the confounding "riddle" of the parable into an explanation. The seeing/not seeing and hearing/not understanding contrasts are stated less emphatically than in Mark or Isaiah 6, and the final purpose is no longer to prevent people from turning and being forgiven by God (Mark 4:12b; Isa. 6:10b). Luke even expands Mark's explanation of the parable (Mark 4:15), indicating that it is the devil who takes away the word **that they may not believe and be saved** (v. 12).

Still, the confounding purpose of speaking in parables is sustained: **so that seeing they may not see, and hearing they may not understand.** Interpretations which argue that Luke meant to remove the offense must also come to terms with Luke 19:42 and Acts 13:40-41 and 28:26, where the prophetic indictments of blindness, unbelief, and deafness prove to be God's will, at least for the present. Those who do not hear are not identified as the "outsiders," as in Mark, but as **others,** i.e., those who are not Jesus' true disciples (8:21). The question of who has truly "heard" the "word of God" is sharply drawn for all who read Luke's account.

11-15—This interpretation of the parable had already related it to the preaching context of the church long before Luke dealt with it. It is not necessary to comment at length on what is itself an ancient commentary, except to note that the allegorical elaboration of the parable draws more attention to the distinct kinds of obstacles to faith and less to the dramatic surprise of the abundant harvest. The several "soils" into which various "seeds" fall seem to be the differentiating factors, inviting closer identification of various conditions of lack of faith.

But Luke sharpens the traditional commentary on the parable by identifying the seed as **the word of God** (v. 11), and then Luke's distinctive questions are whether the devil prevents them from believing and being saved (v. 12, see also 10:17-22), how the word is received but is lost in "time of testing" (v. 13, see 4:13; 11:4; 22:40), how much wealth and the **pleasures of life** prevent the maturation of the fruit (v. 14), and whether they hold fast to the word "in endurance" so that it may bear its **fruit.**

Luke's conclusion in v. 15 strengthens and specifies the appeal for faithfulness which will be fruitful for the kingdom. The "hearing of the word" which is true "hearing" is its reception by those who **hold it fast in an honest and good heart, and bring forth fruit with patience.** As will become clear in 21:12-19, this **patience** is not merely a capacity for waiting, but it is the ability to withstand persecution and rejection while still bearing witness. The tests of the fruitfulness of the word and the faithfulness of the "hearers" will not only be personal and spiritual temptations. They will also be public, and the "faithful and good hearts" of

167

the believers will be disclosed to public scrutiny and attack, just as the devious or "secret thoughts of the hearts of many" (2:35) will also be revealed. The conclusion is still full of promise, confident of the abundant harvest of the mighty word and expecting that a faithful people will endure. The kingdom of this Messiah and his witnesses will be tested, but it will not fail!

Take Heed How You Hear! (8:16-18).   Luke attaches these verses even more tightly than Mark to the parable and interpretation which precede. There is not even a transition phrase, for these words are an explication of what the parable means for Luke's readers. As the discussion of the word "endurance" ("patience") (v. 15) indicated, the hearing of the "word of God" can never be merely a private affair. The way it has been heard will all be revealed, and this "word" is the light with which God intends to illumine and transform the world and its people (see also 2:32; 11:27-36). The "secrets of the kingdom of God" (v. 10) which have been revealed to the disciples are not visions of a distant heaven. They are revelations of how God's rule is active and alive in relatively inconspicuous forms of proclamation, witness, and discipleship. The "word of God" is a dynamic "seed" and "lamp" through which God intends to be at work in the world, and the way it is "heard" makes a difference.

The images of sight and hearing are pressed closer together. Mark's text (4:24) stresses the content of the message, warning to "See [i.e., watch out] what you hear!" Mark is generally more attentive to the objective character of the word of God, even following this passage with the parable of the "seed growing secretly" (Mark 4:26-29). But Luke's warning (v. 18) draws attention to the way the message is received: "See [i.e., watch out] how you hear!" The content is still crucial, but will it be heard in enduring faith which will bear fruitful public witness to the kingdom or not? This is a fair warning about "seeing" and "hearing" the word of God. The passive verbs (**will more be given, will be taken away,** v. 18) again point to God's way of working with differing receptions of the word. Among those who have heard it in good faith ("honest and good heart," v. 15), God will cause the word to grow and prosper. Those who "think they have received it" but have not accepted or understood its dynamic character will have it **taken away,** whether by God directly or by the devil (v. 12).

Jesus' True Family (8:19-21).   Luke has shaped this entire section (vv. 1-21) into an extended discourse on the power of the word of God, especially as it discloses and distinguishes the faithful from the unfaithful. The evangelist now reaches back to an earlier context in Mark (3:31-35) to conclude the discourse. Luke has neglected Mark's suggestions of the alienation of Jesus' family or friends (see Mark 3:19b-21, "he is beside himself"), and he has abbreviated this story of the approach of Jesus' **mother** and **brothers.** Furthermore, where Mark (3:35) identified Jesus' true mother and brothers as those who "do the will of God," Luke speaks of them as those who **hear** and **do the word of God** (v. 21).

The word of God is the will of God. Both of these concepts are central to Luke's testimony to the reality, power, and distinctiveness of Jesus' enactment of God's kingdom. Luke uses the terms "the word of God," "the word of the Lord," "the word of grace [or 'salvation,' or 'consolation']," and "the word" so frequently in the speeches of Acts that they consistently convey his conviction that Christian preaching is a fundamental means of God's reign in the present (see also Luke 1:2; 5:1; 11:28). Luke speaks less frequently of the "will" of God, but God's will is immediately connected with God's reign (see 11:2, also 22:42; Acts 21:14; 22:14). The whole struggle of wills between God and humanity (see especially 13:31-35; 23:18-25) proves to be the medium for God's determined plan and foreknowledge (see Act 3:23; 4:24-28).

Jesus' true kindred are no more determined by physical descent than are the children of Abraham guaranteed their status as heirs to divine promise by their ancestry (3:7-9). The story of the arrival of Jesus' relatives is the occasion for driving home the point. The "word of God" is correctly "heard" when it is obeyed. It is the will of God, the policy of God's dominion, calling for more than casual assent. Although this section does not further specify the content of the word of God, it creates urgency for knowing what God's word, will, and plan are as revealed in Jesus' reign. Faithfulness and even salvation (v. 12) and kinship with the Messiah are at stake in hearing and doing this word.

Jesus, His Commanding Word (8:22-56)

While the previous section (8:1-21) called for obedience in hearing and doing the word of God, these verses provide a demonstration of the character and power of the word in the Messiah's confrontation with powers of nature, evil, sickness, and death. The word of God is no cipher, requiring blind trust. It is the fundamental means of Jesus' exercise of God's rule, and Jesus now continues to reveal its power and saving purpose.

None of the stories in this section is original to Luke. Even Mark's sequence is maintained throughout (Mark 4:35—5:43// Luke 8:22-56), and Luke follows Mark's content and phrasing relatively more closely than in many other places and with fewer alterations than Matthew (8:23-34; 9:18-26). Still Luke has shaped the narrative so that the portrait of Jesus' authority is highlighted in his giving commands and bringing salvation. The efficacy of his declaration of the word of God is demonstrated so that saving faith and obedience to Jesus' command are encouraged.

He Commands Obedience of Wind and Water (8:22-25). **22-23**—With a brief transition back into Mark's sequence (**One day** or "and it came to pass that"), Jesus and his disciples embark on a boat on **the lake.** Luke's grasp of nautical terms and knowledge of the "sea," which in Acts means the Mediterranean, results in some alteration of Mark's language (see all the sailing terms in Acts 27!). Otherwise, Luke has only simplified some details, such as not mentioning that other boats were sailing along (Mark 4:36) and reporting that Jesus **fell asleep** before the **storm** arose. And the danger was real. The boat was swamping.

24—Jesus' disciples awake him with the cry, "**Master! Master! We are perishing!**" Not "Teacher, do you not care if we perish?" as in Mark 4:38. There is no reproach in the disciples' cry, only terror. Calling Jesus **Master** (Gk: *epistata*) may not be to use the most lofty Christological title, but it belongs in contexts where Jesus is being addressed as a person of significant authority, such as a "commander" or "overseer" (see also 5:5; 8:45; 9:33, 49; 17:13!). This is the same title that Peter used once before to address Jesus in a boat (5:5) when he certainly did not know what was coming. Yet "at the word" of the Master, he let down his nets for a catch. The disciples may not have known that Jesus could bring such a miraculous calm, but they must be credited with calling on the right "Master!"

25—**"Where is your faith?"** is a mild reproof (see Mark 4:40, "Why are you afraid? Have you no faith?"), and the "fear" and "wondering" which follows is an appropriate sense of awe at an incredible display of authority. As in the story of the wondrous catch of fish (5:1-11), these disciples could be expected to know something of the traditions of the praise of God who alone could control the powers of the sea and wind (see Pss. 29:3-4; 65:7; 89:9). The specific mention of **waves** (v. 24) may suggest that Luke (or Mark) had Ps. 107:23-32 in mind: "Then they cried to the Lord in their trouble, and he delivered them from their distress; he made the storm be still, and the waves of the sea were hushed."

The concluding refrain is Luke's fundamental emphasis: **"He commands even wind and water, and they obey him."** Only Luke stresses that Jesus has worked by means of his "command." The obedience of the chaotic powers of nature is under the command of his word. Like Mark, Luke sees this as a Christological revelation (**"Who is this?"**), and he has followed Mark (4:39) in speaking of Jesus as **rebuking** the wind (and the waves! v. 24). Jesus' rebuke is a confrontation of powers as when he has struck down a demon or a fever with his word (4:35, 39). But it is also a display of his authority as "Master" to give a command and have it obeyed. And his mastery means salvation for all in the boat. Here is one whose command is the saving word of God, worthy of being heard, trusted, and obeyed.

He Commands the Unclean Spirits (8:26-39).   Once again, the commanding authority of Jesus' word is displayed in this incredible confrontation with a legion of demonic forces who come out to encounter Jesus. This is also a story of salvation and

even of discipleship, but Jesus meets rejection too. As the larger
narrative unfolds, the awesome plight of humans who are **seized
with fear** (v. 37) will prove to be more difficult for the reign of
God than even the most horrendous possession by the forces of
evil.

Since this is the most elaborate and powerful story of possession
in the Gospels, it is necessary to comment on the demonic lore
which is assumed by all of the versions—and in the most detailed
form in Luke. Certain aspects of the traditional story are very
specific to Jewish tradition (e.g., the pigs as an appropriate abode
for unclean spirits), and other features are more generally known
(e.g., the demons' aversion to water, see Luke 11:24 "seeking
waterless places," so also baptism as a rite of exorcism and even
the melting of the witch by water in *The Wizard of Oz* and the
drowning of accused "witches" in colonial New England).

This story is filled with terror for those whose world is filled
with demons, but it also has a delightful twist. Jesus sends the
demons into the pigs, at their request, and then the pigs head
straight for the water! The humor would not have been lost on
those who would fear that the demons had merely hidden out in
a "waterless place" soon to return. Not a chance. Jesus has again
proved to be more than a match for the powers of evil, and his
command may be trusted to be saving. The story is unconcerned
with the economic loss that the herdsmen have incurred, but the
awesome display of divine power confronts the whole countryside
with Jesus' authority. Even the terrors of demon possession may
be more manageable than a revelation of the power and presence
of the reign of God.

Every age and culture has various ways of speaking of the
experience of encountering awesome forces of death, disease, and
destruction. The "naming" of such forces, even in modern scientific terms, is an effort to understand or differentiate even conditions and circumstances over which humans have no real control. The personification of the forces of nature ("even wind and
water obey him," v. 25) and the "naming" of demons (v. 30) may
seem quaint or peculiar to those who are confident that the world
is thoroughly rational. Certainly these stories cannot be "proved"
by strictly rational methods of historiography, and attempts to

"explain" these accounts in scientific or social-scientific categories generally reduce them to the most mundane trivia imaginable.

These stories in Luke 8 are filled with great human terror and hope, but they are also full of confidence that Jesus' word is competent to confront whatever powers or forces of evil people may encounter, no matter how they identify them. Thus modern readers need not abandon the way their own times and cultures "name" the powers of destruction in order to benefit from these more ancient witnesses to the "saving" word of Jesus the Messiah.

By the time Luke retells this powerful tale, it has been well told in the oral tradition and in Mark's narrative. Luke's touches are light, if frequent, merely enhancing certain details and highlighting the episode as another demonstration of the saving authority of Jesus' commands.

26-29—Luke rearranges Mark's account of the initial encounter so that the reader hears all of the details only about the demons' harassment of this poor man (v. 29) after the wild encounter has occurred. All of the screaming and confessing protests ("Who are you to me, **Jesus, Son of the Most High God?**" see also 4:34, 41) turn out to be the tormented demons' violent attempts to avert the saving power of Jesus' word. **For,** says Luke, **he had commanded the unclean spirit to come out of the man.** Now it is clear that this is a power struggle. The demons know they cannot resist the power of Jesus' command, even by "naming" him first.

30-33—This is a desperate negotiation. The demons must yield their name when Jesus demands it, although to give it up is already to relinquish power. **"Legion"** may be an unsuccessful effort to tell a half-truth, revealing a host of demons without any proper names. It is also a fascinating word since it is a Roman military term, but the demons are probably not making any political commentary. It is all that Jesus needs, in any case. The pleading is miserable, lest Jesus **command them into the abyss.** They know they cannot resist his command, but **the abyss** is the bottomless pit of confinement reserved for the enemies of God (see Rev. 9:1-11; 11:7; 17:8; 20:1-3). When Jesus apparently accedes to their pleading and **gave them leave** to go into the pigs, it might seem as if they have tricked him. They are still in the countryside and might soon return. But **the swine rush down** the hill and **drown,** and the demons have merely chosen the means of their own destruction (see above, on demons and water).

34-39—The human epilog of this exorcism is complex and disturbing. The herdsmen **fled** to tell the story everywhere. The major response is not thanksgiving nor even a demand for restitution for the swine. Rather, as Luke emphasizes, **All the people of the surrounding country of the Gerasenes asked him to depart from them; for they were seized with great fear.** They are not possessed by demons, for Jesus' command had been more than a match for a legion of unclean spirits who possessed a man and pleaded with Jesus. But Jesus does not overwhelm them with his power or word. Another method will be required to bring salvation to a fearful humanity.

The man who had been possessed by the unclean spirits, however, is now a disciple, **sitting at the feet of Jesus** (only in Luke), **clothed** and sensible (v. 35). The witnesses now tell how he had been "saved" (v. 36, RSV: **healed**), and he requests to be with Jesus. This is not the desperate pleading of either the demons or the Gerasenes. Still, as he departed, Jesus "released him" with the commission to go home and tell all that God had done for him. The word of acclamation and thanksgiving to God which should have followed the healing is now the charge of the healed man himself. He will be the witness to the reign of God among his own people who are **seized with fear.** The fact that he proceeds to proclaim to the whole town all that **Jesus had done for him** may not be a literal fulfillment of his charge to tell what **God** had done, but it is still correct. Jesus has brought the salvation of God into the region, defeating the powers of evil with his command and leaving a witness to his saving reign among people who are afraid of such authority.

He Heals the Afflicted and Raises the Dead (8:40-56).   Luke completes this section of displays of the saving power of Jesus' word by taking over two stories as they have been woven in Mark (5:21-43). Much like the story of the healing of the paralyzed man with its intervening debate over forgiveness of sins (Luke 5:17-26//Mark 2:1-12), this story begins with an urgent plea of a distraught father for his dying daughter (vv. 40-42a), but the healing is delayed by Jesus' encounter with the woman with a chronic flow of blood (vv. 42b-48). It was hardly an emergency, but with the delay, the child has died before Jesus arrives. The wonder of Jesus' power is heightened into a raising from the dead (vv. 49-56). It is a tale of competing human need, but Jesus brings salvation, peace (v. 48), and new life with his **power** (v. 46) and his word for those who believe (vv. 48, 50).

40-42a—Jesus' return from his journey across the lake is again met with crowds who have high expectations of him (see 8:19-20). **Jairus, a ruler of the synagogue** (vv. 41, 49), is among them, and he pleads with Jesus to come to **his house** (only in Luke!). Luke is especially fond of showing Jesus being welcomed into the houses of the leaders of Israel (see also 7:36; 14:1; contrast 7:6, where the centurion who "built us our synagogue" protests that Jesus need not come to his house). There is no hint of anything but faith in this case. In fact, Jairus abandons all decorum as he begs Jesus to come to deal with the crisis.

42b-48—In the press of the moving crowd, the narrator focuses upon **a woman,** indicating that she **had a flow of blood for twelve years.** Mark (5:28) had even told the reader what she was thinking at the time, but Luke does not become so specific until she later is exposed and explains how she had been healed "immediately" (v. 47). The flow of blood probably indicates a chronic and persistent bleeding that exceeds normal menstrual flow. This condition is distinguished in very specific terms in Lev. 15:19-30, where the pollution of everything and everyone she touches is also indicated. This is a story which enters the realm of powerful religious taboos connected with women, blood, life, and death. She had reason to tremble when her act of touching the hem of Jesus' garment was publicly exposed.

Jesus is unafraid. The awkward moment when he demands to know **"Who touched me?"** is met with Peter's address of him as **"Master!"** Once again this is the title which anticipates a mighty display of Jesus' authority, without the disciples' suggestion in Mark (5:31) that Jesus' question is absurd (see also 5:5; 8:24). Peter may not know what is coming, but Jesus insists that **power** has already **gone forth** from him. Some have argued that Luke even had a "magical" view of Jesus' "power" as if it were a reservoir of energy not directly connected with his saving word (see also 5:17; 6:19). But Luke's telling of the story only raises these possibilities in order to identify the unity of this "power" with the work of the Spirit of the Lord (4:14) which has anointed Jesus and endowed the mission with the saving authority of the kingdom of God.

Jesus' interpretation of the scene is, therefore, decisive. The woman's act is no longer a violation of taboo, rendering everyone unclean. It is an act of profound faith. Her trust has already "healed" and "saved" her, because she has relied implicitly upon Jesus. Like the woman in Simon's house (7:36-50), her act could be open to all kinds of hostile interpretations, but Jesus' word declares her salvation. Even his address of her as **daughter** is not condescending. It is the word which includes her once again in the family of Israel (see the bent woman in 13:16).

49-56—The death of Jairus' daughter now confronts Jesus' authority, and even those who had been hopeful before are silent as the speaker advises Jairus not to **trouble the Teacher** further. But Jesus takes charge, **"Do not fear; only believe, and she shall be** saved!" The mention of being saved is unique to Luke, again elaborating the theme that all of Jesus saving words and work are expressions of his reign. He is worthy of faith and obedience, and his word deserves to be "heard and done" (8:21).

The **laughter** of the mourners (**all were weeping and bewailing**) is more bitter than sarcastic in Luke, since they knew **she was dead.** Jesus has not yet entered the room. When Luke says that at Jesus' call **her spirit returned,** he is also confirming that she was indeed dead. Once again Jesus touches a corpse, unafraid of pollution. Previously it was the only son of a mother (7:11-17). Now it is the only daughter of a father. Luke returns to his theme of the commanding word of Jesus with just a few touches emphasizing that **he directed** them to give her **something to eat** and **charged them to tell no one.**

The element of secrecy is difficult in Luke's account. He has joined Mark in reporting that only Peter, James, and John were permitted to be present along with the child's mother and father, and he has indicated that the crowds outside the room were sure she was dead. In Mark, the command to silence fits with the "secret" of Jesus' messiahship, and the laughing mourners are put out of the room before Jesus acts. But in Luke the matter is more gently stated. Jesus appears to pass them as he enters, and only the insiders who have seen this dramatic act will ever know for sure exactly what he has done. The command to silence then indicates that Jesus' authoritative word and deed were revealed to the disciples, but still hidden from others (see 10:21).

Jesus, The Christ and Chosen of God (9:1-50)

In this section, Jesus' attention is directed toward equipping the Twelve for their proclamation of the kingdom. Their mission will encounter the broader world, and outsiders will raise questions about Jesus' identity. A few stories of public ministry will also be told (vv. 10-15, 37-43), but these will serve primarily to illustrate the instructions Jesus is giving his disciples. Above all, Jesus will be revealed to his disciples as the Messiah of God and the chosen Son of God, and they will be advised that this identity will mean suffering a death for Jesus and service which is obedient unto death for them.

Luke is still following Mark as the source for each of these episodes, but the evangelist has dramatically restructured the story as well as restated details. He has already transferred the story of Jesus' appearence in Nazareth (Mark 6:1-6) to the beginning of Jesus' public ministry (4:14-30), and he has briefly told of John's imprisonment (3:19-20) so that he now reports the Baptist's death only through Herod's comment (9:9: see Mark 6:17-29). All of the stories of Mark 6:45—8:26 are also missing in Luke's account, and source critics will continue to debate whether Luke omitted this material or it was lacking in his version of Mark. In any case, Luke gathers the remaining stories into a narrative which reveals Jesus' identity and mission as Messiah and chosen one while also delineating the character and cost of discipleship.

He Authorizes the Twelve (9:1-6).   **1-2**—The commission of **the twelve** with **power and authority** sets the theme for this section (see the discussion of the twelve apostles at 6:13 and the appointing of the seventy in 10:1). Since they are authorized as agents of the **kingdom of God** (v. 2), the mission to which they are charged will also reveal the character of the reign of God which Jesus is deploying. This is the mission for which the twelve tribes of Israel had been chosen (see 22:30). Their full commission as "witnesses" to the Messiah's gracious dominion will be given later after Jesus death and resurrection (24:46-48; Acts 1:8), but even now the mode and manner of their action is integrally related to the message they announce.

Theirs is a mission of powerful healing (**demons** and **diseases**) and authoritative declaration of the reign of God. When the RSV translates this as **to preach the kingdom of God and to heal,** the reader may need to be reminded that such Christian "preaching" is an announcement of God's kingship or rule, and the mission of the disciples (and the Messiah!) is a revelation of how God has chosen to exercise that dominion. Healing is already a central clue both of the great power which is at work and of the saving character of that authority. This is not an "authoritarianism" which will only enslave people further with heirarchies of power.

3-5—The Twelve are to travel light, relying upon local hospitality (see 10:4-5; Acts 9:43; 16:15). Even the "staff and bag" of the wandering philosophers of the era are denied them. They are "carriers" of a word from God, a testimony which exerts a claim and a warning even on those who are unwilling to receive the messengers. Thus the **shaking off of the dust** (see 10:11) is a symbolic act indicating that they have taken nothing from these people. They have merely left them with the declaration of God's reign, and now the matter is between that town and the king himself (see the discussion at 9:51-55).

He Provokes Herod (9:7-9).   Luke's retelling of Mark's story about **Herod** is subtly stated, and commentators disagree on how to take Luke's treatment of the tetrarch. Mark presents Herod himself thinking that Jesus was John come back to life, which suggests a very troubled conscience (Mark 6:16). But Luke's Herod merely repeats the variety of rumors about Jesus as a resurrected John, Elijah, or a prophet of old (see also 9:19), **and he sought to see him.** The ominous tone of this ending is the first

clue that this ruler who beheaded John will have no less a malevolent purpose in wishing to "see" Jesus than did his father in
Matthew (2:8) who professed wishing to "worship" him when
murder was on his mind.

This is Herod Antipas who was first named by Herod the Great
as the heir to his kingdom, but who then received only the te-
trarchy of Galilee and Perea (Luke 3:1; Josephus, *Ant.* 17.317-
318). Josephus reports that he executed John the Baptist out of
fear of "sedition" (*Ant.* 18.118), and this Herod was famous for
striving unsuccessfully to be named "king of the Jews" by the
Romans. He and his illegitimate wife were finally deposed and
banished when they chafed at his being treated as less than a
"king" (*Ant.* 18.240-256).

Herod's **perplexity** is still relatively controlled, although such
matters could never be taken lightly by oriental princes. Even
the rumor that a prophet or a righteous martyr had been **raised
from the dead** could be dangerous if people believed that God
had intervened against a despot. It is impossible to tell what
Herod Antipas had in mind, but such "perplexity" is a Lukan
literary alert that a vital issue is at stake. Only Luke uses this
verb, and in three other passages in Acts it indicates a kind of
"wondering" or "amazement" which observers, adversaries, and
the apostle Peter feel in the presence of God's initiatives (Acts
2:12; 5:24; 10:17).

In Luke's story this is an early warning that the Herod who
killed John will prove to be an adversary of Jesus (see also 13:31-
35; 23:6-12; Acts 4:25-27). As the Messiah pursues the deployment of his kingdom, the rulers of the world will take notice.
Herod will certainly never correctly understand who Jesus is,
even when he and Pilate will sarcastically treat Jesus as "the king
of the Jews" (23:1-38). But Herod has now been provoked, put
on the alert. His "perplexity" thus gives voice to the crucial question which this section addresses with care, "**John I beheaded;
but who is this about whom I hear such things.**"

He Feeds the Five Thousand (9:10-17).   Luke closely follows
Mark's account of the return of the twelve (Mark 6:7; Luke 9:1)
apostles (Mark 6:30; Luke 9:10) and the subsequent feeding of

the **five thousand.** Luke does not transmit Mark's details of the way the logistics of the crowd contributed to the problem of hunger, nor the emphasis on Jesus' sympathy for these hungry "sheep without a shepherd" (Mark 6:30-34). Instead the continuing witness to the "kingdom of God" and the ministry of healing sets the context for the story (v. 11). Nevertheless, the power of the traditional story must be grasped before assessing more specifically how Luke interprets it.

This is the only story of a wondrous feeding which Luke tells. Mark's story of the feeding of the four thousand (8:1-10//Matt. 15:32-39) falls within the largest section of Mark (6:45-8:26) which Luke does not transmit. These feeding stories were full of scriptural symbolism before they were written in any of the Gospels, and the evangelists probably did not need to draw a picture to remind people how God had previously accomplished wondrous feedings in the wilderness. Furthermore, the linguistic connections with the "Lord's supper" were probably woven into the telling in an early stage ("He **took** . . . **blessed** . . . **broke** . . . **gave,**" v. 16).

The traditional story seems to be an implicit answer to the questions of Ps. 78:19-20: "Can God spread a table in the wilderness? . . . Can he also give bread, or provide meat for his people?" Of course, this psalm was itself a commentary on the stories in Exodus 16 of God's feeding of the whole congregation of Israel in the wilderness. Was Jesus fulfilling the exodus (see 9:31 below)? Furthermore, the prophet Elisha once commanded a man who had "twenty loaves of barley and fresh ears of grain in his sack" to "give to the men that they may eat." His servant objected, "How am I to set this before a hundred men," and the prophet repeated the command, adding, "for thus says the Lord, 'They shall eat and have some left.' " And it happened (2 Kings 4:42-44). Was Jesus acting as Elijah returned or as one of the old prophets raised up (see the reports which precede and follow this story in vv. 8 and 19)?

Even the numbers of **men** and of **baskets** of remaining food have suggested less likely associations with the exodus organization of Israel into groups of thousands, hundreds, fifties, and tens (Exod. 18:21,25; see also from Qumran: 1QS 2:21; 1QSa

1:14-15), and more likely associations with the twelve tribes of Israel (see 22:30).

Christian proclaimers have explored these connections with profit since before the synoptic accounts were composed, and the evangelist would probably not object to most attempts to demonstrate that Jesus fulfilled scriptural precedents (see Luke 24:27-44 where Jesus' instruction in scriptural interpretation is closely connected with his taking, blessing, breaking, and giving of the bread). Luke joined the early Christian tradition in proclaiming that such a wondrous feeding was a sign confirming Jesus' messianic role in Israel. Furthermore, Luke's use of the story may indicate the evangelist's emphasis more exactly.

As a sequel to the Herod episode, this story is an answer to the tetrarch's question (v. 9, only in Luke): "Who is this about whom I hear such things?" The links with the prophets of old are clearly part of the question and the answer which the story provides since Jesus' miracle follows the form of the Elisha story but far outstrips its proportions. But Luke's introduction emphasizes that this prophetic activity is part and parcel of the **kingdom of God** which Jesus is declaring in Herod's region (and perhaps beyond, since the village of **Bethsaida** may have been outside of Galilee, although Luke does not seem aware of that).

At any rate, this story provides only a symbolic answer to Herod's question, since it is then followed by Jesus' questions. The question has now been intensified for the reader, and the definitive answer will soon (9:20) be given.

He Is Revealed as the Christ of God and Predicts His Suffering (9:18-22). Throughout this chapter, Luke pursues the intimate relationship between Jesus' identity and role as Messiah and the disciples' calling. Luke's version thus requires that this powerful story of Peter's confession, which includes Jesus' passion prediction, be connected with Jesus' words of warning to his disciples (see vv. 23-27). Luke is indeed concerned with answering the repeated question of who Jesus is (vv. 9, 18, 20), but this answer is consistently explored in terms of what it means to be the follower and witness of such a Messiah of God, Son of man, chosen Son of God, and Master (vv. 20, 22, 26, 35, 44, 49).

Yet two problems must be addressed before Luke's distinctive use of these stories may be explored more fully, i.e., Luke as a historical source and Luke as a restatement (redaction) of Mark.

The problem of the historical accuracy of this material simply cannot be ignored, especially since this is the crucial text where Jesus elicits Peter's confession of him as "Christ" and where he first predicts his passion and the impending suffering of his disciples. Each of the Synoptic Gospels deals differently with Peter's confession and Jesus' passion prediction (Matt. 16:13-23//Mark 8:27-33; see also John 6:67-71), and clearly each version is told primarily to communicate the meaning of the memory for post-Easter Christian communities. All of them know that Jesus was crucified on the "charge" of being "the king of the Jews," and they are sorting out what it means that he truly was the "Messiah"—yet wrongly executed—and vindicated by God. The variety in the versions certainly reflects such post-Easter interpretations and has led many commentators to conclude that the whole scene is so thoroughly Christianized that no historical core can be reconstructed with high probability.

Historical research is, of course, always a matter of probabilities, and those who insist that the "truth" of the story must be scientifically "proved" have undertaken a perilous task. It is especially difficult to establish just what may have been said by whom in a conversation probably conducted in Aramaic some 35 to 50 years before the Gospels were written. And when the nuances of that conversation are the very medium of Christian witness, it is clear that the stories are themselves more a living testimony to the truth than a archival record.

On the other hand, historical skepticism should not be allowed to obscure the conserving character of first-century transmission of the Jesus stories. Memories of "what happened" were no doubt dramatically affected by the intervening crucifixion and resurrection of Jesus as well as by the circumstances of Christian missionizing. Yet both "eyewitnesses" and "servants of the word" (see Luke 1:2) were bearers of first- and second-generation memories of "those who have accompanied us during all the time that the Lord Jesus went in and out among us" (Acts 1:21).

Furthermore, it is not difficult to see that as Jesus moved from Galilee to Jerusalem his path was increasingly dangerous. The intimidation of the oriental despot Herod Antipas was as real as the execution of John, and the uneasy confederation of Pilate and the high priests in Jerusalem was hardly eager to receive Galilean (!) prophets or kings who would come in the name of the Lord or under any other banner. Unless Jesus is to be regarded as naive or ignorant, he surely would have seen that his mission faced the real peril of Roman crucifixion, and his followers would be subject to the same threat. Historical scholarship will debate exactly which titles or roles Jesus and his disciples ascribed to him and what they came to mean after his resurrection, but all the tradition remembers him as an active agent, proclaiming God's righteous dominion and enacting the fulfillment of scriptural agenda. Exact historical data may be elusive, but Jesus' own acts and words were the foundation of the story by which Christians declared the gospel of God's righteous and gracious rule.

The second problem which emerges forcefully at this point in the story is that of Luke's modification of Mark. Luke has apparently omitted large portions of Mark (6:45—8:26). Speculations concerning this omission often interpret Luke's silence only in the light of various views of the character of these materials in Mark. Since Peter's confession and the subsequent three (!) passion predictions (Mark 8:31-33; 9:30-32; 10:32-34) are so powerful in Mark's story, Luke tends to be interpreted as having "changed" Mark or having reduced the apocalyptic impact and Christological clarity of Mark's story. This passage is an important instance of the need to assess Luke's story on its own terms. The interpreter must observe the alterations of the Markan source, but press to see chap. 9 of Luke as integral to the whole "central section" (9:51—19:27) of Luke's presentation of kingship and discipleship. Luke has not only disrupted Mark's structure of passion predictions, which turn on the narrative hinge of Peter's confession, but he has multiplied the predictions of Jesus' impending passion within his presentation of the extended "way of the Lord" (first, 9:22//Mark 8:31-33; second, 9:44//Mark 9:30-32; third, 12:50; fourth, 13:22-33; fifth, 17:25; sixth, 18:31-34//Mark 10:32-34).

18-19—By setting this episode in the context of Jesus' **praying,** Luke again emphasizes divine guidance at a crucial juncture of the narrative (see 6:12; 11:1-13). Jesus' question of Peter picks up Herod's question of just a few verses earlier (v. 9), and Peter first recites almost the same words as were reported to Herod (vv. 7-8), including Luke's specific note that **one of the old prophets** had arisen. As Chaps. 1–2 show, Luke is fascinated with the testimony of the prophets of old.

By all of these popular accounts, Jesus is already viewed as a divinely authorized agent, even as one whom God has already raised from the dead to come back to Israel with the word of God. As Luke 7 also shows, there is nothing wrong or even inadequate with regarding Jesus as a "prophet," for he is indeed the fulfillment of the prophetic roles of Elijah and Moses (see also Acts 3:22). But he is not merely one of those great prophets from the past returned. Something more decisive, more eschatological is at stake, and even his prophetic role is fundamentally new (see also 16:16).

20-22—Peter's confession of Jesus as **"the Christ of God"** is as central to Luke's account as Peter's differing words are to Matthew (16:16-20) and Mark (8:29-30). Matthew's glorious commendation of Peter's confession stands in contrast to Mark's immediate command to silence, and Luke's brevity is like Mark's. The term **the Christ of God** is, however, as crucial to Luke's testimony as can be imagined. It is the title which articulates the hopeful expectations of faithful Simeon (2:26) and the crucial phrase on the lips of those who accuse Jesus as he dies (along with "his Chosen One," 23:35, see 9:35 below!).

As the crucifixion of Jesus "the King of the Jews" (23:38) and the speeches in Acts (3:18; 4:26) also show, **the Christ of God** is specifically the anointed royal figure in Luke-Acts, i.e., the king who is anointed to exercise God's reign. All of that may not yet be clear to Peter or the reader at this stage of the story, depending on how carefully the many allusions to the kingdom and authority of this "Son of God" (1:35; 3:22; 4:3, 9, 41; 8:28) and "Christ" (2:11, 26; 3:15; 4:41) have been noted. In Luke the command to silence is also not a rebuke suggesting any possible misunderstanding of Jesus' messiahship (see Mark 8:32-33). But Jesus has now been acclaimed as **the Messiah of God** by his own followers, and the strict charge to silence prevents this "hidden knowlege" from circulating abroad prematurely. First Jesus must instruct his followers on what this role and authority will mean for him and for them.

The passion prediction is thus tied immediately to the charge of silence without even starting a new sentence. It is an explication of the need for secrecy at present. God's way of pursuing the royal program of this Messiah will not conform to anyone else's plan. Only after rising will the Messiah show his disciples from the Scriptures that it was "necessary that the Christ should suffer these things and enter into his glory" (24:26-27). In this passage, however, all the synoptic evangelists recite an earlier tradition which speaks of the necessity of the suffering of **the Son of man.** They also agree that this prediction about **the Son of man** interprets Peter's confession of Jesus as Messiah.

This is the heart of early Christian creedal material. The events of the passion are summarized by means of the specific identification of Jesus' adversaries (elders, chief priests, and scribes). These groups probably composed the Sanhedrin in Jerusalem, and Luke will pick up the list again when the passion story begins (20:1//Mark 11:27; see also 22:52, and note the adversaries of the apostles in Acts 4:5; 23:14; 25:15). It is difficult but important to note that even the pre-gospel traditions saw the conflict with Israel's leadership as a "necessary" conflict over how God's will would be exercised. Something of the profound struggle among various Jewish groups, including the Christians, is revealed in this concept.

The most difficult "secret" in Luke is not so much the question "Who is Jesus?" but "Why was it necessary that the Messiah Jesus be crucified?" Thus Luke links the revelation of Jesus' identity as closely as possible with this traditional word of Jesus that the Son of man must be crucified at the hands of the leadership of Israel and raised by God. This motif of "necessity" will reappear constantly throughout the rest of the narrative, and it is still a "secret" at this point in the story. It is the secret which is the clue to the reign which Jesus has been anointed to inaugurate.

He Warns His Disciples (9:23-27).   Jesus' words to his disciples (vv. 18-22) are now expanded into an address **to all** (v. 23) concerning discipleship, linking a series of five sayings to his passion prediction. These sayings have no necessary connection to one another, since each may be recited quite apart from the context. But they are now an extended commentary on the kind of peril and promise which loyalty to Jesus' kingdom entails. Very real earthly dangers and deprivations are contrasted with rewards from God's salvation and rule which are not yet evident in the present order.

The statements are still "apocalyptic" in Luke—in the sense of what is "hidden" and "revealed"—but the present reality of this revelation is much more evident than in Mark. The follower must **take up the cross daily,** indicating a life of struggle and witness, rather than only a specific moment of truth. This fits with Acts 14:22 where Paul and Barnabas "strengthen the souls of the disciples" in Antioch, "encouraging them to continue in the faith, and saying that through many tribulations we must enter the kingdom of God." There is no concept of the expiation of the wrath of God or a "satisfaction given in exchange for life" (see Mark 8:37). But for the righteous, suffering at the hands of the unrighteous is to be expected. Indeed, this is consistent with God's way of lordship in the world.

The disciple is alerted that the loss of life for Jesus' sake should be no surprise, rather this fits the way of the kingdom. While Mark speaks of loss of life for the sake of Jesus "and the gospel" (8:35), Luke regards this loss for Jesus' sake as on behalf of the "kingdom" (see 18:29). God's way of righteousness is not shameful, although even the religious leaders of Israel may denounce people publicly and condemn them to death (see 9:22 above). Jesus, who has predicted his own death and vindication, will soon be exalted as Lord and will be the Son of man exercising dominion and judgment among the angelic powers of heaven (see Dan. 7:13-15 and Stephen's death in Acts 7:56).

The last judgment will be a display of the reality of this unexpected reign of righteousness, a time when the **glory** of this **Son of man** will be revealed along with the **glory** of God and the heavenly court. For the faithful, that is not the only revelation of God's reign. **Some** in Jesus' presence would **see the kingdom** before their deaths.

The question of who "sees" and "hears" and who does not has been raised again. But even more specifically Luke has raised the question of when this promise will have been fulfilled in his narrative. Did the disciples, or at least **some** of them, see the kingdom revealed in the transfiguration which follows (vv. 28-36)? Or is this the "seeing" which only a few are given when Jesus' kingly power is revealed on the cross (23:39-43, 47-48)? Or is this the seeing of those to whom the risen Christ and then exalted Lord reveals his will and reign in Luke 24 and Acts 1 (see also Acts 7:54-60; 9:1-9; etc.)?

Luke's rehearsal of these traditional sayings is a vital witness to a community where suffering posed a challenge to the kingdom of righteousness and mercy they proclaimed in the name of the Messiah Jesus. This is not a glorification of suffering, as if it had redemptive powers in itself. The present and future reality of the reign which God inaugurated in Jesus is assured because the disciples are suffering only as the Messiah himself did. The whole testimony to the vindication of Jesus by God in his resurrection and exaltation is at the same time a profound word of encouragement grounded in the conviction that Jesus is and reveals God's gracious way of ruling in the world.

He Is Revealed as the Chosen Son of God (9:28-36).   This is one of the most powerfully symbolic stories in the New Testament, and Luke has taken a strong hand in exploring its symbolism within his narrative. The larger context of meaning is straightforward. Both Herod (9:9) and Jesus (9:18, 20) have raised the question of Jesus' identity, and Peter's inspired answer (9:20) is now complemented by the testimony of the voice of God (9:35). The more ambiguous features of the narrative may be wondrous accompaniment of the central revelation, the specific significance of which should not be pressed too rigorously, i.e., **the mountain,** the dazzling **white raiment,** the "exodus" of which **Moses and Elijah** speak, the **sleeping** and **waking** vision of Jesus' **glory,** the **booths,** and the **overshadowing cloud** of presence. These images burst upon the reader with great force indicating an encounter with transcendent realities which may be only partially understood. This is an "epiphany" story or theophany (see the discussion at 5:1-11), and all the details must be understood within the central revelation of Jesus as the Chosen Son of God.

28-31—Linking this story to Jesus' previous words (**after these sayings**), Luke emphasizes that Jesus took the select three, **Peter, James,** and **John,** to **the mountain to pray** (v. 28; see also **as he was praying,** v. 29). **The mountain** is a location of revelation and prayer (6:12), even if it is not named. Jesus' dazzling face and garments are indirect indications of God's presence as he reflects God's splendor just as Moses' did on Mount Sinai (Exod. 34:29, see 2 Cor. 3:7). It is not possible or necessary to explain how Jesus, the disciples (see v. 32), or we recognize the **two men** talking with Jesus as **Moses and Elijah** (contrast the anonymous "two men" in Luke 24:4 and Acts 1:10). Although the precise symbolic significance of Moses and Elijah is also elusive, their presence is clearly momentous.

In Luke-Acts, where Jesus fulfills the scriptural promises of the Elijah and Mosaic prophets (see especially 7:11-17 and Acts 3:22-23), the appearance of these two great figures is already testimony that he is not merely "John" or "Elijah" or "one of the old prophets arisen" (9:8, 19), but they are bearing witness to Jesus as one who fulfills and surpasses their roles (see 7:26-28 and 16:16). They are now heavenly figures, each of them having had a most unusual exaltation or departure at the end of life (see 2 Kings 2 and Deuteronomy 34).

31-33a—Luke has composed these verses in a remarkable supplement to the traditional story (Mark 9:2-10) which now tells the reader what Moses and Elijah were discussing with Jesus on that mountain. The word which the RSV translates here as Jesus' **departure** is literally "exodus," but that word is no less ambiguous in Greek than in English. It can mean "death," as in the English euphemism of "the departed." In Luke it could also mean Jesus' entire **departure** of death, resurrection, and exaltation to heaven, since all of these are integral to God's saving plan (see Luke 24:26, 46-49; Acts 1:6-10; 2:36; 10:38-42).

This interpretation fits especially well with the emphasis that this "departure" was something which Jesus "was to fulfill in

Jerusalem." Luke will also speak of the fulfilling of the days of Jesus' "exaltation" as Jesus' purpose in heading for Jerusalem (9:51), and Jesus will later announce the "baptism" with which he is to be baptized and of his "constraint" until it is "fulfilled" or **accomplished** (12:50). Jesus' "exodus," "exaltation," and "baptism" are all highly symbolic Lukan words which lead the reader forward to understand Jesus' death, resurrection, and assumption into heaven. Was it perhaps even more specifically an "exodus," i.e., a fulfillment of the departure from Egypt? Luke's story supports an interpretation of Jesus' death and resurrection as a deliverance, and Luke's Jesus speaks of fulfilling the Passover in the kingdom of God on the other side of his death (22:15-18). Probably Moses (and Elijah?) would know of such matters. But it is at least clear in this passage that Moses and Elijah are revealing the way that "the Christ should enter into his glory," and the context (9:22, 44) demonstrates that such glory will be attained through suffering (see 24:26 and see the discussion at 23:46 of Jesus' death as the "departure" of the righteous of Wis. 3:2).

Since **Peter and those with him were heavy with sleep,** it is not clear that they caught on to what was said about Jesus' "**departure,**" but they did **see his glory** and the two figures standing with him. This is a "dream vision" experience in which the readers see and hear all, while observing that Peter and the disciples may have only grasped portions of the revelation. Did they understand how Jesus' "**departure**" was integral to his **glory** which is glimpsed here as it will only later be fully revealed?

33b-34—Having now removed Moses and Elijah from the scene, Luke picks up Mark's (9:5) narrative with Peter's comment about building **three booths, not knowing what he said.** Is his remark simply misguided, as Mark (9:6) suggests: "For he did not know what to say." Luke's use of the participle could mean that, or it could indicate that Peter suggested three booths, "although he did not realize what he was saying."

The matter could only be settled with a clearer concept of what the **booths** meant to Luke, but it is at least worth suggesting that Luke may have been illuminating a lack of understanding rather than attacking a "misunderstanding." If the three **booths** were just monuments to the disciples' experience or if they indicated a mere "nationalism" of the Feast of Booths, Peter's suggestion must be rebuked. And, clearly, no booths were ever built. But the Feast of Booths may have been regarded by Luke as a time when Israel ritualized the "exodus" and "wilderness" experience by living in temporary shelters during the harvest. This "catechetical" practice of remembering God's restoration would then be an appropriate background for the "exodus" which Jesus was about to fulfill. At least, the evangelist leaves the tantalizing possibility that Peter said more than he knew (see discussion at 23:37, 47).

34-36—The descent of the **cloud** brings an even more profound stage of ambiguity and revelation, and the participants are enveloped in the cloud. The cloud is a sign of divine presence— even saving presence—since it shields the humans from the purging splendor of God (see Exod. 24:15-16; 40:34). Thus even while Jesus and the disciples are "in" the cloud, the **voice** speaks to them **out of the cloud.** This is the "voice from heaven" of 3:21, confirming and further specifying Jesus' identity and role.

Matthew and Mark report that the voice identified Jesus in the same terms as at the baptism: "**This is** [cf. 'you are'] my beloved **Son**," although now instead of concluding with "in whom [you] I am pleased" (Matt. 3:17//Mark 1:11//Luke 3:22) the word is "**Listen to him!**" (Matt. 17:5//Mark 9:7//Luke 9:35). Only Luke alters the basic utterance of the voice from heaven: "**This is my Son,** *the Chosen One!*" Such innovation is a stunning clue that Luke's restatement of God's word is filled with significance.

The "Chosen One" is a dramatic definition of what it means to be the Son of God. In Isaiah (see 42:1; 44:1; 45:4), "Jacob my child" (or "my servant") and Israel "my chosen" are parallel statements of the identity which God confers on the servant. There is little evidence of a tradition of "the suffering servant" in the intertestamental reading of Isaiah. But clearly Isaiah indicated that the chosen "servant" or "child" of God would suffer, and Luke understood Jesus as fulfilling this prophecy (Acts 3:13, 26; 4:27, 30; see also Luke 22:37 and Acts 8:30-35). Of course, Jesus is the "Son of God" in Luke and certainly that means Jesus' royal authority and status (see discussion at 3:22 and 4:3, 9). But as "the Chosen One" Jesus will exercise the dominion of God through suffering. It is certainly no mere coincidence, therefore, that only in Luke is the crucified Jesus taunted for being "the Christ of God, his Chosen One" (23:35).

The silence of the disciples **in those days** concerning all that they had seen is related to this central revelation. As will become even clearer after the next passion prediction (vv. 44-45), only Jesus (and Moses and Elijah) and the reader who knows how the story came out could possibly understand the disclosure of Jesus' identity and role that has been given. The disciples are not stupid or hard-hearted, at least not yet (see vv. 41, 45, 47). They simply cannot understand, and God is both revealing and hiding the strategy of the kingdom which Jesus is about to carry forward in **his departure.**

He Heals a Possessed Boy (9:37-43a).   Luke presents Jesus as moving directly from the mountain of transfiguration into a confrontation with a father and his afflicted son. Mark's intervening words about the coming of Elijah (9:11-13//Matt. 17:10-13) and his extended discussion with the possessed boy's father about his faith and unbelief (Mark 9:20-24) are missing from Luke's story. Instead the story is a simplified disclosure of Jesus demonstrating the power to heal, which his disciples lack. The authority of God's dominion over the oppressive power of unclean spirits is revealed.

37-40—The distressed and pleading father approaches Jesus out of a large **crowd** and gives a graphic description of the boy's affliction. The seizures he has experienced would probably be called epileptic in the modern world, but such diagnostic categories from medical science should not be used to reduce the terrifying urgency of the story. Many afflictions, diseases, and uncontrolled conditions are still experienced as encounters with awesome forces, and their occurrence is no less frightening for parents or loved ones. Prayer may often be the only remedy available, although all other avenues must be pursued (see Mark 9:29). Once again, Luke emphasizes that this is an **only child** (see 7:12; 8:42), and the father is desperate, while refusing to give up hope. The father appeals directly to Jesus because his disciples were unable to heal the boy.

41-43—Jesus' remarks about the **faithless and perverse generation** (see Deut. 32:20) are directed exclusively at his own **disciples,** and the question of how long he would **be with and bear with you** is a reminder that Jesus will not be around forever (see 9:31 and see Moses in Deut. 31:16-19). The details of the violent seizure are important signs in such stories that the healer has indeed encountered and engaged the unclean spirit in the struggle for the "possession" of the boy. When Jesus **healed the boy, and gave him back to his father** (see 7:15), the praise is properly given to **God.** This is truly a display of God's **majesty** or "greatness," revealing God's dominion through his Messiah, Son, and Chosen One (9:22, 35). And has the **faithless and perverse generation** of Jesus' disciples yet grasped what they have seen?

He Again Predicts His Passion and Warns His Disciples (9:43b-50).   **43b-44**—Still following Mark, Luke has tied this second passion prediction directly to the preceding story. All are still **marveling** and praising God's majesty while Luke's Jesus seizes their attention with a word they will not be able to comprehend. **"Let these words sink into your ears!"** This is a kind of prophetic oracle, an alert or warning such as the Lord said to Moses concerning what would happen in the future (see Deut. 31:28; Exod. 17:14). It does not mean that the word will be understood, for the problem of hearing may be a problem of the hardened heart (see v. 47), whether directly caused by God (see 10:21), an evil agent (see 8:12; 10:18; 22:3, 31), or by human agency (see the range of options in the story of God and Pharoah: Exod. 7:3-4, "I will harden Pharaoh's heart . . . Pharaoh will not listen to you"; 7:13-14, "still Pharaoh's heart was hardened, and he would not listen to them"; 8:32, "Pharaoh hardened his heart this time also").

The words which follow are an abbreviated form of the passion prediction focused exclusively on the impending (**is to be,** "is going to be") betrayal of the **Son of man** into human hands. This is a traditional saying, but in Luke it includes no reference to Jesus' execution or resurrection (see Mark 9:31//Matt. 17:23). In 22:22 (Mark 14:21//Matt. 26:24), Luke will again focus on the "necessity" of the betrayal of the Son of man, carefully distinguishing God's will and agency from that of culpable humanity and the power of Satan (see also 22:3-6, 31-32). In this passion prediction, the disciples and the reader are alerted together to **"let these words sink into your ears!"** because the story of Jesus' betrayal will reveal a complex interaction of divine, demonic, and human wills and acts.

45—Luke has no illusions that people will quickly grasp what is going on in the story. They may be quick to praise God's majesty or greatness immediately after they have been unable to perform a healing (vv. 37-43), but they do not comprehend Jesus as he uses this encounter as the occasion to predict human betrayal. And Luke states their problem from three angles: **they did not understand, it was concealed from them, and they were afraid to ask.** In 18:31-34, Luke will again expand Jesus' passion prediction with a threefold statement of the disciples' problem: "They understood none of these things; the saying was hid from them, and they did not grasp what was said."

Human ignorance is a kind of explanation, perhaps even an excuse, but only for a limited time (see 23:34; Acts 13:27; 17:23, 30). Now neither the disciples nor the readers of Luke could claim that they had never been warned of human betrayal of this Son of man who revealed the greatness or majesty of God. And why could they (we) **not understand?** Who **concealed it from them** (us)? Is this the work of the devil or God or human self-deception? The passive voice in this case is probably as ambiguous as in Exod. 7:13-14, "Pharaoh's heart was hardened." But the context makes clear that Jesus as the Messiah of God's reign is warning his followers that they will find themselves at enmity with God's saving reign. Like the "day of the Lord" in the prophets (see Joel 1:15; Amos 5:18-20; Zeph. 1:14-18), the revelation of the reign of God will be a time of judgment (see 10:14; 11:31-32; 19:44) as well as salvation.

46-48—Again abbreviating Mark, Luke interprets this debate among the disciples over who is the greatest by treating it as Jesus' diagnosis of **the thought of their hearts.** The revelation of who is truly the "great one among you" points once again to the "greatness" or "majesty" of God (v. 43). If the disciples properly understood their own praise of God, they would not be caught in the silly and perverse debate over greatness. Having just healed one boy, Jesus now takes another **child** to his side and instructs his disciples that the **least of them** is the place where the greatness of God's majesty, Messiah, and reign are to be found (see also Matt. 25:31-46). This is not merely a moral instruction advising Christians to be humble. It is a revelation of where and how the reign of God is present in all of its greatness. Only in the last line does Luke "apply" it to the disciples indicating that God's "way of ruling" in the world is also their charge and claim to greatness (see also 22:24-30).

49-50 This strange little episode concludes the immediate scene and entire section (3:1—9:50) with one more emphasis on the independence of the kingdom, even from the control of the immediate circle of Jesus' disciples. As will become clear in 11:23, following Jesus is a much more exclusive matter than following the disciples. In Acts 8, Luke tells interesting stories of the apostles sending Peter and John to Samaria to ratify the ministry which Philip had already begun, but he also indicates that the attempt to buy the power of Jesus' name is forbidden (Acts 8:14-24). The apostles do not control the power of the name, but those who attempt to usurp it for their own advantage are also in grave danger (see Acts 19:11-20). At this point in the Gospel, however, the stress is on Jesus' commendation of those who are acting as agents of the kingdom whether or not they are authorized by apostolic authority (see also the prophecies of Eldad and Medad in Num. 11:26-30).

■ The Way of the Determined Messiah (9:51—19:27)

> When the days drew near for him to be received up, he set his face to go to Jerusalem.
>
> (Luke 9:51)

This portion of Luke has been called the "travel narrative," and it constitutes a significant expansion of Mark's narrative. Only a small portion of Mark (9:41—10:12) has been omitted in Luke's version, but Luke continues from 9:51 to 18:15 before resuming the use of Mark. On the basis of observing the material shared with Matthew and its sequence, scholars have shown that Luke is using "Q" extensively. Nevertheless, these chapters are best understood as Luke's composition, since the evangelist develops the schema of an extended journey as the occasion for interpreting "the way of the Lord." As the Messiah moves intentionally toward "fulfilling his exodus in Jerusalem" (9:31), his disciples are instructed in what it means to follow him, and his opposition is further exposed.

To speak of this as a "schema of an extended journey" is not to deny that Jesus in fact traveled from Galilee to Jerusalem. No doubt he did. In fact, John's Gospel (2:13; 5:1; 7:10) suggests three such journeys "up to Jerusalem." Mark (10:32-33; 11:1, 11, 15, 27) has also emphasized Jerusalem as the destiny of his travel, but Luke has stretched out this journey into an odyssey, or a "pilgrim's progess," or more precisely an "exodus." Jesus' travel has become a literary device for gathering a host of stories, sayings, and episodes into a sequence which has direction and purpose.

Several interesting attempts have been made to demonstrate that Luke has structured these chapters with particular care. Some have argued that Luke is depicting Jesus as a "second Moses" and that the sequence of the stories follows the outline of the instruction of Israel in Deuteronomy. It is true that both Deuteronomy and Luke 9:51—19:27 have catechetical purposes, revealing the way Israel is to walk, and Jesus' instructions often seem related by similarity or contrast to Moses. Luke also regards Jesus as fulfilling the Deuteronomic (18:15-18) promise of the "prophet like Moses" (Acts 3:22). But the outline of Deuteronomy simply does not dictate the sequence of these episodes.

Again some outlines of these chapters have been built on a "chiasm," suggesting that Luke's narrative is constructed in the shape of an X where the intial and terminal elements are carefully balanced all the way to the center (i.e., A B C D E : E´D´C´B´A´). This proposal does help the reader to see that Luke begins and ends the section with ominous words concerning Jerusalem (A: 9:51-56; A´: 19:11-27) with counsel on discipleship (B: 9:57—10:24; B´: 18:31—19:10) and questions about inheriting eternal life (C: 10:25-42; C´: 18:15-30) lying inside. The narrative also then centers on another ominous word concerning Jerusalem (13:22-35). But this outline becomes overly ingenious, with various scholars debating about how the sections should be cut and labeled. At least such proposals demonstrate that Luke has a sense for the literary balance of the beginning and ending of the section, and the references to Jerusalem occur at structurally significant points.

In fact, Luke's repeated reminders that Jesus is traveling toward Jerusalem (see 9:51-56; 13:22-33; 17:11; 18:31; 19:11, 28; see also "going on" in 9:57; 10:1, 38; 11:53; 18:35; 19:1) often seem to be rather artificial, since it takes Jesus so long to arrive. This is a clue that Luke has used the schema of the journey as a device for pulling a variety of traditional stories within a narrative framework which is going somewhere. Thus, while it is difficult to argue too rigorously for the significance of the arrangement of particular stories within given portions, Luke has clearly organized this larger section into a three-phase journey (9:51—13:21; 13:22—17:10; 17:11—19:27). And the "way of the determined Messiah" provides a revelation of God's dominion and a catechesis in discipleship.

Jesus Faces toward Jerusalem (9:51—13:21)

He Sets His Face (9:51-62)

The Journey Begins (9:51-56).   This is a remarkable example of Lukan composition in which the literary, scriptural, and theological objectives of Luke's Gospel (see the introduction to this commentary) are meticulously pursued. A woodenly literal English translation of these verses may help indicate their freighted symbolism and punning:

"And it came to pass in the fulfilling of the days of his being taken up (received up, death, exaltation) that he set his *face to go unto Jerusalem.* And he sent messengers *before his face.* And *when they had gone* they went into a village of the Samaritans to prepare for him. But they would not receive him because *his face was going unto Jerusalem.* And when his disciples James and John saw that they said, 'Lord is it your will that we call fire down from heaven to consume them?' But having turned, he rebuked them. And *they did go* unto another village."

Luke is again imitating the style of the Greek Scriptures (see 1:5—2:52), at the same time repeating the words **face** (Gk: *prosōpon* 3 times), **go** (Gk: *poreuomai* 4 occurrences) and **Jerusalem** (twice). The word *to go* is certainly not a technical term, but Luke is sounding an element about Jesus going on his way which will be thematic for the entire section (see also 9:57; 10:38; 13:31,33; 17:11; 19:28). Similarly the repetition of the word **face** enhances the image of Jesus' intentionality and determined "will" as he now moves toward Jerusalem.

51—The Greek noun (*analēmpsis*), which is translated as "being taken up" (**received up,** death, exaltation), is the second of three symbolic terms for Jesus' whole mission (*exodus*, 9:31; *baptisma*, 12:50). This *analēmpsis* again (see 9:31) is something for which "the days are fulfilled" and which will occur in Jerusalem. It is his death, but more. In Acts 1:2, 11, and 22, the verbal form of this term (*analambanein*) is used to speak of Jesus being "taken up" or "received up" into heaven in his exaltation (see Acts 2:33 and Luke 24:51). At this point the term is more evocative than specific, requiring the reader to follow the story forward to see what all will be "accomplished" or "fulfilled" in **Jerusalem.**

But **Jerusalem** is clearly the goal. This Jesus who **sets his face to go to Jerusalem** is a picture of intentionality, much like a determined or commissioned prophet of old. Isaiah says, "For the Lord God helps me. . . . Therefore I have set my face like a flint" (50:7). And the charge to Ezekiel is even more stunning: "The word of the Lord came to me: 'Son of man, set your face toward Jerusalem and preach against the sanctuaries; prophesy against the land of Israel' " (Ezek. 21:1-2; see also 20:46, the south; 25:2, the Ammonites; 28:21, Sidon; 29:2, Pharaoh). Jesus is already fulfilling a prophetic role under divine direction, and a confrontation of wills with Jerusalem looms ahead.

52-56—This is an encounter with Jesus' emissaries in which **the Samaritans** refuse to receive him and thus refuse to receive the God who sent him (see 9:48; 10:16). It is a test, just as if a city on the projected route of a conquering emperor would reject his embassy and close the gates against him. And if they are rejecting the prophet or agent of God's word and will, then what will be their fate? In 2 Kings 1:9-12 the answer is clear when a threatened Elijah says repeatedly, "If I am a man of God let fire come down from heaven and consume you and your fifty," and it happens. The disciples know the prophetic precedent.

Why the Samaritans reject Jesus is not clear. Perhaps it was that he was going to Jerusalem whereas they revered Gerizim as the holy temple mount (see John 4:19-20). Or perhaps Jesus' determination to go to Jerusalem implied a confrontation with the Roman order which they were not ready to join. Or perhaps just his prophetic mission ("his face was going unto Jerusalem") was enough to put them off. Even glimpses of Jesus' divine authority could be fearful (see 8:37).

As with his mission in Galilee (see 4:14-30), Jesus first encounters rejection in Samaria. He does not "will" to bring immediate **fire** and brimstone on Nazareth, nor upon Samaria. Luke 10:12-16 soon indicates that those cities which reject Jesus' ambassadors and thus him and God are in grave peril. **Fire from heaven** would not be excessive (see Sodom in 10:12). But now is the time for repentance, and Jesus himself will continue his ministry among Samaritans (see 10:33 and 17:11-19). And in the book of Acts the ministry of the apostles will proceed from Jerusalem to Judea and Samaria (see Acts 1:8; 8:1-25). Jesus' rebuke of the disciples is a restraint of the judgment which still could come, because it is God's will that Samaria, Judea, Galilee, and all the world be saved and not destroyed.

There Is No Retreat (9:57-62).   This passage flows directly from the preceding introduction to the whole section, and it continues the awesome display of Jesus' unflinching will and command. Luke has written the introduction to these sayings from "Q" in the same language he has just used: "And as they did go on the way . . . ." This is the "way of the Lord," and they are now **going** on it with this determined Jesus. His uncompromising words are thus further evidence of his singularity of purpose. They are even more compelling than in Matthew 8, especially since the third command is unique to Luke.

Attempts to soften or psychologize these warnings about leaving house (vv. 57-58), family duties (vv. 59-60), and even family bonds (vv. 61-62) without looking back are misguided. Jesus is frighteningly clear. Volunteers who plan to follow Jesus out of their "free will" must be warned of the impossible demands of the course upon which Jesus has embarked. It will be no less demanding of him.

57-58—Following the **Son of man** on this "way" will not be easy. This first exchange is like the warnings in 14:27-33 about counting the cost of discipleship. Jesus knows what the cost is for him as **the Son of man.** The title here sounds like a proverbial usage, meaning a "human person" or even "I." But in the context of chap. 9, the Son of man is the one who will be "delivered into the hands of sinful men" (9:44). Thus homelessness is only an aspect of the way of the Lord which leads to crucifixion (see 14:27).

59-60—Jesus even violates the profound Jewish obligation of proper burial for one's father (see Gen. 50:5; Tob. 4:3). Priests could even touch the dead if they were relatives (Lev. 21:1-3). Only the most strict Nazarites were prevented from touching the corpses of their family because "his separation to God is upon his head" (Num. 6:6-8). But Jesus does not speak of the problem of ritual purification. He commands a kind of separation from the all the "dead" who are not following. Let them **bury their own dead.** But, says Luke's Jesus alone, **"You go, and proclaim the kingdom of God"** (see 9:62). The mission of heralding God's righteous rule controls and directs Jesus as well as those who follow him.

61-62—When Elijah called his successor Elisha, he allowed him to return to his house to bid his family farewell (1 Kings 19:19-21). Not so with Jesus. He has "set his face to go to Jerusalem," and his determination allows no backward glance. It is important to state again that attempts to accommodate these demands miss the point that the determined will of God is here revealed. Those who aspire to volunteer for this mission must be warned that to be "fit" or "straight" for God's righteous rule is an impossible standard. Jesus is indeed going to fulfill this "exodus," *analēmpsis*, and "baptism," although none of his disciples will be proved truly faithful or worthy of the kingdom he enacts.

The disciples who "did not understand" his passion prediction and from whom "it was concealed" (9:45) now hear the word straight. Whether they still were able to understand the awesome mission which Jesus was undertaking is doubtful.

He Sends Out Seventy (10:1-24)

Jesus now advances his kingdom campaign by sending out another group of emissaries in advance of his coming. Like the Twelve in 9:1-10 and the messengers in 9:52, the **seventy** are a larger cadre of officially authorized delegates who herald the approaching king and kingdom. They fulfill the urgent and unswerving mission of the kingdom to which Jesus has just called his followers (9:57-62).

By gathering a host of traditional sayings from "Q" into his narrative framework, Luke has thus explicated the intensity of the demands on the disciples in terms of the immediacy of the confrontation with the cities. The kingdom is more than a challenge to persons, requiring them to abandon old values and loyalties. It is a mission of God and of God's Messiah to houses and communities and regions.

Luke's literary hand is most evident in the introduction to this section (v. 1) and the close connection which is made between Jesus' summary word (v. 16) and the return of the seventy (v. 17). As with the sending and return of the Twelve (9:1, 10), the time of their mission passes as Jesus speaks without any specific stories of their activities being told. The fact of their mission and its interpretation by Jesus are the crucial concerns.

The Charge of the Seventy (10:1-12).   1—Only Luke mentions this second major embassy of the kingdom, and only Luke introduces the **seventy**. The textual conundrum of whether Luke spoke of "70" or "72" cannot be solved with certainty. It could reflect an earlier disagreement in the versions of the Scriptures as to whether there were 70 (MT) or 72 (LXX) nations in the world descended from Noah after the flood (Genesis 10). Perhaps the passage is an allusion to the 70 elders chosen by Moses from the 12 tribes of Israel (Exod. 24:1, 9; Num. 11:16, 24; plus Eldad and Medad = 72?, Num. 11:26-30). A direct connection with the 72 translators of the Scriptures into Greek (Ep. Arist. 46–50) is less probable. The problem is interesting, however, as a glimpse into the early stages of scribal copying of Luke's text. Whether Luke wrote "70" or "72," one group of scribes apparently felt it was appropriate to "correct" the number by deferring to the scriptural or traditional number known to them. The symbolic significance of the number was clearly regarded as important.

There is no hint of a "Gentile mission" at this point in Luke's Gospel. This is still a campaign which is headed for Jerusalem. To be sure, the towns mentioned in the words of warning (vv. 13-15) were not exclusively Jewish. There have already been "hearers" from Sidon (6:17; see 4:26 for Sidon as an alien town) and Jesus has withdrawn with his disciples to Bethsaida where they were warmly welcomed (9:10-11). Luke is aware that the mission to Israel will take Jesus into "other cities" (4:43), and the **seventy** are now simply going to the **towns** and **places** where Jesus is **about to come** (10:1). The problem of the "Gentile mission" will require the more direct treatment it receives when the Holy Spirit does a new thing in Acts 10.

Traveling **two by two** was probably standard practice for early Christian missionaries (see Acts 8:14; 13:1; 15:32, 40), and this entire passage may well have been read as a handbook on evangelization. As such, it is remarkable for its vision of simplicity, clarity on the message of peace, and refusal to allow the messengers to use force or exercise judgment. This is not merely a "method" to make proselytes. It is a definition of the authority of the messengers in terms of the message of the kingdom they bring.

2-4—In Matthew (9:35-38) Jesus' words ("Q") are offered as consolation to sheep without a shepherd. In Luke, they are counsel to the 70, demonstrating that both proclamation and prayer are instrumental to God's mission. God's **harvest** is not so much the last judgment (see Matt. 13:30, 39) as it is the long-promised gathering of the people of God (Isa. 27:12). Even so, the time is short. The task to which the 70 have been appointed is nothing less than God's project of salvation in history. They could never operate on their own authority. They must realize that they are lambs in the midst of wolves because God's reign of justice and mercy is set upon (see Luke 2:29-35; Acts 4:25-28). The image of Israel as God's flock among the wolves of the nations was well known. The Cynic and Stoic "spies of God" also traveled around with their staffs and cloaks and bags (see 9:3-5). Later Jesus will refer back to these commands to demonstrate that they had no unmet needs while allowing specific equipment for a new occasion (22:35-36, see discussion). But the ambassadors of this kingdom were on urgent business, going directly to their assigned towns with no socializing on the way.

5-7—Although no "greeting" is allowed while on the way, a particular word is commanded upon entering a **house: "Peace be to this house!"** This is more than a greeting (see also Matt. 10:12). It is the same salute which King David's servants extended to the Calebite clan that stood on the fringe of Israel: "Peace be to you, and peace be to your house, and peace be to all that you have" (1 Sam. 25:6). It is an official declaration of the presence of the kingdom, and it confronts the people of the house with God's salvation and authority. It is a word of blessing. Luke could never conceive of a form of Christian evangelism which opened with a threat, whether direct or implied (contrast 1 Sam. 25:13), yet this **peace** is a force or effect of God's presence which the disciple conveys. If it is received by a **son of peace** who is open to it, it remains with that person. If not, it returns and belongs to the disciple. Of course this peace is not the personal possession of the disciple, but it returns to the Messiah as God's agent who bears and conveys the word and work of God. Even the modest practice of remaining in one house is a sign that this is truly an embassy of peace and salvation. There is nothing coercive or abusive in their behavior. Those who trust the word of peace are treated with respect.

8-12—The mission to **towns** is similar, but now the declaration is the more public announcement of the presence of the kingdom. Coupled with healing the sick, the declaration of God's dominion is a word of salvation and blessing. For those who receive it as such, this embassy comes in a spirit of peace and good will. The appearance of the disciples of Jesus is an event of great consequence because they bear the very authority and power of the

Lord of heaven and earth, but only for the accomplishment of good.

Judgment on those who reject such an embassy is reserved for God. The disciples are only authorized to announce the word of warning that the advent of God's reign becomes a threat to those who reject it. Only Luke again ties this peril to the approach of the kingdom in the presence of its ambassadors. This kingdom is a power with which to contend, the very strength of God (see also 11:20), and the disciples merely separate themselves quickly and cleanly from the place, even wiping off **the dust of** that **town** from their **feet** (9:5). It is liable to a fate worse than the fire and brimstone of Sodom.

The Warning of Cities (10:13-16).   **13-15**—These verses are a elaboration of the theme of judgment. The prophetic denunciations are severe, virtually verbatim to those in Matt. 11:20-24 without Matthew's final reference to Sodom (see v. 12 and Matt. 10:15). The **mighty works** are evidence of the power of the kingdom, putting cities on notice of the need for repentance. This **repentance,** even in **sackcloth and ashes,** is not merely remorse for sin. **Repentance** in Luke means turning around to receive the reign of God which is present in the Messiah and his disciples. This is also the call of the apostles in Acts (see 2:38; 3:19; 17:30; 26:20). The peril for those who do not repent in the face of this authority is grave.

16—Once again the authority of the disciples is clearly identified as that of the Messiah and of God who has undertaken this campaign. The disciples do not possess their own authority. Neither does Jesus. This is a very common theme in the New Testament (see Matt. 10:40; 18:14; Mark 9:37; John 12:44-45; 13:20; Luke 9:48). But Luke sharpens the tradition, for now it is not generally about "receiving" Jesus' representatives (see 9:5, 48; 10:8, 10). The question is rather whether they **hear** the disciple and therefore the Messiah. The efficacy of the "word" (see chap. 8) is again central, for the declaration of God's reign is itself an event in which the authority of God is exercised.

The Fall of Satan (10:17-24).   Luke has filled these few verses with theological content, using the tradition with mastery and making one of the most ample theological statements of the entire narrative. By means of his expansion on v. 16, he has revealed the success of **the seventy** as a triumph of God's reign over the powers of **Satan.** He has then resumed his use of "Q," drawing first upon materials in the same sequence as Matthew (vv. 21-22//Matt. 11:25-27) and then reciting sayings which occur elsewhere in Matthew (23b-24//Matt. 13:16-17). Perhaps Luke has merely preserved the sequence of "Q" in these verses (21-24), but these words of blessing on the disciples stand as a private revelation which further highlights the significance of Jesus' words of thanksgiving (vv. 21-24). Thus vv. 17-20 establish the inspired character of the moment, vv. 21-22 convey a unique insight into the relationship of Father, Son, and Holy Spirit, and vv. 23-24 confirm to the disciples (and the reader) that **you** have just seen and heard a most privileged revelation.

17-20—The context is the return of **the seventy** (or seventy-two, see 10:1). As in the sending and return of the Twelve (9:1-6, 10), Luke uses the return to move the narrative forward. But this time the return itself is an occasion of great significance. The Twelve told Jesus "what they had done" (9:10), but we hear the report of **the seventy** in specific terms.

Their **joy** (v. 17) is itself a sign (see 1:14, 44; 2:10; 8:13; 24:41, 52), and Jesus directs them to recognize that the real meaning of this **joy** is that they are now participants in the sovereign reign of God (v. 20), just as citizens in a city or kingdom would have their **names** enrolled. And Jesus (v. 21) **rejoices in the Holy Spirit,** just as King David danced in inspired joy on the triumphant procession of the ark (2 Sam. 6:1-23). Jesus is rejoicing in the dynamic power of God's presence and dominion which have been **revealed.** Jesus is not merely telling them to rejoice because they are clearly "going to heaven." That may be the emphasis of Matt. 7:22, where Jesus teaches that even those who have performed exorcisms in his name may not escape the final judgment (see also the reference to the "book of life" in Rev. 3:5). But Luke is more concerned with the correct understanding for the present of their joy at subjecting the demons, and Jesus interprets their victory as a demonstration of how God is at work.

The **subjection** of **the demons** (vv. 17, 20) is an event of great significance. In 9:1, Jesus gave this authority to the twelve, and now **the seventy** exercise it in his **name.** Jesus' name is understood in Acts to be a manifestation of his presence and power, even after he is exalted to heaven (see Acts 3:6; 4:7, 10, 17-18, 30; 5:40; 9:27). But the power of Jesus' name for subjecting the spirits was only accessible to those who were authorized to use it (see Acts 19:13-14). The success of the disciples is, therefore, a sign to Jesus that his dominion was encountering and conquering the very domain of Satan. Scriptural tradition is filled with images of God's conquest of principalities and powers (see Isa. 14:12, "how you are fallen from heaven . . . you who laid the nations low"), and intertestamental literature is well acquainted with the hope of the binding of Satan or Beliar (see Test. Levi 18:12, "And Beliar shall be bound by him, and he shall give power to his children to tred upon the evil spirits").

The image of treading upon "serpents and scorpions" is also an assurance of the conquest of the **all the power of the enemy,** which draws upon traditional images of scourges (see Deut. 8:15; Luke 11:11-12; see also Ps. 91:13; Isa. 14:29-30; Gen. 3:15). In Acts 28:1-5, when Paul is unharmed from the bite of a viper, the pagans make the mistake of thinking that "he was a god." While Luke probably saw this as a literal fulfillment of the promise of divine protection, he certainly did not regard Jesus' words as an invitation to put God to the test with ordeals of handling deadly snakes. On the contrary, Jesus specifically warns the disciples not to dwell on the victories as their own but to be joyful to be enrolled in God's campaign.

21-22—Luke now links the scene of the victorious return to the praise of God from "Q" by depicting Jesus as **rejoicing in the Holy Spirit.** This is the only use of such a phrase in the New Testament, but it fits well with Luke's vision of how Jesus manifests and implements God's reign in the world. The **Holy Spirit** which "anointed" Jesus as the Christ (3:22; 4:18; Acts 10:38) and led Jesus "full of the Holy Spirit" in the wilderness (4:1) is the presence and authority of the Father's promised reign (see 24:49; Acts 1:5; 2:33). Thus the praise of the Father which follows is a glimpse into the unity of purpose and will among the Son, the

Father, and the Spirit. The early church will carefully ponder such a text to develop later concepts of the "economy" or "communication" of the Trinity.

The "Q" sayings are themselves remarkable for the direct address of God as **Father** and Jesus' straightforward identification of himself as **the Son.** Jesus addresses God as "Father" in other prayers in Luke (see 11:1; 22:42; 23:34, 46), and he speaks of God as "my father" (2:49; 22:29) and "your father" (6:36; 12:30, "Q" passages). Still there is no other portion of Luke with so much explication of the relationship between God and Jesus. The words about "the Father" and "the Son" sound more like the Fourth Gospel than any of the Synoptics (see John 3:35; 6:65; 10:15; 13:3; 14:7-13; 17:25), but the identification of God the Father as "the Lord of heaven and earth" is consistent with Luke's usage of Jewish prayer formulas (see Acts 17:24!).

Jesus presents both the revelation and the hiding of God's saving reign as due to God's "good pleasure" (see 2:14; RSV: **gracious will**) and the "choice" or "will" of the Son. But the narrative will show (see 13:31-35; 23:25) that this is not merely a matter of God's "wish" or "pleasure." It is God's will to both **reveal** and **hide** because a struggle of wills is central to what is happening in the deployment of the kingdom. Paul will also argue that it was God's design to foil **the wise** and powerful by revealing to the weak and foolish that the gospel of the cross of Christ is the power of God (1 Cor. 1:18-25), while "none of the rulers of this age understood this [wisdom of God]; for if they had, they would not have crucified the Lord of glory" (1 Cor. 2:8). So also it would be "in ignorance" that Israel and her rulers together with "the kings of the earth" would gather against the Lord and his anointed in crucifying Jesus. And all of this would be part of the hand and plan of God (Acts 2:17; 4:26-28).

23-24—In Luke, therefore, the traditional word of blessing to those who do **see** and **hear** is spoken privately to the disciples. Not only the "prophets and righteous" have "yearned" in vain to see and hear (Matt. 13:17), but **prophets and kings** have "intended" or "willed" to see and hear without success. This insight or understanding can come in no other way than by the grace of God. Even the disciples have no cause for being pleased with themselves at their powers over the demons. Neither does their having seen the saving power of the kingdom at work grant them a superiority over others. It is all a gift, a blessing, and the rejoicing is also a praise of God alone.

He Teaches the Way of the Kingdom (10:25—11:13)

This cluster of stories presents Jesus teaching "on the way." The encounter with the **lawyer** (vv. 25-28) sets the context with a discussion of observing the Law and inheriting eternal life. The parable of the "good Samaritan" (vv. 29-37) provides an object lesson in loving and serving the neighbor; the exchanges with Mary and Martha (vv. 38-42) deal with the priorities of serving and hearing the word of God, and Jesus' instruction on prayer (11:1-13) depicts the confidence with which all people may love and serve God. The first two stories are integrally connected, but the whole section does not appear to be tightly structured. Still, as a sequel to the preceding revelations of the kingdom with their grand visions of the work and being of God, these instructions in discipleship provide practical counsel. They also provide a brief interlude before more substantial conflicts and tensions confront Jesus' "way" (11:14-54).

The Good Samaritan (25-37).   It is difficult to gain a fresh perspective on a text which is so familiar as this parable. Even the traditional title, "The Parable of the Good Samaritan," so controls its meaning that interpreters overlook the fact that no one is called "good" anywhere in the passage, nor does Luke use the word "parable." The story is so well known that newspersons and legislators who have no idea of what it meant to be a "Samaritan" will speak of passing "good Samaritan laws" and people being "good Samaritans." This story is still much alive in the oral tradition, which is a happy fact even if many interpretations may be a bit unusual. This is all the more reason for attending to the way the evangelist has given a distinctive setting and meaning to the story. It is more than a morality lesson. It is Jesus' instruction in the observance of the Law of God in accord with the kingdom of mercy and service which he has inaugurated.

Luke weaves the story into a series of exchanges between Jesus and **a lawyer** who **stood up to put him to the test** with his question **"Teacher, what shall I do to inherit eternal life?"** (v. 25). Jesus answers with a question (v. 26). The lawyer answers (v. 27), and Jesus commends his answer with a command to practice (v. 28). He agains opens with another question (v. 29). Jesus responds with a story (vv. 30-35) which raises a question (v. 36). The lawyer answers (v. 37), and Jesus commends his answer with a command to practice (v. 37).

This **lawyer** is no attorney or even a legalist. Even the words "law" and "lawyer" could obscure the character of the scriptural debate which is being conducted. He is an interpreter of the Scriptures, the Law of God. This is a "test question" which Jesus the teacher must answer as would any of those who were the expositors and interpreters of the revelation given to Moses and the prophets. That does not mean it is a hostile "test" or distrustful (see by contrast 20:27-40), and Jesus enters into the debate so that the give and take of the questions becomes the means of instruction of all who hear or overhear the dialog.

25-28—The question about **inheriting eternal life** will be raised again by a "ruler" who addresses Jesus as "Good Teacher!" (18:18). This is certainly a question about the hope of life after death, but it is also about how to live now in accord with God's will and reign (see especially 18:25-30). When the question is what one **must do,** Jesus merely points to the commands of the Scriptures.

In deferring to the Scriptures, however, Jesus asks two questions: (1) **What** stands **written in the** Torah?" (2) **"How do you read?"** These questions may be merely complementary, but the matter of "how" the Scriptures are to be read could divide Israel as well as the Torah of Moses could unite them. This interpreter and Jesus, however, agree by combining Deut. 6:4 (which is part of Israel's creedal "Shema," "Hear O Israel: Deut. 6:4-9) with Lev. 19:18b concerning the love of neighbor as one self. Notice that these are the "first" and "second" commands in Mark 12:29-31 and Matt. 22:38-39, and the love of neighbor was widely accepted as the summation of the Mosaic Law (Gal. 5:14; Rom. 13:9; James 2:8). The Synoptics display slight variations of the command to love God with one's whole heart and soul and strength and mind, but these are no more significant than differing modern translations of the Lord's Prayer. The will of God is no secret, and Jesus agrees. Furthermore, the combination of the two commands was a "reading" of the Law which Jesus commended: "You have answered correctly. Do this and you will live!" Jesus does not suggest that the Law of Moses was difficult to observe (see Acts 15:10). Jesus' own commands were even more severe (9:57-62; 6:20-49). Still there is no debate about what one must **do.**

29-37—The plot thickens as the questioner is determined to **justify himself.** This is a consistent theme in Luke: carefully observant or "righteous" people press on to "justify themselves" before God and their neighbors (see 16:15; 18:9-14, 18-30, comment at 18:14) on the basis of their standards of keeping the Law. Even the question **"And who is my neighbor?"** quickly raises the matter of cases. The scholars of the Scriptures debated such questions often. In Lev. 19:18, "neighbor" clearly refers the "the sons of your own people." These considerations could be extended to the sojourner (Deut. 10:19) since God cares for the fatherless, the widow, and the sojourner. But the limits of such consideration were open to debate, and the level of obligation was different in differing cases.

Here is where Jesus turns the whole matter around. He does not stop with suggesting that even Samaritans should receive the love due the **neighbor,** which would be shocking enough since the animosities were so severe (see 9:51-54 and John 4:9: "Jews have no dealings with Samaritans"). Rather it is the **Samaritan** in the story who is the one who **has compassion,** fulfilling the Shema after the pattern of God's love (see Deut. 10:12-20; see also 7:13; 15:20). Detailed assessments of whether the **priest** and the **Levite** were afraid of contamination from a **half-dead** man who looked dead are only further rationalizations. The point is simple enough for a child to see. Compared to the Samaritan, the "righteous" and observant religious leaders of Israel fail to love a neighbor, which is what the Law commanded. And there is no suggestion that the victim was not a Jew. The question "Who is my neighbor?" is exposed as a self-justifying question which

obscures the obligation of loving the neighbor. And Jesus highlights this obligation by the still more scandalous question of
"Who **proved** to be the **neighbor**?" so that the **lawyer** is compelled to commend the Samaritan as fulfilling the Mosaic Law
by his mercy beyond the priest and Levite.

Now that is what it means to observe the Law. "**Do this, and
you will live**" (v. 28). "**Go and do likewise**" (v. 37). The Samaritan's
mercy, risk, generosity, human concern, and even practical attention to the needs of the afflicted reprove those who want to
set limits, but they are also object lessons in human scale of God's
reign of grace and mercy which Jesus is deploying.

Mary and Martha (10:38-42).   This episode is also very familiar, but considerably less popular, especially with women who
have so often been told to fulfill their Christian vocation by **serving** and then hear Jesus' criticizing Martha's concern for serving.
Apart from the specific concerns of women readers and hearers
of this story, however, the story has a point to score. If the "lawyer" in the preceding story was criticized for trying to decide
whom he did not have to treat as a neighbor, these words of Jesus
correct those who try to make their service obligatory for everyone else. Both are forms of self-justification or self-concern.

Jesus' respect for **Mary** and **Martha** is evident. As in the Fourth
Gospel, where Mary and Martha are engaged in a theological
discussion about the resurrection (John 11:1—12:8), Mary **sat at**
the Lord's **feet** as a disciple in this story (see Paul as a disciple
at the feet of Gamaliel in Acts 22:3). From what is known of the
status of women in first century Palestine, such opportunities for
women to participate in "teaching" were most exceptional. The
Greek text states the matter even more pointedly by depicting
Mary as "hearing his word" (v. 39, RSV: **listened to his teaching**).
She is a disciple who has heard the word of God, one of the
blessed (10:24).

The story also reflects the place that Jesus gave to being served.
Although he has just praised the Samaritan for his great concern
for human need, he has also instructed his disciples to expect
little and not be a burden on a household (10:4-9), and he will
later stress that his role as Son of man is to serve and not to be

served and so is theirs (12:37; 22:27). Those who would become
anxious and troubled over serving the agents of the kingdom are
missing the object of the mission.

The good portion, in this case, is the freedom to be a hearer.
Mary has not even asked what she must "do to inherit eternal
life," as if some task were the qualification. The kingdom is a gift,
received by hearing the word in faith. The logic of what one must
"do" is simply misguided in such an instance. The opportunities
for service will come in great abundance and challenge in due
time.

The Kingdom Prayer: (11:1-13).   Luke has composed a discourse on prayer by setting the scene with Jesus at prayer (v. 1),
reciting the kingdom prayer or "Lord's Prayer" which Jesus taught
his disciples (vv. 2-4; see also Matt. 6:9-13), introducing an en-
tertaining account of shameless begging (vv. 5-8), and concluding
with traditional sayings of encouragement to rely on God's grace
(vv. 9-13, see also Matt. 7:7-11). The stunning conclusion is that
the Father will give the Holy Spirit (v. 13) to those who ask, and
this is the answer to the prayer for the kingdom itself (v. 2). This
passage concludes the straightforward teaching on the way of the
kingdom which began in 10:25, and the controversy and opposition soon become more intense (11:14-54). But with the mention
of the **Father** (v. 2) or **heavenly Father** (v. 13) and the assurance
of the giving of **the Holy Spirit** (v. 13), Luke has also resumed
his explication of the relationship of Father, Son, and Spirit of
10:21-22.

1—This is a Lukan introduction in which the **Lord** at prayer
is asked by his disciples to **teach** them **to pray.** The comparison
as John taught his disciples indicates that Jesus' followers are
requesting more than general instruction in how to pray. In Luke's
presentation they are asking for instruction in the kind of prayer
that is appropriate to "the present time" (see 12:56) of Jesus'
inauguration of the kingdom, just as John properly taught his
disciples at the end of the era of the Law and the Prophets (see
7:28; 16:16). This setting stands in contrast to Matthew, where
the negative examples of the "hypocrites" and "the Gentiles"
prompt Jesus to teach the prayer. There is no hint of a polemic
in Luke's version.

Luke is consistently eager to identify divine guidance and authority being given at important junctures in the context of prayer (see the list of passages and comments at 3:21). At this point in the narrative, the Holy Spirit has come upon Jesus and anointed him (see 3:21-22; 4:1, 14, 18; Acts 10:38) and Jesus can thus rejoice in the Holy Spirit (10:21) like King David before the ark (2 Sam. 6:1-23, see also the comments on Luke 3:21-22). But this Holy Spirit has not yet been sent by the exalted Jesus as the "promise of the Father" on Jesus' disciples (see 24:49; Acts 1:4, 8; 2:1-21). Jesus now teaches his disciples the prayer of the kingdom.

2-4—The address of God as **Father** has troubled some people as too specifically male and authoritarian. Of course this prayer comes from a patriarchal culture, and the whole Gospel of Luke is a testimony to the authority and power of God's reign at work in Jesus. But Jesus' use of the word **Father** was probably shocking to first-century ears because it was not as authoritarian or regal as they expected. Instead of praying to the "Sovereign Lord who made heaven and earth" (see Acts 4:24) or the King of the Universe, as in many other contemporary prayers, Jesus prayed and taught his disciples to pray to God as **Father** or "your Father" whose pleasure it is to give them the kingdom (see 12:30, 32). Luke does not preserve the Aramaic word *Abba* by which Jesus was remembered to have addressed God as Father (see Mark 14:36), but he clearly shares the understanding of the early church that it is God's own abiding Spirit which invites and authorizes the kind of intimate speech that characterizes trusting children and loving fathers (see Gal. 4:6; Rom 8:15). The simplicity and confidence of speaking to God as "Father" may even be a critique of patriarchal structures of authority (see Matt. 23:9-10; see Luke 22:24-30 on altering the authoritarian language of kingship). In any case, Luke's understanding of the address brings the followers of Jesus within the intimate identity of will and purpose which characterized Jesus, the Holy Spirit, and God.

The petition that God's name be sanctified is consistent with scriptural convictions that God's holy name has been maligned by a sinful people and must be vindicated by God's judgment and eventual restoration of the chosen people (see especially Ezek.

36:22-28; 20:41; 38:23; Lev. 11:45; Deut. 32; Isa. 5:16). The passive voice is still a plea that only God can be the actor. The
righteousness and mercy of God may be discounted in a world
where willful and sinful powers and people seem to hold the
upper hand.

The petition for God's **kingdom** to **come** is therefore a restatement of the first petition. God's reign is not merely a future event
(see Mark 9:1). It is already being deployed in Jesus' mission (see
9:27; 10:9, 11; 17:20-21; 19:38, but see comment on its future
coming in 22:18). It is unlikely that Luke knew the additional
petition for God's will to be done on earth. Since that petition
corresponds so directly to Luke's convictions, why would he have
omitted it? God's will is another aspect of God's reign, and it is
exactly the exercise of God's will on earth which is being contested
in the plot of Luke-Acts. The next story will also indicate that
the forces of Satan are also under the onslaught of the arrival of
God's kingdom (11:17-20; see also 4:5-6).

The prayer for **bread** is obscured by the unusual Greek word
epiousios, which is translated **daily**. It is possible that in "Q" this
Greek word already had rich associations with the bread of the
heavenly banquet or the Lord's Supper. Scriptural associations
are also possible with the daily bread from heaven or the manna
in the wilderness (see Exod. 16:4; Ps. 78:24). But even with Luke's
understanding of Jesus' "exodus" to Jerusalem (9:31), such themes
are not developed. Rather, in Luke's story this traditional prayer
would emphasize that both the Son of God (see 4:6-8) and his
disciples (see 10:7-8, 38-42) would trust God and not require elaborate provisions.

In the next petition, Luke appears to have modifed "Q's" prayer
about "debts" to a plea for forgiveness of **sins,** now linked with
"our" forgiveness of "debts." On the one hand, Luke's version
seems to be less difficult than Matthew's (6:12) apparent claim of
accomplishment: "because we have forgiven our debtors." But
Luke's wording may tie the hope of the forgivness of sins more
directly to the disciples' remission of financial debts (see 6:36-
38). In 17:1-10, however, it is clear that the mutual forgiveness
of sins is expected to be a regular practice of the community even
if it requires great faith. There is no place for pride in this position,

only the recognition that those who pray in the way of the kingdom are themselves caught up in a system of grace and forgiveness. No case is made for people receiving or dispensing what
they or others "deserve."

In Luke, the petition about **temptation** or "testing" has particular impact. Jesus himself was "led" by the Spirit in his wilderness "tests," but Satan did the testing (see 4:1-2). Although
different Greek verbs for "leading" are used in these two contexts,
even the thought of God "leading" the faithful into testing is
awesome. Earlier Jesus had spoken of people whose faith prospers
quickly but in time of "testing" they fall away (8:13), and he
commended his apostles for faithfulness in his trials (22:28). On
the Mount of Olives (22:40, 46), Jesus twice exhorts his disciples
to "pray that you may not enter into temptation" (or "testing").
People put Jesus to the test (11:16), and Ananias and Sapphira
are accused of putting the Spirit of the Lord to the test by lying
(Acts 5:3, 4, 9; see also Acts 15:10). This cluster of words indicates
that the kingdom of God is caught up in a struggle of powers,
and the faithful must pray to God to be protected from the trials
of Satan (see Judas in 22:3 and Jesus' prayer for Peter in 22:31).
This is not a struggle for humans to enter armed only with their
"free will." Praying to be delivered from such "testing" is acceptable even when God's will may be accomplished through it
(22:39-46).

5-8—These verses are only in Luke, and they provide some
relief from the intensity of the kingdom prayer while offering
assurance of God's attentiveness. It is one of Luke's two stories
of "shamelessness" in prayer (see also 18:1-8), and both are com-
ical stories in the tradition of the kind of "shamelessness" for
which the Cynic philosophers were famous. The man making the
request is some kind of midnight fool, and the man in the house
only responds to hush the noise. Not even their friendship can
handle such ridiculous behavior. If even a poor **friend** responds
to such a shameless request, who could imagine how the loving
Father will respond to people who approach him in indelicate
circumstances? The point is not that God will only respond to
people who bang on the door at all hours, but prayer in many
forms is appropriate to people in need, people who do not have

the luxury of propriety. The story anticipates the next verses, which reveal the surpassing grace of the heavenly Father.

9-13—Luke now brings in material from "Q" to elaborate the indirect point about confidence in prayer to God. Verses 9-10 are tightly worked sayings in which the passive voice reveals the work of God: **it will be given you, it will be opened** to you. Verses 11-12 then raise pointed questions which assume that even **evil** human fathers would never give **serpents** and **scorpions** (see 10:19) to **children** who asked for food. Only Satan gives such scourges. On the one hand, the modern reader may be offended to hear human fathers called **evil.** On the other hand, Luke's Jesus may seem to be too optimistic in the light of what is known of the evils of abusive fathers. But this passage is relying upon the conviction that "fathers" at least know how to look out for their own (see 6:32-34 for a similar logic and comparison). Then the contrast of v. 13 is a strong affirmation of the surpassing grace of God's gift of the Holy Spirit.

The Holy Spirit is the "promise of my Father" (24:49; see Acts 1:4). The Holy Spirit will authorize and empower the disciples in the baptism of Pentecost (Acts 1:5,8) and will be bestowed on repentant Israel and even the Gentiles (Acts 2:38; 4:31; 5:31; 10:45-47). The Holy Spirit will bear witness along with the apostles under accusation (Acts 5:32; see Luke 21:12-19). By giving the Holy Spirit to the followers of Jesus, God will answer their prayer for the kingdom.

He Meets Opposition (11:14-54)

Having taught his disciples more of the way of the kingdom and promised the giving of the Holy Spirit, Jesus again encounters opposition to his reign. Not that all of the episodes in the rest of this chapter are filled with overt hostility. Some even praise Jesus (vv. 27-28) and share their tables with him (vv. 37-44), but Jesus refuses to be accepted on their terms. He presses the mission of the kingdom even as it provokes some to oppose him in very ominous ways (vv. 53-54).

Satan's Kingdom (11:14-26).   This passage is an excellent example of the evangelist's perceptive use of traditional material.

The story of the charge that Jesus exorcises by means of the powers of Beelzebul appears to be derived from "Q" (see Matt. 12:22-30), although Mark (3:22-27) also has a version of the story but with fewer verbal correspondences. In both Matthew and Mark the point of the story is Christological, since it drives to the revelation that as the "stronger one" Jesus is the "Son of David" (Matt 12:23) or "Son of God" against whom blasphemies have been uttered (Mark 3:11, 21, 22, 30). But Luke depicts Jesus and his powers as confronting Israel with a test and a crisis. By means of a rewritten introduction (v. 14), an expanded restatement of the work of the "mighty one" (v. 21) and the use of a prophetic word of warning as a conclusion (vv. 24-26, "Q"), Luke alerts the reader that the opposition of "some" in Israel to Jesus' reign portends even worse bondage and destruction for her house.

14—The transition from the preceding section is a simple introduction to another event on the way, although the presence of the Holy Spirit with Jesus has been underscored with the promise of its coming to the disciples (v. 13). Thus the reader knows that the exorcism which is briefly reported is a display of the Holy Spirit's power to heal (see 4:18; 5:17). Since this is the only healing of a person who is mute/deaf (Gk: *kōphos*), it is also an explicit scriptural fulfillment (Isa. 35:6) which Jesus has claimed about himself: "the mute/deaf (Gk: *kōphos*) hear. . . . And blessed is he who takes no offense at me!" (7:22-23). Before reporting the offense, moreover, Luke indicates that **the people** (crowds) **marveled.** As will become painfully clear in the account of Jesus' death (see especially 22:1-6), Israel is divided by Jesus, but **the people** or the "crowds" would wish to protect him.

15-16—In Matthew (12:24) the opponents are Pharisees. In Mark (3:22) they are scribes. But in Luke, even his opponents are divided, and they are unnamed. **Some** charge him with exorcising by means of the power of **Beelzebul, the prince of demons.** This is a glimpse into the demonic lore in which double agents of Satan could feign exorcism. The politics of the principalities and powers could be devious as "false messiahs and false prophets" (see Matt. 24:24), and the "Lord of the flies" or **prince of demons** was not to be taken lightly.

Others, says only Luke, **sought from him a sign** in order **to test him.** This is not a "testing" as when one seeks to "discern the spirits" (1 John 4:1; Luke 12:2, Gk: *dokimazein*). This is the "tempting" and "testing" which the devil himself did to Jesus (4:1-33) and concerning which Jesus has just told his disciples to pray (11:4). By introducing the quest for a sign as a "test," Luke anticipates Jesus' word concerning "this evil generation" which "seeks a sign" (11:29). Thus the opposition of **some** or **others** evokes judgment on all (see discussion at 13:31; 19:39-44). Jesus is himself the **sign from heaven** in the sense that in him **the kingdom of God has come upon you** (v. 20, see also vv. 29-32).

17-20—Jesus now introduces three **if . . . then** arguments, offering flat assessment of the consequences of **their thoughts** (v. 17). This is all traditional material, but small touches indicate that it is now the "house" of Israel which is being tested. It is the internal division of that **kingdom** and "house against house" which the whole dialog diagnoses, and the case develops from the particulars of each subargument. First, it is ridiculous to accuse Jesus of **casting out demons by Beelzebul,** because then his kingdom would be **divided** (v. 18). That is not what is happening in Jesus' ministry, but God's kingdom is in conflict with Satan's. Second, Jewish exorcists have always invoked God's power, and Jesus is ready to be judged by the same standards (v. 19). Can they not distinguish an ally in the struggle against Satan from an enemy? Third, in Exod. 8:19 even the Egyptian magicians could tell that the plagues Moses wrought were the work of **the finger of God,** and they could not match such authority. Although "Pharaoh's heart was hardened and he would not listen to them," the magicians had warned that Pharaoh was contending with God. Now Jesus is alerting his hearers to the work of **the finger of God.** Jesus is already moving beyond a defense to a warning, lest they also "be found opposing God" (see Acts 5:39; 11:17).

21-23—Luke's expanded version of the saying about the strong man makes it clear that Jesus is God's **stronger man** invading Satan's **palace** (Matthew and Mark read "house"). The royal imagery again fits with Luke's emphasis on a conflict of principalities. This is also an expansion on the implied reference to Isa. 49:24-25 where the question and answer are all about God's strength to enter the very realm of a mighty foe. "Can the prey be taken from the mighty, or the captives of a tyrant be rescued? Surely, thus says the Lord: 'Even the captives of the mighty shall be taken, and the prey (LXX: *skula;* Luke. 11:22, "spoil") of the tyrant be rescued, for I will contend with those who contend with you, and I will save your children.' " God's campaign of salvation is at work in Jesus who is "mightier" than Satan, but will Israel join Jesus in this struggle or oppose him? Given the scope of the conflict, there is no neutral ground.

24-26—These verses are thus a warning that the **house** of Israel could end in a worse state than when Jesus undertook this raid of Satan's domain on their behalf. The lore of the demon seeking safe haven in **waterless places** (see comments on 8:33) reflects a profound respect for the tenacity of evil forces. If this could be true on the personal level, the salvation of the people could also be in jeopardy.

These prophetic oracles must be remembered as dire warnings to the people of God. They should never be used as vindictive attacks on the Jews by which Christians justify themselves. Their force in Luke's narrative, however, is to sound an alert that even as the light of Jesus' saving reign begins to dawn, the forces of opposition quickly begin to marshal their troops.

The Word of God (11:27-36). These verses at first appear to be a loose collection of traditional materials. No forceful connections are built into the narrative, and the pieces are diverse: an acclamation of blessing and a word of correction (vv. 27-28), "Q" warning sayings about **the sign of Jonah** coupled with two pronouncements about the **greater** one (vv. 29-32), and a composite group of sayings about **light** apparently drawn from different contexts in "Q" (v. 33: Matt. 5:15; vv. 34-36: Matt. 6:22-23). Nevertheless, the flow of the chapter is not lost. Luke has incorporated these pieces into an extended presentation of Jesus as a test and a sign to Israel. This presentation fits Luke's view of Jesus both as the "light for revelation to the Gentiles" to the "glory of Israel" and as the "sign spoken against" (2:32-34). Luke again explores the consequences of that **sign** and **light** for those who see and hear.

27-28—Using a traditional blessing, **a woman in the crowd** praises Jesus by declaring the blessedness of his mother in the very physical terms of childbearing and nursing. The mention of **the womb that bore you, and the breasts that you sucked!** correctly prevents the tendencies of some Christian pieties to deny the reality of Jesus' human birth and physical needs. These words do not mean that in Luke women are only blessed by their ability to be mothers. On the contrary, Jesus' response to this "blessing" again stresses that the "blessedness" of Jesus' true "mother" and "family" (see 8:19-21) belongs to those who **hear the word of God and keep** (8:21, "do") **it.** The story of Jesus' annunciation clearly identified Jesus' mother Mary as one who heard the angel's "word of God" in faith, and her blessedness included her maternity (see 1:28, 48, 42: "Blessed are you among women, and blessed is the fruit of your womb!"). The story of Mary and Martha also emphasized the priority (10:42, "the good portion") of listening to the word of Jesus' teaching. This is the mark of true "blessedness" or "favor with God."

29-32—Luke now picks up a traditional saying from "Q" to mark the contrast to true "blessedness." Refusing to hear the word of God in repentance stands under condemnation. Luke sets the scene by declaring that Jesus spoke this word in the face of growing crowds. Matthew (12:38) indicates that it was "the scribes and Pharisees" who were seeking a sign (see also Mark 8:11-12). But in Luke, Jesus' reproof reaches back to 11:16 where "others, to test him, sought a sign from heaven." Now addressing the crowd, Jesus diagnoses the **evil** of **this generation** in terms of "not hearing" or "testing" the word of God's rule which he bears (see also the judgments on "this generation" in 7:31 and 9:41).

In Luke **the sign of Jonah** for the Ninevites is **Jonah** himself, and **the Son of man** is the sign which God has given **to this generation.** This traditional use of the term **Son of man** is for Luke a direct reference to Jesus. The future tense (**will be**) is best understood here as an indication of the confrontation which Jesus is and will be provoking. This hint of the future also fits with Jesus' impending mission: "the Son of man is to be delivered into the hands of men" (9:44; see 9:22; 18:31; Acts 2:23, "the hands of lawless men"). **Jonah** was the one who confronted **Nineveh** with the word of the Lord. His message and he were the **sign** God gave. For Luke, Jesus is "the sign spoken against" (2:34). Nothing is said about Jonah's three-day sojourn in the whale or Jesus' three days in the ground (Matt. 12:40). His person and his message are inseparable. To seek a sign from heaven is to reject the sign that he is and to refuse to hear the word he bears.

In the sequence of the next two sayings (contrast Matt. 12:41-42), the mention of the **queen of the South** precedes another reference to Jonah. Both sentences which follow are also linked back to v. 30 by the repetition of the words **this generation** (30, 31, 32). The coming of **the Son of man** to **this generation**, therefore, is an occasion of judgment. The **queen of the South** and **the men of Nineveh** become witnesses for the prosecution, indicting **this generation**. The parallel is forceful. If the Queen of Sheba (1 Kings 10:1-11) and the Ninevites came to believe and bless God (see 1 Kings 10:1-11) and even **repent** (Jonah 3:6-10) on the basis of Solomon's wisdom or Jonah's preaching, will they not condemn **this generation** since **something greater than Solomon/Jonah is here?**

33-36—Jesus is not only the "sign spoken against." He is also the "light for revelation to the Gentiles and for glory to thy people Israel" (2:32). Luke arranges the traditional sayings about the **light** and **lamp** so that the theme is sounded at the beginning (v. 33) and resumed at the end (v. 36). The one who is "something greater than Solomon/Jonah" brings God's "wisdom" and "word" to shed light and scatter darkness. Luke's conclusion of v. 32 emphasizes that one sets up a light in order that **those who enter may see the light.** Luke's persistent question of why people do or do not **see** is close at hand.

The physiology of "seeing" was understood differently in the ancient world, but their poetry still captures immediate human experience, just as when people still say that "the sun rises in the East." The "good eye" and the "evil eye" were thought to spread light or darkness throughout the body and mind of the person. This situation is described in Matthew's version (6:22-23) with the conclusion that "If then the light in you is darkness, how great is the darkness!" In Luke it is a word of warning: **Be careful lest the light in you be darkness!** As the beginning and ending emphasize, God sent this **light** to overcome darkness; or as Simeon says, to be the salvation of the Gentiles and the glory of Israel (see also Isa. 49:6).

When this light illumines, it encounters darkness as a power, a force with which to contend. The evil eye of an "evil generation" sheds this darkness abroad in the body. This is where the light confronts and uncovers the "secret thoughts of the heart" (2:35). When **your body is full of darkness,** it is not only difficult to see the light and to hear the word of God and keep it, but a battle is pitched.

The end of the passage, however, is not a word of judgment and gloom. Only Luke's version of these words about the good (Gk: *haplous:* clear, **sound,** healthy, guileless) eye ends with the promise of the complete banishment of darkness. The **something greater** of the kingdom will surpass Solomon's wisdom and Jonah's preaching in its power to invade the "palace" of Satan and to drive out the darkness (see 11:21). The illumination of this **light** is more than instruction or new data. It is the power of the Spirit of God bringing the salvation of the kingdom.

Woe to the Pharisees (11:37-54).   This series of encounters with people beyond the circle of Jesus' disciples (see 11:14-15, 27, 29) concludes with Jesus' sharp words of indictment against the **Pharisees** and their **lawyers.** The passage is a collection of **woes** drawn from the tradition (see Matthew 23), now organized by Luke into an extended **reproach** (v. 45) within the narrative context of Jesus' visit to the house of a Pharisee. Following directly upon Jesus' indictment of "this generation" (vv. 29-32) and the contrast between internal "light" and "darkness" (vv. 33-36), these words now diagnose the hypocrisy and uncleanness of Jesus' opponents. It is important to note that Matthew 23 reports these words of woe against the "scribes and Pharisees, hypocrites" collectively in the context of Jesus' last temple speech and shortly before his arrest (see also Luke 13:34-35 and Matt. 23:37-39). But Luke distinguishes the **lawyers** from the larger group of **Pharisees** and does not use the word "hypocrites." His warnings against the "scribes" in 20:45-47 also differ from Matthew's. Here Jesus' woes are warnings of implicit rejection rather than final verdicts as in Matthew.

The passage is structured around six "woes," three to the **Pharisees** and three to the **lawyers,** with preliminary words of warning to the Pharisees about their concerns for externals (vv. 39-41) and an expanded word to the "lawyers" about their complicity in the rejection and killing of the prophets (vv. 48-51). Jesus' general words of rebuke of the practices of the Pharisees (vv. 39-44) become even more severe when he addresses the interpreters of the Law (vv. 45-52), accusing them of perverting their calling as witnesses. Small wonder that the story which began with the Pharisee's hospitality (v. 37) concludes with the whole group seeking to provoke him into a grave mistake (vv. 53-54).

37-38—Jesus is in the house of **a Pharisee,** participating in their **table** fellowship once again (see 7:36-50). As will be especially apparent in Chap. 14, table fellowship is a sign of acceptance, even election, since it is limited to those who observe the scriptural food laws concerning what is clean and unclean. The "holiness" of Israel was closely tied to the separation of this people from those who ate meat sacrificed to idols or animals which the Levitical codes named as unclean. And the Pharisees were especially concerned with the details of such observance. The Pharisees were not aware of modern understandings of hygiene for the prevention of disease. Handwashing was a matter of ritual purification, of observance of the law of God. As Luke sets the scene, the only thing about Jesus that fills this Pharisee with "wonder" is that **he did not wash.** This is a theological issue. How could Jesus be a teacher of Israel, let alone **the Lord,** as Luke identifies him here?

39-41—Jesus' first words are in the form of an oracle of "woe" in Matt. 23:25-26, but in Luke they are a direct response to the host. The emphasis on what is going on "inside the body" continues from vv. 33-36. Actually Jesus speaks about **the outside of the cup and the dish,** which fits with the Pharisees' extension of matters of purity to the cleansing and storing of the tableware. But the **inside** and **outside** of the human vessel is the primary issue, as vv. 40-41 make clear.

The question is how the law and will of God are best observed, and Jesus is critical of the Pharisees' preoccupation with details of observance because it has just blinded them to him as the living fulfillment of the Law and the Prophets. To call them **fools** is particularly severe, since their goal was to be wise in their observance of the Law and not indifferent like the fools (see Ps. 14:1; Prov. 6:12). Jesus is entering into an argument which also was pursued among the Pharisees, and he is taking a strong position. External observance is secondary and will frequently lead to preoccupation with detail while missing what is crucial. At its core, the Law is simple, while still testing the heart of humanity. The sacrifice of a contrite heart (see Ps. 51:10, 17; see Luke 10:27) is the giving of alms, and all things are then clean on the outside (see also Mark 7:15, Rom. 14:14, 20, 23). The attempt to control the Law by a list of things to be done, even a long list, perverts the Law by missing the dynamic character of God's will and reign.

42-44—Now Jesus launches into the three **woes** against the **Pharisees.** These are prophetic denunciations, filled with the extravagance of prophetic indictment. Of course Jesus means what he says, but it is dangerous for others to read these words merely as a description of the Pharisees and thereby to "justify themselves" at the expense of the accused. Each item on this bill of particulars is specific to Pharisaic practices: careful **tithing** from the herb gardens, recognition as leaders in **the synagogues,** and concern for avoiding hidden pollutions even as they **walked.** Now all of these practices are cited against them. The charge is that they have neglected the heart of the Law, justice and the love of God, while busy with little observances.

It is painful when our "virtues" and "pieties" are exposed as hypocrisies, but Jesus speaks in accord with the old prophetic refrain denouncing false religion: "What does the Lord require of you but to do justice, and to love kindness, and to walk humbly with your God?" (Mic. 6:8; see Amos 5:23-24; Hos. 2:19-20; 6:6). **These** things **you ought to have done without neglecting the others** (v. 42). The crowning blow is the suggestion that these religious leaders themselves are **like** hidden **graves** which pollute others without their knowing it! This is not merely a charge against their own purity (see Matt. 23:27), but a warning of the hazard their inward impurity poses to others.

45-52—The second set of three woes is directed against the **lawyers** or authoritative interpreters of the Law of God. As Luke

introduces these oracles, their spokesman includes them in the
reproach against the Pharisees. The impression is that Luke sees
these words as a more harsh condemnation for the scholar class
among the Pharisees. Each of the woes is more elaborate.

The **woe** concerning the **loading** of people **with burdens hard
to bear** is echoed in Acts 15:10: "Why do you make trial of God
by putting a yoke upon the neck of the disciples which neither
our fathers nor we have been able to bear?" In Acts this is not a
rejection of the Law itself, but it is a charge that they have made
the Law a "yoke" and a "burden." It is a response to the "believers
who belonged to the party of the Pharisees" who were insisting
on circumcision for all Gentiles (Acts 15:5). That is, Christian
Pharisees had continued to regard certain observances as necessary for inclusion in the people of God or for salvation. Peter's
speech concludes (Acts 15:11) with a testimony to salvation by
"the grace of the Lord Jesus" for both Jews and Gentiles. That
meant the burden of the Law had been lifted and people were
not required to bear it to be saved.

In Luke 11:46, the **woe** has the edge of indicting the authoritative interpreters for increasing the burden without interest in
helping the people keep the Law. It is the religious leaders who
have made God's Law more oppressive for people while being
unwilling to lift a finger for them. The scholasticism of the scriptural interpreters appears to be receiving the brunt of the attack,
and the scholars and learned students of every generation should
take notice.

The second of the woes against the **lawyers** is even more expanded, building in intensity through v. 51. Again this is a traditional prophetic indictment. Jeremiah 7:25-26 had already
warned, "From the day that your fathers came out of the land of
Egypt to this day, I have persistently sent all my servants the
prophets to them, day after day; yet they did not listen to me,
or incline their ear, but stiffened their neck. They did worse than
their fathers." In Deuteronomy 31–34, Moses recited the history
of Israel as a testimony against them, and this refrain is carried
further in Stephen's speech in Acts 7:51-52: "You stiff-necked
people . . . you always resist the Holy Spirit. As your fathers did,
so do you. Which of the prophets did not your fathers persecute?

And they killed those who announced beforehand the coming of the Righteous One, whom you have now betrayed and murdered." This is not an anti-Jewish polemic. It is a classic prophetic indictment and call to repentance. Israel knew well that the struggle of wills between God and the people had a long history.

But now this charge is tailored for the interpreters of the Law. How did they **build the tombs of the prophets** and become complicit in the rejection and killing of God's messengers? They were to be **witnesses** for God and God's righteous will (see Isaiah 43–44; 49; Deut. 6:20-25) lest God's prophet be a witness against them (Deut. 31:19-22). The precedent of **Zechariah** is such a case: his prophetic testimony provoked a conspiracy to murder him, and the threat of divine vengeance was declared (2 Chron. 24:19-22). These **lawyers** have again sealed up the testimony, perhaps with convoluted interpretation.

The role of **Wisdom** is noteworthy. Wisdom is presented as an agent, almost an independent being alongside of God. This reflects the personified Wisdom of Proverbs (1:20-33; Chap. 8) and the Wisdom of Solomon (Chap. 7, see also Luke 7:35). It is she who sends **prophets and apostles** and messengers of God's reign, but they encounter only persecution and deadly rejection. God's wrath will then surely be visited on the perpetrators ("be required of this generation").

This theme will reappear throughout Luke-Acts. It is pre-Lukan tradition, but it is also basic to the evangelist's conviction that the fate of Jerusalem and Israel are at stake in Jesus' mission. If the people of God are found to be complicit in the death of a righteous person or a prophet, it will be grave. And if it is the one who is Messiah and Lord, then what will God do (see Acts 2:36-37)? Only repentance and faith in the name of the Lord Jesus can save.

The third **woe** again brings the offense of the interpreters front and center. This is how they participate in the rejection of God's prophets and apostles. They do not open the testimony of the Scriptures, but lock it away in regulations or obscurities. Instead of helping people bear the burden of the Law, they add to it. Instead of being witnesses to God's righteous will, they fight the messengers. Instead of opening the **scriptures** they seal them away under their control. Alas, the calling of each generation of religious leaders has become the list of charges against them.

53-54—These verses are Luke's narrative conclusion to this harsh recitation of woes. It is not a surprise to see that Jesus' prophetic words are themselves a prophecy, fulfilled as soon as they are uttered. The long shadow of the prophetic words about those who kill and persecute God's ambassadors also reaches forward to the passion narrative. Luke does not say that the Pharisees were planning to kill Jesus, nor does he later include them with Jesus' adversaries at his trial and death. But they are now "building the tomb" at least by their setting themselves in a posture of trying to catch him in what he says. The forces of opposition are gathering strength.

He Calls for Readiness and Repentance (12:1—13:21)

This section is an extended presentation of Jesus' teaching of his disciples and the multitudes. It is not tightly structured, but moves along by persistently identifying the audience of succeeding portions: **He began to say to his disciples first** (v. 1), **"I tell you, my friends"** (v. 4), **one of the multitude said to him** (v. 13), **he said to his disciples** (v. 22), **"Lord, are you telling this parable for us or for all?"** (v. 41), **he also said to the multitudes** (v. 54), and **some present at that very time. . . . He answered them** (13:1). It is a collection of of teaching materials which has been largely drawn from "Q" and Luke's own traditions.

These teachings follow the troubling disclosures of opposition to Jesus (11:14-54). The story is still filled with urgency, but now it is elaborating what Jesus' mission means to the faithful. No easy path is promised. Genuine struggle and trials lie ahead for Jesus' disciples as well as for him. Nevertheless, the key to the whole section probably lies in a word of Jesus which only Luke conveys: **"Fear not, little flock, for it is your Father's good pleasure to give you the kingdom"** (12:32).

The reader is never reminded within this lengthy section that Jesus is still journeying to Jerusalem. There is also no suggestion that this is one continuous "speech." The ease with which these traditional sayings may be pulled out of their literary context may itself be a signal that their occasional character is still preserved in Luke. These are materials which were recited in various situations and sequences as the community interpreted its own experiences. Conflicts with the synagogues (v. 11), anxiety about food and clothing (v. 22), and division in families (vv. 51-53) probably were immediate problems in the Christian communities which preserved these sayings. Perhaps the evangelist did not need to do much more than rehearse these "words of the Lord to his followers" as instructions in discipleship.

Still, the literary context of Luke's narrative offers an interpretation of these sayings as words for those who are following the "way of the Lord" (see comments on 9:51). Thus Jesus' teaching in 10:25—11:13 has led to his encounter with opposition (11:14-54). This second teaching section (12:1—13:21) then speaks to the faithful before the mission to Jerusalem resumes (13:22). The literary device of following the journey is strained, but not broken.

Hidden and Revealed (12:1-12).   This section is a collection of sayings which explores several dimensions of what is **hidden** and **revealed** (vv. 1-3), who only appears to have power over people and who truly does (vv. 4-7), and when public confession of Jesus will be required (vv. 8-12). The Pharisees have just been criticized (11:37-53) for their actual pollution under the guise of a concern for purity. Things are not as they seem for the disciples either, but for them disclosure is to be welcomed. Even if the religious authorities and rulers seek Jesus' followers out in order to expose them (vv. 2-3), kill them (vv. 4-7), or bring charges against them, there is nothing to fear. These are opportunities for witness, and the power of the Holy Spirit is at work.

1-4—Verse 1 is a transition, linking the sayings which follow directly to the harsh encounters with the Pharisees and lawyers. A new phase has clearly begun, and the evangelist has marked the transition with a summary statement about the immensity of the crowds. The mention of "myriads" (RSV: **many thousands**) is directly paralleled in Acts 21:20 where again "tens of thousands" of Jews are "believers," that is, Christian Jews who observe the

Law. Luke is fond of reporting impressive numbers (see Acts 2:41; 4:4; 5:14; 6:1, 7; 9:31; 11:21, 24; 12:24; 14:1; 16:5; 17:4, 12; 19:10, 19-20, 26; 28:23). Here the growing press of the crowds begins to compound the danger to Jesus because of the animosity of Pharisees who are lying in wait for him (11:53-54; see also 19:48; 20:6; 22:1-6).

Jesus' word **"Beware of the leaven of the Pharisees"** is traditional, reflecting customary Jewish views of the impurity of leaven (see Exod. 12:14-20). In Mark 8:15, the "leaven of the Pharisees and the leaven of Herod" is interpreted as hardness of heart. Matthew 16:6, 11 warns of the leaven of the Pharisees and the Sadducees, which is then identified as "the teaching of the Pharisees and the Sadducees." But in Luke, Jesus is not elaborating on the failings of their teaching, but warning his disciples against **hypocrisy.**

The sayings about **revealing,** making **known,** and **hearing in the light** and public proclamation from **the housetops** are thus words to the disciples about their own sincerity. The hidden **hypocrisy of the Pharisees** is only an object lesson, and Jesus' words from "Q" which appear in a very different context in Matthew (10:26-33) move beyond the conflict to instruction to his followers to avoid deception and cover-up. These sayings would bear repeating merely as good political counsel, but the persistent use of the passive voice (**will be revealed, be known, be heard, be proclaimed**) is prophetic. God will do the revealing.

4-7—Jesus is now speaking to his **friends** (only in Luke). In John 15:13-15 the significance of Jesus' disciples being his "friends" is elaborated in terms of his close relationship with God, just as the Stoic philosphers spoke of the "sage" as a true "friend of the gods" and as a "spy of god" in the world. Jesus' **friends** are thus more than his "personal friends." They are colleagues with Jesus in God's mission, and they need to know the truth about whom to fear and whom not to fear.

In "Q," Jesus' words were already clustered around the verbs **do not fear** (v. 4) . . . **but fear** (v. 5) . . . **fear not** (v. 7). It appears that Luke has elaborated this theme at the beginning and end of v. 5 by the additional words of Jesus, **"I will warn you whom to fear . . . yes, I tell you, fear this one!"** (see also v. 11, "Do not be anxious!"). Similarly the specific assurance at the end of v. 6 that none are **forgotten before God** is probably a Lukan emphasis. The evangelist is highlighting the point that everything takes place *coram deo*, in the presence of God. God is the one **to fear.** Nothing may be hidden from God (vv. 2-3), and God's reign and authority extend beyond life itself.

The point of the section, however, is clearly not to intimidate the disciples, but to assure them in the face of intimidation. People who threaten others with death always attempt to destroy all human dignity. They treat innocent people like "vermin" or birds for target practice, and they demean their bodies. Finally they will seek to take away human hope, for that is the final touch with life. Often through history such tyrants have slaughtered the victims' children before their eyes so that they would die knowing that there would be no one left even to remember them.

Behind these counsels to the believers to **fear not** lay real experiences of intimidation and killing, and the assurances address exactly such terrors: there is still a life and a judgment to come, they are not forgotten, and **even the hairs on their head are numbered.** All of this is in the form of second person address, so that it is not merely a description or a doctrine, but a word to **you** who know such fears. Perhaps the Christians in Luke's community knew such terrors themselves, but certainly these words of the Lord have spoken immediately and directly to martyrs of subsequent generations.

At the same time, the Christian teachings of future judgment and life after death are anchored in this passage (including vv. 8-12) and many like it. The hope of resurrection is grounded in the faith in God's justice which will vindicate those who suffer and die at the hands of cruel and godless people. It is an "apocalyptic" hope both in the sense that it is found in those passages which predict a future judgment, but also because resurrection is a final "uncovering" of the truth. All hypocrisy, deceit, and covert violence will be disclosed at once. Not only is all of life conducted in the open before God (vv. 2-3), but those who seek to play God by arbitrarily persecuting the innocent and even killing the witnesses to God's reign will not prevail. These persecuted ones are the **friends** of Jesus and of God, of much more value than the oppressors could ever see, and God will yet convene the heavenly court (see also Daniel 7 and 11 and Rev. 20:4-6).

8-12—Luke has masterfully combined the first two verses (vv. 8-9//Matt. 10:32-33) from "Q" with two other traditional sayings of Jesus concerning the "sin against the Holy Spirit" (v. 10//Mark 3:28-30//Matt. 12:31-32) and the promise of the assistance of the Holy Spirit (vv. 11-12//Mark 13:11//Matt. 10:19-20). All of the material is traditional, but Luke offers a further exposition of the connection between the confrontation with the human courts of judgment and the divine court. Like Isaiah 6 before him, Luke's picture of this heavenly court is enhanced with the attending angels of God (vv. 8, 9; see also 15:10, "joy before the angels of God").

In Matt. 10:32-33, Jesus speaks in the first person, "Everyone who confesses me, . . . I will confess. . . . Everyone who denies me, . . . I will deny." In Luke, the subject of the second clause is **the Son of man: "Every one who acknowledges me . . . the Son of man also will acknowledge. . . .** Everyone **who denies me . . . will be denied."** Perhaps Luke is merely reciting the tradition, and all that is meant is that **the Son of man** is a synonym for *Jesus.* The term **Son of man** is also used in two similar passages in Luke where it is lacking in Matthew: 6:22 (Matt. 5:11, "me"); 9:22//Mark 8:31 (Matt. 16:21, "he"). In Matt. 16:21, the term "Son of man" is dropped from the Markan (8:31; see Luke 9:22) material, and thus Matthew may have again avoided the term in this context while Luke preserved it from "Q."

In Luke, the term **Son of man** is more than a synonym for "I," since the role of the Son of man in judgment (Daniel 7) is so crucial to the whole context. As will become clear in 17:24-25, Jesus is that Danielic Son of man in Luke's Gospel. Thus Luke would not object to understanding that these references to the Son of man mean Jesus, but this is Jesus in a specific role, as eschatological judge.

Christians are called to speak out, to testify, to confess Jesus, probably in public contexts of trial. Verse 11 indicates that they must be ready to speak this word before **synagogues, rulers,** and **authorities.** This is consistent with the charge to the disciples in Acts 1:8, "You shall be my witnesses," and numerous scenes in

Acts show that the testimony to Jesus as Messiah and Lord could involve legal and physical peril. But to be silent would be to "oppose God" (see Acts 4:19-20; 5:39).

The most complex and difficult aspect of this text is the distinction between the assurance that forgiveness may be given even for speaking **a word against the Son of man,** while **the blaspheming of the Holy Spirit** is unforgiveable. Within Luke-Acts, Peter's threefold denial of Jesus causes great remorse (22:62), but Jesus already anticipated his "turning again" when he predicted Peter's denial (22:32). On the other hand, Ananias and Sapphira were struck dead for "lying to God" and "tempting the Spirit of the Lord" (Acts 5:4,9), and Simon the magician verged close to the unforgiveable sin by trying to buy the "power" or "gift" of "receiving the Holy Spirit" (8:19-24). In Mark 3:29, blaspheming the Holy Spirit is understood to be committed by those who charge Jesus with having an unclean spirit. In Matt. 12:32, speaking against the Holy Spirit is itself the unforgivable sin.

In Luke, where the dynamic character of the Spirit's role is so thoroughly developed, it appears that **blaspheming against the Holy Spirit** is committed by the misuse of the power of the Spirit or the challenge of the power of the Spirit. These are not merely problems of the disciples failing to fulfill the commission, but of attempts to usurp or co-opt the authority and power of the Holy Spirit.

The presence of the Holy Spirit is not merely an otherworldly reality. It is the very means of the earthly exercise of the dominion of the exalted Lord Jesus. The power at work is awesome. But the assurance of the concluding promise of this passage also rests in that strength. The Holy Spirit is not to be taken for granted or tempted or used like a private possession. People do not possess the Holy Spirit when they have received the gift.

But the Holy Spirit does possess or dwell in them. The Spirit remains present with them, even providing the counsel and words when the time of their testing comes (21:12-19). In Acts 4:8, Peter's speech on trust before the "rulers of the people and the elders" is directly inspired by the Holy Spirit, and the "boldness" of such "uneducated, common men" as James and John causes the rulers to wonder (4:13). Thus Luke is confident of the continuing power and presence of the Holy Spirit with those who bear witness to the lordship of Jesus even in the face of vicious charges or death.

The Peril of Wealth (12:13-21).   Between assurances to the disciples against anxious concern (vv. 11-12, 22-30), Luke interposes another section of warnings. In vv. 1-12, Jesus was contrasting the folly of fearing persecutors with the wisdom of fearing God and assuring his followers of God's abiding concern for them. Now the question is not whom to fear, but whom or what to trust. Where is the source of true security and treasure? Once again, the warnings come first.

The discourse has apparently been assembled by Luke out of diverse traditional sources of the sayings of Jesus. Verses 13-15 were probably an independent memory piece, a typical question-and-answer dialog with the teacher which ends in two pronouncements. One is a word of direct address, "Beware of greed!" and the other is a proverbial saying which explicates the warning, "Life does not consist in the surplus of possessions!" The story of the "rich fool" which follows is then used by Luke as an object lesson which directly illustrates the proverb. This is a "parable" in the general sense of a morality story, but it also begins to transform the world of moral advice. (See the discussion of Jesus' most distinctive usage of "parables" in Luke 15).

This moral instruction is not especially original with Jesus. Its force is even enhanced by the recognition that the wisdom traditions and psalms of Israel constantly warned against the false security of wealth. The Greek and Latin moralists did the same. A few samples from Israel's heritage must suffice to indicate that Jesus' teachings were fully in accord with the scriptural conviction that wealth could delude people into false confidence. Psalm 39:6 and Eccles. 2:18-19 caution that all the wealth people gather together will be left to others at death. Sirach 11:18-19 is almost a paraphrase of this parable, but written two centuries before Christ: "There is a man who is rich . . . when he says, 'I have found rest, and now I shall enjoy my goods!' he does not know how much time will pass until he leaves them to others and dies."

(See also 1 Enoch 97:8-10 and 1 Samuel 25, where the rich fool "Nabal" rejects King David, feasts and drinks like a king, and dies.)

13-15—Jesus is addressed as **Teacher** and asked to be the "divider" (see the Gospel of Thomas 72) of an estate. This serious business of adjudicating estates has never been easy, as any probate attorney knows. In first-century Palestine, the traditional "laws" which governed such disputes were scriptural, especially Num. 27:8-11 and Deut. 21:16-17. The "teachers of the law" were thus also the "lawyers" in the public sense of probating estates.

This appears to be a detail rather directly conveyed from the memory of the historical Jesus, and it is fascinating that Jesus refused the role of **judge or divider.** He clearly had no reservation about claiming authority as an interpreter of the Scriptures, and the Gospels are confident of his role as the Son of man who will exercise God's final judgment. Furthermore, Jesus is consistently portrayed as concerned with justice, especially for the poor and the widow before the unrighteous judge (18:1-8). It is idle to guess whether Jesus thought this petitioner was undeserving or whether he thought the whole case was only a greedy fight and thus refused to take sides.

In Luke's narrative, however, Jesus, who is the Messiah and Son of man as well as the teacher of the Law, does not usurp the existing structures for resolving such questions. He rather takes the request as an occasion for a warning, and he remains in the role of a teacher. The division of estates is too often the source of divided families because of jealousy and greed, and the meaning of life begins to be measured in the quantity of possessions. Once again the scene is portrayed against the broader canvas of divine judgment, and the hazard that "I might not get my share!" pales next to the peril posed by jealously and greed to the meaning and worth of **life** itself.

16-21—Greed is one of the perils of wealth, but the delusion of security is another. The previous exchange came to a focus on what is the substance of **life** (Gk: *zōē*, v. 15) and these verses revolve around the close synonym "soul" (Gk: *psychē*, vv. 19-20). Here the rich fool even talks to his **soul** and says, "**Soul** . . .," advising his *psychē* that enough is enough! It is time to take it

233

easy and enjoy! He is not a picture of endless greed. He is not commended for tearing down his storehouses to build larger ones, but neither is he condemned for that, at least not directly. The foolishness of the man is that he thinks this hoard is enough to bring security and happiness to his **soul.**

Wrong! The soul is not merely his own concern, and he could never accumulate enough to bring security to his soul. He is not the one to give it orders, because it is not his own possession or under his control. Of course when God **requires** his soul, he dies; and all of his earthly goods falls into the hands of others. But the question of what happens to all the hoard (**whose will they be?**) is quite secondary. The **fool** did not understand that God would "ask back" his soul, to which he was giving such bad counsel about security and pleasure.

The last line substitutes **himself** for **his soul** and indicates the ultimate folly of listening to this man talk to himself. He had done an excellent job of looking out for **himself** (his **soul,** his *psychē*), even knowing enough to quit accumulating. His foolishness was not mere greed, but self-concern, "enlightened self-interest," that could not see beyond the self. Even his "self-understanding" turned out to be foolishness rather than wisdom because it blinded him to the truth. His life, his soul—he—was accountable to God.

The Security and Treasure of the Kingdom (12:22-34). Most of these sayings come directly from "Q," but they have particular promise in this context in Luke. Read directly after the warnings against the dangers of greed (vv. 13-15) and false security (vv. 16-21), they are assurances of God's promise of adequate supplies (vv. 22-31) and true security (vv. 32-34). Furthermore, these verses conclude by harking back to the counsel at the beginning of the chapter about appropriate and inappropriate "fearing" (Gk: *phobeomai;* vv. 4, 5, 7, and 32). Inside that beginning and ending, the theme of "not being anxious" is picked up again from the conclusion of the first section (Gk: **merimnao;** vv. 11, 22, 25, 26). These are words of consolation for Jesus' followers (v. 22: "he said to his disciples") as they venture into the life of trusting God along the way. The conclusion of the whole section, therefore, is the promise of God's gift of the kingdom (v. 32) as the basis of freedom from need to hang on to possessions (vv. 33-34).

22—The logic of the section is announced with **therefore,** which ties these words back to the negative examples which precede, but also forward to the appeals which Jesus is about to make. Why should Jesus' followers not be **anxious** about the "soul" (Gk: *psychē,* note that the RSV has translated this as **life)** or the **body?** If the previous story proved anything by its negative example it is that neither body nor soul may finally be secured by human efforts (see the parallel between "soul" and "life" in that passage). And Jesus had just said that "life is more than an abundance of possessions" (v. 14). **Therefore,** all that follows is a further explication of vv. 13-21.

23—The case is also developed positively. First, **life** is interpreted in terms of both **body** and "soul" (Gk: *psychē).* The RSV may make the right decision in translating *psychē* again as **life,** since in modern usage the word "soul" is filled with all kinds of nonbiblical notions of dualism and immortal "sparks." The English cognate "psyche" also misses the point since it often implies only "psychological" states. What is shocking here is that Jesus speaks about the "soul" (Gk: *psychē)* as where the **food** goes, and the *body* (Gk: *sōma)* as where the **clothes** are worn. Clearly the larger concern is with the substance of **life,** body and soul, inside and outside. And the point is that human life is more than a matter of fulfilling needs. Life is certainly not quantitatively or qualitatively enhanced by more and more attention to creature comforts or the pursuits of luxury. It is not only impossible to finally secure body and soul **(life)** with "enough" (see vv. 16-21), but anxious concern for more and more will not benefit body or soul or keep them together.

24—The ravens are an object lesson in the second reason why disciples should not be anxious about **food** and **clothing.** Not only is there more to life, but God provides. There may even be an irony in the fact that **the ravens** were regarded as unclean birds (Lev. 11:15; Deut. 14:14; see "the Gentiles" in Luke 12:30). The rich fool tore down his barns to build yet larger ones, but the ravens do not have **barns** or **storehouses** for hoarding against the future. Once again (see 12:7), people are more **valuable** to God than **birds**. This is not a discussion about the preservation of endangered species of birds. This is a word of consolation to people who may feel very endangered themselves. It is also not a cavalier statement from a wealthy ruler who remains untouched by suffering: "God will provide! Let them eat cake!" It is a testimony from the Messiah whose own life was imperiled by privation and violence, and it is transmitted in a narrative which is filled with the reality of suffering as well as the confidence of faith.

25-26—The third point in the case against anxiety is that it is not effective anyway. Something seems to have been obscured in the strange mixed metaphor about not being able to add a **cubit** (18 inches) to one's "height" (**span of life**), but the point is clear that people often worry about things that are beyond their control. Perhaps only parents of adolescent boys who try to stuff themselves with food in order to grow very tall would understand the futility which this saying expresses.

27-28—Now the argument moves back to clothing, and the splendor of the wildflowers is the object lesson. It is another argument from proportion. The brevity of the life of vegetation is a common scriptural theme for speaking of the transitory human life (Job 8:12; Ps. 37:2; 90:5-6; 103:15-16; Isa. 37:27; 40:6-8). But now the traditional point is altered to emphasize that even such passing forms of life are gloriously clothed. All the fretting over fashion in the world will not match what God does with the disposable grasses of the field.

29-30—The fifth point begins by restating the issue of anxiety in very specific terms (v. 29), and then two arguments are stated as one. The fact that **the nations** (Gk: *ethnē*) **of the world seek these things** could be a negative judgment. The RSV translates the same phrase in Matt. 6:32 as "for the Gentiles seek these things," and it is clear from Matt. 5:47 that what the "Gentiles" do is no standard for the disciples. In Luke 6:32-34, a similar contrast is drawn between what "sinners" and disciples do. Even if Luke is speaking about **Gentiles** here, the point is that all human beings **seek these things,** but the disciples no longer need to be anxious. Only Luke specifically tells them not to be anxious (RSV: **nor be of anxious mind**). They may understand that God knows they need them.

31—The promise again at the end of the argument makes it all work. Simply telling people not to be anxious or to be content with their lot in life like the birds or the grass could be a cruel, if sentimental deceit. Jesus does not trivialize human needs of food and clothing, of "life/soul" and body. God feeds the birds, and adorns the vegetation in grandeur. But God's way of caring for humanity, God's reign and **kingdom** will be done on God's terms. This reign is not another scheme to get rich or to dominate the world. Nor is it a new spiritual asceticism by which an elite corps of the "poor" will conquer. Its strength is hidden in its being the work of God, and trust in God's promise, faith, is the way of the Messiah and his disciples. Luke is not yet concerned with the possibility of a spiritual elite of the poor so much as with the more obvious human drive to "take yours while there is still some left" or look out for ourselves first and always.

32-34—Now the theme of the whole section (12:1—13:21) is sounded with Luke's crucial addition to Jesus' teachings from "Q:" **"Fear not, little flock, for it is your Father's good pleasure to give you the kingdom."** This wondrous assurance rings out like a hymn. It is linked to the immediate context by the words **Father** and **kingdom** (vv. 30, 31). While the masculine term offends modern gender-conscious ears—for important reasons—the strength and gentle grace of this promise must not be lost (see also "Father" in 11:2). This is not a demand from an oppressive "father figure," but an earnest desire of a loving parent (see also God's "good pleasure" for humanity in 2:14; 10:21).

Even the **kingdom** is not an achievement to be sought, but a gift to be received. Thus the "seeking" for the kingdom which was taught in "Q" (v. 31) is interpreted in terms of a gift to the flock which God intends to bestow. In Acts 20:29, Luke's Paul is keenly aware that the "flock" itself will be under attack. Even as a gift, the kingdom of God does not come without tribulation (see Acts 14:22). So also the simple life of the witnesses to the kingdom who sell their possessions and give alms (see also 10:3-12) will certainly involve conflict with authorities and systems. But God's way of ruling in heaven and on earth has been revealed to proceed from God's gift and grace. Because of God's initiative in Jesus, those who follow this Messiah may live with such hope rather than with persistent human anxieties.

The **treasure in the heavens,** therefore, is an act of earthly faith, living in confidence of the present reality of God's kingdom while it is still contested. It is an investment strategy concerning what will last and what is truly worthwhile. This is not a "heavenly mindedness" which is no "earthly good." It is an earthly faith in the kingdom of righteousness and mercy which Jesus has inaugurated. The ethics of this faith are also stated quite literally here, but not as a way to produce the kingdom. They are rather a real possiblity because in Christ Jesus, the kingdom has been given.

This reign may well seem foolish and vulnerable by the standards of those who have wealth and power, but it is the very strength of God for living in uncertain times with the security of the God's reign. And when this Messiah had been crucified, vindicated, and exalted as Lord and Savior, Luke's testimony could declare that the kingdom had been inaugurated.

Be Ready! (12:35-48).   The interpretation of this section has been subject to much debate concerning its themes of "readiness" and "delay." Clearly most of these sayings were traditional, and scholars debate which of them probably go back to Jesus himself. Others investigate this section as a primary source for the "eschatology of 'Q,' " because of the high verbal agreement here between Matthew and Luke. Lukan scholarship has also treated these verses as a fundamental statement of Luke's conviction of "the delay of the parousia." According to that interpretation, these "words of Jesus" are now less reminiscences of what Jesus said, although Jesus may indeed have said such things. And they are less recitations of the "sayings" tradition of prophetic words of the Lord which the church recites, although early Christian "prophets" and "teachers" probably did proclaim these sayings to their own times. Rather these words are best understood by a careful assessment of the way Luke has modified them and placed them in his story. Thus they are now a proclamation to Luke's own community, addressing the problem of the delay in

Jesus' return with renewed calls for readiness in prospect of coming judgment.

All of these approaches have been instructive for understanding the wealth of meaning such sayings had in those early decades when they were remembered, transmitted, and recorded by Christian evangelists. Furthermore, the scriptural overtones in the sayings frequently mark their theological nuance, indicating how the words of Jesus and the scriptural "words of God" were used to interpret each other.

But this commentary bends every effort to understand what such traditional sayings mean within the narrative or plot of Luke's story itself. Perhaps the evangelist as a redactor has altered the tradition to speak a word to the problems of the church, but it is risky to read each "change" as a direct word to Luke's church. Rather as a narrator Luke has consistently gathered up these words of Jesus into the beginning, middle, and end of the story. This narrative context is directly accessible to the interpreter even if the historical context may only be indirectly inferred. Thus even in this section where the traditional sayings appear to be only loosely "collected," the reader must first seek to understand what these words mean within Luke's story of Jesus. Then the possible significance for Luke's church of such a telling may be explored.

In this context, the call for readiness sounded in these sayings belongs to the urgency of the "hidden and revealed" reign of God. Both the immediate disciples and the larger multitude have been instructed in whom to fear and what not to, what is worth single-mindedness and what anxieties should be forgotten. And now the concern for readiness and watchfulness will be focused on the building tension of Jesus' kingdom campaign as it heads for Jerusalem. Now these words are prophetic, anticipating the coming of the crisis of the "visitation" (see 19:44). In the context of Luke's story, only the ignorant and unfaithful are deluded by apparent delay. These are all words to the faithful, revealing Jesus' sense of determination and alerting the faithful and the reader that the time of the kingdom is already unfolding.

35-38—Jesus moves immediately into these words of alert. He has just spoken about the hazards of wealth and the freedom to live without possessions, and his call for readiness needs no other introduction. Israel had been instructed long before about eating the Passover with "your loins girded, your sandals on your feet and your staff in your hand" (Exod. 12:11), like a firefighter sleeping in full dress. This state of preparation would also be excellent counsel for the church of Luke's time (or the present), since the master could come at any time. But in the story, this counsel is a direct clue that now is the time to be "watchful," for the Lord is the one in charge of the timing.

Only Luke recites these sayings. Perhaps Matt. 24:42 is an abbreviation of these three verses from "Q" or perhaps Luke expanded on the one verse found in Matthew. But the whole point so far in Luke is positive. These servants are **blessed** (vv. 37, 38; see also the disciples in 10:23). The kingdom is to be a gift (v. 32), and the faithful servants will be so blessed that the lord (vv. 36, 37; Gk: *kyrios*, RSV: **master**) will even put on his apron at the oddest hour and serve the servants. Of course, this is exactly what Jesus does in the meal in Luke 22:14-28 along with considerable discussion about Jesus as the one who serves rather than "exercising lordship" over them. The disciples, however, do not do so well then at remaining awake (22:39-46).

39-40—These sayings are almost verbatim with Matt. 24:43-44. Clearly Luke did not merely invent these sayings to fulfill a narrative objective, and these "Q" sayings explore the negative side of the call to be on alert. Certainly this warning about the unknown time of the coming of the Son of man was understood by many in the early church to be a reference to the "second coming" or return of Jesus. This expectation was also directly supported by Luke's account of Jesus "departure" into heaven (Acts 1:11), and it was connected with Jesus' role as the reigning Son of man as revealed in Stephen's vision (Acts 7:56).

It is noteworthy that the warnings in these sayings are all based on the conviction of the last phrase: **for the Son of man is coming at an unexpected hour.** This statement is verbatim in Matthew, and it also fits directly with Jesus' last words on earth in Acts: "It is not for you to know the times or seasons which the Father has fixed by his own authority. But you shall receive power . . . and . . . be my witnesses . . . ." (Acts 1:7-8). Matthew and Luke agree explicitly with the Jesus tradition that speculations about God's timetable are faithless and fruitless. Readiness does not mean second-guessing, but faithfulness in service and constancy in witness. Those who are charged with guarding the house or the flock (see Paul in Acts 20:25-35) must remain at their posts for the duration of their watch. Neither the thief in the night nor the Son of man intends to provide advance clues so that half-hearted watchfulness will suffice. And if the unexpected **thief** is a fearsome adversary, how much more **the master** who is expected but who comes **at an unexpected hour!**

41—This verse is unique to Luke, and it locks these sayings into Luke's narrative by means of a favorite Lukan rhetorical device, the leading question. To whom is Jesus speaking? As noted at the beginning of this section (12:1), Luke persistently identifies the differing audiences of these words of Jesus (see 12:1, 4, 13, 22, 41, 54; 13:1). But now the question is open, answered only by Jesus' further question in v. 42. In Luke's story, these words of warning follow the words of assurance of God's care for the "little flock," and thus they are primarily counsel to the immediate circle of Jesus' disciples. But Peter's question escalates the signficance of Jesus' words, for they clearly have consequence for all people. Suddenly Peter's insightful question includes the readers along with the disciples in the story, for we find ourselves addressed (see also 20:19). Yes, the faithful had better be ready, and they have been warned (see v. 47). But the truth of Jesus' reign is not a private matter, and all the world needs to know this truth.

42-48—Now resuming the use of the "Q" traditions of Jesus' words, Luke presents Jesus' question as the answer to Peter's question. To whom is Jesus speaking? "You tell me! Who will it be?" says Jesus. Only in Luke does Jesus speak in the future tense, and later in the narrative (22:28-30), Jesus appoints the Twelve to their offices. And in Acts 6 the restored Twelve will further delegate the tasks of distributing daily portions to those in need.

The feudal images of **lord** and **master** and **servants** and **stewards** which abound in this material (see also 19:12-27; 20:9-18) are shocking to modern sensibilities. Betrayal of trust and abuse of authority among subordinates are still well known, but physical beatings and mismanagement with lavish parties seem excessive. So also the idea that **the master** would administer more **beatings** (or even kill his enemies, as in 19:27) on his return offends many readers. But the point is that Jesus intended to shock his hearers with extreme examples drawn from the culture of their own experience. The stakes are this high. The faithful and wise manager will be vindicated by the master and given even more responsibility (vv. 42-44), but those who betray their trust can expect a harsh judgment befitting their betrayal.

Verses 45-46, derived from "Q", describe the behavior of unfaithfulness and indicate that **punishment** will follow. Once again only the wicked servant speaks of the master's **delay** in coming (see also 19:11-26). Yet Luke is not particularly interested in the servant's miscalculation. His abuse of his authority is rather the specific concern.

In vv. 47-48, Luke expands on the theme, moving beyond the tradition in "Q". The passive voice of the verbs (**shall receive a severe/a light beating . . . to whom much is given . . . will much be required**) further explicates the punishing work of the master (v. 46). God or the Son of man will mete out punishment appropriate to the offense. This differentiation of punishment intensifies the peril of Jesus' words especially for those of **us** who are on the inside (see v. 41) because those who have the advantage of "knowing" also have a responsibility that exceeds that of the ignorant.

This concept of levels of accountability and culpability is certainly not original with Luke. The proverbial character of the concluding statements indicates that such notions were not even original with Jesus. But such aphorisms gain new force when understood within Jesus' charge to his disciples. This is not merely a statement that those who have more to work with can be expected to produce more. Luke would agree with such a view (see 19:11-27). But this is a charge to Jesus' followers that the "blessing" of having seen and heard what they have (see 10:23-24) also entails a heightened responsibility before God and the Son of man. And within Luke's story, the "knowledge of the will of God" is the central revelation. In the speeches in Acts (see

3:17; 17:30), Peter and Paul will also indicate that repentance and forgiveness are given by God to those who acted in "ignorance," even in killing the Messiah. But once the truth has been proclaimed and made known, the peril of more severe judgment increases.

The Time of Judgment (12:49-59). These last verses in the chapter are Luke's gathering of Jesus' words of judgment. There is no relief, nor is there any response from Peter or the multitudes or Jesus' adversaries throughout this section. The force of each set of sayings is compounded by this context. Whether Jesus is speaking "to us or to all" (v. 41), he is revealing that the "will and plan" of God is at work in him as a driving power which wreaks division among people (vv. 49-53). People would do well to catch on, to observe what is happening before their very eyes (vv. 54-56), and they should be instructed that divine judgment will not be delayed (vv. 57-59).

49-53—In these verses Luke offers a rare glimpse into Jesus' own sense of urgency of his mission (see also 13:31-35). The theme is still the "will of God" (see v. 47 above, Gk: *thelēma*), but now it is Jesus as the agent of God's will. "I have come to hurl fire on the earth, and how I am determined (how I will that: Gk. *thelo*) it already be ignited. I have a baptism to be baptized and how I am constrained until it be fulfilled" (compare the RSV). Jesus is not merely "wishing" that something might happen. He is caught up in God's will and plan as announced before by John that the Messiah would baptize "with the Holy Spirit and with fire . . . to gather the wheat . . . and burn the chaff with unquenchable fire" (3:16-17). No aspect of the Messiah's mission will fail of fulfillment including the **baptism** and the **fire,** but how it shall all be **accomplished** is still hidden in the will of God. Perhaps even Jesus does not yet know how all of this will take place.

The Christian reader may be tempted to diminish the theme of judgment and peril. After all, the baptism of fire will prove to be fulfilled in the fiery baptism of the Holy Spirit at Pentecost, the fulfillment of the promise of the Father (Luke 24:49; Acts 1:4; 2:1-4). But Jesus is the bearer of the prophetic word, and the "constraint" and "determination" he feels are that of the will of

God. Before him, Jeremiah had announced God's will in God's words: "Behold, I am making my words in your mouth a fire, and this people wood, and the fire shall devour them!" (Jer. 5:14), and Jeremiah could not restrain the word he bore, "There is in my heart as it were a burning fire shut up in my bones, and I am weary with holding it in, and I cannot!" (Jer. 20:9).

Moses and Elijah had spoken of the "exodus" which he was about to fulfill in Jerusalem (9:31), and the evangelist had announced the fulfilling of the days of his "exaltation" (9:51, Gk: *analēmpsis*) in Jerusalem. So also, Jesus now speaks of the **fire** of his word and the **baptism** which **constrains** him. He is interpreting his own mission in sharply prophetic terms, and the peril of judgment is deeply felt. Neither Jesus' contemporaries nor the Christian reader should be deluded. Even God's will to save and to fulfill the promises confronts and exposes resistance and rejection and provokes deep divisions.

Every kind of division is envisioned, especially the kind which penetrates to the household. No doubt such divisions were very real in the households of Israel where the early Christian mission found a hearing. No easy **peace** was possible there, perhaps especially after Israel's terrible calamities at the hands of the Romans made toleration of diversity within the family of Israel less possible. Of course Luke proclaims Jesus as God's act of peace for the earth (see 1:79; 2:14, 29; 7:50; 8:48; 10:5; 19:38; 24:36 [some manuscripts]; Acts 9:31; 10:36!), but when rejected, Jesus will bring destruction rather than peace (see 19:41-44). The two-edged sword of the word and mission of God which Jesus bears will cut Israel to the quick. Those who would reduce Jesus to a sentimental savior of a doting God have not come to terms with the depth of divine passion, of the wrath and love of God which is revealed in Jesus' word, will, and obedience even unto death.

54-56—These words are often read as a general comment on "interpreting the times," but their intensity is compounded by the context as well as by the sharp charge against **you hypocrites** (see also 13:15). There is nothing cool or dispassionate here, only an indictment which draws upon the observation of common intelligence. People are clever enough to anticipate the weather by watching the clouds and the winds. Such "discernment" of the face of earth and heaven is known to them, but they do not know how to "discern this present moment" (Gk: *kairos*). These words echo the charge against "this generation" which "seeks a sign" but is unable to discern the ultimate sign it has been given (11:29-32). The prophetic force of the words uncovers a deeper ignorance or blindness, and their direct address speaks out to the present reader as well as to Luke's first readers and Jesus' audience. If you are so clever in predicting the weather, why are you unable to discern the very presence of God's reign in your midst? This is yet one more disclosure of the divine will along with an exposure of human rejection of God's reign. If the whole of Luke's narrative were not confident of God's saving triumph, this haunting question could only demonstrate the validity of divine judgment (see also 13:1-5).

57-59—These words also assume that the state of the human heart is dire in the prospect of the coming judgment. Jesus is the "visitation" of divine righteousness (19:44), just as John had seen. Those who wished to "flee from the wrath to come" (3:7) knew the justice that was required. Matthew also related these proverbial sayings to the righteousness of Jesus' reign, and neither of the evangelists minimizes the consequences of disobedience. Does Jesus literally mean what he says in this context? Absolutely yes, says the evangelist, and the demand for righteousness is fundamental to Jesus' prophetic mission. Yet both vv. 56 and 57 open with a negative question: **"Why do you not . . .?"** The evangelist is sharply aware that finally the hearers are able neither to **interpret the present time** nor to **judge for yourselves what is right** in the sense of performing justice. Thus these sayings have the effect of condemning every **you** who hears. The only hope lies in the "baptism" with which Jesus is constrained until it is fulfilled, but at the moment it appears that this too is merely a blazing denunciation which will consume the dross of human ignorance and unrighteousness.

The Time to Repent (13:1-9).   This section flows directly out of the preceding warnings of impending judgment. The ominous tone continues with three illustrations of judgment, two drawn from contemporary experience (vv. 1-5) and one from a parable of an unproductive tree (vv. 6-9). The first verse is also crafted by Luke to supply an immediate link with the preceding sayings: **There were some present at that very time** (Gk: *kairos*). Jesus has just charged that his hearers "Do not know how to discern this time" (12:56, Gk: *kairos*), and now they present him with the raw data of current experience and outrageous suffering at the hands of a cruel tyrant. The implied question is, "What does it mean? Why is this happening in the present time? Why did these people suffer?" Jesus' words then offer a three-part answer, each with a concluding call to repentance. Each conclusion is stated conditionally, for the outcome depends on whether or not the people repent.

2-3—Jesus' word on the Galileans:
    "Unless you repent you will all likewise perish."
4-5—Jesus' word on the casualties in Jerusalem:
    "Unless you repent you will all likewise perish."
6-9—Jesus' parable of the fig tree:
    "If it bears fruit next year, well and good; but
    if not, you can cut it down."

All of this material is preserved only in Luke, since the story of the cursing of the fig tree (Mark 11:12-14//Matt. 21:18-19) is a very different episode. Luke has also structured these sayings carefully in the narrative, perhaps even drafting the conditional conclusions so that the parallelism of the calls to repentance will intensify the effect. Luke's use of these sayings in his story is the primary concern in this commentary, but these sayings are so compelling and important in their own right that other dimensions of their "meaning" must also be explored before assessing Luke's distinctive emphasis.

This passage is a classic testimony on the problem of divine justice. It is a theodicy, dealing with two cases where faith in a moral universe has been badly shaken. The crowd introduces the first instance and Jesus brings up the second. Capricious violence by **Pilate** against religious pilgrims from Galilee and some kind of construction accident in **Jerusalem** threaten the conviction of all religious people that evil people are punished and the righteous rewarded. Such common hope is expressed throughout Israel's Scriptures (see Job 4:7; 8:20; 22:4-5) and stated succinctly in Prov. 10:25, "When the tempest passes, the wicked is no more, but the righteous is established for ever." But then is the converse true? Does that mean that those who suffer are the more culpable, the greater sinners?

In John 9:1-3, Jesus confronted a similar problem with the case of the man born blind, and John reports that he rejected simplistic notions that the man's blindness was due to either his sin or that of his parents. God's justice was not at stake, but God's glory was about to be revealed in a healing. So also in Luke's story, Jesus emphatically rejects simplistic notions which justify God by blaming the victims of caprice or casualty. But these are signs and warnings, and larger questions of divine justice and mercy are at stake. The significance of such current events does not lie in their being demonstrations of the sinfulness of those who died but in their call to the whole people to **repent.**

Such prophetic interpretation of current events was probably characteristic of Jesus, just as prophets before him and Galilean contemporaries interpreted the signs of the times. All the Gospels remember Jesus as possessing a dynamic view of God's will and mission in Israel's history. Perhaps these sayings were even part of Jesus' prophetic testimony concerning Jerusalem's eventual fate at the hands of the Romans (i.e., **Pilate**) and peril of destruction (i.e., the falling **tower** in Jerusalem as a omen of Jerusalem's future; see also 19:41-44; 21:5-24). The identification of Judah and Jerusalem as an unfruitful fig tree was even a traditional image portending judgment (Jer. 8:13; Mic. 7:1).

It is important to note that **Pilate** is not vindicated at any level of the tradition, even if his act is a sign of divine vengeance. Commentators have struggled to identify both of these cases in terms of known historical events. All that can be demonstrated from Josephus is that Pilate's cruelty was well known and included attacks on Samaritan pilgrims (Josephus, *Ant.* 18.86-87), introduction of Roman standards into the temple (*Ant.* 18.55-59), and the seizing of temple funds (*Ant.* 18.60-62). Even if this specific slaughter of Galilean pilgrims is otherwise an untold story, it fits with Pilate's reputation of disdain for religious practices (see 23:1-25).

247

Among the early Christians these Jesus traditions were probably subject to further symbolic interpretations. Not only could the first two cases be seen as signs of Jerusalem's future, but the vinedresser who pleads for three years for the fruit tree was probably understood as a figure for Jesus' ministry in the vineyard of Israel (see Isa. 5:1-7). Once Jerusalem lay in ruins, these words were probably remembered as prophecy fulfilled and used as warnings for the continuing need for repentance.

Within Luke's story, however, these calls to repentance follow directly on the powerful warnings of judgment which Jesus has just spoken (12:35-59). The stress lies on the conditional conclusions: **unless you repent you will all likewise perish . . . if it bears fruit . . ., but if not, you can cut it down.**" No legal casuistry is allowed, as if it were a question of who are the "worse sinners" or "worse offenders," because Jesus refuses to talk about "them" abstractly. He is still speaking to "you" who hear him (see 12:41, 42-59), and the possibility of destruction is still future (**you will**) but a real possibility. The audience and the readers are commonly addressed, and their (our) response to Jesus' mission and reign is the critical test. These grim deaths are not "explained" in themselves, but they are occasions for Jesus to confront the hearers with the call to faith and obedience.

The parable of the vineyard is clearly allegorical, used by Luke to reinforce the calls to repentance. Even the concept of **bearing fruit** is an image for true repentance (see Luke 3:8, 9; Acts 26:20, "deeds"). Whatever "delay" is envisioned is not a source of consternation, but a sign of grace. "Time for amendment of life" is a gift of divine forbearance, and the **manure** and tending of the soil are investments to save the tree by restoring its productivity.

Just as the narrative builds steadily toward a confrontation which appears to be unavoidably tragic, these calls to repentance are reminders that from God's point of view destruction is not inevitable or necessary. The possibility of repentance appears to be more remote than the threat of destruction, and the hope that the tree will bear is not bright. Nevertheless, the time of Jesus' ministry is an extended, prolonged campaign to save Israel, and the possibility of averting destruction is still real (see by contrast 19:41-44).

The Bent Woman (13:10-17).   Jesus has been teaching, pro-phesying, and talking almost constantly since the beginning of his journey toward Jerusalem in 9:51. Even his exorcism of a demon in 11:14 was only mentioned as the occasion for more instruction, but now Luke relates a healing story. The context is still that of Jesus' **teaching** (v. 10), and the brief story (vv. 11-13) again prompts an instructive debate between Jesus and **the ruler of the synagogue** on the proper observance of **the Sabbath** (vv. 14-17). The evangelist has thus woven this healing episode into the fabric of Jesus' extended discourse so that it now illustrates the sad state of division in Israel which Jesus had predicted and provoked (12:49-53, see 13:17).

Only Luke tells this story, and it fits well with his distinctive emphases. In 7:36-50, the healing of "this woman" (7:44) provides an occasion for instructing Simon the Pharisee in the grace of the kingdom, and now the healing of **this woman, a daughter of Abraham** (13:16; see also "woman/daughter" in 8:43-48//Mark 5:25-34) leads to Jesus' exposition of the Scriptures for the **ruler of the synagogue.** Only Luke will also later identify Zacchaeus as a "son of Abraham" (19:9), and these surprising identifications correspond with the warning and assurance of John the Baptist at the beginning of the story: "Do not begin to say to yourselves, 'We have Abraham as our father'; for I tell you, God is able from these stones to raise up children to Abraham." (3:8-9//Matt. 3:9). Jesus exposes religious pride and labels it **hypocrisy, putting his adversaries to shame** and causing **the people** to **rejoice** (v. 17).

10—Luke introduces the **sabbath** question as directly as in 6:1-11, where Jesus was demonstrated to be the Son of man who is lord of the Sabbath and in 6:6-11 where he healed on the Sabbath (see also 14:1-6 below). But he also presents Jesus once again teaching **in the synagogue** (see 4:14-30, 31-38, 44; 6:6-11). This is the fulfillment of the hopes of Israel, the Messiah teaching in the synagogues and later in the temple (19:47—21:38). But is it an occasion of joy or judgment?

11-13—Luke fills us in on all the particulars of the woman's disability, including the length and severity of the problem (v. 11). Perhaps the number **eighteen** is a memory link to the pre-ceeding story of the eighteen casualties (v. 4), but the point here is simply that she had suffered from a spinal disorder for a very long time. The woman with the twelve-year flow of blood and the woman with the eighteen-year back problem would understand each other's need.

But here **Jesus** took the initiative. He recognized her plight and addressed her directly, which was probably a violation of synagogue customs in itself. Then to heal her, he touched her. This is almost as shocking an act as when he touched the litter of the dead man from Nain (7:14) or when the woman with the flow of blood touched him (8:44-46). Luke's sense for the human dimensions of these encounters is most impressive. We are drawn directly into the drama of the moment and instructed by her appropriate response, **praising God.** As the sermons in Acts will verify (see 2:22-24; 10:38), such healings are mighty works of God, and God is to be praised (see also the lame man in Acts 3:8).

14—But the healing provokes controversy (see also 5:17-26; 6:6-11; 7:36-50; 11:14). It is important to note that Luke's Jesus is not predisposed to dislike a **ruler of the synagogue,** since he had responded well to Jairus who had the same title (8:41). But now this **ruler of the synagogue** is **indignant,** and his ire has religious justification. He opens a public discussion by addressing the people with his objection drawn from Deut. 5:13 and Exod. 20:9-10. He is not specifically identified as a Pharisee, and his zealous defense of the sanctity of the Sabbath would have found approval among other carefully observant traditions.

15-17—Jesus' response is equally sharp, and it is also based in a scriptural interpretation. The word **hypocrite** is biting, especially for those who were so preoccupied with consistency in observing the Law. In 12:1, Jesus had warned his disciples to "beware of the leaven of the Pharisees which is hypocrisy" and in 12:56 he called "hypocrites" those unable to "interpret the present time." He is not merely accusing them of being "legalists," but attacking a kind of scriptural interpretation which prevents them from discerning the present saving activity of God. They have boxed in the Law so closely that even God's healing of **this woman** cannot be praised.

But he does not merely call names. He introduces an argument drawn from current discussion of "case law" or precedents. At

Qumran and among the rabbis the debate was pursued about how strictly the Law had to be observed in the care of domestic animals. Only the most rigid would suggest that you could not untie an animal in order to water it on the Sabbath, and thus Jesus is taking up this reasonable accommodation and arguing from the lesser case to the greater: if you would unbind an animal on the Sabbath, would you not the more unbind **a daughter of Abraham?** (See also 12:24, 28, and compare the discussion at 14:5-6). The suggestion that it is Satan who has bound the woman in her disability is significant. Jesus is challenging the dominion of Satan, and those who are piously defending the Sabbath have not discerned what is happening. More is at stake than mere human religiosity. Jesus has suggested that his critics are in danger of aiding Satan in his reign of bondage. He has put them to "shame" (v. 17), just as the makers of idols are put to shame and confounded upon the revelation of God as Savior in Isa. 45:15-16. By contrast, the people join the woman in joy and praise to God, recognizing that Jesus has done glorious things.

The Hidden Kingdom (13:18-21)   These two compact parables of the kingdom of God complete the immediate context with a word of hope and furnish a conclusion to the first phase of Jesus' journey to Jerusalem which began at 9:51. They offer considerable relief to the words of judgment and warning which have characterized much of this section because they are an assurance that no matter what the obstacles, the kingdom of God will not fail to prosper.

Luke has pulled these two parables together from diverse contexts in Mark (Luke 13:18-19//Mark 4:30-32) and "Q" (Luke 13:20-21//Matt. 13:33). Both of them are parables of remarkable growth, drawn from natural examples, and conveying a dynamic sense of the "kingdom of God" as a divine "force" or "energy" or "strength." These are not pictures of a kingdom as a place or a realm, whether on earth or in heaven. These are images of the way God's dominion accomplishes its purposes and grows far beyond all expectation although it is not obviously powerful or imposing.

18-19—The image of the great spreading **tree** is also found in Dan. 4:10-12 and Ezek. 17:22-24; 31:2-9 as a promise of greatness and prosperity, but only Jesus' parable contrasts this promise so sharply with the very modest beginnings of the **mustard seed.** In Jesus' own time, such an image was probably a prophetic promise that God would prosper the mission of the kingdom as the fulfillment of the grand promises of Ezekiel, and such an assurance must have continued to be signficant as Jesus' followers continued to experience resistance and rejection (see Luke 8:4-15). Luke also presents the parable in that light, but the context provides an even more vivid contrast to such growth since so much judgment and rejection precedes it. Although much of the narrative is preoccupied with the opposition to Jesus, these parables again resound with confidence in what God is doing.

20-21—The parable of the **leaven** says the same thing, but it does have an ironic ring in this context in Luke since "the leaven of the Pharisees" or hypocrisy has so recently been mentioned (see 12:1, 56; 13:15). While that "leaven" was an uncleanness, just as the Pharisees understood leaven to be, the "leaven of the kingdom" is its fecundity, its power and strength. Jesus' image is provocative and probably shocking, but it is also confident that the whole lump will be transformed, even if not much but opposition seems to be happening at the moment.

Jesus Journeys Toward Jerusalem (13:22—17:10)

In v. 22 of Chap. 13, Luke marks a resumption of Jesus' **journey toward Jerusalem.** No dramatic new stage of action or time is reached in the story. But Luke's summary statement in this verse at least reassures the reader that the evangelist is conscious of (1) the journey, (2) the goal of Jerusalem, and (3) the teaching which Jesus is pursuing along the way. Jesus is not arriving quickly, but his journey is a literary device for extensive instruction to Jesus' followers in "the way of the Lord."

He Prophesies the End (13:22-35)

The Last and First at the Great Banquet (13:22-30). After v. 22 mentions the resumption of the journey, vv. 23-30 present a collection of Jesus' sayings on "the few" and "the many," "the insiders" and "the outsiders," and "the last" and "the first." This entire discourse is prompted by **someone's** question (v. 23), **"Lord, will those who are saved be few?"** Jesus' extended answer is a sharp challenge to the questioner. As has been noted before, Luke is fond of using leading questions and revealing comments as narrative occasions (see the comments at 1:18, 34; 4:22; 10:29; 12:41, and note the comments below at 13:31; 19:39). In this instance, Luke has pulled together sayings from "Q" which occur in various contexts in Matthew (7:13-14, 22-23; 8:11-12; 19:30// Mark 10:31). The effect is a discourse of sharp warnings for those in the story (and for the readers) who would take their (your) privileged connection with Jesus as a guarantee of "salvation" and participation in **the kingdom.** Speculations about how **few** or **many** would be saved are rejected by Jesus' prophetic declarations of divine freedom. Thus the warnings to repentance (13:1-9) resume and stand in tension with the assurances of the gift and growth of the kingdom (12:30; 13:18-20).

24-25—Luke appears to have pulled these verses together around the repetition of the word **door.** Perhaps the traditional saying was about the narrow "gate" (Matt. 7:13), but the image of the householder arising to close the **door** has already modified what is **narrow** about this entrance. That is, entrance is not merely limited by keeping "on the straight and narrow way" of moral behavior or observance of the Law. The time within which one may be admitted is also limited. Jesus escalates a traditional ethical exhortation with an eschatological warning. Such freedom of God and messianic authority are a challenge to those who only desire a system of moral or legal observance.

Luke's story of Jesus is consistently confident of God's saving purposes and of the ultimate gift and triumph of **the kingdom** (see 12:30, 35-40; 13:18-21), but Luke is also persistently aware of the danger that people may cut themselves off from this kingdom and salvation. Jesus may even be the cause of offense, while God's good pleasure is that Jesus be the "glory to thy people Israel" (2:32; see 2:34-35). Jesus' words here do not simply mean "try harder and harder" (RSV: **strive;** see 2 Macc. 13:14, "fight to the death") to get in because the moral standards are high.

Rather the charge is to "be disciplined" (Gk: *agōnizesthe*) in following the way which the Lord has opened now to the kingdom feast. One day the door will be closed. Then no one, not **few** (v. 23), not **many** (v. 24), and not **you** (v. 25), will be able to enter. **26-30**—The messianic banquet is a traditional image which Luke will develop at length in Chap. 14 (see especially 14:7-23), and it is one of the richest biblical pictures of **the kingdom of God.** This is the feast which God prepares (see Isa. 25:6-8; 55:1-2; 65:13-14). To be on the guest list of this royal banquet means election and salvation. It was a historical hope of hungry people and an eschatological vision of the world to come (see the Magnificat in 1:53). Yet the question of just who will be included in that feast is explored further as an answer to the question of "few" and "many" or "us" and "them."

Luke casts this material (until v. 30) in the form of a reproof to **you** (contrast Matt. 7:22-23), omitting all positive references to "many" (contrast Matt. 8:11; 19:30). Whether or not Luke has altered the tradition, the force of these words is now a sharp warning to "you" who are asking the question or listening to Jesus' answer in the narrative (and perhaps to "you" who read the story). Merely having eaten and drunk in Jesus' presence or having heard his teaching is no more a guarantee than having "Abraham as our father" was in the time of John the Baptizer (3:8). Those who are counting on ritual are no better off than those counting on race. In Matt. 7:22, those who are excluded also raise more specifically Christian claims: "Did we not prophesy in your name and cast our demons in your name, and do many mighty works in your name?"

But Luke remains with distinctive Jewish questions of election, focused on meal practices, teaching, and identity within the lineage of Abraham. This warning applies to all who are present for Jesus' teaching and his frequent meals (see Chap. 14) in his journey to Jerusalem. John had called the multitudes a "brood of vipers" (3:7), and Jesus uses an equally uncomplimentary scriptural phrase, **"Depart from me, all you workers of iniquity!"** (Ps. 6:8, LXX 6:9: "workers of lawlessness"; see Luke's use of the same Greek word "iniquity" in 16:8,9; 18:6; Acts 1:18; 8:23).

Weeping and **gnashing of teeth** are traditional contrasts to joy and festivity. These are the people who were **thrust out** of the feast, or who were "destroyed from the people" (Acts 3:23 speaks of this judgment on those who did not listen to Jesus, the prophet like Moses). Of course the patriarchs, **Abraham, Isaac, and Jacob, and all the prophets** are included in the royal feast. Luke is eager to identify this **kingdom** as the fulfillment of the promises made to the patriarchs and prophets (see Acts 3:13, 7:32; Deut. 1:8; 6:10, 9:5, 27; 1 Kings. 18:36, 2 Kings. 13:23).

But Luke is also entering into a more ancient discussion of how God will provide this feast for "all peoples" (LXX, Isa. 25:6-8, "all nations," "all the Gentiles"), not merely Israel. Was not such meal fellowship restricted to "kosher" practice, i.e., to those who observed the Law with great care? At least within the Septuagint of Isaiah 25, this great feast was already more than a picture of how all the Gentile nations and their wealth would flow to the benefit of vindicated Israel (see Isa. 60; 52:10, etc). In that text, the feast was already a vision of God's reign over all the nations and Israel's reproach was removed, precisely in God's inclusion of the nations.

Neither ethnic identity nor even acquaintance with the Messiah is a ticket to the feast. Yet, neither God nor the Messiah is capricious, and the door is still open in the present time, the time of repentance (12:56). This is the banquet which God hosts, and God's hospitality may not be questioned. All along God has planned that it would be very inclusive and that the "light for revelation to the Gentiles" would truly be the "glory to thy people Israel" (2:32), and thus the eschatological banquet will shock those who might expect that admission would come only through "the narrow door" of observance of the Law.

Thus the reversal of expectations may be predicted (v. 30): "They are [RSV: **some are**] **last who will be first,** and they are [RSV: **some are**] **first who will be last.**" While Matthew says "many," Luke remains silent, not even saying "the last are those . . .," etc., but leaving the translators to struggle to supply a subject to the clause. Still the point is clear. Speculative questions about how "few" or how "many" will be saved or included in the feast of the kingdom are rejected. Rather "you" are to remain in readiness and repentance, not assuming special privilege indefinitely, and to be prepared for God to exercise great grace and freedom in who is included among the elect!

Jerusalem's Dire Future (13:31-35).   This brief passage of five verses is a Lukan masterpiece. The evangelist has drawn upon a "Q" saying of Jesus which is a lament for Jerusalem (vv. 34-35//Matt. 23:37-39), provided a distinctive context for that lament by a report of a threat from Herod, and used the whole as a prophetic anticipation of Jesus' "end" in Jerusalem toward which his journey is headed. Furthermore, this scene is a display of the complex struggle of wills which characterizes the entire story: the intention of Jesus' adversaries, the determination of the Messiah, the unwillingness of Jerusalem, and the fulfillment of the will of God. The pathos of the lament is caught up in God's passion to save, which is pitted against human determination to resist, even when the results will be tragically destructive.

31-33—These verses are Luke's composition, but literary skill does not mean fictionalizing. They are probably based upon a traditional report of a threat from **Herod** Antipas (vv. 31-32a) as well as remembered words of Jesus (vv. 32b-33), and they are linked with the vocabulary of the "Q" saying of Jesus which they introduce (vv. 34-35). The word plays on the Greek terms "to go" (Gk: *poreuesthai*) and "to will" or "intend" (Gk: *thelein*) hold the passage together and sound the critical themes. As noted above at 9:51-55, Luke uses the common word "to go" as a literary device to indicate that Jesus was obedient only to God's will as he set his face "to go" to Jerusalem. Now again, this is not merely a question of Herod's "wishing" or **wanting,** but a powerful clash of wills and intentions. Only a wooden English translation can keep these associations alive:

> Get out and *go* for Herod *intends* to kill you. . . . Now you *go* and say to that fox . . . for I am accomplishing healings today and tomorrow and on the third day I accomplish my course (I am accomplished). Nevertheless, I must *go* today tomorrow and on the following day because . . . Jerusalem, Jerusalem, how often I have *intended* to gather you . . . and you did not so *intend.*

It is not possible to tell if the **Pharisees** are sincere in their apparent effort to protect Jesus from **Herod.** Jesus was still in Herod Antipas's territory in the north, and Luke's report (9:9) of Herod's question when he "sought to see" Jesus was already ominous, "John I beheaded; but who is this about whom I hear such things?" (see also the comments on Herod at 23:6-12). As in 19:39, Luke is careful to state that only **some Pharisees** offered such "protective" counsel, but in both cases Jesus rejects it sharply. Once again (see 13:22 above), a leading comment or question provides the context for Jesus' sharply different and prophetic interpretation of what is really happening. It certainly is unlikely that any Pharisees would have delivered Jesus' message to Herod or conveyed his insulting epithet, **that fox.** Even to repeat such a name which had no romance but implied a "varmint" could be dangerous to one's health. Thus even if they meant well, or thought they did, Jesus refuses to accept such counsel.

Jesus' mission has a content and a timing which comes from God. It is God who determines when and where Jesus **must go,** not Herod or the Pharisees. In 4:43 (only in Luke), Jesus insists on moving on because "it is necessary that I preach the good news of the kingdom of God to the other cities also; for I was sent for this purpose." This necessity and this being "sent" are divinely directed, and thus Jesus' "action" and "being directed" are a unity of will. These verses repeat the rhythm of Jesus' "acting" and "being acted upon." Almost as if v. 33 were an elaboration of v. 32b, both speak of Jesus first as acting in controlled phases (**today, tomorrow** and **the third day//today, tomorrow** and **the day following**). Then both use symbolic language to express his being acted upon (I am accomplished, RSV: I finish my course//for it is not fitting for **a prophet** to **perish** outside of **Jerusalem**). In 18:31, Luke will return to the theme of "accomplishment" in a commentary on Mark's third passion prediction: "Behold, we are going up to Jerusalem, and everything that is written of the Son of man by the prophets will be accomplished" (see also 12:50; 22:37).

And why is it not "fitting" for a prophet to perish outside of Jerusalem? This is not merely a question of what is "proper" or "appropriate." Such words would hardly be adequate for speaking of wrongful deaths in any case. No, this is a matter of historical precedent and prophetic analysis. It is not merely "predictable" that Jerusalem would be the place of such conflict, although such a political judgment could also make sense. But the following traditional saying interprets why Jerusalem is the "fitting" or "necessary" place for such a death, and the matter is tied up with the prophetic sense of history as the arena where God contends with a people which is often set against God's kingdom.

34-35—This saying is reproduced from "Q" almost verbatim by both Matthew (23:37-39) and Luke, but in Matthew's context Jesus has been pursuing his ministry in Jerusalem for some time. Thus Jesus' lament about **"how often would I have gathered"** expresses his frustration at the reception he has received in Jerusalem. The effect is very different in Luke's narrative, where Jesus has not been in Jerusalem since his circumcision as an infant (2:21-38) or his encounter with the teachers in the temple as a boy (2:41-51). Luke has been stressing Jerusalem as the goal of Jesus' mission, and his journey has just been renewed (9:51; 13:22). Now the misguided effort of "some Pharisees" to tell him where or when to "go" merely provokes Jesus' declaration that he is constrained to "go" only to Jerusalem and only according to the timing of God's accomplishment. His "lament," therefore, is a prophetic oracle. It predicts Jerusalem's dire future, and it diagnoses the counsel of these religious leaders as the kind of implicit rejection which will predictably, necessarily lead to Jerusalem's destruction (see further the comments at 19:41-44).

The traditional oracle is itself filled with prophetic tradition. Intertestamental Jewish interpretation had also developed the theme that Israel had been guilty of **killing the prophets,** expanding on the calls of repentance in the Deuteronomistic historians (see the comments at 11:37-54). Now the repetitive cadence of the lament compounds the effect: **"O Jerusalem, Jerusalem, killing the prophets . . . and stoning those sent."** This is the language of prophetic indictment, already anticipating what will happen as much as reciting what has happened—which is also the effect of Jesus' words about "How often I have intended

to gather . . . but you did not so intend"; RSV: **How often would
I have gathered. . . . And you would not.**
The image of **gathering the brood** is a scriptural picture of
divine protection. God hovers like a eagle protecting Israel on
the way in the wilderness (Deut. 32:10-14). Even more, in the
temple the outstretched wings of divine protection sheltered Israel and the oppressed (Ps. 17:8; 57:1; 61:4: "Let me dwell in thy
tent for ever! Oh to be safe under the shelter of thy wings!").
Jerusalem and all of Israel depended upon the brooding presence
of God, and later Josephus would report the omens of divine
departure which marked the impending doom of the city and
temple (see *War* 6.288-315). But these convictions were as old
as Jeremiah's oracle (22:5-6), "If you will not heed these words,
I swear by myself, says the Lord, that this house shall become a
desolation. . . . I will make you a desert, an uninhabited city!"
Thus Jesus' announcement of a "house forsaken" (Matt. 23:38,
"desolate") is a recited oracle, declaring a new fulfillment of the
departure of God's protecting presence from Jerusalem and the
"house" or temple of God's abode.
     The last phrase is also scriptural, drawn from the festal Hallel
psalms and declaring blessing on "the one who comes in the name
of the Lord (Ps. 118:26). This allusion was already in "Q," but it
takes on new significance in Luke's narrative. Occurring at this
early stage in the story, this conclusion to Jesus' prophetic oracle
creates "end stress" or anticipation of Jesus' eventual arrival in
Jerusalem. **"You will not see me until you say . . .!"** Exactly as
Jesus approaches Jerusalem in his festal royal procession, the
multitude of his disciples call out this psalm with the additional
identification of him as "the King!" (19:38). That will be the critical
moment of Jerusalem's "visitation" (see the comments on 19:44),
and it will again be the moment when "some Pharisees" suggest
that Jesus alter his mission (19:39).
     This passage stands in the midst of Jesus' journey to Jerusalem
which began at 9:51 and will conclude at 19:28-44, climaxed by
his entry and cleansing of the temple in 19:45-46. It is a reminder
that the way of the determined Messiah is God's mission which
will not, can not be deterred. But it is also a prophetic sign that
the Messiah is well aware of the resistance and tragic rejection

which lie in the path of God's saving purpose. The Messiah is caught up in God's passion, love, and judgment, and the struggle of wills is far from completed.

He Announces a New Protocol (14:1-35)

This chapter appears to be presented as a series of encounters and discourses in the setting of a dinner or banquet. The meal setting is mentioned explicitly at 14:1 and repeatedly identified until 14:24. Chapter 15 begins with a retrospective accusation that Jesus "receives sinners and eats with them." Perhaps Luke intended to include Jesus' discourse to the multitudes in 14:25-35 as an extension of the banquet speech "on the way" (14:25, "they were going along together; Gk: *synporeunonto*). Surprisingly, no other setting is introduced for Jesus' further discourses until the journey begins again in 17:11. Are Jesus' words in 15:1—17:10 also part of an extended banquet discourse?

The question is significant to understanding Luke's narrative because the evangelist may be suggesting that Jesus was holding forth at some length in the manner of a king at a banquet. The Greek tradition of the "symposium" and the oriental stories of conversation, riddles, and discourses at royal banquets provide rich comparisons. In the intertestamental Letter of Aristeas, the king and his guests carry on a question and answer session about the goodness of God, virtue, divine sovereignty, prayer, banquet etiquette, generosity, and nobility for many days and over a hundred verses (vv. 187-300). The format for such discussions of wisdom, theology, and ethics was familiar.

But to the extent that Luke is aware of such a literary convention, the content of Jesus' teaching stands in remarkable contrast with the kind of conversation that is expected in such elite groups. In particular, Jesus' messianic freedom in challenging traditions of who is invited and what is acceptable behavior appears even more shocking against such a backdrop. And the central question will be that of God's favor or election as reflected in the persons with whom one shares meal fellowship. In Let. Arist. (vv. 286-287), the king asks, " 'How ought one to conduct himself at banquets?' The reply was, 'By inviting men of learning, with the ability to remind him of matters advantageous to the kingdom and the lives of their subjects . . . because these men are beloved of God.' " (trans. R. J. H. Shutt).

Jesus is beginning a discourse on the protocol of the kingdom of God, and the guest list of those "beloved of God" is remarkable. The banquet setting probably extends through Chap. 14, and the revelation of the gracious extravagance and freedom of this reign extends at least until the end of the section (17:10). The Messiah is challenging accepted views of who is "elect" of God, now, in the ongoing struggle of the dominion that is emerging, and in the resurrection of the just which is to come.

Another Sabbath Test (14:1-6).   This is the fourth episode of conflict in Luke over Sabbath observance (see also 6:1-5; 6:6-11; 13:10-19). It is a story of a healing, but the force of the story is invested in the conflict. Only Luke tells this story, and Luke has introduced it with care as in a setting of a dinner at **the house** of a **Pharisee** where **they were watching him.** Whatever happens in this scene, the reader knows that Jesus is being tested, but once again soon it is **you** who are tested by Jesus (see 13:22-30).

1—Such **Sabbath** meals were regularly prepared a day earlier, and noted guests and visiting teachers were invited. Even outside of this banquet chapter, Luke is fond of portraying Jesus at meals (see 7:36-50; 9:13-17; 10:38-42; 11:37-54; 22:14-38; 24:30-35). The meals with **Pharisees** are consistently scenes of conflict (7:36-50; 11:37-54), and the motif that the Pharisees were **watching him** is repeated in Luke's story (6:7; 11:53-54; see also the animosity of "the chief priests and the scribes and the principal men" in 19:47; 20:20).

2-4—The **man** with **dropsy** appears on the scene with no explanation. It is unlikely that someone with a condition of edema would have been invited. Such abnormal accumulation of body fluids with unsightly swelling and disfigurement was not understood as it is now as a medical symptom of a wide variety of conditions, many of them serious. It was perceived as a condition of impurity, probably as a divine judgment. Whether he slipped in or was brought to put Jesus to the test, the confrontation is clear.

Only **Jesus** speaks. When he raises the question of whether it is **lawful to heal on the sabbath,** the interpreters of the Law and the Pharisees remain **silent.** They are also unable to reply at the end of the story (v. 6). Luke has told us that they are watching him, but Jesus is the one who raises the hard questions, and answers them implicitly (so also in 6:8-9 where Jesus "knew their thoughts" and raised the question; contrast 6:2 and 13:14-15 where first the "ruler of the synagogue" objects and then Jesus raises the second question). At this point, he simply **heals** the man, and sends him away. We learn almost nothing about him or the severity of his condition or how he responded.

5-6—Jesus' second question is an expansion on his first. As in 13:15, Jesus introduces a classic issue in the interpretation of Sabbath observance, where another scriptural command created dispute. That is, Deut. 22:4 commanded a person to assist if someone's "ass or ox" had "fallen down by the way," and Exod. 21:33-34 declared the liability of digging a pit if someones "ox or ass falls in it." Furthermore, Exod. 23:5 required a person to assist even "one who hates you" if their animal had fallen. So the interpreters debated which command took precedence on the **sabbath**—the command to pull out an animal or the command to rest on the **sabbath.** At Qumran where the "strict constructionists" dominated, it was declared that one could not pull out a beast on the Sabbath, but a person who fell into water or fire could be helped, even with implements (CD 11:13-17).

Jesus, therefore, raises the question with the implied expectation that assisting in such need is the most appropriate. The manuscripts differ, however, on exactly what he asked. If he asked about an "ass or an ox," as the RSV (1965 edition) had it (but see the footnote), he is merely taking a position on the more permissive side of the ususal scriptural debate. That is, they are wrong at Qumran. Beasts should be pulled from pits. But if he asked about a **son or an ox,** (see the RSV, 1971 edition), which is the reading of equally reliable manuscripts, then he is combining the questions of "people" and "beasts," and his verdict is that even the most rigid interpreters would agree that a person in need should be assisted.

This discussion is even more cryptic than the debate in 13:15-16, for there Jesus expanded the point to say that this "daughter of Abraham" should be released from her bondage on the Sabbath much more than a thirsty beast should be led to water. But the flow of the argument is again from the lesser to the greater, and it seems more likely that Jesus' cryptic question should already mention both the **son** or "child" and the **ox** in the same breath. That combination would be the brilliant stroke which would silence those who **were watching him** so that **they could not reply to this** (v. 6). In 20:34-40, Jesus will exercise a similar tour de force in a debate with the Sadducees, showing himself to be more than a match for them on their own grounds. In Luke's presentation, Jesus does not merely disagree with certain views, he demonstrates magisterial understanding of the methods of interpretation and exposes the shallowness and hypocrisy of those who object to him or seek to entrap him.

Seating Charts and Guest Lists in the Kingdom (14:7-14). As indicated in the introduction to Chap. 14, this whole section may be viewed as a royal banquet discourse, but this discourse differs sharply from traditional banquet wisdom where it is the learned and virtuous who are to be invited because they are the "beloved of God" (see Let. Arist. 286-287, quoted above). In these verses, the questions appear to be merely matters of banquet etiquette. But the larger context, with its reference to "eating bread in the kingdom of God" (v. 15), and the concluding reference to the "resurrection of the just" (v. 14) indicate that these sayings are declarations of the protocol of the kingdom.

No great imagination is necessary to perceive the radical policies of the kingdom implicit in these declarations about meal practices. Seating assignments and guest lists are still very sensitive matters in state dinners as well as at weddings and recognition banquets, and the risks of embarrassment and insult run high. In some measure, Jesus was merely repeating the practical wisdom of every age which warns against overreaching one's status. As it says in Prov. 25:6-7, "Do not put yourself forward in the king's presence or stand in the place of the great; for it is better to be told, 'Come up here,' than to be put lower in the presence of the prince." But Jesus' counsel is also a prophetic declaration which he is bold to announce at someone else's banquet and which drives to the heart of a traditional scriptural question of who is truly "invited" or "elect" to share the meal fellowship of the kingdom.

Both of his declarations, one to the guests (vv. 8-11) and one to the host (vv. 12-14), have the same structure of proverbial counsel.

When you are invited // give a dinner . . . *do not* sit in a place of honor // invite your friends *lest* a more eminent man be invited // they also invite you in return. . . .

But when you are invited // give a feast . . . go and sit in the lowest place // invite the poor . . . *then you will be* honored // blessed. For everyone who exalts himself . . . // Because they cannot repay . . .

Thus when Luke speaks of these words of Jesus as **a parable** (v. 7), he may be referring only to their form in the broadest possible sense of the "parables" as "proverbial sayings." But, in the context of Chap. 14, these words may also be regarded as "parabolic" in the narrower sense of being surprising revelations of the kingdom.

7-11—Oriental customs as to who reclined where at table were even more serious matters of honor than modern egalitarian seating charts, and they were frequently given religious connotations. At Qumran, even the entering procession was strictly established with the priests and the Levites and all the people one after another, each "according to the perfection of their spirit . . . that every Israelite may know his place in the Community of God according to the everlasting design. No man shall move down from his place nor move up from his allotted position" (1QS 2:4ff.).

Still these verses in Luke are by themselves simply prudent counsel, like the wisdom of Proverbs cited above. Only v. 11 indicates that this counsel has new meaning, especially with its future tenses in the passive voice. In 18:14, this aphorism will recur as the conclusion of the story of the Pharisee and the tax collector. There it is more clear that the passive voice refers to

God as the one who "justifies" and **exalts** the **humble.** In 14:7-11, such a conclusion is only a clue that this homey wisdom is to be understood as a glimpse of the great reversal of accepted values which the kingdom brings (see also 1:51-53).

12-14—This is more than proverbial wisdom. It is a reproof of the host, but it is also a prophetic revelation of God's surprising way of ruling. Once again the conclusion (v. 14) provides the rationale (**because**) which is the disclosure that God's way of keeping the records of "who owes whom" is both different from human custom and ultimate. Such a "kingdom policy" was also stated explicitly in 6:27-36 where the promised reward for an exercise of economic generosity was grounded in God's mercy. In Deut. 14:29 such an appeal to generous sharing of food with the "Levite and the sojourner, the fatherless, and the widow" had already been linked with God's blessing. But when the list goes beyond the poor to include **the maimed, the lame** and **the blind,** a new level of kingdom protocol is revealed.

In the priestly code of Lev. 21:17-23, the list of those who may not "offer the bread of his God" includes those with a host of specific disabilities and diseases along with the "blind or lame." Again, at Qumran this list became the basis for those who were excluded from the assembly and even from participating in the eschatological struggle against the evil powers. "No man smitten with any human uncleanness shall enter the assembly of God . . . no man smitten in his flesh, or paralysed in his feet or hands, or blind, or deaf or dumb, or smitten in his flesh with a visible blemish" (1QSa 2:5-7, 1QM 7:4). This tradition may also clarify Luke's reason for including in this section the story of the healing of the man with edema.

Jesus' words on who is to be **invited** are more than a criticism of his host's etiquette. They are a revelation of the protocol and priorities of the kingdom of God. Those who desire their feasts to be in concord with God's will or anticipations of God's great feast are not counseled to practice religious exclusion, preserving themselves, God, and the feast from the pollutions of the diseased and disabled. Rather let the extravagant grace and generosity of God's reign transform such self-serving religiosity into the inclusion of all those who have been prevented. This is the protocol of the kingdom, and it will be revealed in the last judgment along with the vindicating **resurrection** of those who have been justified by such righteousness.

The Blessing and Urgency of the Feast (14:15-24).   The banquet discourse continues, now shifting from criticism of the guests (vv. 7-11) and the host (vv. 12-14) to a more direct statement of how the feast of the kingdom will be conducted. Once again prompted by a leading comment of someone present (v. 15), the traditional parable (vv. 16-21a), and its sharpened conclusion (vv. 21b-24) sound Luke's consistent theme that the blessing of the kingdom is at the same time a peril for those who resist, reject, or even seek to postpone it. The force of the entire exchange, therefore, is that of a prophetic warning with little direct pastoral comfort. Yes, those who **eat bread in the kingdom** are **blessed,** but woe to you if you do not come when **invited.**

Luke may have derived this parable from "Q," although the verbal correspondences with the closest parallel in Matt. 22:1-14 are minimal. It seems quite unlikely that Luke would have altered a story of a wedding feast hosted by a king if "Q" contained it. Matthew probably introduced that specific royal identification along with more elaboration on the "mixed crowd" of "both bad and good" and the king's subsequent sorting (see also Matt. 13:47-50). The apocryphal Gospel of Thomas (v. 64) also includes a version of the parable in which the details are closer to Luke's version than to Matthew's. This is indirect evidence that Luke's version corresponds more closely with pre-Gospel traditions, whether transmitted in memory or manuscript. Still Luke's use of the story in this context is part of a distinctive presentation of Jesus' prophetic revelation and warning of the urgency and claim of the reign he was announcing and enacting.

Considerable debate has been invested in the possible connection between this parable and the list of conditions in Deut. 20:5-8 which would exempt one from holy war, i.e., having built a new house but not yet dedicated it, having just planted a vineyard but not yet enjoyed its produce, having just married but not yet "taken" his wife, and being fearful. Such a possibility is enhanced by the conviction of the sectarians at Qumran that the eschatological banquet would be a celebration of victory in holy war, and the suggestion is a fruitful reminder that discussions of banquet protocol were widely understood as primary metaphors of how God rules. The conditions of discipleship which follow in 14:25-33 also have the stringency of the holy war tradition. But the pleas for exemption from conscription which make military sense in Deuteronomy do not apply so directly here. Only the case of recent marriage is a direct parallel, and it is certainly less compelling when life and death are not at stake. These "excuses" are more general and less convincing reasons for refusing hospitality, and they are not accepted as legitimate.

15—This leading remark is Luke's familiar literary device which locks a traditional saying into the narrative. In this case, the announcement is exactly right, and Jesus' words are not a rebuke (contrast 11:27-28). Rightly understood, this declaration is a testimony of faith. Nevertheless, it is also a platitude, and as a general statement it is at least inadequate and may even be misleading since it may obscure the dynamic character of God's reign. It may miss the point that the question is still open as to "who" or whether "you" will share the feast. Thus Jesus' response (vv. 16-24) is not a rebuke of a true statment, but it is a warning against false comfort.

16-21a—The intensity of the scene is increased by the fact that all of these people have been invited before, and they are begging off at the critical moment when the host has everything ready. Of course, each one has a reason which may even sound somewhat legitimate, and no doubt the servant must nod and smile and maintain the semblance of oriental decorum. But these are rejections, and the servant and his master know it. Now, what will the lord (Gk: *kyrios*) do?

21b-24—The wrath of **the master** of the house (Gk: *despotēs*) is as profound as his invitation had been genuine, and his response is decisive and immediate. He swiftly changes the guest list, sending the servant to gather the **poor and maimed and blind and lame,** which is exactly the list Jesus had just counseled his host to invite (14:13). This is a list intended to reproach those first invited, but it is also now the protocol of the feast. And when these are not enough, the "lord" sends the servant to gather the most unlikely riffraff, even if he must **compel** or "constrain" them by insisting (see Gen. 19:3). This does not mean conversions at the point of a sword, but it does reveal the unswerving will of the host. His **anger** intensifies his determination, and his two compulsions are combined in one will: he is not going to let those who rejected his invitation either prevent his feast (v. 23b) or participate in it (v. 24).

The blessedness of eating bread in the kingdom of God may not be taken for granted. This is a glimpse of divine wrath, which is even more severe in Matthew's version (Matt. 22:11-14; compare Luke 13:22-30; 19:11-27). Jesus' mission and God's purposes are not casual, and those who would sentimentalize the kingdom or presume on God's grace must take notice, including the person who declares those who eat the bread of the kingdom to be blessed.

The allegorical character of this story is clear—and frightening. But in which setting should the application be made? Is this the historical Jesus alerting Israel that his ministry is God's invitation to the banquet? Is this the early church and perhaps Luke's community declaring that "now" is the time of the second invitation and the time for repentance is limited? Certainly the story speaks to both of these settings and a host of subsequent contexts. But Luke presents this story as a prophetic word within his narrative. Jesus is warning that the opposition he is encountering is a sign of further rejection which lies ahead for him and for his followers. Some will come in, but they will probably be an unlikely lot by the standards of the religious leaders. Then the eventual turning to the Gentiles in Acts will also be a fulfillment of God's will, even if it is also a severe judgment on those who were first invited (Acts 13:46; 18:6; 28:23-28).

Counting the Cost (14:25-35). Luke's transition to this section of the discourse offers an indirect reminder of the journey, since these great crowds are "going along with him" (Gk: *syneporeuonto*). Still, the substance of the discourse which began with the healing of the man with dropsy in 14:1 continues to be "election" or the protocol of the kingdom with regard to those who have excluded themselves as well as those who have now been invited. In Matt. 22:1-14, the parable of the royal feast concluded with the harsh exclusion of one who had come to the banquet without the proper garment. Having just emphasized the mixed crowd which will be included in the banquet of the kingdom (vv. 15-24), Luke's Jesus now sounds a similar warning to Matthew's story against presuming on their election. Even as the setting changes, the discourse begun at the banquet continues.

This section is thoroughly structured. Since the parallels to Matthew (10:37-38//Luke 14:26-27) and Mark (9:49-50//Luke 14:34-35) are scattered and weak, Luke probably did not derive the structure from "Q" or Mark. Perhaps the repetitions in the section would suggest a memory pattern, and the possibility of other written sources (such as "L") can never be excluded. But the structure also serves to undergird the flow of Luke's narrative, particularly as the repetitions in vv. 26-33 are tied into the conclusion in vv. 34-35. Thus the structure may be assessed as indicating Luke's use and grasp of these sayings of Jesus.

25—Luke's transition and introduction
26—Case #1: If anyone does not hate . . . it is not possible to be my disciple
27—Case #2: Whoever does not bears their own cross . . . it is not possible to be my disciple
  28-30—Illustration: Cost of building a tower
  31-32—Illustration: Cost of going to war
33—Case #3: Whoever does not renounce all . . . it is not possible to be my disciple
  34-35a—Similitude: Valuable and worthless salt
35b—Conclusion: Let the one with ears to hear hear!

All three of the conditions which are stated in the three cases are radical, uncompromising, and fearsome. None of them should be reduced in their claim, since the whole point of this entire section is to alert those in the crowds (v. 25) who are able to hear (v. 35b) to the extremely high costs which discipleship may entail. Yet these are prophetic warnings and disclosures of the magnitude of the claim of the kingdom. In Exod. 32:25-29 and Deut. 33:8-9, Levi furnishes the precedent for those whose loyalty was tested to the extent that they were compelled to put their own people to the sword, and his priestly ordination rested on this act of holy war. Once again, Jesus' teachings about the kingdom resound with the radical requirements of holy war. The stakes are that high!

Nevertheless, it would be incorrect to regard these commands as initiation requirements or ordeals which all who enlist in this kingdom must first perform to qualify. Nothing in the story supports such an understanding. But those who do become Jesus' disciples should know that the securities of family bonds, personal dignity and life, and possessions will be at risk. And the costs of loyalty to this Messiah and his reign will be high.

25-26—The list of family members varies among accounts (see also Matt. 10:37-38 and Gosp. Thomas 55, 101), but only a legalist would worry about having **hated** everyone on the list. The same concern about divided fidelities arises elsewhere in Luke where Jesus himself identifies who his true family members are (8:9-21) and commands a would-be follower not to return to bury his father (9:59-60). In 18:28-30, Jesus assures those who have left "house or wife or brothers or parents or children for the sake of the kingdom of God" that their sacrifice will not be in vain. But Luke's version escalates the traditional demand for loyalty to the kingdom with the phrase **Yes, and even his own life.**

Verse 26 then fills out this demand. "Self-hatred" has not been identified as a religious virtue. But the disciple of Jesus is one who follows in the way of the teacher, even as he goes to Jerusalem to die by crucifixion. Life, salvation, and security are not to be found in self-preservation, but in obedience to the way of the Lord, which Jesus himself pursued. As noted in the comments at 9:23-27, loyalty to Jesus and his kingdom often involved a very real peril of family rejection, dishonor, and even execution, perhaps by crucifixion. Other Christian witnesses and martyrs have also discovered that these words are not merely psychological intensifications. They are notices of the kind of struggle Christian discipleship often entails.

28-32—The illustrations are very practical, and they are traditional themes. In Prov. 24:3-6, one instructed by wisdom builds a house wisely and wages wars with wise counsel. It is simply foolish to undertake a task without carefully (i.e., **sitting down,**

vv. 28, 31) calculating what will be necessary. "If it doesn't pencil," say the shrewd minds of today, "don't do it." In 16:1-9, Jesus again commends the practical intelligence of very crafty people, without approving of their practices. But at least "the sons of this world" are not stupid. Neither should those who are counting on the coming of the kingdom be foolish. But they would do well to recognize and calculate (!) the high **cost,** even to them, which loyalty to that dominion requires.

33—Now the third cost is identified in terms which are very familiar in Luke's Gospel, the **renouncing** of personal possessions (Gk: *huparchonta heautou,* see comments at 6:20, 24). Attachments to family, personal safety, and financial security are all at risk in this building project (vv. 28-30), this campaign (vv. 31-32) of the Messiah and his kingdom. This is not a "kingdom" which people can build or a battle they can wage on their own. But even as followers of this Messiah, no one ought to "sign up" for the duration without understanding the costs involved.

34-35a—The point is simply that if "the salt of the earth" (to borrow Matthew's term for the disciples, Matt. 5:13) is to be worth anything, it must have savor. Debating whether **salt** could ever **lose** its flavor is a theoretical modern question based on a chemical understanding of the properties of sodium chloride. Whatever kinds of "salt" they may have had in first-century Palestine, the similitude only depends on the fact that some things that looked like salt or some "salts" had no value at all. Such "salt" was not even worth adding to the compost heap or the manure pile. It wasn't worth dung! In Luke's context, this shocking comparison drives directly to the point that those who are eager to join Jesus' entourage better understand where it is going. If they do not count the costs, they may not only become a laughingstock. They may have nothing to contribute, but be like **salt** that is not "salty," more worthless than waste, which can at least be recycled.

35b—Let the **one who has ears to hear, hear!** The whole passage is summarized. And if further comment is needed, look at the discussion of the poignancy of the commands to "hear" in 8:8, 10, 18.

He Declares God's Love of the Lost (15:1-32)

This chapter is one of the great treasures of Christian literature. The parable of the prodigal son ranks with the "Christmas gospel" (2:1-20) and the parable of the good Samaritan (10:29-37) as the best known of the stories of Jesus, and only Luke tells any of these. The parable of the lost sheep (15:1-8) is told also by Matthew (18:12-14), but the parable of the lost coin (vv. 9-10) is only in Luke. The compilation of these stories of "the lost and found" (vv. 4, 6, 8, 10, 24, 32) is the work of Luke, and the effect of joy and rejoicing (vv. 6, 7, 9, 10, 22, 24, 32) compounds as one story follows another. Each parable is a wondrous revelation of the extravagance of God's concern for the **lost** and **joy** at **repentance,** but taken together they are a sustained testimony to God's passion and freedom in seeking the lost and the splendid **joy of heaven** over the salvation of people who appear to be insignificant and wayward.

The literary context of this collection of parables is also significant. The banquet discourse of Chap. 14 has included words of promise for "the poor and maimed and blind and lame" (vv. 13, 21), but this reversal of the ususal protocols of "election" has been largely a prophetic reproof. The tone of the whole discourse has been persistently that of warning. Now, in the opening verses of Chap. 15, Jesus is criticized once again for the company he keeps at table (see also 5:29-32). But Jesus does not respond with sharp prophetic warnings or declarations of reversal. These parables are unadulterated words of promise. Even the complex conversation with the disapproving elder son (vv. 25-32), which touches again on the criticism of Jesus, is a display of gentleness without any compromise of the gracious determination which pervades the chapter.

The outline of the entire chapter manifests Luke's skill in composition. Not only does the vocabulary repeat the critical themes as noted above, but these three parables constitute a coherent response to the objection of **the Pharisees and the scribes** at the beginning of the chapter (vv. 1-3). The parables of the shepherd (vv. 4-7) and the woman (vv. 8-10) are so parallel that they complement and interpret each other. The more ample parable of the father and his sons (vv. 11-32) heightens the power of the chapter by dealing with a human story of a lost child (vv. 11-24) and by returning to the realization that even God's joyful love may be criticized (vv. 25-32). Luke's larger concern for interpreting the tragic mystery of the rejection of Jesus has not been forgotten. But before Jesus returns to stories about money—which will again warn and scandalize his opponents (Chap. 16)—Luke 15 offers another unqualified assurance of God's "good pleasure to give you the kingdom" (12:32).

The Lost Sheep and the Lost Coin (15:1-10).   The outline of these verses demonstrates how thoroughly parallel they are in content as well as structure. This parallelism could be the result of Luke's shaping the "lost coin" parable after the model of the "lost sheep," and the concluding references to **repentance** are probably Lukan. But it seems probable that both parables were traditional pieces, told in similar terms, and if one were remembered in the oral tradition, the other would be too.

On the other hand, the historical origins of these traditions remain problematic, and using the parables as avenues to reconstruct the teaching of the "historical Jesus" must be pursued elsewhere. It is more possible and productive in this commentary to assess the effect of these parallels within Luke's story, no matter what their prior histories. Noting contrasts between Luke's "final version" and possible earlier nuances of meaning will thus be pursued primarily in order to grasp Luke's message.

1-3—Luke's introduction to the whole chapter is dramatic. If all (Gk. *pantos*) **the tax collectors and sinners were all drawing near to hear him,** it would seem to be a large group. That they were coming **to hear** is a direct link back to 14:35 where "those who have ears to hear" were commanded to hear. Luke is again emphasizing that large groups in Israel did "hear" Jesus, and yet Jesus' following was not among the recognized religious authorities. The murmuring of **the Pharisees and the scribes** over Jesus' meal fellowship with **tax collectors and sinners** will appear again when "all murmured" at his eating with the "sinner" and "tax collector" Zacchaeus. These issues of meal fellowship were serious considerations within Israel, long before the question of eating with Gentiles appeared (see Acts 10 and 15; Gal. 2:12-13).

3-7//8-10—The parables of the lost sheep and the lost coin can be virtually superimposed on the same outline.

Which man/woman . . . having 100 sheep/10 coins, if he/she loses one . . . does not leave/sweep . . . and go after/and seek . . . until he/she finds it? And when he/she has found it . . . he/she calls together his/her friends and neighbors saying, "Rejoice with me, for I have found my sheep/the coin . . . which was/I had lost.' Just so, I tell you, there will be more/is joy in heaven/before the angels of God over one sinner who repents. . . ."

In both cases, however, the parable itself seems to have a different thrust from its application, which begins **Just so I tell you.** Perhaps it is more accurate to say that both parables primarily convey images of the determined concern of God to find the lost while the conclusions draw more attention to the necessity of repentance as the occasion of returning or being **found.** The parable of the lost son and the loving father (vv. 11-32) will explore this tension between "returning" and "being found" in still more explicit terms. Thus it will be productive to explore both dimensions of these stories as a Lukan introduction to the deeper question of salvation by God's grace and the necessity of repentance.

The glory of both parables lies in their astonishing picture of God or God's way of ruling. This shepherd and woman are the central figures of both stories. What they do and say conveys the drama, not the wayward sheep or lost coin. They are images of determination, perhaps even obsession with the lost. Many scriptural precedents exist for speaking of God as the shepherd of Israel and even as the faithful shepherd who seeks and restores the lost (Ezek. 34:11-16; see also Jer. 31:10-14; Isa. 40:11).

But this shepherd and woman are not merely examples of virtue. It may even be possible to question why the shepherd puts the 99 at risk by leaving them **in the wilderness.** And why does the **woman** make such a large scene over the loss of an insignificant **coin?** And why do they call in their men and women **friends** for a celebration? Some interpreters have suggested that the shepherd feared punishment for losing a sheep or that he "must

have" put someone in charge of the 99 or found a safe place for
them to herd up. Others have argued that the woman was very
poor or she may have lost this little coin from a necklace of sentimental value. But none of this is in the stories, and these efforts
only demonstrate that the behavior of these two requires an explanation which is not merely moralistic.

These are human behaviors of determination which go beyond
the rational, and the friends and neighbors will recognize their
profound relief and the joy in their extravagance when they find
the lost item. Anyone who has lost the car keys knows about this
compulsion to find the lost, and the joy of finding may exceed
the mere recovery of the object. This is the time for a party!

These parables are glimpses into the heart of God. They are
drawn from human experience, but experience in which determination, extravagance, and joy exceed normal practice. A shepherd who is obsessed with finding that one lost sheep may take
inordinate risks, and a woman who loses a coin may take her
house apart knowing that it "has to be here." And so it is with
God, and God's Messiah acting in obedience to God's will. The
determination, the risky behavior of eating with sinners and tax
collectors, and the extravagant **joy** of **heaven** put the moralists
and religionists on edge and to shame.

The conclusions (vv. 7, 10) sound the note of joy which the
parables already imply, but they also indicate that God finding
the "lost" person is more complex than a shepherd finding a **sheep**
or a woman **a coin.** After all, both the sheep and the coin are not
responsible or willful agents. No suggestion is made that the
sheep (or the coin) was "bad." But it is probably Luke who has
introduced the mention of **repentance,** and Luke's conviction is
that the image of the parable must be elaborated if the force of
this parable is to be caught within this larger story of the revelation of God's will and the disclosure of human rejection.

Yes, God's passion and compassion is to save, even at great risk
and with displays of determination. That is why Jesus "set his
face to go to Jerusalem" (9:51) and why his priority has been not
to call "the righteous" but "sinners" to repentance (5:31). The
greater **joy in heaven over one sinner** than **over ninety-nine
righteous persons who need no repentance** (v. 7) is not cynical.

It does not imply that the **ninety-nine** are all hypocrites. But it does declare God's freedom and determination to save sinners (and tax collectors) without criticism for irreligion, immorality, or extravagance.

In Luke's presentation, **repentance** is not a good work (see 15:20). Repentance is itself a gift from God for Israel and later for the Gentiles (Acts 5:31, 11:18). God, the Messiah, and the Holy Spirit are of one will and one dominion in seeking to find the lost and lead sinners to repentance. But committed and compassionate as God's will is, it is not coercive. It always requires the hearing of faith. Thus repentance is a miracle of God's tireless grace and of faith, and the courts of heaven rollick with joy when this mission is accomplished and one sinner repents. It is not simple, even for God.

The Lost Son and the Loving Father (15:11-32). This magnificent story is known by all the English-speaking world as "the parable of the prodigal son," even by people who never use the word "prodigal" in other contexts. Since the word "prodigal" refers primarily to the son's extravagant wasting of his inheritance, that traditional title draws attention to the son's immorality, perhaps even stressing a moralistic interpretation. But then the elder brother's understanding may have the last word. He had the moral of the story well in hand. Perhaps the German-speaking tradition has a more adequate title, "the parable of the lost son." Clearly Luke ties all three of the parables of this chapter together around the theme of the "lost and the found" (vv. 4, 6, 8, 10, 24, 32).

But the parable is centered on the father: **There was a man who had two sons** (v. 11, see also the shepherd, v. 4, and the woman, v. 8). He is present at the beginning, middle, and end of the drama, and the most remarkable aspect of the story is his extravagant love. His elder son might say that this is the story of the prodigal father and the immoral son, since the father was so lavishly generous in giving to an undeserving son. The question which counts is whether to accept the elder son's interpretation or the father's, just as the question in the context is whether to agree with the objections of the Pharisees and the scribes or to accept Jesus' insistence on the propriety of his eating with tax collectors and sinners (v. 2).

This is a human story. Its power and appeal arise from the reality of the characters. None of them is a plaster saint. The **younger** son is headstrong, demanding, wasteful, and perhaps even manipulative in his return. The **elder son** is petty and angry, but his protests have the logic of simple justice and good order. And the **father** has not been very sensible. He might well have listened to the wisdom of Jesus Ben Sira, "To son or wife, to brother or friend, do not give power over yourself, as long as you live; and do not give your property to another . . . it is better that your children should ask from you than that you should look to the hand of your sons . . . in the hour of death, distribute your inheritance" (Sir. 33:19-23). Or again, "Give to the godly man but do not help the sinner . . . for the Most High also hates sinners and will inflict punishment on the ungodly" (Sir. 12:4-6). Instead, he gave away the inheritance early to a son who wasted it. He rushed out to receive the son in lavish joy. He even interrupted as the younger son tried to give his repentance speech. And then he had to plead with the elder son that his behavior was **fitting** or "necessary" (v. 32). He is not the model of prudence, but he is the picture of parental love. When the wayward son or daughter appears at the door, all the moral speeches and all the worry, anger, and disappointment may be swept away. "Thank God, you're alive! Welcome home!"

This is also a story about God, and the humanity of the story is central to its theology. It is thoroughly anthropomorphic or anthropopathic, envisioning God in terms of human experience and feelings. But the prophets of Israel had taken the same shocking and embarrassing risks before, revealing but not capturing God in the human image. When Jer. 31:18-20 spoke of the repentance of wayward Israel, it was in terms of the yearning of God's heart for "Ephraim, my dear son, my darling child." And the theme of God's loving compassion was expanded in Hosea 6 and 11 in profoundly human terms: "It was I who taught Ephraim to walk, I took them up in my arms. . . . How can I give you up, O Ephraim! How can I hand you over, O Israel! . . . My heart recoils within me. . . . I will not execute my fierce anger, I will not again destroy Ephraim; for I am God and not man, the Holy One in your midst, and I will not come to destroy." (Hos.

11:1-9). In the kingdom of God, the only force which is more powerful than God's justice is God's mercy. And no one may criticize God's mercy, for it will surpass even what the most religious would find acceptable. Then because God is God, no human standard may be invoked in judgment.

11-13—The plot is established. The **younger** son is headed for trouble, and everyone knows it. He took the inheritance which he just received and turned it into cash (RSV: **gathered all he had**) and went away, far away. Exactly how he **squandered** the money is not clear, even if the elder brother accuses him of whoring (v. 30). When the RSV says **in loose living,** it is translating a rather vague term which says "living in an unsalutary way" (Gk: *asōtōs*). Certainly that is not good, and he did blow the inheritance. But it is not so lurid as the elder brother and many interpreters imagine.

14-19—Now things get worse, even lurid. He did not cause the **famine,** but he did not save his money to meet such problems either. Feeding pigs and eating pig food! According to Leviticus (11:7-8) pigs were not even to be touched. The shame for a Jewish boy might have been worse than the starvation. So now he starts to talk to himself, but it is not an especially noble soliloquy. He is sobered (RSV: **he came to himself**), but he is primarily concerned to get something to eat, at least as much as his **father's servants.** So he practices a speech which is designed to evoke his father's sympathy. It is not possible to tell how sincere his repentance is, and apparently all he hopes to receive from his confession is a servant's fare. He did not understand much about his father's love when he demanded his inheritance and left home, and he is not prepared for the reception he is about to receive as he returns in failure. And it is true that he has no "right" to anything from his father and no "worthiness" as a son to bank upon. Assuming that he is not trying to manipulate his father, the best he could expect is a little pity.

20-24—Instead of pity, the father overwhelms him with grace. The artists in Christian history have often caught this while the theologians were moralizing and allegorizing, and the picture is incredible of the father, filled with **compassion** (see also 7:13), "running" down the road, that is, abandoning all decorum before the servants, the neighbors, himself, and God, then hugging him and kissing him (Gk: he fell on his neck). Forget morality! This is love! And it is foolish and joyful. Only a distraught, grieving parent could imagine such release.

The younger son has not anticipated this scene. He has just been assaulted with love, and still he starts into his prepared speech. After all, he had rehearsed it to the pigs, and it was a pretty good speech. But his father is in no mood to sober up and listen to such somber talk. According to the best manuscripts of v. 22, he interrupted before he hears (and we hear for the second time) the whole drab speech. He is uninterested in a discussion about who is **worthy.** He stops the boy at the word **son,** and never hears about how he is supposed to treat him as a servant. Nonsense! The father is already stirring up the servants for a royal welcome. "A **robe,** a **ring,** and **shoes!** Right now! And **kill the fatted calf!** This is a homecoming!"

There are times when eating and merrymaking are disapproved (see 12:19), but this is different. This is like the joy in heaven before the angels of God (vv. 7, 10) because the father has found and regained his son. This is not merely a banquet. It is a party!

25-32—Apparently they started the party before the **elder son** got home from work, even the **music and dancing.** It does not seem fair. It isn't fair. All the laughing and singing reaches his ears before the news. His question, therefore, creates great tension in the story; even Luke's use of the optative makes the moment more tentative (see also 18:36; Acts 21:33): "And what have we here?" The poor servant is caught, but his answer reaches out to include the elder brother in the joy, "**Your brother** . . . **and your father** . . . **because he has received him safe and sound.**"

It does not work. He is **angry.** This is not his party, and he does not later use the word "brother" or "father" to address or speak of either of them. Now it is the father who leaves the party and pleads with him, and this time the father listens to the whole speech. And it is a bitter speech ("I have slaved for you all these years and never disobeyed"), a resentful speech ("yet you never gave me even a kid so I could have my own party with my friends"), and a self-justifying speech ("but when this son of yours came, you killed the fatted calf"). He not only refuses to join the joyful celebration, he also is cutting himself off from his brother and his father.

Yet the father still calls him **"Son."** He assures him that his place in the family is secure (**"you are always with me"**) and his legal rights are protected (**"everything I have is yours"**). The only way the elder son would be excluded from the party or the feast (or the kingdom!) would be if he insisted on excluding himself.

But the father will not back down on his grace. The last line is firm: **"It is fitting** (Gk: *edei*) **to make merry and be glad because. . . ."** This expression is not merely an appeal to propriety, but in Luke it is usually translated, "It is necessary that . . ." (see 2:49; 4:43; 9:22; 11:42; 13:14, 16, 33; 17:25; 18:1; 19:5; 21:9; 22:7, 37; 24:7, 26, 44). Often it is the central clue that the will of God and fulfillment of the Scriptures are at stake. In this case the "necessity" need be no more than the human reality of a lost son returned home, but it is also a strong expression of the father's will.

Thus Luke brings the reader full circle to the occasion for these parables of Jesus. The Pharisees and scribes also could not tolerate Jesus feasting with tax collectors and sinners. Certainly they did not want to participate, but Jesus was declaring that this is the kind of joy and feasting which God and the angels found most "fitting." It was not done to exclude the righteous (see 5:31; 15:7, 10), and they should not exclude themselves (see also Acts 3:23). But the grace and love of God were at work in this joyful mission of bringing back the "lost," and neither God nor the Messiah was about to stop.

Those who merely desire justice and morality will always find Jesus and his kingdom offensive. Of course he is about the tasks of righteousness, and his good news to the poor and oppressed deals with their immediate realities of sickness, hunger, and misery. But in the midst of all of Jesus' calls for self-sacrifice and renunciation of goods by his disciples (14:25-35), he reveals that this is not merely a program of equitable redistribution of resources. Something greater than distributive justice and more profound than fairness is at stake. The joyous freedom of God to be God is to show mercy on the sinner and to seek the lost. God surpasses all human religious systems and redefines all standards of righteousness by such mercy.

He Warns of the Dangers of Money (16:1-31)

This chapter is another display of Luke's gathering of traditional stories around a theme. The contents of the first 12 verses are only found in Luke, then vv. 13, 16-17 are from "Q," and v. 18 appears to be based on Mark 10:11-12. In the midst of these diverse materials, Jesus has another confrontation with **the Pharisees** (vv. 14-15), which ties all of this discussion about money and the Law into the larger narrative framework of Luke. That is, Jesus' words to his **disciples** (vv. 1-13) and **the Pharisees** (vv. 14-31) are part of the larger discourse on God's will and reign. The banquet setting is no longer prominent, although it is noteworthy that the parable of the lost son just concluded with a feast (15:22-32) and the story of Lazarus begins with the rich man's feast (16:19-21). Furthermore, this section ends with yet one more meal setting (17:7-10). Thus even as the discourse moves on to questions of money and the Law, the theme of the banquet is not lost.

The Dishonest Manager (16:1-9). The meaning of this whole story revolves on how the master's "praise" of the **dishonest steward** in v. 8 is to be understood. The debate has several positions related to where the story is perceived to end, but either **the master** is **commending** the **steward** for his prudence in a difficult situation or merely complimenting him for being as amazingly **shrewd** as he is **dishonest.**

If the parable concludes with the commendation of the steward in v. 8a, it may seem more probable that the master has reversed himself. His praise is straightforward because the manager has found a way to achieve collections through discounts of exorbitant interest charges or perhaps even through cutting his own commission. This interpretation redeems the steward as a model of someone who faces reality and makes necessary adjustments. But it also depends upon a series of rather speculative suggestions as to how the commodity and interest economy worked. Furthermore, it tends to discount vv. 8b-9 as secondary comments or applications of the parable by the evangelist.

Dealing with the parable in its literary context all but requires that it be read straight through v. 9, with vv. 10-12 standing apart as a further commentary drawn from another traditional saying of Jesus. But then the parable has an ironic conclusion with a biting tone, and this appears to be the better reading. The whole story is a display of the **shrewdness** of the **sons of this world,** which is indeed impressive. But beware ordering your affairs that way if you wish to enter the **eternal habitations.**

1-2—The situation is clear. This manager is at least mismanaging the master's resources. It is not yet clear if fraud is involved, but the later identification of him as the **dishonest steward** indicates that this is not mere incompetence. In fact, he is quite competent, but he plays the game cleverly only to his own advantage. At any rate, he is notified that he is fired, and there is never a suggestion that the master reconsiders that decision. He must hand over the books.

3-4—This is another of the self-centered soliloquies in which he talks to himself as do other persons of questionable character in Luke (see 7:39, Simon the Pharisee; 12:17, the rich fool; 15:17, the younger son; 18:4 the dishonest judge). He is like Fagin in *Oliver* "thinking it out again" when compelled to change the scene. He is not repenting, just lamenting that he does not have a legitimate option. So he figures out a new way to continue playing the same dishonest game to his advantage. He moves fast while he still has control of the accounts because his goal is to accumulate obligations which he may call in after he has lost his position (v. 4). His purposes are strictly self-serving.

5-7—These are **his master's debtors.** Nothing is said about their owing him anything. Of course, once he has discounted all of their debts to the master, they are in his "debt." He uses his office one last time in a scam which will benefit the debtors directly. And they know and he knows that they now **owe** him. That's the way the world works!

8-9—The master is not ignorant. When he receives the accounts, he can see he has been taken. But it is all over. Both the creditors' notes and the books agree that the debt has been discounted. They have not done anything illegal and probably the manager also had such authority as long as he was in charge of the loan accounts. So the master can only compliment the **dishonest steward** for being shrewd or clever (Gk: *phronimōs*). After all, it is sad but true that **the sons of this world are more shrewd** (Gk: *phronimōteroi*) than the sons of light. Just think what could happen if people were as clever in pursuing the justice and mercy of the kingdom as they are in looking out for themselves!

The word **commend** or "compliment" could be sincere praise of a job well done, and if it is done "prudently" it would appear to be a good moral example. But this is **shrewdness** such as generally characterizes the worldly wise in contrast to **the children of light** who walk in accord with the light of the gospel (see Eph. 5:8; John 12:36; 1QS 1:9-10; etc.), and this is only a grudging compliment. "I must admit that you figured it out once again even after I fired you!" But he is still the "manager of unrighteousness" (Gk: *oikonomos tēs adikias*), and he is still fired.

The word of counsel in v. 9, therefore, is a double-edged counsel for people who know all about "smart money" and clever dealing, but the stakes are raised impossibly high. If you are impressed by a shrewd fellow like this who wrote the book on how to manage unrighteousness, go ahead. Build up the "network" of friends who are obligated to you on the basis of the **mammon of unrighteousness** (on **mammon,** see vv. 10 and 13 below), and see what they can do for you, not when you are fired, but when you are dead! Good luck!

Love, Money, and the Constraint of the Kingdom (16:10-18). These verses include a diverse collection of traditions, and interpreters are divided on whether or how the section holds together. The most significant interpretative proposal has been offered by those who view Luke-Acts as a project in "salvation history." In this school, v. 16 has been held up as a major thematic statement of Luke's eschatology or understanding of the plot of the whole historical drama. The epoch of **the law and the prophets** comes to an end with **John,** then the epoch of Jesus and **the kingdom** begins, and perhaps the sending of the Holy Spirit after

Jesus' "departure" marks yet another epoch. But then this major thematic statement of Luke's eschatology seems to be adrift in a wash of unconnected statements.

But if Luke's project is more focused on soteriology than eschatology, perhaps the coherence of this section is more apparent. That is, this collection of sayings does not provide much in the way of a context for a major statement about the phasing of the divine plan, but it does hold together in addressing issues of conflicting loyalties and in its revelation of opposition to God's will. Verses 16-17 are more than thematic statements about phases. They are declarations of the uncompromising claim and evident force of **the kingdom of God.** God's will has not changed, nor have **the law and the prophets** been surpassed. But in Jesus, God's reign has come in strength, renouncing divided loyalties (vv. 10-13), revealing idolatries (vv. 14-15), and raising standards of obedience (v. 18).

10-13—These traditional words of Jesus are apparently attached to v. 9 as further expositions of "unrighteous mammon" (v. 9, "the mammon of unrighteousness"; v. 11, **unrighteous mammon; v. 13, mammon**). As standard wisdom aphorisms, they are not particularly original or interesting. Only their theological applications (v. 11b, **true riches;** v. 13b, **God and mammon**) raise these sayings above the level of truisms.

Verses 10-12 are found only in Luke, and they underline the irony in the conclusion of the story of the unrighteous manager (v. 9). No one who is a manipulator could be commended as a example for "the sons of light" (v. 8), except as for contrast and comparison. When the third person general statement of v. 10 (**he who** . . .) becomes direct address in v. 11 (**you**), the point is driven home that **you** do not qualify for managing the **true** riches of the kingdom by the kind of "creative accounting" practiced by the unrighteous manager. Verse 12 then moves the logic further with a still more personal implication in the form of a question. If you are not trustworthy with someone else's goods (such as those of God's reign), who will give you your own? These are words of warning, requiring honesty and faithful management, first of all of the true riches of the kingdom. Self-serving schemes are denounced.

Verse 13 is taken almost verbatim from "Q" (Matt. 6:24). Only
the word **servant** seems to be an addition, tying the saying into
this context. Once again the general statement (**no servant can**)
moves to direct address in the application (**You cannot serve God
and mammon**). The possibility of "having it both ways" is sternly
renounced.

The theological application of the old aphorism about **two masters** is not original with Luke, but it is thoroughly consistent with
his presentation of Jesus. This is where early Christian ethics and
faith converge, and the issue is idolatry—not merely equity.
Nothing was more basic than the first command of the Decalogue,
"You shall have no other gods before me!" (Exod. 20:3; Deut.
5:7), or more central than Israel's confession, "Hear, O Israel: the
Lord our God is one; and you shall love the Lord your God with
all your heart, and with all your soul, and with all your might!"
(Deut. 6:4). Jesus' interpretation of the old saying about **two masters** sharpens the contrast between worldly "shrewdness" in **unrighteous mammon** and faithful service of God. As in the temptation story, where the newly anointed Messiah refused to do
obeisance before the devil's claim to worldly dominion (4:5-7),
the issue is that of serving God or a false god. No accommodation
is offered for living in the "real world" where compromise and
manipulation are the rules of the game. Such attempts to live in
both worlds are simply not consistent with God's rule.

14-15—The problem with **the Pharisees** is that they are too
much like the rest of humanity. In Luke's narrative they play the
role of the adversaries, and here they are offended by such un-
compromisng talk. Jesus has just escalated money matters into
questions of idolatry, and they "sneer" in disapproval (see also
the rulers at the cross, 23:35). Luke says that they were **lovers
of money,** which explains how he has pulled all of this together
as an illustration of how those who "love" and "serve" mammon
(v. 13) are exposed as idolaters when forced to choose. Jesus'
theological application of the proverb of two masters has proved
to be a prophetic word, disclosing the secret thoughts of the heart
(v. 15, **God knows your hearts**) of those with divided loyalties
(see Simeon's word, 2:35). In v. 15, therefore, Jesus merely concludes the prophetic diagnosis of the condition which has been
exposed.

You who respond with sneers to Jesus' theological interpretation of the proverbial maxim are those who **justify yourselves before humans.** Luke does not use the language of "justification" as constantly as Paul, but this is not a casual concern for Luke either. In 7:29, the tax collectors and people who were gratified by Jesus' praise of John "justified God" because they had been baptized by John. By contrast in 10:29, the Law interpreter who was testing Jesus soon found himself "desiring to justify himself." And in 18:14, the penitent tax collector is the one who is "justified" (by God) rather than the self-righteous Pharisee. Self-justification before others is the antithesis of being justified by God or justifying God. But **you** who sneer are exposed as hypocrites, for God's discernment of the heart and judgment is final.

This confrontation is fundamental to Luke's interpretation of these sayings of Jesus within the larger story. The Lukan theme of Jesus' prophetic word exposing the self-justifying hypocrisy of the heart unifies the collection of sayings. The Pharisees bear the brunt of the scene, and certainly Luke has sharpened Jesus' judgment by identifying them as "lovers of money." But the reader must remember that this charge serves a literary purpose in a larger narrative and must proceed with some caution in knowing how to take this charge. The assumption that this is a straightforward historical description of all Pharisees is dangerous. If "they" are made into scapegoats, the force of the whole section may be lost. The reader may be tempted to practice another kind of self-justification at the expense of the Pharisees. Not only is this an implicit anti-Semitism for modern Gentile Christian readers, but it is an effort to escape the theological claim of Jesus' prophetic word. This passage indicts all who practice self-justification and all who love money. **The Pharisees** are only colleagues in such idolatry.

16-17—The declarations of these verses are major statements of the whole of Luke's story, and they are integral to this section. Three related points are scored in the course of these few words. (1) **John** the Baptizer marks the transition from the old economy of **the law and the prophets** to the new regime of the declaration of **the kingdom** itself. Only Luke speaks in these terms of "proclaiming the kingdom" (Gk: *euangelizesthai tēn basileian tou*

theou, 4:43; 8:1; Acts 8:12). Matthew's version of this saying from
"Q" (Matt. 11:12-13) counts the time of the kingdom as commencing with John ("from the days of John until the present . . ."),
but Luke seems to count **John** as the last and greatest of the
prophets who stands at the end of that era and on the brink of
the time of the kingdom (see the discussion at 3:18-22; 7:26-28).
In Luke's usage of the traditional word of Jesus, these phases in
God's way of ruling the world are consistent with the larger contours of the narrative, beginning with John and Jesus in the infancy stories. And since Jesus began his ministry (4:14), the time
of the proclamation of the kingdom has begun.

(2) Luke understands the kingdom of God to be a force with
which to reckon, whether accepted or rejected. The last phrase
in v. 16 should probably be translated with emphasis on the passive force of the verb: "And everyone is constrained [Gk: *biazes-
thai,* "forced, compelled"] into it [the kingdom of God]." The
passive voice is again an indirect way of speaking of God's activity.
Everyone is constrained by God. The word is different in Greek,
but this is the same difficult vision of the will of God which is
encountered in Jesus' being "constrained" (Gk: *synechesthai*) until his "baptism" is accomplished (12:50) or the lord of the feast
"compelling" (Gk: *anangkason*) people to enter (14:23). God does
not merely invite people into the kingdom, as if they could take
it or leave it. They are commanded to enter, and to choose otherwise is to reject the kingdom.

(3) This kingdom is a new reality, but it does not mean that
the commands of God in the Law and the Prophets are thereby
annulled. Not so much as a pen stroke on a single letter has been
wiped away. Even if God and the Messiah have extended grace
to the tax collectors and sinners who do not keep **the law,** that
does not mean that God's commands for obedience are null and
void. God's mercy has been extended to those outside of **the law,**
but the law's role for setting a standard of obedience continues.
It may even be increased.

18—Luke now adduces a case which verifies the third point,
drawing upon Synoptic tradition (see Matt. 19:9//Mark 10:11-12,
and see also 1 Cor. 7:10-11). All of these traditions are primarily
opposed to remarriage after **divorce.** Paul and Mark's version of

this word of the Lord speaks to both the wife and the husband, which probably reflects a legal circumstance in the Hellenistic world where a woman could take an initiative in divorce. Matthew's version allows for remarriage after divorce only on the grounds of unchastity, but none of these Christian traditions even comments on the more liberal allowances for divorce and remarriage in Deut. 24:1-4.

Luke's version follows the Jewish tradition of dealing only with the legal rights of the man (see the view of the wife as property reflected in Exod. 20:17; 21:3, 22; Jer. 6:12; Num. 30:10-14), but the man's "rights" are sharply curtailed. Remarriage after **divorce** and marriage of **a divorced woman** are **adultery.**

This is no more radical than the declaration about the unfaithfulness involved in the love of money (v. 13). Perhaps modern readers would think that the charge of "adultery" is worse than "idolatry," but such comparisons are wrongheaded. The point is that the appearance of the Messiah and declaration of God's kingdom is an intrusion which reveals all human hypocrisies. Quiet little divorces because "I found someone else" and investing one's life in the money game are exposed and condemned. The kingdom of God compels people to enter or to reject God's law and mercy by denying the reality the Messiah has uncovered. The determined will of God is at work.

The Rich Man and Lazarus (16:19-31).   This story begins with no introduction. It is a remarkably powerful story which has contributed graphic detail to popular depictions of hell and heaven in the afterlife, and it is a fearsome warning of a time when repentance is no longer possible. Since the subsequent sayings are introduced as addressed to the disciples (17:1), this story is probably intended for the Pharisees who were the last audience mentioned (16:14). Or perhaps the Pharisees are again merely overhearing (along with the readers) Jesus' discourse as when they responded to his words to his disciples (14:1-3, 15).

But the context of the story is decisive. Two fundamental points are scored by this story, and both points are expositions of themes which are central to this chapter. (1) The story concludes with the warning that **if they do not hear Moses and the prophets,**

neither will they be persuaded if someone should rise from the dead (v. 31, also vv. 29-30). Since Jesus has just been emphasizing the continuing validity of the Law and of the will of God revealed in "the law and the prophets" (v. 16), this conclusion reinforces the teaching that the Scriptures are valid and vital revelations of God's will. The question of the relationship between the revelation in the Scriptures and the new era after Christ's resurrection is only sharpened.

(2) Chapter 16 has been particularly attentive to questions of money or mammon (vv. 9, 11, 13, 14). This story of the reversal of the fortunes of a rich man and a poor beggar provides a confirmation that "what is exalted among human beings is an abomination in the sight of God" (v. 15).

It should also be noted that the popular appeal of this story is related to its familiar form. Every generation has had its collection of tales, example stories, and nervous jokes about someone who died and met St. Peter or approached the river Styx or went to hell. Interesting parallels to this story have also been found in Egyptian and Jewish stories of a poor man being blessed and a rich man punished after death. Jesus was also telling a story, with no indication that he was describing an actual case and no claim that this is a detailed view of the physical architecture of Hades or the specific means of angelic transport of the blessed to Abraham's bosom. How all of this scene relates to a "last judgment" remains unclear, since the lore of the afterlife is not always fully consistent with the teaching of resurrection. But if too much speculation about the state of the dead on the basis of this story is inappropriate, there is no question but that the story assumes and teaches divine judgment and resurrection.

19-21—The contrast between the earthly lives of the two men is developed in detail. Royal splendor and rich feasting are contrasted with the misery and hunger of a man who had to be laid at the **rich man's gate.** The literary art of the story stimulates the imagination, inviting even more graphic description: a banquet honoring the great man at the Hilton with the street people picking through the dumpster out back. The typical scene is all too familiar. The rich man is not depicted as especially evil, perhaps he even makes sure that the surplus from his **table** gets to **Lazarus.** He is living the good life, but he is not even aware that this is not all simply his due, or his blessing. He is receiving his consolation (6:20-24).

It is important to note that the **rich man** is not named (see the textual variant) while **Lazarus** is. Since the Gospel of John tells of Jesus raising his friend Lazarus from the dead, questions about possible connections between these stories abound. Other commentators have been interested in the fact that the name "Lazarus" may mean "helped by God." But none of this figures in the story. **Lazarus** may simply be a Jewish name that came to Jesus' mind. But it is interesting that by having a name "Lazarus" becomes more of a person, although he says nothing in the story, while the **rich man** only achieves a pathetic identity through his words.

22-23—Death is not merely an equalizer. It is a doorway to a world where earthly appearances are an "abomination" (v. 15). The heavenly messengers (see also the joy of the angels in 15:10) **carry** the **poor man** once again, but now to the blessed state of the chosen people and children of **Abraham.** The **bosom of Abraham** is a figure for the closest contact possible, a picture of acceptance and love (see the "beloved disciple" in John 13:23-25). Lazarus was not only a genuine child of Abraham (see 3:8), but he would be at the head table with Abraham for the great feast (13:28-29). He has been gathered to his ancestors in the most intimate way possible (see Gen. 15:15; 47:30; Deut. 31:16); and, as Jesus will later argue, Abraham and Isaac and Jacob are alive to God and proofs of the resurrection (20:37-38).

The rich man, on the other hand, simply **died and was buried.** Of course this means he received a proper burial, and more will be said about him. But the literary effect of this short phrase creates a sharp contrast with the expansive account of Lazarus' exaltation.

24-26—The rich man's misery and **torment** is primarily important as a direct display of the reversal which has now taken place. Jesus' words of 6:20-24 are now given pictorial form. The rich man still calls Abraham his **father** (3:8), and Abraham speaks to him as **child** (Gk: *teknon;* RSV: **son**). But now neither Abraham nor Lazarus can do anything for him. Abraham simply reminds him of the sharp contrast between then and now. He had good things and is now in **anguish.** Lazarus had evil things and now is comforted. Even the chasm is not merely lateral. In v. 23, it is clear that he must look up (see 1:52-53).

27-31—The rich man makes a second request, again involving Lazarus. Perhaps he has not yet caught on that he is not in a position to give directions as to what Lazarus should do. But the argument focuses on his plea that his brothers be warned, and **Abraham's** (he is also their **father**) refusal. This time it is not physically impossible, as with the barrier of the chasm. Now the point is the validity and adequacy of **Moses and the prophets.**

The vocabulary is signficant. He begs that Lazarus might **warn** his **brothers,** and the term (Gk: *diamartyrēsthai*) means "to bear witness." In Acts, the apostles are identified as the "witnesses" (1:8, *martyres*), and Peter's Pentecost speech to the Judeans and "all who dwell in Jerusalem" is a witness and a warning that Jesus had been raised from the dead in fulfillment of the Scriptures (see Acts 2:40, *diamartyrēsthai*). The rich man's hope is if someone brought news from the dead, they would **repent** (Gk: *metanoein*), but Abraham declares that unless they **hear** (Gk: *akouein*) Moses and the prophets they would not be persuaded (Gk: *peithēsthai*) even if someone should rise from the dead. "Repenting," "being persuaded," and believing are matters of "hearing," and the testimony of Moses and the prophets is warning enough.

In the context of Luke's story of Jesus, Abraham's word is both an endorsement of the continuing validity of the Scriptures (16:16-17) and a prophetic warning that many in Israel will repent neither on the basis of the Scriptures nor on the testimony of Jesus' resurrection. Luke will also later emphasize that the risen Christ taught his followers how to read and understand the Scriptures in the light of their fulfillment in him (see comments at 24:26-27, 32, 44-48). In fact, God did what Abraham did not do. Christ was raised from the dead, and his apostles were sent as the witnesses to call Israel to repent on the basis of both the Scriptures and one raised from the dead. God does not give up easily on the lost, even those who are persistently unable to "hear."

He Encourages Faithful Obedience (17:1-10)

Luke rounds out the second major section of Jesus' journey to Jerusalem (13:22—17:10) by collecting the diverse sayings in these verses into a brief discourse **to his disciples** (see also 6:20; 9:14; 12:22; 17:22). Clearly these sayings circulated independently of each other. They are still easily separated, and they appear in quite diverse contexts in Matthew and Mark. But in Luke, these sayings mark the resumption of Jesus' counsel to his disciples (16:1-13) which has been interrupted by a sharp exchange with the Pharisees (16:14-31). Now, taken together, they constitute a discourse on faithful obedience or at least an exchange with the disciples/apostles (see v. 5). And Luke's Jesus counsels his followers: (a) "Beware of sinning, especially if it causes other to sin!" (vv. 1-3a), (b) "Be quick to forgive!" (vv. 3b-4), (c) "Have faith!" (vv. 5-6), and "Do not look for recognition for simple obedience!" (vv. 7-10).

1-3a—After Luke's careful identification of the **disciples** as the audience for these words, he moves into a traditional saying of Jesus about the dire fate of anyone who causes one of the **little ones** to stumble. The first phrase may also be Luke's rather complex transition: "It is impossible (Gk: *anendekton*) for stumbling blocks (Gk: *skandala*) not to come." The reality of evil in the world is not taken lightly, but the point of the phrase is that it introduces the word of woe and warning which follows. The structure is repeated in 22:22, "The Son of Man goes as it has been determined, but woe to that man by whom he is betrayed." These two-sided warnings envision a broad context of powers and events beyond human control, but people are still responsible actors in the drama. Luke provides another glimpse into this complex problem when Jesus addresses Peter in 22:31 and says that Satan desires to "have you that he might sift you like wheat, but I have prayed for you that your faith may not fail" (see vv. 5-6 below).

The consequences of causing one of the **little ones** to stumble are grim. In this context where Jesus is speaking to his disciples about the snares of sin and then about one brother sinning against another (vv. 3-4), the "little ones" are Jesus' followers, the community of faith (see also 10:21). The image of being drowned with a **millstone** tied to the **neck** needs no more explanation than the old gangster practice of setting a victim's feet in concrete before being thrown into the sea. Yet this threat of harsh punishment is not directed against anyone who betrays the leadership, but against those who cause one of the "little ones" to fall away. Once again the priorities of the kingdom invert the world's standards (see also 22:24-27). Verse 3a is thus a concluding word of warning, "Watch yourselves!" It highlights the importance of faithful relationships among Jesus' followers and serves as a transition to the following verses.

3b-4—Although a sin which causes another disciple to stumble is gravely serious, the community is called to practice forgiveness, not retribution. The "reproof" or **rebuke** of the offender is a call to repentance, not a vindictive attack. The tone of these verses is controlled by the emphatic use of the future tense in the last line, "If he repents you *will* forgive him." The number—**seven times in** a **day**—is not a limit (see Matt. 18:22, "seventy times seven"). It is merely an index of the extravagance of forgiveness. No member of this community of faith can be lost, and failing to forgive a repenting sinner could be a sin which would cause one of the "little ones" to stumble.

5-6—Luke sets the traditional word about faith like a mustard seed (see Mark 9:28-29; Matt. 17:19-20) in the context of this discourse. Now it is a comment on the disciples' sense of peril of causing someone to sin and challenge to practice forgiveness. They interject a plea to **the Lord: "Increase our faith!"** Luke identifies them as **the apostles,** which means the Twelve who are Jesus' closest disciples and delegates (see comments at 6:13; 22:30; 24:9,33).

Jesus' answer is an amazing affirmation of the power of even the smallest **grain** of **faith.** Quantity is not so important, but the reality of faith is. It would be equally foolish to debate whether Matthew's version of a faith that moves mountains (see also 1 Cor. 13:2 and Zech. 4:7) is more powerful than the **uprooting** and transplantation in **the sea** of a **sycamine tree.** The roots of that tree were known to be so extensive that they were not to be planted within 12 yards of a cistern. The whole point is that faith can do what it is impossible to do.

This is not merely a notion of intense believing or positive thinking. In Luke, faith is always faith in God or God's Messiah Jesus (see especially 5:20; 7:9; Acts 20:21; 24:24; 26:18), and it is closely correlated with the presence of the Holy Spirit (Acts 6:5; 11:24). Faith is a power because it is the link to the power of God. It is God's means of healing and forgiveness (Acts 3:16; 15:9). Thus Jesus' prayer for Peter was that his "faith may not fail" (22:32), and Jesus' haunting question is not whether God's vindication will be delayed, but "When the Son of man comes, will he find faith on earth?" (18:7-8).

Jesus has warned his disciples of the grave consequences of causing others to sin (vv. 1-3a), and he has commanded an impossibly high standard of the practice of forgiveness (vv. 3b-4). Their plea, **"Increase our faith!"** is understandable, but Jesus' response is a word of assurance. There is no need for desperate quests for "more" faith, as if it could be quantified or possessed. It is God's Spirit and reign working through the means of faith which makes all things possible, and this community of faith (or even of "the faith," Acts 6:7; 13:8; 14:22; 16:5) is called to sustain such faith "on earth" confident of the abiding presence of the Spirit and the kingdom of the Messiah.

7-10—If desperate pleas for "more faith" are excluded on the one side, boasting at obedience is forbidden on the other. These words of Jesus are used by Luke to fill out the discourse, and they assume particular force in this context. This is not a denigration of **the servant** or a pronouncement of human worthlessness. The Jesus who is among his disciples as "one who serves" (see 22:24-27) is not "putting them in their place." But the exclusion of boasting is the obverse of the assurance that the power to do the impossible comes from God.

The general theme was well known in Jewish piety. Two sayings from the *Pirke Aboth* of the Mishnah attributed to Antigonus of Socho and Yohanan ben Zakkai express it well: "Be not like slaves that serve the master for the sake of receiving a bounty; but be like slaves that serve the master not for the sake of receiving a bounty; and let the fear of heaven be upon you" (1:3). "If you have achieved much in the Law, claim not merit for yourself; for this purpose you were created" (2:8). Jesus' words do not alter this counsel much, and they simply assume the social stratification of the ancient world.

But in the context of this discourse, these words reinforce the assurance Jesus has just given his apostles. The question has been, "How can we do what has been commanded?" The answer is, "Through the power of God at work in faith." Thus those who do **what is commanded** cannot boast of their own achievement. Not only have they only done what was commanded (vv. 7-10), but they are dependent on God all the while. The logic is like that in Jesus' word in 10:20, "Do not rejoice in this, that the spirits are subject to you; but rejoice that your names are written in heaven." The servant has no "rights" or independent authority over against the master and no cause for self-justification for obedience. But the faithful servant may all the more have faith in the power of God to accomplish what would otherwise be impossible.

Jesus Approaches Jerusalem (17:11—19:27)

Once again Luke's Jesus resumes the journey **to Jerusalem** (see 9:51; 13:22). The beginning of this third phase of the journey is explicitly marked by the geographic summary in 17:11, but deciding exactly when the journey concludes proves more difficult (see comments at 19:11, 28, 45). Furthermore, Luke's suggestion that Jesus **was passing along between Samaria and Galilee** is rather confusing to a careful map reader. Still, the general southward movement is clear, and the mention of Samaria provides a link into the first story of the grateful Samaritan.

Luke has again collected a wide variety of traditional stories and sayings within this portion of the journey, and it would be wise to refrain from overstating the importance of the literary structure for interpreting the section. The wide variety of outlines which commentators propose may indicate either that Luke has no tight structure here or that the interpreters have not identified it convincingly. But since it will be argued that Jesus' entry in

295

the festal procession commences his mission in Jerusalem (19:28—23:56), it is at least possible to highlight the contours of 17:11—19:27.

The section may not be tightly structured, but it does move forward in three cycles of stories, punctuated by prophetic words. (1) Luke 17:11—18:8 includes healing and proclamation of the kingdom but concludes with warnings of coming judgment and the poignant question of whether the Son of man will find faith on earth. (2) The subsection 18:9-34 offers more teaching and further glimpses of division leading to the prediction of the suffering and death of the Son of man. (3) Luke 18:35—19:27 presents additional stories of healing and salvation, but again concludes with the severe story of the destruction of the king's enemies. Throughout this whole section, therefore, Luke continues the theme that the mission of Jesus reveals the kingdom and discloses the resistance and rejection of God's plan by many in Israel.

He Proclaims the Kingdom and Predicts the Judgment (17:11—18:8)

The Ten Lepers (17:11-19).   This is a story of healing, salvation, and judgment. It is a complex story, in which the pre-Lukan tradition may still be identifiable, since vv. 11 and 19 are rather obvious additions by the evangelist. But even within the traditional core (vv. 12-18), the vocabulary and syntax appear to be thoroughly Lukan. The evangelist has not merely composed an introduction and an epilog but has emphasized the response of the Samaritan **foreigner** in contrast to that of **the nine** who are presumably from Israel. Thus all are healed of leprosy, but the thanksgiving of the foreigner is a sign of saving faith which in effect judges the lack of response of the others. As in 7:9, the conclusion could have been, "Not even in Israel have I found such faith."

12-14—This is the second story of a healing of leprosy (see 5:12-16), but the healing story itself is amazingly brief. This time Jesus does not touch the **lepers,** but they remained at a distance, as the Law required (see Leviticus 13–14, especially 13:45-46).

They call him **Master** (Gk: *epistata*), which is a term only used in Luke and otherwise only by the disciples when they are in some consternation (5:5; 8:24, 45; 9:33, 49). It is not clear that their cry for **mercy** was a plea for healing, but they would have known that the commanded trip to the priests implied they were about to be cleansed. Their obedience to a command given at a distance is reminiscent of Naaman's reluctant obedience to Elisha's command which produced his healing from leprosy (2 Kings 5:10-14; see Luke 4:27). And when the healing happened as they went on their way, the reader expects a chorus of acclaim or thanksgiving to conclude the miracle story.

15-16—Only **one** of the **ten** who were **cleansed** (v. 14) or **healed** (v. 15) turns around to **give thanks.** The standard miracle story is already altered. This is not an astonished crowd (5:9, 26; 7:17; 9:43), but one man who praised God (v. 15) and gave thanks to Jesus (v. 16). Jesus speaks only of praise for God (v. 18), but Luke clearly regards this gesture of worshipful praise of Jesus to be exactly correct. Like the Gerasene from whom the demons were driven (see 8:39-40), this man praised God by glorifying Jesus. The healing story itself is now complete. Only the last line of v. 16 indicates that more must be said: **Now he was a Samaritan.** The emphatic style again suggests the hand of the evangelist. Luke is about to interpret the significance of this traditional story.

17-18—Jesus' three questions overshadow the whole scene. They are rhetorical questions, in the sense that the answers are painfully obvious. The reader feels the embarrassment along with the audience in the story. The three questions compound the indictment. Since the one who returned is so strongly identified as a Samaritan and a foreigner, **the nine** must be Israelites or Jews. This is treated as a further indictment, as when the faith of a Roman centurion outshone that of those in Israel (7:9). It is also another instance of Jesus encountering both rejection and faith, now among the Samaritans (see the rejection in 9:52) while before it was among the Jews (rejection, 4:14-30, followed by stories of faith; see 4:42—5:1). In the book of Acts, the mission of the apostles of Jesus will proceed from Jerusalem to Judea and Samaria, and faith will be found in both Judea and Samaria (Acts 8:1, 5-8, 14). Jesus' questions, however, first sound a reproach to all those who have received the benefits of his healing and restoration without any change of heart, any repentance or returning to glorify God.

19—The concluding word is a commendation. Perhaps it is more a statement of fact about the saving power of faith. When Jesus dismisses him with the declaration, "Your faith has saved (Gk: *sesōken*) you!", he is not simply speaking about the healing. The word "saved" may mean "healed" (8:36), but all were healed (v. 15, Gk: *iathē*). This is the "salvation" which comes through faith (see the discussion at 8:48 and 17:5-6), and this man has "seen" that he was healed and returned, giving thanks to God. He is not merely delighted to be free from leprosy. He is aware that his healing is a blessing from God, and this bond of faith in God has brought him within the kingdom. He has discerned the saving reign of God and is sent out with the blessing of the Messiah.

Luke does not diminish the miracle of the healing of the lepers, but he again stresses the greater miracle of faith. Against the backdrop of those who only want a healing and those who are not even grateful for that, this "foreigner" is an exemplar of "saving faith" which "sees" the work and reign of God. That is the greater blessing (10:23).

The Presence of the Kingdom (17:20-21). This exchange with **the Pharisees** is such a famous and disputed passage that it must be treated separately, but it must also be read in close connection with the subsequent words on the coming day of the Son of man (17:22-37; 18:8). Luke has again used a comment or question of the Pharisees as an occasion for Jesus to utter a word of correction or reproof, followed by prophetic words which reveal the future (see 13:31-35; 19:39-48). In this case, the audience shifts from the Pharisees (vv. 20-21) to the disciples (vv. 22-37), and Jesus' words about the presence of the kingdom (vv. 20-21) stand in juxtaposition to his declaration about the future day of the Son of man (vv. 22-37; 18:8). Each section probably comes from distinct traditions and the shift in tone and tense is perceptible. But this shift is a precise reflection of Luke's eschatology. The kingdom has indeed come in the person and reign of the

Messiah, but the public revelation of his judgment as the Son of man still lies in the future.

The question which **the Pharisees** raise is eschatological, assuming that the **coming** of **the kingdom of God** lies only in the future: "**When?**" Jesus' answer is a reproof of their question, but it is a correction and not a wholesale rejection. This is a similar scene to Acts 1:6-8, where Jesus' answer to his disciples offers a specific reproof of their desire for a timetable without denying that God will indeed "restore the kingdom to Israel." There the problem is that the "times and seasons" are not subject to human understanding or speculation. In this passage, the Pharisees' apocalyptic speculation is also misguided. If the question is "When?" in the sense of what **signs** should be **observed** or "Where?" as if it could be located somewhere else, the questioner has misunderstood the nature of God's reign.

It is possible that Jesus' answer is an even more specific reproof of the Pharisees, because the word "observation" (Gk: *paratērēsis*, verb: *paratērein*) could mean the "observation" of religious practices and feasts (see Gal. 4:10, "You observe days, and months, and seasons, and years"). Later Rabbinic texts suggest that keeping the Law ("observing the Torah") was understood by some as the necessary condition for the coming of the kingdom or the Messiah. If this is the meaning of "observance" in this passage, Jesus would be saying that keeping the Law will not bring the kingdom. But the issue seems to be more narrowly that of the "observation" of watching for **signs.**

It is more likely that Jesus' affirmation about the nearness of the kingdom is a paraphrase of a passage in Deuteronomy which would have been familiar to the Pharisees about the nearness of the word of God of the commandments: "neither is it far off. It is not in heaven . . . neither is it beyond the sea. . . . But the word is very near you; it is in your mouth and in your heart, so that you can do it" (Deut. 30:11-14). Or perhaps Jesus' words echo the assurance of Isa. 45:14 when the Egyptians and Ethiopians say to Israel, "God is with you" (LXX: *en soi*).

The central point is that **the kingdom of God** is not only a future apocalyptic event. Nor is it merely an internal or spiritual reality which could be contained "within you," but it is as close to these Pharisees as Jesus is standing. Even as Jesus speaks, God's reign is "here and now," "in your very presence." If they could but receive him, God's reign would also be "within them." The RSV translates the critical prepositional phrase (Gk: *entos hymōn*): **The kingdom of God is in the midst of you.** This is consistent with Luke 10:9, 11 where the kingdom "has drawn near to you" in the preaching of the apostles and with Luke 11:20 where Jesus' exorcizing by the "finger of God" is the sign that the kingdom of God "has come upon you." But in all these cases, the kingdom has come in fact. Whether that reign brings salvation or judgment depends on how the Messiah Jesus is received (see again Simeon's oracles in Luke 2:29-35).

Perhaps vv. 20b-21 contain traditional words of Jesus which Luke has given decisive meaning as responses to this apocalyptic question. Or perhaps Luke has composed the whole section in order to establish a clear contrast with the sayings about the Son of man which follow. In either case, God's reign is not merely future. It is now here in the presence and person of the Messiah Jesus. To ask about when it will come is to miss the point that God's reign has been inaugurated in Jesus. Its future public manifestation, however, will be discussed in other passages (see 21:31).

The Coming Day of the Son of Man (17:22-37).   This section is the necessary sequel to Jesus' reproof of the question about the kingdom (vv. 20-22). The kingdom is not **coming,** but the day of the Son of man is (for the contrast, see the comments on 21:31). Luke depicts Jesus as continuing an eschatological discourse with his disciples following the prompting of the Pharisees (see the notes on vv. 20-22 above). The evangelist has drawn upon traditional sayings of Jesus which occur in Jesus' speech to his disciples at the temple in Mark 13 and Matthew 24 (drawing upon both Mark and Q). Luke will also provide a fuller eschatological discourse when Jesus is at the temple in Chap. 21, following the Markan outline of the speech. But in Chap. 17, Luke uses some Markan fragments and several sayings from Q, which occur in Matthew as testimonies to the "coming" (Gk: *parousia*) of the Son of man (Matt. 24:27, 37, 39). Luke never uses the word *parousia* in his narrative, but speaks consistently of the coming "day"

or the **days** of the Son of man (vv. 22, 24, 26, 30; see also 18:8,
"when the Son of man comes").

In the context of the travel narrative (9:51—19:27), this eschatological discourse is prophetic, just as Jesus' response to the
Pharisees in 13:31-35 anticipated his oracles of 19:41-44 and provided a warning of coming conflict. Again Jesus' prophetic declarations concerning the "days which are coming" build the ominous sense of what is "coming" both for Jesus as Son of man
within the narrative (see v. 24) and for Jesus' followers who will
in time be yearning for the revelation of Jesus as the Son of man
in judgment. This passage sets Jesus' death within the unrolling
"days of the Son of man," awaiting the apocalypse of the final
judgment of the "day of the Son of man."

22-23—Jesus speaks to his **disciples** about the coming **days,**
promising only unfulfilled longings and deceptive messengers
until the day of judgment. Verse 23 is adapted from Mark 13:21,
but there the deceivers announce the appearance of "the Christ."
In Luke they merely declare the appearance **"here"** or **"there"**
of **one of the days of the Son of man.** This mention of **here** or
there is repeated from v. 21, tying these sections together lit-
erarily (see also v. 37, "Where?"). But speculation about "where"
the Son of man appears is no more profitable than attempts to
locate the kingdom.

One of the days appears to be an expression for "the first of
the days" (see Luke 24:1; Acts 20:7) or the commencing of the
end. In 21:27-28, this picture is filled out by Jesus in terms of
the dire cosmic signs which will precede this coming of the Son
of man. This expression is thus distinguished both from the longer
period of "the days of the Son of man" (v. 26; see the days of
Noah and the days of Lot, vv. 26, 28) and from "the day when
the Son of man is revealed" (v. 30, see also v. 24, "the Son of
man in his day). The point is that Jesus' followers will long to see
this period begin, and it will not happen immediately (see also
21:9).

24-25—No prophetic insight will be needed to see the coming
of **the Son of man in his day** when it occurs because it will be
like **lightning** flashing from one end of **the sky** to another. In
Matt. 24:27, this image is applied to the "parousia" of the Son of

man, and it is more probable that Matthew added this technical term (see also 24:37, 39) to "Q" than that Luke omitted it. But Luke has added v. 25, indicating that **first** Jesus' suffering and death must occur before this cosmic revelation.

This has been called the fifth passion prediction in Luke (see also 9:22, 44; 12:50; 13:32-33). In the cases where Luke is following Mark's three passion predictions (see 9:22, 44; 18:31; and 22:22a), it is specifically "the Son of man" who suffers. In this passage, Luke is drawing upon "Q" traditions about the coming **day** of **the Son of man,** and Luke introduces the passion prediction without specifically saying that the **he** who **must suffer and be rejected by this generation** is the Son of man. But clearly Luke has accepted and developed Mark's conviction that Jesus suffers as the Son of man (see also 24:7). Here is where Luke correlates that role with Jesus' fulfillment of the role as judge at the end (see Dan. 7:13). In Luke, Jesus' death is itself part of the eschatological drama.

26-30—The analogy with **the days of Noah/Lot** and **the days of the Son of man** is thoroughly drawn. These were extended periods which preceded the critical day, and people were busy with all of the affairs of daily life. The list of activities is interesting, but thoroughly mundane. The point is that they were oblivious to the coming destruction throughout these **days,** and so they will also be **in the days of the Son of man** (v. 26). **Noah** and **Lot** were aware that the world had been altered, but for an unrepentant world it was business as usual throughout these **days** until **the day when Noah entered the ark** (v. 27) or **the day when Lot went out from Sodom** (v. 30). That critical day was the time of judgment and destruction, and **so it will be on the day when the Son of man is revealed.**

This "revealing" or disclosing (Gk: *apokalyptesthai*) of the Son of man is as public as lightning flashing across the heavens (v. 24) or the flood (v. 27) or the rain of fire and brimstone (v. 29). It will have the same (or more, see 10:12) dire consequences on those who have rejected the kingdom which Jesus and his disciples have proclaimed as the destruction of Sodom had on its inhabitants. Like the "day of the Lord," this "day of the Son of man" should not be "desired" (v. 22) without knowing the calamity it will bring (see Amos 5:18-20).

31-37—These verses lay out the destruction and salvation which this **day** brings. The images of salvation are not as prominent. Luke appears to have inserted v. 33 to tie this whole scene into Jesus' other words of salvation and destruction as based not on self-seeking but on self-denial. As is clear from 9:24, this does not mean masochism but faithful following of Jesus even to death. There will be no other way to look out for oneself on "the day of the Son of man." And then salvation will be the work of God. The passive voice of the verbs (**one will be taken and the other left,** vv. 34, 35) indicates that God is the rescuer, or perhaps this is the Son of man as the agent of divine judgment.

But the dominant theme of these verses is the judgment of destruction. Verse 31 announces there will be no hope of rescuing one's possessions, and no time to **turn back.** This is counsel to those who hope to be **taken** as Lot's family was from Sodom or Noah's from the impending flood. Even now in the travel narrative, Jesus is constantly instructing his disciples to break their attachments to their possessions, land, and family. Verse 32 is thus a severe and cryptic reminder that **on that day** it will not merely be a question of whether one who looks back is "fit for the kingdom" (9:62). Then it will be a fatal mistake.

The judgment is immediate and final. There are no scenes here of the Ancient of Days or the Son of man in session of judgment. In Luke 21:27-28, the heavenly manifestation of the Son of man is the sign of approaching "redemption," but this passage envisions no processes. The whole emphasis is on how sudden and decisive God's action will be. Verse 36 is omitted in most English versions since it has very weak manuscript evidence and appears to have been added from Matt. 24:40. But Luke still has two cases, the men in a **bed** at night and the **women grinding** at the same mill. The one who is **taken** is saved (Gk; *paralambanein,* see John 14:3), and the one who is **left** is like those outside the ark or those remaining in the city of Sodom.

In v. 37, the disciples' question "**Where, Lord?**" prompts Jesus' word from Q about **the eagles** gathering over a body. In Matt. 24:28 this word is a further explication of the public character of the appearance of the Son of man. It will be as obvious as lightning or great birds circling the carrion. But in Luke, Jesus' words about the eagles is the direct answer to the question, Where are the ones who are left? The answer is they are left like dead carcasses for the vultures to find, wherever they are. If you want to know where they are, look for the circling birds. The day of the Son of man is "darkness and not light" (Amos 5:18-20) for them.

The Vindication of the Widow (18:1-8). The harsh predictions of the coming of the day of the Son of man (17:22-37) must now be related to the situation of Jesus' disciples. Luke has set the parable of the unrighteous judge (vv. 2-5) into the context of this discourse on the coming of the Son of man in order to encourage the faithful to continue in prayer (v. 1), to assure them that they are not dealing with a judge who will delay their pleas in indifference (vv. 2-7), and to raise the sharp concluding question about whether they will have kept the faith when the Son of man comes (v. 8). In Luke's narrative, therefore, the passage as a whole is integrated with the eschatological discourse which precedes it, but the sharp contours of the parable still protrude and catch the reader off guard.

1—This verse is Luke's introduction, presenting the **parable** as Jesus' words on the necessity of **prayer** and **not losing heart.** In the story this probably refers back to 17:22 where the disciples would "long to see the first of the days of the Son of man, but would not see it." As noted above, Luke does not speak of "the delay of the parousia," but the section is full of concern as to how long the "days of the Son of man" (17:26) will continue until "the day of the Son of man is revealed" (17:30, 24). Luke appears to be addressing a circumstance in his own community of loss of hope in the final judgment. Prayer is therefore the necessary means for not yielding to temptation (11:4b) or experiencing the failure of faith (22:46). The present time is the period of ongoing struggle with tribulations (see Acts 11:19; 14:22; 20:23), and the faithful long for vindication.

2-5—The parable is another of Jesus' surprising stories in which a model of unrighteousness is used to speak indirectly and by contrast of God (see also the unjust manager 16:1-9). It is hopeless to make this **unrighteous judge** (v. 6) into any moral exemplar. Of course, he yields to pressure, but to suggest that this means that believers must bang on heaven's door until God relents is to miss the point (see also the "shameless friend" in 11:5-13). Instead of using the justice and mercy of God to set a standard for the exercise of human justice, as the moralists do, Jesus uses the injustice and indifference of an unjust judge to reveal the contrast to God's reign.

The description of the **judge who neither feared God nor had regard for any person** is similar to the harsh judgment Josephus rendered against King Jehoiakim: "unjust and wicked by nature, neither reverent toward God nor kind to people" (*Ant.* 10.83). His disdain for the **widow** is also especially reprehensible and shows disdain for God because God is the judge who "will not ignore the supplication of the fatherless, nor the widow when she pours out her story" (Sir. 35:12-15). Luke is particularly sensitive to the plight of the widows (see 2:37; 4:25-26; 7:12; 20:47; 21:2-3; Acts 6:1; 9:39, 41), reflecting a host of scriptural precedents where God is their advocate (see Exod. 22:22-24; Deut. 10:18; 24:17; Ps. 68:5; Mal. 3:5).

This judge not only refuses to give her justice, but when he starts talking to himself, his speech shows nothing but shallow self-interest. He finds her to be a bother, and perhaps her continuing return is "wearing him down" or "giving him a black eye" in public. The word which the RSV translates as **wear me out** (Gk: *hypōpiazein*) can even mean physical assault, but the reader is not likely to be impressed with the extravagance of his self-pity. The man is no good.

6-8—When Jesus, **the Lord,** speaks, he interprets the parable with three distinct comments. First, in v. 6 Jesus tells his hearers, "Just listen to what the judge of unrighteousness says!" The phrase may be translated as **the unrighteous judge,** indicating that he is "unrighteous," but this judge in not merely personally unjust. He is actually adjudicating "unrighteousness" rather than justice (see also "the manager of unrighteousness" in 16:8). That is how the world of the "mammon of unrighteousness" (16:9) works, and the faithful should not be surprised.

Second, God's reign of righteousness is the exact contrast, and Jesus develops this contrast in vv. 7-8a. The widow could not get prompt justice, but the questions in v. 7 indicate that God's **elect** will not receive such disregard. God's reputation of justice for the **widow** (see above) also includes the "chosen ones." This is the only time Luke uses this identification for the faithful, but "Chosen One" is a central designation for Jesus (see 9:35; 23:35). God's protection of the "chosen servant" (see Isa. 42:1) is also not obvious to the world, but the resurrection of Jesus will be God's act of vindication. The word translated **delay** in the RSV (Gk: *makrothymein*) could also mean "to be forbearing" or "to be patient," but the issue is how **long** they must endure injustice. The close parallels with Sirach 35:18 (LXX: 35:19) suggest that this may be a traditional phrase, but then the issue is still that God will not delay. The unrighteous will even feel God's impatience. And v. 8a confirms that the point of the whole is that God will deal speedily to vindicate those who cry out in prayer.

The third comment, in v. 8b, turns the whole discourse back to the coming "day of the Son of man." No, the faithful need not fear that God will delay or disdain their petitions. Heroic efforts are not necessary to catch God's attention, even in prayer. The necessity of constancy in prayer is bound up with the human problem of "losing heart" (v. 1) or "losing faith" before the day of the full public revelation of God's judgment. This is the real issue, and the reason why people must continue in prayer. God will never fail or be distant, but the elect must pray that their faith not fail (see 22:32, 40).

He Proclaims the Kingdom and Predicts His Passion (18:9-34)

The larger context is that of the third and final phase of Jesus' journey to Jerusalem (17:11—19:27), and this phase moves with a rhythm of stories, sayings, and healings, punctuated three times with prophetic warnings and predictions (17:22—18:8; 18:31-34; 19:11-27). Luke 18:9 marks the beginning of the second segment of this phase, and at 18:15 Luke will resume the usage of Mark, which was discontinued when the journey began (9:51). But neither these schematic details nor Luke's sources prove to be decisive, except to document Luke's persistent concern. The controlling motif of the larger context continues to be crucial: Jesus is instructing his disciples in the way of the kingdom as he travels toward his fateful arrival in Jerusalem. Thus this second cycle of stories in 18:9-34 again moves from stories which reveal the character of God's kingdom (vv. 9-30) to prophetic warnings that God's way of ruling will be beyond human understanding (vv. 31-34).

The Pharisee and the Tax Collector (18:9-14).   9—Once again Luke introduces a story with a clear indication of its proper audience (see 15:1; 18:1; 19:11), and the reader "overhears" the telling. This story is particularly effective because its introduction addresses those who **trust in themselves** and think they are **righteous.** Of course, the **Pharisee** is such a person in the story, but that does not mean that Jesus was only speaking to Pharisees. In fact, Jesus' story also addresses all those Christian readers who have justified themselves at the expense of the Pharisees, counting themselves to be more righteous in their humility than the self-righteous Pharisees. But the whole point is that no self-righteousness or self-justification counts before God. Despising others is also the regular corollary of self-righteousness, and the story which follows explores the themes of the regard of self and others before God.

10-12—The two who are introduced are standard contrasting types in Luke's Gospel, the **tax collectors** and the **Pharisees** (5:29-32; 7:29-30; 15:1-2). Jesus' fellowship has offended the Pharisees before, and Jesus will soon again show extravagant acceptance to a tax collector (19:1-10). Here Jesus presses the contrast, probably to the point of a caricature, not in order to glorify the tax collector, but in order to illustrate the folly of trying to impress God with one's virtue and the danger of elevating oneself by demeaning others.

The Pharisee **prayed with himself.** In fact, both were praying privately, but the Pharisee is actually talking to (Gk: *pros*) himself. He clearly likes to hear himself pray, and his prayer approximates the tone and terms of such scriptural prayers as Pss. 17:3-5 and

26. But those psalms envision an urgent need for vindication from God in the face of accusers. This prayer only asks God to endorse what the man already has concluded, and his surpassing the requirements of the tithing Law (Deut. 14:22-23) clearly leaves God in his debt. If the economy of God's rule and righteousness were merely a quantified observance of the prescribed rules, the Pharisee has made his case. But this is not even close to how the kingdom works or what prayer is about.

13—**The tax collector** simply throws himself upon God's mercy. His body language is that of Semitic humility and contrition, standing afar, averting his eyes (Enoch 13:5: "they did not raise their eyes to heaven out of shame for the sins"), and beating his breast (see discussion at Luke 23:48). This is not merely a case of someone with a poor self-image. This is a man who regards God's justice as real, knows he does not measure up, and counts on God's mercy to be even greater (see also certain psalms from Qumran, 1QS 11:2-5: "as for me my justification is with God," 1QS 11:10-12; 1QH 11:15-22). That is why he is an exemplar of faith. He has understood the dynamic character of God's reign and its ultimately gracious character. His prayer is that of those who "justify God" (7:29-30), making no claim to rights before God, and it is consistent with the proper usage of the prayers of repentance of Psalms 34 and 51.

14—The conclusion demonstrates that this is more an example story (see also 10:29-37; 12:16-21; 16:19-31) than one of Jesus' striking Gospel parables. But the point is that this is how the reign of God works, and the primary force of the story is to correct misunderstandings. It is a polemical example against those who seek to "justify" themselves (see 10:29). The traditional maxims about the humbled and the exalted are thus more than mere moralisms (see also 14:11). They are statements in the passive voice about how God's justice and reign reveal human self-righteousness as hypocrisy and work vindication for those who merely trust God's grace. This may not be as ample a presentation of "justification by grace through faith" as Paul offers, but Luke's Jesus concurs that the only "vindication" or **justification** which matters is God's.

The Children and the Kingdom (18:15-17).   Suddenly Luke
resumes following Mark. After a long departure from using Mark
as a source (9:51—18:14), Luke picks up almost where he left off
in Mark 10:1. But while Mark's story of the blessing of the children
follows Jesus' teaching on marriage and divorce (Mark 10:2-12),
Luke presents these words within Jesus' extended instructions
on the way of discipleship. Mark's two passages on Jesus and the
children (9:36-37; 10:13-16) thus occur in close proximity in that
narrative, but these episodes are widely separated in Luke (9:46-
48; 18:15-17). Furthermore, Mark presents this encounter as another of Jesus' sharp words of reproof of his disciples' lack of
understanding (Mark 10:14), but Luke treats Jesus' words as at
most a correction of the disciples. In Luke, Jesus' words are
primarily further instruction in the character of the kingdom of
God.

The two statements of vv. 16-17, therefore, interpret each other
as parallel affirmations about the kingdom. What does it mean
that **to such belongs the kingdom of God?** It is now a further
explication of the kind of reception which was just described in
the example of the penitent tax collector (18:13-14). Those who
have no claim to make before God, except trust in God, are the
ones to whom the kingdom belongs. This is not so much a comment about children, and perhaps this is why Luke does not
report that Jesus "took the children in his arms and blessed them"
(Mark 10:16).

In the next story Luke speaks further of "entering the kingdom
of God" (18:24, 25; see also Acts 14:22 and perhaps Luke 13:24).
This phrase implies both the present and the future reality (see
18:30), but it is a comment about those who "belong in" the
kingdom as well as those to whom it belongs. God's way of ruling
in the world and in heaven is surprisingly difficult for those who
have achieved the world's wealth (18:24-25). Thus it is no surprise
that those who follow in this way of faith will face tribulation in
this world (Acts 14:22). But while God's rule is virtually impossible
for all who would justify themselves, it is also naturally easy for
those who trust as children.

Much has been written in Christian history about this passage
as an argument for the baptism of children. The fact that only

Luke refers to them as **infants** (v. 15) has increased the level of interest. Certainly this passage is a strong statement of not "preventing" children (see also not "preventing" baptism in Acts 8:36; 10:47; 11:17), but the question of infant baptism does not appear to have been at stake in Luke's telling, but the character of God's rule.

The Rich Ruler and the Peril of Wealth (18:18-30). This story is another of the complex traditional accounts of Jesus the rabbi and interpreter of the will of God. It is strikingly similar in form to 10:25-39 where a "lawyer" asks one question, which Jesus answers with a question and an answer. Then the interlocutor asks another question or raises an objection, and Jesus presses the discourse to a much more profound level. In these stories someone addresses Jesus as **Teacher** (7:40; 9:38; 10:25; 11:45; 12:13; 19:39; 20:21, 28, 39; 21:7; see also John the Baptist 3:21), and Jesus accepts this traditional role of authority (see 22:11). Then Jesus engages the person, and all who overhear the exchange are instructed.

Luke is fond of this format, but clearly he did not create it. This story is almost a verbatim reproduction of Mark 10:17-30. Thus the parallels to 10:25-39 noted above do not demonstrate Luke's literary editing, but they reflect the structures of oral recitation. These stories have a regular rhythm which revolves around the questions, highlighting the drama and authority of Jesus' teaching.

Here again the issue is what one must **do** to **inherit eternal life,** and as long as that is the question, Jesus' words are unremitting in their radical demand. Even the words of promise which conclude the passage (vv. 29-30) do not offer much relief. In vv. 31-34, Jesus' passion prediction will reveal that salvation lies in what God is about to "do." For the moment, however, no one understands how all of that fits. They are too preoccupied with what they must "do."

18-20—In Luke, this **ruler** could be a local synagogue official (8:41), a magistrate (12:58), a leader of the Pharisees (14:1), or an official connected with the bureaucracy of the high priest (23:13, 35; 24:20). The context of encounters with the Pharisees and the character of the exchange would suggest that this is a standard dialog among teachers of Israel. The questioner appears to be sincere.

Jesus objects to being addressed as **Good Teacher,** since only **God** is good. God's goodness is a consistent scriptural theme (Pss. 34:8; 106:1; 118:1, 29; 1 Chron. 16:34), and Jesus is identified with God's will (10:21-22, 2:49) without displacing it (11:27-28). This is not what the ruler intended to discuss, but Jesus gives him a brief lesson in proper reverence and humility. The exchange is full of fascinating possibilities of meaning. Was Jesus indirectly attesting his link with God? ("How did you know I am good?") Or was he distinguishing himself from God? ("Don't set me up as the moral authority! We both know that only God's will sets the standards for eternal life.") The dynamics of the address and response become clear only in the larger context, and later Jesus' reponses will become adversarial (19:39-45; 20:1-7, 21-26, 27-47). At this point, however, Jesus' words merely increase the intensity of the exchange and elevate the questions of morality to theology.

Jesus' first answer is a theological endorsement of **the commandments.** The will of God is no secret, and obedience to God's commands is the way of life (see also 10:27-28). This is the way of life for Israel (Deut. 30:15-20), and the way to eternal life for the Israelite. Jesus is repeating one of the central convictions of Pharisaic Jewish tradition: the observance of the commandments is the way to life now and in the world to come. The simplicity of Jesus' answer is a disclosure that the Law of God is truly a gift, to be kept and observed. But if people cannot receive God's commands as a gift, how shall they "inherit" the gift of eternal life itself (see also 10:25 and Acts 13:46-48)? People do not want simply to "inherit" eternal life, they want to "earn" it. The question of what must I "do" may already reveal a distrust, a need to control, and an inability to live depending only on God's promise.

21—The simple answer does not satisfy. Like the lawyer in 10:29, this ruler could not let it rest. He does not seek to "justify himself" with another question (10:29), but he brushes aside Jesus' summary of the Commandments (see Deut. 5:16-21; Exod. 20:12-16; and compare Luke 10:27) as too routine. He displays the persistent need of religious people to achieve some higher righteousness which would make their claim to salvation indisputable, even by God.

22-23—Luke does not suggest that Jesus' words were uttered out of affection (Mark 10:21), but they were a direct response to what Jesus had **heard** from the ruler. In a delicate play on the words **lack,** "everything," and **treasure,** Jesus diagnoses that this man who has everything still "lacks" the one thing which only disposing of "everything" he owns can remedy. He is seeking "all this and heaven too," but the inheritance of eternal life is not merely another thing to possess. His worldly goods are preventing him from entering into the kingdom campaign which is unfolding before him in Jesus' ministry. He wants to buy or earn an insurance policy to protect himself and his substance, but Jesus identifies the **treasure in heaven** with God's care for the poor and his messianic mission. God's will and purpose defines the treasure of heaven and the inheritance of eternal life. The peril of wealth is that it offers a misleading assurance of treasure and security (see 12:13-34 and the comments on 16:9).

As will become clear from the story of Zacchaeus which follows (19:1-10), Jesus deals differently with the "righteous" and the "sinners," even when they are wealthy. Their expectations and central concerns differ, and the "righteous" presume they are qualitatively right. Only matters of degree need to be deliberated. Their question is, "How much more must I do?" or "How much will it cost?" Then Jesus' answer is a radical statement of the Law. "Everything you have!" The contrast between Zacchaeus's joyful abandon (19:6-9), and the ruler's sorrow is instructive. The ruler is concerned from the beginning about what he will be required to relinquish, but the tax collector never asks what is demanded. Thus Luke's Jesus reveals the thoughts of many hearts once again (2:35) in judgment and blessing.

24-25—Jesus' verdict on this scene is another declaration of the peril of wealth (see 6:24; 8:14; 12:13-34; 16:1-31). These verses serve as a transition to a second cycle of questions and answers on the same topics with the faithful (vv. 26-30). The statement of "difficulty" is a hyperbolic expression. It is as impossible as selling snowballs to Eskimos! To argue that the **eye of the needle** could have been the night gate of the city where it was difficult to bring in a camel is to miss the point. Perhaps the image does imply a picture of the rich man's bulky cargo. But Jesus is marveling, and his speech is poetically extravagant. His earlier "woe to you that are rich" (6:24) reveals, however, that he is returning to a theme of utmost seriousness. It is humanly impossible (v. 27) for the wealthy to enter into God's reign, now or in the world to come (v. 30).

26-27—Now the theme of vv. 18-23 is taken up by the faithful, **those who heard** what Jesus just said. This is no longer a challenge to the teacher, but the questions and answers are matters of life and death, of despair and assurance. **"Then who can be saved?"** is a more pressing form of the ruler's inquiry. It is important to note that "being saved," "inheriting eternal life," and "entering the kingdom of God" are virtually interchangeable throughout this passage (see also 10:25-28; 13:23-24). But the whole Gospel of Luke insists that salvation in the world to come is not separable from entering the reign of God now (v. 30). Thus these phrases which are already filled with traditional meanings also interpret each other. Jesus' teaching on wealth and security is not merely a matter of the necessary preconditions for future reward. He is speaking about the present real circumstances which are consistent with the reign of God which he is inaugurating.

Because it is God who is at work, it is **possible** that even a rich man could be saved. Humanly incredible, but possible for God. The Zacchaeus story will be an object lesson of such a miracle. Gabriel and Mary had a discussion earlier about what is "possible for God" (1:37), and this passage again reflects the phrasing of the Lord's words to Sarah in the Septuagint (Gen. 18:14). The word of hope lies in what **God** can do, not in what humans must do (v. 18).

28-30—Peter's response is discouragingly like that of the ruler (v. 21). He points to what "we" have already done. In Mark's account, this is the third time that Peter and the disciples both understand and miss what Jesus is saying so that Jesus' passion predictions are sharp correctives to them (Mark 8:27-33; 9:14-32; 10:23-34). Luke has again picked up that Markan sequence, but he has not been criticizing the disciples for missing the point.

He will soon emphasize that the disciples were not understanding **these things** (v. 34).

Jesus' response to Peter (vv. 29b-30), therefore, is more of a word of assurance and an attempt to instruct someone who does not understand. Luke has also stripped Jesus' words to Peter of their dramatic links with the passion (in Mark 10:29, "for my sake and for the gospel") and has removed their more concrete promises of reward (Mark 10:30; "will not receive a hundredfold . . . houses and brothers and sisters and mothers and children and lands, with persecutions"). Jesus' words are not weakened in Luke, but their focus is changed. This is an assurance of great reward for all who have given God's reign their allegiance and sacrificed to do so. Luke has picked up Jesus' usage of the traditional Jewish distinction between the present age and the age to come (see the comments at 20:34), and he has presented it as a further explication of Jesus' earlier encouragement to the faithful to let go of their possessions and trust God for the gift of the kingdom and its benefits (12:22-34).

The Prediction of the Passion (18:31-34).   Luke ties this next crucial piece of Markan tradition into his narrative by relating it even more closely than Mark to the preceding discussion (see also Luke 9:22). Mark presents Jesus' passion prediction after an interlude of their amazement and fear (10:32a), but Luke depicts Jesus as directly **taking the twelve** aside. Thus his pointed warnings about what lies ahead for him stand in contrast to his words of assurance to them (vv. 27-30). Whatever comfort they derived from Jesus' assurances, Luke stresses that they had no idea what to make of his dire predictions (v. 34; 9:45). The salvation they so earnestly desire (v. 26) is about to be won, but not by what they "do." It is God who is at work here in the midst of an opposing humanity.

This is the third passion prediction in Mark, closely tied to the threefold revelation of Jesus' messianic identity and the character of discipleship (Mark 8:27—9:1; 9:30-41; 10:32-45). But for Luke, this is the sixth prophecy of the passion (9:22; 9:43b-45; 12:50; 13:31-35; 17:25), and most of Jesus' journey to Jerusalem has intervened since the last passion prediction drawn from Mark

(Mark 9:30-31//Luke 9:43b-45). As noted at 17:25, Luke has expanded upon Mark's emphasis on the suffering of the Son of man (see also 24:7). Although he follows Mark quite consistently in this passage, Luke has woven the saying into the fabric of his narrative with care. For Luke there is no "messianic secret," but there is a profound mystery of why Jesus the Son of man and Messiah (see 24:26-27, 46-47) had to suffer.

31—This is Jesus' statement to **the twelve** of what is about to happen as the journey to Jerusalem reaches its goal. This is not merely another trip "up" to Jerusalem or the temple (2:42; 18:10; Acts 3:1; 15:2; 21:12, 15; 24:11; 25:1, 9). This is a journey of obedience, of fulfilling his "exodus" (9:31) which he was to accomplish in Jerusalem. He has been on this purposeful journey since 9:51 and will complete it only when he "goes up" at 19:28. Thus only Luke explicates this **going up** as the fulfilling of all **that is written of the Son of man by the prophets.**

As many interpreters have noted, the search for Old Testament prophetic passages which speak of a suffering Son of man is unfruitful, and Luke does not provide any specific texts. But it will be the revelation of the risen Christ which will demonstrate to his followers that the suffering and death of the Messiah was the fulfillment of "everything written about me in the Law of Moses and the prophets and the psalms" (24:44-46, 27). In this prediction of the passion, Luke is laying a foundation block for understanding Jesus' "words which I spoke to you while I was still with you" (24:44). The prophetic words of Jesus and the scriptural prophecies together declare the active reign and will of God in the coming passion.

32-33—These words explicate in greater detail how the prophetic oracles will be fulfilled. It is probable that at some levels of the recitation of these words, their association with Isa. 50:6 was conscious. In Acts 8:30-35, Luke was clearly aware that the text of Isaiah 53 was actually about Jesus. Furthermore in Acts 4:25-28, the gathering of the Gentiles and peoples of the earth against the Lord and his Messiah spoken of in Psalm 2 was about Jesus' death. Thus Luke's use of Jesus' predictions about his coming humiliation and death at the hands of the Gentiles is already an explication of "everything written of the Son of man by the prophets" (v. 31). But this is where the lines blur between history, the interpretation of history, and Christian proclamation. Even as the evangelists recite the common memory of Jesus' passion predictions, they nuance what he said to help the reader grasp what really was about to happen, and they emphasize that **none** of this was clear to his disciples at the time.

It is interesting that in this passage Luke omits Mark's references to Jesus' condemnation to death by the high priests and the scribes (but see 9:22). It is the betrayal of this Son of man into the hands of **the Gentiles** which stands at the focus. It is apparently at their hands that he will be humiliated and reviled, and they are his executioners. Certainly this does not exonerate those who betray him (see 22:32-38), but many agents will be at work. And, above all, this will be the fulfilling of the Scriptures. It will be the accomplishing of the will of God (see also Acts 4:28).

34—The mystery of God's reign is shrouded in the death of Jesus the Son of man and Messiah. This verse is an echo of 9:45 where the words of the earlier prediction of the suffering of the Son of man were similarly incomprehensible to the disciples. Now "the twelve" did not understand, the matter **was hid from them,** and they did not know what it meant. The passive voice, "it was hid," is again the most telling, for this is a "theological passive." Jesus is telling them what God has not yet revealed to them. These are the "secret matters" which will yet be made known, and they must be "heard" with care so that they may later be explicated (8:17-18). In fact, this is exactly what the risen Christ will reveal through the interpretation of the Scriptures. But for now, the "secret" of the coming passion is beyond their understanding. Even the Christian reader who knows how the story comes out must wonder. God was about to do a deed which would be unbelievable, even if someone, even the Messiah himself should declare it in advance (see Acts 13:41). The humanly impossible is possible for God (18:27).

He Proclaims the Kingdom and Predicts the Destruction of His Enemies (18:35—19:27)

The last three episodes of the journey to Jerusalem are set in Jericho, and Luke will stress the proximity to Jerusalem. None of these stories has any other necessary connection to that geography or to each other, but together they comprise the last of the three cycles of stories (17:11—18:8; 18:9-34; 18:35—19:27) which have all moved between proclamation of the kingdom and prediction of judgment. Having arrived at the very doorstep of Jerusalem, Jesus again displays his messianic fulfillment of the program he announced in Luke 4 (18:35-43), declares forgiveness and salvation to an outcast of Israel (19:1-10), and warns of the dire consequences which would be rightfully in store for those who reject his reign (19:11-27).

The Healing of the Blind Man (18:35-43). Luke draws this story from Mark, but his dependence on Mark does not control his usage of the episode. Having followed Mark quite carefully since 18:15, Luke now takes more initiative with his source, dropping a major section (Mark 10:35-45), placing this healing within Jesus' entrance to Jericho rather than his departure (Mark 10:46), and supplementing this healing with another encounter in Jericho (Luke 19:1-10) and the stern warnings of the "parable of the pounds" (19:11-27). Some commentators have observed only Luke's omission of Jesus' words in Mark 10:45 concerning giving his life as "a ransom for many," as if Luke had selectively omitted just this detail to alter Mark's "theology of the cross."

It might be closer to the mark to suggest that Luke's omission of Mark 10:35-45 is consistent with Luke's depiction of the disciples. While they did not understand Jesus' passion prediction (see 18:34), neither did they misinterpret his words so extremely as Mark suggests. Some traces of Mark 10:41-45 seem to show up in Jesus' words to his disciples on service in Luke 22:24-37 where Jesus is both correcting and instructing the Twelve, and Luke agrees that a proper understanding of discipleship is immediately linked with understanding Jesus' identity and dominion. But arguments as to why Luke did not use a portion of Mark will remain speculative and may distract from more concrete observations of the testimony which Luke's narrative offers.

Here the entrance to Jericho is a clue to the near approach to Jerusalem (see 10:30). A map of Palestine will show how far Jesus has come and how close he now is to Jerusalem. But as the comments on 17:11 indicate, what is most important is how Luke's story dramatizes the "way of the Lord" rather than its specific geography. The Messiah is nearing the conclusion of his lengthy journey. This Son of David (vv. 38, 39), Son of man (19:10), and royal ruler (19:15, 27) now displays his authority before his entrance into Jerusalem as the King who comes in the name of the Lord (19:38).

35-38—Luke enhances the drama of the story with a more elaborate introduction. He omits the name of the **blind man** (see Mark 10:46, "Bartimaeus, . . . the son of Timaeus"), but he develops the scene of a large crowd preceding Jesus into **Jericho.** The blind man hears the crowd, asks what was happening, and is told by the multitude that **Jesus of Nazareth is passing by.** He is already crying out for **Jesus, Son of David,** and being rebuked by the crowd before Jesus himself appears. As with the Zacchaeus story which follows, the large crowd is itself part of Luke's picture of Jesus' dramatic procession.

No reason is given for the blind man's identification of Jesus as **the Son of David.** This is clearly a pre-Lukan royal-messianic title, but it fits Luke's conviction of Jesus' royal Davidic identity (see 1:32; 1:69; 2:4, 11; 3:31; 6:3; and 20:41-45). The blind man is an oracle (compare Simeon 2:26, 30). He sees what many others have failed to recognize, and he cries out for an audience with this Davidic ruler who is about to pass by. The **rebuke** of the crowds displays their lack of understanding (see 18:17), but it serves to heighten the drama of the story. He merely intensifies his cry.

40-43—Jesus is every inch a king. He stops this procession (literally, "he took his stand"). He orders the man brought, and he asks him what he wants. The whole healing story is surprisingly brief. Only Jesus' word is needed, **"Receive your sight!"** This verb (Gk: *anablepsein*) is repeated three times in these verses, and it recalls Jesus' citation of Isa. 61:1 in Luke 4:18 and the probable allusion to Isa. 35:5 in Luke 7:22 (see also Acts 9:17-18). This is more than a miracle of physical healing. It is a fulfillment of the role for which the Holy Spirit has "anointed" Jesus, the recovery or receiving of sight of the blind.

Some interpreters have argued that there is little evidence that a Davidic king was expected to be a healer, unless the stories about the powers of David's son Solomon may be allowed (see Josephus, *Ant.* 8.41-49). But Luke clearly understands this healing by the "Son of David" as a demonstration of Jesus' messianic authority. It fulfills his anointing (see 4:18). The implicit trust of the blind man in the "Son of David" is a kind of "seeing" which brings him the healing he sought (see also "your faith has saved you" in 7:50; 8:48; and 17:19). The concluding glorification of God resounds with the praises which the shepherds declared at the birth of the Messiah in the city of David (2:11, 20). The miracle Jesus performs causes people to praise God because this is the reign of God at work through God's Messiah (see also 5:25-26; 7:16; 8:39; 13:13; 17:15).

The Salvation of Zacchaeus (19:1-10).   This story is a Lukan masterpiece, a wonder story of the first order. Here God and the Messiah Jesus accomplish what is humanly impossible (18:27)— a rich man is saved! This story provides a telling contrast to the self-concerned righteousness and sadness of the rich ruler (18:18-24), and it complements the healing of the "daughter of Abraham" (13:16). Zacchaeus, the wealthy tax collector rejoices in his salvation, restored as a child of Abraham (3:8) and displaying the fruits of his conversion/repentance (3:8) with extravagant generosity. Following the story of the healing of the blind man, which is also a story of salvation ("your faith has saved you/healed you," 18:42, Gk: *sesōken*), the story of Zacchaeus is an elaboration of the theme of salvation, healing, and restoration.

Even the form of the story is that of a healing, as may be seen when the story is compared with such classic healings as that of the paralyzed man (5:18-26) or the blind man (18:35-43). The narrative format introduces the characters and indicates the man's condition: **he was a chief tax collector, and rich.** In Luke this may be a more serious diagnosis than that a man who was paralyzed was brought to Jesus or that a blind man was begging. The obstacles to access to Jesus are overcome by lowering the man through the roof, his crying out to the entourage, or by climbing the tree. Jesus receives these dramatic actions as signs of faith, and when grumbling from the bystanders increases the drama, he performs the "healing." Then a chorus of acclaim from the crowd or the "saved" person or Jesus himself indicates what has transpired in the wondrous encounter.

Of course, being a rich tax collector is not a physical malady, but it is a perilous spiritual condition in Luke's understanding. The angel Gabriel's conviction that "nothing is impossible with God" (1:37) not only echoes Gen. 18:14 but has taken a new turn in Luke 18:24-27. Now the reader could debate which is more "impossible" or more "miraculous," that a blind man regained his sight or that a rich man was saved. But in fact, this Son of David (18:38-39) and Son of man (19:10) accomplished both. Verses 8, 9, and 10 thus present three elaborated conclusions to the "wonder," demonstrating its reality and relating its meaning to the larger context in Luke's narrative.

1-4—All of this is important narrative detail in the novelistic style of wonder stories. It is impossible to tell which elements may have been part of a pre-Lukan version, since everything except possibly his name counts so heavily for Luke. **Zacchaeus** is a good Jewish name (see Ezra 2:9; Neh. 7:14; 2 Macc. 10:19) literally meaning "innocent" or "clean," but he was a wealthy collector of tolls, which meant that he participated in the bureaucracy of Roman control. From many points of view he was neither "clean" nor a good Jew. But, like the woman who disrupted Simon's banquet (7:36-50) or the woman who touched Jesus in the crowd (8:43-48), Zacchaeus risked ridicule by **climbing a tree to see** Jesus. That is the only reason his short **stature** is interesting. What is most remarkable about him is not his height but his faith as displayed in this absurd position. Perhaps a child would climb a tree, but a wealthy bureaucrat who was already despised by many as a collaborator and a cheat?

5-7—Luke does not explain how Jesus knew his name, but he called **Zacchaeus** by name and invited himself to his **house.** Jesus' words are freighted with Lukan nuances. "Today it is necessary for me to stay in your house." The emphasis on **today** will resound again in v. 9, alerting the reader to the present reality of salvation (see 2:11; 4:21; 5:26; 23:43; see also Deut. 6:24; 26:16-19). Furthermore, **today** is identified as a crucial phase in the regulated journey of the Messiah ("I must go today," 13:32-33). This "necessity" may not be the full-blown revelation of God's will, as when the Son of man or the Messiah "must suffer" (17:25; 22:37; 24:7, 26, 44), but it is part of the deployment of the kingdom or will of God (see also 2:49; 4:43). Jesus is not merely acting on a whim. He is enacting the will and reign of God and is under some constraint from his mission to go to this house (see also 7:40; 19:31). Thus he tells Zacchaeus to **make haste;** he does make haste and receives Jesus joyfully.

The note of joy is the signal of Zacchaeus's conversion. He receives Jesus and his command with open heart, in striking contrast to the sadness of the rich ruler (18:23) and the subsequent murmuring of the crowds (v. 7). Joy is the response of faith (1:14; 2:10; 10:20; 13:17; 19:37; 24:41, 52). This is a tax collector who abandoned his pride and received the Messiah with joyful freedom (see also 18:10-14).

8—His speech is a remarkable confirmation of the salvation which he has received in trusting Jesus. He is able to let go of his wealth. He does not ask, "What must I do to be saved?" or "How much must I give up now?" And Jesus sets no conditions. It may be significant that he exceeds even what the Law required, i.e., restitution plus 20% for extortion (Lev. 5:16; Num. 5:7) or fourfold reparations for stealing sheep (Exod. 22:1). But the point is probably that no one is discussing amounts. This is a free response of letting go, with no deliberation of "rights" or "obligations." Zacchaeus knows full well that **the poor** are the proper recipients of this grace (4:18). He does not think to pay Jesus, but **half** of his net worth is pledged away. It is not even clear whether he has actually defrauded anyone. This is not a scene full of remorse. He has **stood** to give a speech of thanksgiving and has done so while still talking in the percentages and numbers of a business person.

9-10—Jesus' two statements are verdicts of approval on Zacchaeus's speech. Jesus has enacted the same mission to which he directed his disciples by entering this house and bringing the kingdom as a present reality (9:4; 10:7-9). The whole household has been blessed (see Acts 10:2; 11:14; 16:31; 18:8). His first verdict thus confirms that **salvation has come to this house** *today* (see v. 5 above). This tax collector may no longer be regarded as a traitor, for his faith has confirmed him to be **a son of Abraham** (see also 3:8; 13:16; and Gal.3:29).

Jesus' final word is one more declaration of his authority to exercise such grace in restoring the lost (see also 5:30-32; 7:34; 15:1) so that the whole episode becomes another demonstration of the message of Luke 15. By including this last traditional word in this context, Luke highlights the Christological or soteriological revelation of the story. This is **the Son of man** who carries forward God's mission to bring back **the lost** and the strayed (see Ezek. 34:2, 16).

The Parable of the Pounds (19:11-27).   This frightening story marks the conclusion of Luke's "central section" or "Way of the Determined Messiah" (9:51—19:27). The opening verses (9:51-54) of this section had begun with the disciples' eagerness to call fire down from heaven to consume the Samaritans who would not receive Jesus, but Jesus rebuked them, later promising that cities which reject the kingdom will yet face a worse fate than Sodom (10:12). Now, **near to Jerusalem,** Luke reports that **they supposed that the kingdom of God was to appear immediately** (19:11), and Jesus' parable supplies a complex corrective to such expectations by indicating that (a) harsh opposition still lies ahead in the coming of the kingdom, (b) the judgment which will come with the kingdom could be fearsome, and (c) those who are faithful servants and disciples have important responsibilities in the meantime.

This story is so filled with probable historical allusions that it has been a springboard for speculation about the circumstances of Luke's community. It is likely that Luke's rendition of this story was an indirect comment on speculations in his own time about when Christ would return (see also Acts 1:6-11) and painted a harsh picture of the coming judgment for those in Israel who still had not received Jesus as king. As the book of Acts shows, Luke regarded the proclamation of repentance unto forgiveness in Jesus' name as God's grace to Israel and the Gentiles, but the Messiah's return would mark the end of that era of grace (see Acts 2:38-40; 3:17-26; 5:31-32; 17:30-31). No doubt a crucial part of Luke's purpose in writing an "orderly account . . . that you might know the truth" (1:1-4) was to assist his readers to understand how the Jesus story helped them understand their "present time" (12:56).

But the passage must be interpreted first of all within its context in the narrative. Then more elaborate suggestions may be explored about how the story corresponds to what may have been happening in Luke's world or community. In this instance, the parable of the pounds scores a vital point within the story. It serves notice that Jesus' arrival in Jerusalem will not meet with universal acclaim. Having just witnessed the salvation of a "son of Abraham" (19:2-10), the crowds must now hear a sober word of warning. The campaign which follows faces harsh opposition.

Luke appears to have combined two kinds of traditional materials in the construction of this ominous episode, a **parable** from "Q" about **servants** who are entrusted with funds in the master's absence and a story about a ruler who went to a far country to receive a kingship and who dealt out punitive judgment on his opponents when he returned. The parable is well known from Matthew's (25:14-30) account of the "talents," where it is thoroughly elaborated by Matthew so that the master's return "after a long time" is clearly the last judgment when the good servant is invited to "enter into the joy of your master" (25:21, 23). Luke's version has enough differences in detail and vocabulary to suggest that it may not be drawn from the same written source, but the same parable provides the substructure so that no disciple can miss the point that active stewardship is expected.

But the story about the king has been grafted onto this parable, and in vv. 12, 14, 15a, and 27, the elements which alter it into a story about a king can still be isolated. Of course, in Matthew 25 this parable was already a story about "the kingdom of heaven," but now it is a depiction of what kings do. As 19:38 shows, Luke is emphatic in identifying Jesus as "king."

This alteration increases the political drama of Jesus' entry into Jerusalem. The practice of a person of the nobility going to **a far country** to receive a kingship was well known in the oriental regions of the Roman Empire. Herod the Great was named "King of the Jews" by the Romans, and Josephus tells that his son Archelaus went to Rome at his death to receive his kingship while an embassy from Jerusalem pleaded that he not be named king. Archelaus also dealt harshly with his opponents upon his return (*Ant.* 17.299-303, 339-344). By contrast, Herod Antipas, who participated in Jesus' trial (23:6-12), spent and ended his whole career trying to receive the title "king." What then does Jesus' identity as "king" or "King of the Jews" (23:3, 38) mean to Jesus' servants or his opponents?

Luke's retelling of this parable, therefore, is a two-sided prophetic warning. For the followers of Jesus it is an assurance that the kingdom is indeed coming, a call to faithful service, and a warning that they should not presume an easy judgment (see also 17:8; 21:36). For the opposition, which is soon to emerge much more adamantly in the narrative, this story is a reminder that they will be contending with the one whom God will vindicate and exalt as Messiah and Lord; he will receive the kingship. If Jesus were to act as kings predictably act in the face of rejection, his opponents would have nothing to expect but destruction and death. Jesus raises the stakes high by means of an overtly political parable which all could understand, but he does not thereby limit the kingdom of God or his own reign to be exercised by the known rules of oriental kingship.

11-12—Jesus' words are spoken against a backdrop of the expectations of those who have just heard his words to Zacchaeus. The proximity to **Jerusalem** creates the occasion, and since 9:51 (or 9:31) the reader has known that the climax lies ahead in Jerusalem. Now the climax is presented, not as a sudden resolution, but as a decisive encounter within a more extended process. In this process, Jesus' "departure" (9:31) or "being received up" (9:51) becomes his "being taken up into heaven" (Acts 1:11) so that his exaltation to heavenly dominion still anticipates his "return" to earth in judgment and dominion in Israel (Acts 1:6-8; see also the discussion of the day and days of the Son of man in 17:22-27).

13-15—The traditional parable begins in v. 13 and resumes in v. 15b. The elements about "kingship" in vv. 12, 14, and 15a

stand out largely by comparison with Matthew 25, but they increase the tension in this context, since this king is immediately
confronted with hatred and sedition. This is no longer merely a
story of how well the servants handled the master's assets.

Within the parable, the **pounds** or "minas" are not a large sum,
probably less than $20 each. The point is simply that the master
is entrusting each of them with a small investment. In Luke, each
initially receives the same.

16-26—The only elements in these verses which make them
stand out from the traditional parable of stewardship is that the
faithful servants are rewarded with authority over **cities** (vv. 17,
19). Certainly such a political reward heightens the encounter,
but later, in vv. 24-26, the man who achieved the greatest return
is only given the **wicked servant's** pound. Nothing is said about
cities, yet **they** object as if this additional award of $20 were
significant. Thus the traditional parable about the "pounds" has
only been altered slightly in Luke's recasting.

The master is not a direct picture of God or the Messiah, but
he is a worldly wise businessperson who puts his servants to their
tasks and expects performance. Like the master who expects service from his servants in 17:7-10, he is severe and demanding.
His servants know that, and he does not apologize for it (vv. 21-
22). They are given a task, and they merely indict themselves by
complaining. This is presented as a realistic picture of the authority which masters had over their servants, and the picture is
still realistic in many circumstances. The "boss" does not allocate
his resources on the ground of treating everyone equally, but he
gives the money to the person who produces a return. It is his
money, after all. The rules of this game are simple and well known
in the world of business: go with the producers. But if that is the
way masters realistically behave, how much more "right" would
the Lord and Messiah have to expect performance from his servants on his return?

27—Luke again escalates the traditional parable to the political
level. It is not only businesspeople who operate by a demanding
code; the same is true of kings. They do not tolerate seditious
embassies (v. 14). They execute their enemies when they have
the opportunity. Again, this is not a direct picture of what Jesus

will do, but it serves notice that Jesus is aware of the way the "real world" works. And would not the Lord and Messiah have the same right simply to **slay** his enemies if he chose to exercise it?

The end of this journey of the Messiah toward Jerusalem is at hand, and the threat of fire from heaven or the slaying of Jesus' enemies remains a realistic possibility. Jesus is not at all naive about the conflict which is coming, nor does he have delusions that all of his disciples will prove faithful with what is entrusted to them. In time the apostles will proclaim to Israel and the Gentiles that they have in fact been complicit not only in opposition to the Lord and his anointed, but in his shameful execution (Acts 2:36; 3:13-15; 4:27-28; 7:52-53; 13:27-29). Common experience would suggest that a boss would be severe and a king cruel.

And what about God? Certainly God would be in the right to be severe, even to slay those who oppose the reign of God's Messiah. Without diminishing the real possibilties of such judgment, Luke's story of Jesus moves into the confrontation in Jerusalem, the death of the Messiah, and his resurrection and ascension still confident of God's determined will to save Israel and the Gentiles.

■ Jesus' Visitation of Jerusalem (19:28—21:38)

> Would that even today you knew the things that make for peace! But now they are hid from your eyes.
>
> (Luke 19:42)

In this fifth section of Luke's narrative, the Messiah reaches the goal of his journey, but this climax appears to reveal only a failed mission. Jesus' triumphal entry evokes joy, but also provokes resistance and soon hostility. He implements his rule and restoration in the temple, but Israel is divided and her leaders are the adversaries of his reign. Jesus' tears and his prophetic words reveal the pathos of God, but the will of the Messiah is resolute. The section moves from acclamations of God's rule to prophetic declarations of the dire fate of Jerusalem and the temple. Jesus' life is in peril, but it is Israel's future which is more gravely threatened. The "visitation" of God's Messiah is the moment of Israel's judgment.

The King Who Comes in the Name of the Lord (19:28-48)

This entire section should be read as a unit. It is a turning point in the story, marking the completion of the extended journey of the determined Messiah (9:51—19:27) and the beginning of his intentional and obedient mission in Jerusalem (19:28—23:56). Jesus' arrival is God's "visitation" of Jerusalem (19:44) in blessing (19:38) and in judgment (19:41-44). The goal of his arrival is the temple (19:45-48) which he cleanses and where he will teach (19:47—21:38) until he is arrested through a plot. In the midst of significant acceptance by the people as well as fierce rejection, the Messiah is the presence of the reign of God in Jerusalem for this brief period.

The Royal Procession (19:28-40)

All four Gospels tell the story of Jesus' entrance into Jerusalem, complete with dramatic acts and scriptural acclamations with royal overtones from the crowds. Historians have examined these accounts with great care in an effort to identify what kind of event this arrival actually was and what Jesus' own understanding of it may have been. The minimalists argue that Jesus was merely part of a host of pilgrims streaming in for the festival, perhaps being feted as a celebrated rabbi by riding a mule. More ambitious interpretations have suggested that Jesus was enacting a kind of royal procession according to the script of Zech. 9:9, advancing a messianic claim and provoking a conflict with the authorities in Jerusalem. But it is not necessary to resolve the historical question or to read the mind of Jesus to know that Luke understood this as an intentional act. In his account, Jesus is the Son of David entering Jerusalem in royal procession.

This passage is drawn from Mark 11:1-10, but heavily edited by Luke and thoroughly integrated into his narrative. The first verse (v. 28) is linked directly back to the royal episodes in Jericho (**and when he had said this**), and even the verb "to go" (vv. 28, 36; Gk: *poreuesthai*) strikes a familiar chord at the conclusion of the travel narrative (see the discussion at 9:51 and usage at 9:57; 10:38; 13:31, 33; 17:11). Luke's expanded version of the praise of the **multitude of his disciples** also resounds with preceding recitations of Jesus' "mighty acts." Even the traditional word of blessing from Psalm 118 now fulfills Jesus' prophecy of 13:35 and is supplemented with a specific identification of him as **King.** Finally, Jesus' words to the Pharisees both remind the reader of a similar rebuke in 13:31-35 and anticipate the oracle of judgment which follows. Luke has clearly mastered the tradition in his presentation of Jesus' climactic royal entry.

28-29—The traditional geographic details concerning **Bethphage, Bethany, Jerusalem,** and the Mount of Olives (**the mount that is called Olivet**) receive no further comment in Luke. Even Jesus' **going up** to Jerusalem may only be a reference to the rise from Jericho, which is 800 feet below sea level, to Jerusalem, which is 2500 feet above sea level. It is tempting to ask whether Luke or the pre-Lukan tradition drew attention to the Mount of Olives because of the prophecies in Zechariah 14 where the coming of "the Lord your God" to this mountain is the Lord's becoming "king over all the earth." The restoration of the holiness of the temple promised in Zechariah 14 would also mean that "there shall no longer be a trader in the house of the Lord of hosts on that day." Certainly modern interpreters are not the first to see such symbolic possibilities in Jesus' dramatic action, but the evangelist does not call attention to them. Only the theme of the extension of the journey is highlighted.

30-36—Luke follows Mark's account more closely in these verses. The tradition is already replete with allusions to Zech. 9:9, and Matt. 21:4-6 draws out that allusion so specifically that it appears that Jesus rode both the foal and its mother. But neither Mark nor Luke identify the source explicitly, and the interpreter must wonder how far back in the tradition the allusion to Zechariah lies. Similarly, none of the evangelists explains how Jesus knew where this beast was to be found or what the dialog would be with someone who would ask. The common point seems to be that Jesus was fully in charge, and it was he who set up the scene in fulfillment of the text from Zechariah. The fact that this was to be a "new foal" on which no one had sat appears to suit the special royal function of the animal. The evangelists do not envision a demonstration of welcome which simply arose spontaneously as Jesus approached.

Even the repetition of what people would say and what the **owners** did say expresses the conviction that Jesus was staging this entrance. The "owners" are the "lords" or "masters" (Gk: *kyrioi*), and Jesus is the "Lord" or "Master" (Gk: *kyrios*). Thus Jesus is exercising the special prerogatives of royalty or a figure of great authority in commandeering the animal. He does not need a signed requisition. He is the Lord, or at least he is on the Lord's business, and he does not meet further objection.

They who brought the colt, spreading **their garments** on it, and they who **spread their garments on the road** appear to be part of a growing company who are rolling out the carpet for Jesus! In 1 Kings 1:33-35, David's son Solomon is similarly "mounted" (Gk: *epibibazein*, see Luke 19:35) on a mule as he is taken in royal procession to be anointed king in David's stead and "ruler over Israel and over Judah." And when Jehu was anointed king, "every man of them took his garment, and put it under him on the bare steps, and they blew the trumpet and proclaimed, 'Jehu is king' " (2 Kings 9:13, see also Josephus, *Ant.* 9.111). Luke has omitted the mention of the "leafy branches" (Mark 11:8) which provided one more link with the "festal procession with branches" of Ps. 118:27. But this is still a thoroughly royal procession before any words are spoken.

37-38—The content of the acclamation leaves no ambiguity, and these verses are distinctively Lukan. **The descent of the Mount of Olives** is the last moment before the ascent to Jerusalem, and **the whole multitude of the disciples** joins in praise. This is no minor following. Luke has been alerting the reader to the crowds (18:15, 36, 43; 19:3). Their rejoicing and praise of God resounds with the praises which began with the angels (2:13, 20; 18:43), and it centers around all the "mighty works" which they have "seen." This phrasing also echoes 7:22 and points back to 4:18, for it is the fulfillment of the anointed one's role which has been "seen and heard" by those who have faith. The traditional citation of Psalm 118 also fulfills Jesus' own prophecy that they would not "see" him until they say, "Blessed is he who comes in the name of the Lord" (13:35). If even a shred of unclarity remained as to Luke's grasp of the meaning of that fulfillment, he adds, **The king!** This is a royal procession, fulfilling what Luke regards as a royal psalm and acclaiming Jesus to be God's king entering Jerusalem.

Even the liturgical phrases of **Peace in heaven and glory in the highest** link back to the angel's declaration at the birth of Christ the Lord of "Glory to God in the highest and peace on earth" (2:14). The fact that "earth" is not mentioned in this case is not evidence that Jesus' reign is only heavenly. The whole scene is a declaration of the presence and power of the reign of God on earth, entering Jerusalem, just as it is also exercised in heaven.

39-40—These "certain" **Pharisees** who object remind the reader of the "certain Pharisees" who tried to counsel Jesus to avoid Herod's wrath in 13:31-35. They appear in Luke to be especially cautious that Jesus avoid any appearance of "political" confrontation, sharing the caution of many religious people in later generations. Of course they were right, in the sense that they understood that such a demonstration as this could provoke violent reaction from the people in power, whether Herod, the high priests, or Pilate. Just as Jesus should be counseled to avoid Herod's territory, he should be advised to silence his disciples. Such a demonstration could be misunderstood.

Or worse, it could be understood! Jesus was entering Jerusalem as **the King** of God's own choosing. This was a confrontation with the brokers of power, and Jesus was unafraid. He was about to move directly to the temple and drive out those who sold. God was coming in strength in the person of this Messiah, and Jesus was not about to be deterred by those who counseled caution.

His final word, therefore, is a sharp prophetic oracle. It is stated in an unusual form called the "future more vivid construction" where the "if" clause is followed by a future indicative which has nothing tentative about it. "If these be silent, then the stones *will* cry out." This is not merely a pathetic fallacy to the effect that the rocks will praise God if no one else does. This is a word of warning as the words about the "stones" in 19:41-44; 20:6; and 21:6 will soon show. If and when the acclamation of Jesus as king falls silent, Jerusalem will be doomed.

The words of apparent restraint and sensible judgment of these "certain Pharisees" again receive the full brunt of Jesus' rejection. As in 4:23-27 or 13:31-35 (see also 11:45-46), Jesus is not about to be deterred from his mission by well-meaning wisdom which is implicit rejection of his messiahship. He is the king, and he knows full well the conflict which lies ahead. He has been predicting his passion when no one could grasp what he was saying. But he will not accept attempts to silence the acclamation which is Israel's true hope. Luke does not indict all Pharisees, and he even suggests that those who spoke came out of the vast multitude of disciples who were properly acclaiming Jesus. But the words of these few provoke Jesus to pronounce an oracle of destruction, uttered through tears (vv. 41-44).

Prophetic Lament (19:41-44)

These verses are unique to Luke, and they fill the transition from the triumphal entry of the king to his cleansing of the temple with profound pathos. In Mark 11:11-25, Jesus entered Jerusalem, surveyed the temple, and departed. On the following morning, his cursing of the fig tree preceded his cleansing of the temple, and nothing is said in Mark of Jesus' tears. But Luke's account condenses Jesus' entrance into one trip and compounds the emotional impact by moving quickly from an oracle of warning to the Pharisees (v. 40), to tears for the city in the midst of a dire oracle of doom (vv. 41-44), to a dramatic act of cleansing the temple (vv. 45-46), and to Jesus' teaching in the midst of hostile adversaries (vv. 47-48). The emotional load is almost too much to comprehend, but it is crucial to Luke's message. The arrival of Jesus is the divine **visitation** of Jerusalem, intended to be her salvation, but tragically turned into her destruction by a humanity opposed to God's Messiah.

Luke's depiction of Jesus as the prophet-Messiah reaches its peak in this episode. The oracle is filled with scriptural allusions drawn largely from Jeremiah 6:6-21; 8:18-21; 15:5; and 23:38-40; as well as Ps. 137 (LXX, 136):9; Isa. 29:3-10, and 2 Kings 8:11-12. The phrases are heaped up from the old prophetic oracles of judgment against Israel, Jerusalem, and the temple, the words which were uttered in connection with her first destruction at the hands of the neo-Babylonian Empire. Reading those texts with care may be the best commentary for grasping the archaic force of Jesus' words in this setting. The ancient word of the Lord, spoken before in divine anguish of love and wrath, is now uttered again by the prophet-Messiah as the visitation of God's reign confronts Jerusalem. If this Gospel was written in the wake of the Roman destruction of Jerusalem, Luke's recitation of these oracles would have had particular force. The fate of Jerusalem was bound up with her acceptance or rejection of the reign of God's Messiah, and the sad tragedy was that in an attempt to keep the peace by silencing Jesus, the tragic consequences of destruction were brought upon Jerusalem.

It is important to note that other late first-century sources struggle to understand how Jerusalem's destruction could fit with God's purposes and justice. The Jewish historian Josephus is much more condemnatory than Luke, suggesting that God went over to the Roman side (*War*, 6.399, 401, 411-412). Josephus even said that "God perverted their judgment so that they devised for their salvation a remedy that was more disastrous than destruction" (*War*, 4.573). But Luke treats the problem of why Jerusalem did not know the time of her visitation in much the same way as the "ignorance" of the disciples concerning Jesus' death (9:45; 18:34). Only God and God's Messiah know, and the grief is great. This is closer to the spirit of the non-Christian book 2 Baruch: "Do you think that there is no mourning among the angels before the Mighty One, that Zion is delivered up in this way? Behold, the nations rejoice in their hearts. . . . Do you think that the Most High rejoices in these things or that his name has been glorified?" (67:1-3).

The form of these verses in Luke also reinforces the depth of the lament. The lament is structured into (1) a declaration of what is not the case (**would that** . . . **but now,** v. 42), (2) a series of phrases stating the dire consequences (**for** . . . , vv. 43-44a), and

(3) a final reason or indictment (**because you did not know,** vv. 44b, see also the discussion of the structure of 23:28-31). The harsh phrases cascade like a litany of judgment connected only by a repetition of the word **and.** "And your enemies will cast up a siegework . . . and they will hem you in . . . and they will raze you to the ground . . . and your children in you . . . and they will not leave stone upon stone in you" (compare the RSV). These may be phrases drawn from a pre-Lukan source or a chain of prophetic warnings used like a scriptural litany after the destruction. But it is certainly possible that Jesus himself could have uttered such warnings against Jerusalem, as did other prophets in his era. Whatever their origin, these oracles fit with Luke's conviction that although Jesus is about to go to his death, the tragic blindness in this story is not his. The lament is for Israel and the tears must be shed primarily for Jerusalem and her children (see 23:28). Like the prophets of old, the prophet-Messiah is caught up in the pathos of God, even as it is God who will become Israel's adversary (see Jer. 8:18-9:11; 22:8-23; Isa. 29:3).

The last phrase states the reason for all of this woe in another classic prophetic formula, **because** (Gk: *anth' hōn*) **you did not know the time of your vistation.** The word **because** is a strong expression meaning literally, "this for that," indicating retributive justice. This is the expression used repeatedly in Jeremiah to speak of God's judgment on the city and temple (see especially Jer. 22:8-9; 23:8; see also Ezek. 5:11; 6:11; and see the tone of judgment in Luke 1:20; 12:3; and Acts 12:23). As Luke has testified (1:68; 7:16), God's **visitation** was intended to be the redemption and salvation of God's people. But now it has turned tragically into a visitation of judgment (see the ominous oracle of the "time of visitation" in Jeremiah 6:14-15 (LXX: *en kairō episkopēs*; see also Jer. 10:15; 11:23; 51[28]:18; 48[31]:44).

Cleansing and Teaching in the Temple (19:45-48)

Luke ties these verses closely into the preceding oracles. As noted in the comments above, Luke has shortened Mark's account so that Jesus' lament over Jerusalem drives directly into his action. His grieving and his wrath are not separable, but are two

aspects of the passion with which he advances into Jerusalem.
The specific mention of **those who sold** suggests that the allusion
to Zech. 14:21 may indeed have been conscious at some stage in
the telling of this story (see the comments on 19:28-29 above),
but the reference is only indirect (see also the temple as a house
of prayer in Isa. 56:7). The account is very brief in Luke, and the
absence of such details as the overturning of the tables and the
reference to the "nations" or "Gentiles" is surprising. The remaining details thus stand in bold relief: Jesus wept for the city,
drove the traders from the temple, and proceeded to teach in it
in the face of grave hostility from the **chief priests and the scribes
and the principal men of the people.**

The temple was not merely a religious building. It was the
most important Jewish institution which the Romans and their
predecessors tolerated and controlled within their governance of
the region. The high priests were appointed annually by the
Roman procurator, and the treasury of the temple was always in
jeopardy from some tyrant or administrator who was looking for
funds. Furthermore, the temple was the site of considerable financial exchange as pilgrims purchased sacrificial animals and
sought to have proper currency for paying the temple tax. Thinking about the social and political role of the temple in an occupied
land may help the reader of the Gospels understand that this was
not merely a case of turning a church into a bazaar. In the ancient
world, sharp distinctions between what was religious and what
was political would never have had much meaning anyway. But
people did have strong convictions that certain political and economic aspects of temple practice were contrary to its primary
function as **a house of prayer.**

Jesus was not the only one who was unhappy. The passage from
Zechariah 14 and the text of Isaiah 56 (so-called trito-Isaiah) reflect
the views of Jews in the era after the exile who were eager that
the restoration of Israel should involve a much more purified
cult. The sectarians at Qumran also withdrew from the practices
of the "wicked priest" in Jerusalem and dreamed of a reconstructed temple in a restored kingdom (see the Temple Scroll).
The leaders in Jerusalem and the high priests in particular had
often been criticized, and yet they were compelled to keep the

peace in the temple if they did not want trouble from the Romans. Thus when Luke presents the Galilean prophet-Messiah Jesus entering in royal procession, weeping over Jerusalem's fate, and driving the traders from the temple, he is portraying a provocative act which will not go unnoticed by the rulers.

The description of the response of the different groups in vv. 47-48, therefore, will prove programmatic for the rest of the narrative. Luke has not related all of the details of Jesus' deeds, but he has pressed the story for its social consequences. **The chief priests and the scribes and the principal men of the people** will seek **to destroy** Jesus. Until they succeed, **the people** will prove to be his only line of defense. The Pharisees will be notably absent after this episode (see the comments at 11:53-54). Eventually all will be complicit in Jesus' death, including **the people** and the disciples, but for now the prophet-Messiah will receive a favorable hearing from the people while he teaches in the temple. This is a story of both faith and opposition, and the faith of Israel must not be missed.

Conflicts While Teaching in the Temple (20:1—21:4)

This section is constructed on the framework of Mark 11:27—12:44. Only the story of "the Great Commandment" (Mark 12:28-34) is omitted from this context, probably because Luke had already conveyed that saying within the introduction to the parable of the good Samaritan (Luke 10:25-28). These conflict stories probably contained historical details from Jesus' own teaching and encounters with various authorities in Israel, and they may have been collected in a pre-Markan cycle of stories which emphasized God's authorization and inspiration of Jesus' teaching. Even the four types of questions contained in Mark's sequence may have been something of a standard catalog by which Jesus' surpassing wisdom was displayed.

In Luke's usage, however, the recitation of these stories had the primary effect of highlighting the growing conflict between Jesus and the rulers of Israel, with the people standing in the middle. The summary statement in 19:47-48 stages the scene with Jesus as the protagonist, the "chief priests, scribes, and principal men" as the antagonists intent on "destroying" Jesus, and the people hanging on his words. Three times these adversaries confront Jesus with questions which are intended to expose, entrap, or ridicule Jesus (20:1-8, 19-26, 27-40). None of the questions is sincere, and yet Jesus consistently provides answers which have genuine instruction for those who are willing to hear it. The people who are eager to hear are instructed along with the readers, and then Jesus proceeds with prophetic teaching (20:9-18, 41-44; 20:45—21:4) which further exposes the hypocrisy of his opponents and assails their authority.

The whole section displays conflicting claims among those who are the teachers of Israel, and the temple setting makes this conflict even more dramatic. These are stories which early Christian communities would have treasured as disclosures of the triumph of messianic teaching over the attacks of the temple leadership.

Conflicts over Authority in Israel (20:1-19)

This section is the first of three rounds of conflict. The temple authorities take the lead intending to expose Jesus. But he is more than a match for them. He quickly silences them and turns the encounter into an occasion when his adversaries and the people are instructed together in the peril which killing him would pose to Israel. He wins the conflict, hands down, but is he heard (v. 16)?

John's Authority and That of Jesus (20:1-8).　　In Mark's account, this conflict story follows a more extensive version of the cleansing of the temple and the story of the disciples seeing the fig tree which Jesus had cursed "withered away to its roots" (Mark 11:12-26). There the question, "By what authority do you do these things?" (Mark 11:28) drew attention to these highly symbolic acts. Luke's version, however, emphasizes Jesus' "daily teaching" in the temple (19:47; 20:1), and offers only a minimal account of Jesus' cleansing of the temple. Luke knew that Jesus' driving out those who sold from the temple was a provocative act, but he suggests that Jesus' adversaries would only be able to "destroy" him by a successful attack on his teaching (19:48). Thus in Luke it is Jesus' **teaching** and **preaching in the temple** which provide the setting for the adversaries' question, "**By what authority do you do these things?**" (20:1-2). The whole episode becomes a display of Jesus' ability to refuse to answer that question in a way which would serve his adversaries (v. 8) while still forcing them to provide an indirect and affirmative answer for **the people.** The story is fully satisfying for those who believe Jesus' authority comes from God, and frustrating for those who oppose him.

1-2—Only Luke presents the conflict in the setting of Jesus' **teaching the people in the temple and preaching the gospel.** As noted above (19:47), "the people" will prove to be Jesus' greatest allies, remaining faithful to him even after his own disciples have betrayed or denied him, until all finally are complicit in his death. The term **the people** is used more than 80 times in Luke-Acts with very specific connotations. "The people" are consistently the people of Israel. They are Jewish, and they are generally the faithful who are looking to God for salvation (see comments at 1:10, 17, 21, 68, 77; 2:10, 31-32; 3:15; 7:29). They will prove to be a "divided people," with those who reject Jesus eventually "destroyed from the people" (see Acts 3:9, 23—4:1), but the many who repent will be the restored people to whom the Gentiles will be added by God (Acts 2:37-47; 15:12-21; 26:17).

The RSV states that Jesus was **preaching the gospel,** but the verb (Gk: *euangelizesthai*) is used frequently by Luke merely in the sense of "preaching" or "proclaiming," and it may be the kingdom of God (4:43; 8:1; 16:16) which Jesus preaches (see also 4:18; 7:22; 9:6) or "Christ Jesus" or "the word" which the apostles proclaim (Acts 5:42; 8:4, 35; 11:20; 15:35; 17:18). Luke rarely uses the noun **gospel** (Acts 15:7; 20:24). Luke's presentation is focused on Jesus' authority as "teacher."

The adversaries are identified (in Mark's words) as **the chief priests and the scribes with the elders** which is only slightly different from 19:47 ("the chief priests and the scribes and the principal men of the people") or 20:19 ("the scribes and the chief priests"). The identification of "the Sadducees" (20:27) will be much more specific, and they are distinguished from "the scribes"

(20:39). But a major point of the chapter is to group Jesus' adversaries together among the various "official" leadership groups (see also 20:46 and 22:1-6). These are the people who have public recognition as the leaders and teachers of Israel, and they are identified in various ways with the institution of the temple. Luke does not explain just which people had **priestly** offices or which were **scribes** of the Pharisees or Sadducees or whether the **elders** were members of the Sanhedrin (see 22:66). Nor does Luke indicate that they were defending the sanctity of the temple. The threat which Jesus poses is his recognition by the people as an authoritative teacher. The double question is, therefore, a single, frontal assault from the official teachers, "Who do you think you are?"

3-6—Jesus answers their questions with a question about **John.** It is a ploy in a deadly game, but more than a ploy. As a teacher, Jesus has answered questions with questions before, pressing predictable tests deeper (see 10:25-26; 18:18-19). This time the reader knows that the question is part of an intention to destroy Jesus (19:47), and even the fact that Jesus eludes the trap is satisfying. But who is interrogating whom? Jesus is willing to come clean, but they must too. The question about John requires them to exercise their authority as teachers of Israel, to discern whether his **baptism** was from God or humans. If they are sincere in challenging Jesus' authority to teach, they must risk opposing popular opinion about John. Or they must risk a politically dangerous endorsement of the prophet who was executed by Herod Antipas. The question is especially powerful in Luke's narrative because the ministries of John and of Jesus have been so thoroughly intertwined since their infancies (see the outline of Luke 1–2; 3:1-22; 7:18-35; 16:16; Acts 10:37). Only Luke identifies **the people** specifically as the cause of their fear (see also 22:2). Thus they fail to be teachers of the people of Israel out of fear of the people. They turn a fundamental question about God's agency into a merely political discussion to protect their lives.

7-8—Jesus is no longer obliged to answer these "officials" who have abdicated their teaching office. His final word is a simple refusal, which would be unthinkable if they had been sincere or had engaged his question with integrity. Their effort had been to expose this teacher's lack of authority. They had the positions of authority from which to do so. But Jesus rather exposed their lack of authority. Round one goes to Jesus, but the stakes are rising.

The Vineyard and the Tenants (20:9-19).   The religious authorities have challenged Jesus (20:1-8), and now he intensifies the conflict. Luke is following Mark's sequence of stories throughout this section, but this picture of Jesus pressing his adversaries also fits Luke's previous depictions (see 4:14-30; 13:31-35). In Luke's telling, furthermore, Jesus is speaking to **the people** who are "hearing" him eagerly (see vv. 9, 16, 19), but he is speaking "against" the religious leaders who "understand" that they bear the brunt of the story (v. 19). Even if they do not "hear," these leaders know what is happening, and the reader overhears the whole exchange.

Interpreters of this **parable** have long debated whether it is more a product of the early church or derives from Jesus' own teaching. It certainly seems to be a natural Christian allegory, which makes different sense after Jesus, God's only Son, was killed by the religious leaders and Jerusalem was then destroyed. By the time the evangelists tell this story, it has become a prophecy recited after the facts, and it is impossible to determine exactly which details have crept into the telling out of later Christian experience. Probably the scriptural argumentation in v. 17 and the proverb in v. 18 are examples of such Christian enhancement.

On the other hand, several aspects of this "parable" fit very credibly with Jesus' own teaching and situation. The whole parable is an expansion on the prophetic "song of the vineyard" of Isa. 5:1-7, and it is likely that Jesus would have recited such a word of warning to Jerusalem. Clearly this prophet from Galilee regarded the temple leadership in Jerusalem to be less than faithful stewards of God's vineyard, and his mission entailed a challenge to their claim to authority from God. Furthermore, the theme of the dire fate of the prophets was a traditional call to repentance in contemporary Jewish sources (see the discussion at 11:47-52), and many strands of the Jesus tradition indicate that he had no illusions that he would be warmly received or that

Jerusalem's role in God's reign would be simply restored. This story also fits with the symbolic action of his dramatic entrance into the city and demonstration in the temple.

In Luke's presentation, this is an elaboration of Jesus' teaching in the temple. Israel is divided before him. The people are listening eagerly and fearfully to the awesome words of the prophet-Messiah, and the temple leadership is growing more adamant in their opposition. Meanwhile, Jesus' words both illumine what is really happening in the scene and offer instruction in God's reign.

9—Luke's introduction identifies **the people** as the immediate audience. The religious leaders have merely faded into silence (vv. 1-8) while listening close at hand (v. 19). In Isa. 5:1-7, Jerusalem was identified as God's vineyard, having been cultivated by God and expected to bear fruit or be destroyed. This parable of Jesus also begins with a patient process. Luke has fewer details about the construction of the vineyard than Mark 12:1 and thus is less open to allegorical application to Jerusalem. But Luke indicates that the owner departed **for a long while.** This is not an apology for "the delay of the parousia," but it is an emphasis on divine forbearance. God did not rush the vineyard or look for produce before **the time came** (v. 10).

10-12—The three embassies of mistreated servants are easily allegorized as Luke's allusions to the "prophets and apostles, some of whom they will kill and persecute" (11:49; Acts 7:51-53), and clearly this application process began very early in the transmission of this parable. In Mark 12:5, there are "many others, some they beat and some they killed." The Gospel of Thomas (v. 65), which preserves a very primitive form of this parable, has only two embassies before the **son** is sent (see also Matt. 21:33-44), but even there the tenants beat the second servant to the point that they almost killed him. Luke suggests that with each embassy the treatment grew harsher, but he does not indicate that the servants were killed or in peril of death.

Thus far, Luke's account avoids excessive judgment. This is a more credible account of contemporary practices between tenant farmers and an absentee landlord. Of course these **tenants** are clearly wrong, and the **owner** has the right to expect to receive

produce. This is not a story of the rights of oppressed share-croppers. But the owner's patience is also not stupidity. This land-lord continues to deal in an expectation of justice, although his tenants have displayed extremely bad faith in the abuse of his collectors. In Luke, God's patience with sinners is a sign of gracious forbearance (see Acts 2:37-40; 13:17-19; 17:30).

13—The "Lord of the vineyard" engages in a characteristic Lukan soliloquy, **"What shall I do?"** (see 12:17; 15:17-19; 16:3). The reader is drawn into the problem at a level where the soul of the speaker is revealed. This "Lord" takes a great risk in the hope ("perhaps," Gk: *isōs*) that these obstinate tenants will respect his **beloved** son. The allusion to the "beloved Son" within the Gospels is an obvious clue that this is God who identified Jesus as "my beloved Son" at the baptism (Mark 1:11//Luke 3:22) and the transfiguration (Mark 9:7, but "the chosen one" in Luke 9:35). This is a statement filled with pathos, even the pathos of God. In Jesus' view, this Lord has not abandoned hope that the son will be received with respect. Just as Jesus has wept over Jerusalem because the pathos of unfulfilled hopes is genuine, so God, who knows how improbable this mission is, still hopes for a good outcome.

14-15a—The tenants' speech is a total disappointment. This is their private conversation (Gk: *dielogizonto pros allēlous*), revealing the secret thoughts of the heart (see Simeon in 2:35, Gk: *dialogismoi*). Their thoughts are strictly malevolent. Whether such a plan could ever result in the tenants actually taking possession of the vineyard is a subject for historical debate. Legal questions of eminent domain are probably less relevant in that situation than considerations of whether they would be able to make a success out of an insurrection. This landlord appears to lack courage since they have gotten away with so much already. Their decision to **kill the heir** and seize the vineyard is thus the topic of their calculating words.

15b-16—When the tenants act on their worst schemes, the Lord of the vineyard must also act. This part of the story relies on the simple logic of what oriental custom requires. Just as the ruler would slay his enemies who did not want him to be king (19:27), so the landlord will **destroy** these insurrectionists and dispossess them of the the vineyard. And everyone would expect such action, even the people who hear this story, knowing that Jesus is speaking about Israel. That is why they cry out, "By no means!" The expression (Gk: *mē genoito*) is used frequently by Paul (see Rom. 3:4, 6, 31; 6:2, 15; 7:7, 13; 9:14; 11:1, 11) but only here in the Gospels, and it is a strong denial of a real possibility. The RSV catches the sense well, **God forbid!** And that is the question which will loom large in the rest of the story. What will God do in the face of human rebellion and the murder of God's Messiah?

17-18—Jesus invokes a scriptural argument (v. 17) and a proverbial aphorism to drive home the point that divine judgment is exactly what may be expected. These traditional statements do not fit tightly with the parable itself, but they reflect expanding interpretations. Both of them tie the conclusion into the broader narrative context.

The allusion to Ps. 118:22 (**the very stone which the builders rejected**) scores the primary point of transforming the rejection of Jesus by the religious authorities into divine approval (20:1-19). It fits the story in the sense that it was about rejection, and the story was an allegory for Israel's rejection of Jesus. It is intriguing to wonder whether Jesus' death on the charge of insurrection (23:5) was not understood by Luke as especially ironic. It is the tenants, not the son, who practice rebellion, and their revolt is against God's dominion. The allusion to Psalm 118 is also intriguing since this is the same psalm which the crowds recited as Jesus entered Jerusalem as king, thereby fulfilling Jesus' own prediction, which was based on the psalm (19:38; 13:35). The people acclaimed him in the words of that psalm, but those who rejected him must now contend with words of judgment from the same Scripture.

The proverb (v. 18) is a restatement of an old aphorism: "If a stone falls on a pot, woe to the pot. If the pot falls on the stone, woe to the pot. Either way, woe to the pot." But that traditional saying has new power in this context since it is a further word play on the word **stone.** Once again, the "stone" turns out to be the instrument of divine justice. Throughout this section, the "stones" bear an ominous testimony against those who reject "the cornerstone" (see the discussion at 19:44).

19—This statement is carefully recast by Luke so that the several agents in the story are carefully identified and differentiated. The religious leaders are the adversaries, and the people are supportive of Jesus. The drama which has been laid out carefully in 19:47-48 will continue, because Jesus' adversaries are, for a time, frustrated in the execution of their hostile will.

Entrapping Questions about Caesar's Realm (20:20-26)

Luke has tied this story directly to the preceding episode, using vv. 19-20 as a transition which strongly emphasizes the hostility and evil intent of Jesus' opponents. The RSV tries to capture this linkage in English by starting a new paragraph at v. 19 and beginning v. 20 with **So they**. . . . But v. 19 is more correctly the conclusion of the previous story (see also Mark 12:1-12). Luke's thorough rewriting of vv. 20-21 (see Mark 12:13) thus marks a new level of conflict and sets Jesus' words about tribute to Caesar in the more explicit context of political intimidation. As in 20:1-8, Jesus' answer will prove to be both a refusal to answer his adversaries and a profound statement of principle for those who will hear it.

This passage has long been read as Jesus' endorsement of the doctrine of the "two kingdoms." In turn, some interpreters have understood this as ratification of "the separation of church and state." This encounter has been misinterpreted by such imposition of later dogmas from church history and Western civil law. Jesus' words are helpful for recognizing that allegiance to civil authorities is not necessarily hostile to faithfulness to God, but other New Testament texts must be used to sort out proper obedience to civil authorities (see Rom. 13:1-7; Rev. 13:1-18; 1 Pet. 2:13-17; Acts 4:19-20; 5:29,39). All of the Synoptic accounts present Jesus' answer as a deft evasion of a trap. The most immediate effect of his answer is to move the problem back to the questioners. They must decide first what properly belongs to **Caesar** and what belongs to **God**.

Luke is especially aware of the political dangers of the question. Only Luke mentions the **jurisdiction of the governor** and later states that Jesus was explictly charged before Pilate of "forbidding us to give tribute to Caesar" (23:2). The reader is aware that this is a false charge. Neverthless, Jesus' answer could have been interepreted as a refusal to give tribute. The scriptural tradition of the kingship of God testified clearly that God was the Lord and master of the whole world. Did this mean that everything belonged to God, and Caesar was a false god? Israel's psalms were full of affirmations that "the earth is the Lord's and the fulness thereof, the world and those who dwell therein" (Ps. 24:1). In Acts 4:24-30, Luke also interprets Jesus' death as the gathering together of "the kings of the earth . . . and the rulers" against the "Sovereign Lord" and "his anointed." Simple separation of God and Caesar was impossible.

The Roman **coin** itself could be offensive to Jewish religious convictions. In Jesus' era, the denarius (v. 24) not only had Caesar's **likeness,** which was a forbidden graven image (see Exod. 20:4, 23; Deut. 7:5), but it was inscribed with the theological claims of the Roman order. "Tiberius Caesar, son of the deified Augustus, Augustus" was written on one side, along with Tiberius wearing a laurel wreath. On the other side, his mother Livia was depicted as the goddess "Peace" with the inscription, "High Priest." This money was not theologically neutral, although people probably used it every day without much thought. But when Jesus pointed out these features, he confronted all the Jews with the problem. A weak contemporary comparison could be made with the lawsuits in the United States to remove the inscription "In God we trust" from the currency, but the passions stirred there would be mild on both sides compared to those aroused by the use of Roman coins in occupied Palestine.

Josephus tells of another Galilean, named Judas, who in about A.D. 6, "incited his countrymen to revolt, upbraiding them as cowards for consenting to pay tribute (Gk: *phoros*) to the Romans and tolerating mortal masters, after having God for their lord" (*War*, 2.118). Luke is aware of that revolt and indicates that Gamaliel the Pharisee compared it with and distinguished it from the Christian movement. But Gamaliel also understood that obedience to God could mean opposition to human authorities (Acts 5:33-39). Furthermore, in Acts Jesus' apostles withstood the leaders of Israel precisely on the grounds that they were compelled to obey God rather than humans (4:19; 5:29). Certainly Jesus' answer about tribute to Caesar is not a blanket endorsement.

Jesus' word does press the faithful hearers to ponder the question of civil obedience and its limits, and it turns this issue into more than an ethical or political question. It is a question of the First Commandment, a theological question about the sovereignty of God and human allegiances. But in this passage, that discussion is undeveloped. Luke only stresses that Jesus has a second time fended off an attempt to "take hold of what he said, so as to deliver him up to the authority and jusridiction of the governor" (v. 20) or to "catch him by what he said . . . in the presence of the people" (v. 26). Round two goes to Jesus.

20—Luke alters Mark's identification of the adversaries from "some of the Pharisees and some of the Herodians" (Mark 12:13) to "the scribes and the chief priests" (vv. 19-20). Luke never mentions the Herodians, and he omits the Pharisees from the narrative from the arrival in Jerusalem (19:39) until the trial of the apostles when Gamaliel addressed the council in their defense (5:34). He knows of genuine conflict with the Pharisees (see 11:37—12:3), but they are not party to the conspiracy to kill Jesus which is developing in the story. "The scribes and chief priests," however, are the consistent adversaries (see 19:47; 20:1; 22:2). The **spies who pretended to be sincere** are clearly evil, and if the word is translated more technically, they may be pretending to be "righteous" (Gk: *dikaios*). This could even mean that they were pretending to be the defenders of the Law who were pressing the teacher for his "word" (Gk: *logos*). In such a case, their deceit would mean baiting him to implicate himself with the Romans by taking a strict interpretation of the commandments.

21-22—This feigned "righteousness" does seem to be Luke's understanding. The flattery is all in terms of "right teaching" which is not politically motivated, and the issue is whether tribute is **lawful.** These are all the categories of authoritative interpretation of the Law of God, and the question could be profound if it were genuine. It is they who undermine the Law by their insincerity, not Jesus. Luke uses the word **tribute** (Gk: *phoros*, see Josephus above), which was probably the more offensive form of "taxes" (see Mark 12:14).

23-24—Jesus' entire response is based on his perception of **their craftiness** or manipulation of the Law. He asks them to produce the **coin;** apparently they are the ones who are using them. Perhaps they were already embarrassed, and certainly they were already complicit in the political system. To the crowd, Jesus' answer exposes his questioners as people who deal in Caesar's money. Certainly they must pay Caesar's tribute. The nuance of this exchange of flattery and implied insult is too subtle to read with confidence at this distance. But the final phrase drives home the theological teaching of the Law, and it clearly dominates Jesus' understanding.

Tribute to Caesar is not on a par with faithfulness to God. All of Israel and the apostles know that (Acts 4–5). For the moment these people who pretended to be strict interpreters of the Law have been exposed, just when they sought to entrap Jesus. They have been revealed to have already made their compromise with Caesar and Caesar's theologically inscribed coins. The question of what God requires is thus pressed back upon them and upon the readers, and Jesus' respect for the integrity of God's Law and reign is publicly revealed.

Disputes with Sadducees and Scribes (20:27—21:4)

Luke continues to follow Mark's sequence as the conflict with the Jerusalem leadership grows, and the tension is even more unrelieved in Luke. Mark follows the debate about resurrection with the story of the Great Commandment (Mark 12:28-34), suggesting at least the possibility of common ground with the scribes, but Luke retains only a trace of scribal approval of Jesus' words (20:39). This is, rather, the third round of hostile questions directed at Jesus, followed by Jesus' sharp attacks on these adversaries. Even the instruction which Jesus provides to the faithful is minimal since the atmosphere of conflict so dominates the narrative.

Misleading Questions about Resurrection (20:27-40). First it was "the chief priest and the scribes with the elders" (20:1), then their "spies" (20:20). Now the **Sadducees, those who say there is no resurrection,** bring their question. None of these interrogators has been sincere. Jesus is still teaching in the temple, and the official leadership has persistently sought to expose, entrap, and ridicule him. Luke has continually emphasized that Jesus' pronouncements have shown him to be more than a match for such adversaries, and "the people" continue to be his faithful audience and support (19:47-48; 20:1, 6, 9, 19, 26, 45). None of these references to "the people" occurs in Mark (see the textual problem in Mark 11:32), which indicates that Luke's depiction of the setting of these conflicts is drawn carefully and consistently.

The Sadducees are infamous in surviving Jewish texts for their denial of the resurrection (see also Acts 23:8 and Josephus, *Ant.*, 18.16-17, *War*, 2.165). The fact that not much more is known about the group probably indicates more about how offensive the Christians and the Pharisaic traditions found their teaching than it does about what they thought was important. Their priestly origins are generally linked with "the sons of Zakok," Zakok having been a priest in David's reign (2 Sam. 8:17). The legitimacy of the Zadokites as priests was strongly attested in Ezekiel's vision of a restored temple (Ezek. 40:46; 43:19; 44:15-16). Luke also identifies the Sadducees closely with the temple leadership (Acts 4:1; 5:17), and Josephus emphasizes the aristocratic character of the group (*Ant.* 18.17).

Some have suggested that their disdain for the doctrine of the resurrection fits generally with their priestly understanding of the religion of Israel and upper-class contentment with the status quo. Certainly they were not filled with prophetic zeal for reforming the temple and probably were not too impressed with calls for repentance that anticipated God's dynamic reign of righteousness. Their approach to Jesus in this story seems to indicate that they were confident of their own righteousness and right teaching. Josephus also notes that they were ready to dispute any teacher (*Ant.* 18.16).

In this story, the Sadducees raise a complex question based on a ridiculous case (vv. 27-33). They hardly feign sincerity, because they respect neither the teacher nor the teaching on resurrection. Jesus' answer, however, displays surprising mastery of the situation. First he dismisses the question as based on a false concept of **resurrection** (vv. 34-36). Then he engages them in a debate of the real issue of whether the Scriptures testify to the resurrection (vv. 37-38). Luke's conclusion (vv. 39-40) demonstrates Jesus' victory. Round three goes to Jesus.

27-33—The case these Sadducees raise is based on the Semitic practice of Levirate marriage, that is, the marriage of a widow to her husband's brother (Latin: *levir*) when no children had been born to the first marriage. The objective was to perpetuate the first husband's line; the children were his, but the wife then belonged to the brother (see Deut. 25:5-10 and Gen. 38:8, see also Ruth 3–4 and Josephus, *Ant.* 4.254-256). The number **seven** is probably intended as a ridiculous touch. It may also reflect a connection with the story in Tobit 3, where a series of seven husbands die on their wedding nights after marriage to one woman. The Sadducees address Jesus as "**Teacher**," and they refer to **Moses.** But the point is to insult all who think they can base the teaching of resurrection on the Law of Moses.

34-36—Jesus requires them to alter their concept of the resurrection before proceeding. They have assumed simple continuity with the present order, but this **age** (Gk: *aiōn*) in which there is marriage must be distinguished from **that age** (vv. 34, 35), and even the resurrected are no longer mortal (v. 36). This response is reminiscent of Paul's response to the questions, "How are the dead raised? With what kind of body do they come?" "You foolish man!" Paul says, indicating the absurdity of trying to understand the resurrection as a mere extension of previous bodily existence. Then he proceeds with a discussion of the transformation which accompanies the resurrection. Simple notions of resuscitation will never be adequate. Thus Luke's Jesus also continues with surprising comments that are unique to this passage.

Earlier Luke had developed the traditional Jewish distinction between "this age "and" the age to come" with reference to "eternal life" (see 18:30). Now **this age** is described further as the era of normal human activities, of (in that culture, men) **marrying** and (women) **being given in marriage.** The alternative reading in the manuscripts speaks of "begetting" and "being begotten." But for those who are aware of the age to come, such realities are already not ultimate (see 18:24-30). And the age to come is the "age" of the "resurrection from the dead" to which the worthy hope to attain. This is what Luke calls "the resurrection of the just" in 14:14. Jesus does not indicate here what is entailed in being **worthy to attain to that age,** although an appeal to 18:24-30 again would suggest that this is a basic image of salvation which is the work of God.

Mark 12:25 suggested that people, after being raised, do not marry because they are "like angels in heaven." This tradition is well known in Jewish texts, probably reflecting the interpretation of Gen. 6:2-4, where "the sons of God" violated their status by marrying the daughters of men (see 1 Enoch 15:6-9). But Luke develops another theme of Gen. 6:2-4—that humans of flesh were limited to a life span of 120 years lest the offspring of these "sons of God" live forever (see also "sons of God" in Job 1:6; 38:7; Pss. 29:1; 89:6). Now the resurrected cannot die anymore because they are **equal to angels** (Gk: *isangeloi*). The resurrected have become immortal. They have become **sons of God** because they are **sons of the resurrection.** The resurrection is an exaltation, as will also be proved when the resurrection of Jesus inaugurates his exaltation and enthronement as "Son of God" (see Acts 13:33-34 on Psalm 2, and see Acts 2:36).

Jesus' indirect appeal to the passage from Genesis also has some secondary effects in this story. Here is a passage which comes from the first book of the Torah of Moses which the Sadducees accepted without argument. It proves that marriage is not normal in the heavenly court and that God must limit human life because "My spirit shall not dwell in man for ever" (Gen. 6:3). It also speaks of these "sons of God" who were commonly understood to be "angelic" beings. Thus it addresses all of the biases of the Sadducees who had the reputation in Luke-Acts of believing "there is no resurrection or angel or spirit" (Acts 23:8). All of this is done indirectly, but the technical terms **sons of God** and **sons of the resurrection** are thus elaborations of the statement in Mark that the resurrected are like the angels.

37-38—Next Jesus offers a direct scriptural argument for the resurrection, again based on a passage from the Torah. As an introduction to a second argument from **Moses,** Luke's phrase should read, "And Moses also revealed that the dead are raised (in the passage) about the bush." The quote from Exod. 3:6 is God's word from the bush (see also Acts 7:32), and the implication is clear that the dead could not have a God at all if they were simply dead. Thus God is speaking about the living and claiming to be their God. This is a fascinating argument from the Scriptures which displays the deductive reasoning of scribal interpretation. Luke merely supplements the argument with another traditional corollary, "For all live to him."

In 2 Maccabees 6, Eleazar, a "scribe of high position, a man now advanced in years" spoke as a martyr facing the tortures of Antiochus IV Epiphanes. His death was exemplary, consistent with the testimony to the resurrection of the dead which followed in 2 Maccabees 7. But in 4 Macc. 7:8-19, Eleazar is a priestly descendent of Aaron, and his more philosophical speech uses traditional scriptural arguments in an affirmation of immortality: "Only those who with all their heart make piety their first concern are able to conquer the passions of the flesh, believing that to God they do not die, as our patriarchs Abraham, Isaac, and Jacob died not, but live to God."

Both Luke 20:38 and 4 Macc. 7:19 conclude the traditional reference to Exod. 3:6 with an affirmation of life in God. This does not prove that Luke borrowed from 4 Maccabees or that Luke teaches immortality in place of resurrection. But Luke's understanding of resurrection is certainly more complex than re-vivification of corpses. Jesus' answer exposes the foolishness of the Sadducees' question, meets each of their objections with crucial scriptural resouces, and instructs all who hear with a rich composite of traditional teachings. Finally, the identity and agency of this God of the living stands at the heart of Jesus' teaching in the temple.

39-40—In Mark 12:28 one of the scribes observes the dispute, notes that "he answered them well," and proceeds with the question of the "Great Commandment" (Mark 12:28-34); but Luke has retained only the note that **some of the scribes** complimented the **teacher** for answering well. This sounds like a grudging compliment in Luke, since "the scribes" are such strong adversaries in the chapter (see the comments at 20:20, 46). The mention of **some** (Gk: *tines*) is characteristic of Luke (13:31; 19:39), and Luke may understand these "scribes" to be in greater sympathy with the Pharisaic teaching on the subject of the resurrection (see Acts 23:6-8). Still the compliment hardly resolves the underlying conflict with the scribes. The last line indicates that the tactic of entrapping him with questions has simply failed. If they are determined to "destroy him" (19:47), "lay hands on him" (20:19), "deliver him up to the governor" (20:20), or "catch him by what he said" (20:26), they will need to try other methods.

The Messiah: David's Son and Lord (20:41-44).   Jesus now turns the interrogation around. He had followed the first question about John with his bitter warnings of the parable of the vineyard and the tenants. Now he turns the tables on these scholars of the scriptural tradition. First he poses a scriptural conundrum for them to ponder about David's son and lord (vv. 41-44). Then he presses his direct attack on the scribes and all those filled with the pretense of piety (20:45—21:4). They **no longer dared to ask him any question** (v. 40), but he has some for them.

41-44—These verses begin and end with the question of how the Messiah is **David's son.** It is an odd question, since the whole tradition and Luke are so insistent that the Messiah is the son of David (see 2 Samuel 7; Ps. 89:20-37; Isa. 9:2-7; 11:1-9; Jer. 23:5-6; 30:9; 33:14-18; Ezek. 34:23-24; 37:24; Ps. Sol. 17:21; 4QF1 1.11-13; 1QS 9.11; 4 Ezra 12:32; Luke 1:27, 32, 69; 2:4, 11; 6:3; 18:38-39; Acts 2:25-36). Certainly Jesus is not questioning the Davidic identity of the Messiah, but the question is "how" the "impossible" is possible (see 18:27). Jesus insists that **David's son** is David's **Lord,** and David himself knew it.

The reader of Luke-Acts must answer the question first, and Luke has provided David's own answer in Acts 2:25-36. Mark (12:36) reported that David's psalm was inspired by the Holy Spirit, and Acts 2 identifies David as a prophet who foresaw Jesus' resurrection and exaltation. This is how **David's son** became his **Lord** when God fulfilled the promise to "raise [LXX: *anastēsō*] up offspring after you, who shall come forth from your body, and I will establish his kingdom" (2 Sam. 7:12; see also Jer. 30:9). As Acts 2:31-36 shows, what David foresaw was the resurrection of the Christ, which meant Jesus' exaltation to reign as Lord and Christ. Psalm 110 is cited both here and in Acts 2. Thus Jesus' question receives its definitive answer when Peter interprets it as a Davidic prophecy which has now been fulfilled.

Commentators have emphasized that Jewish expectation of a Messiah usually had political implications, and certainly this language of making the **enemies** a **footstool** sounds like oriental practices of humiliating the conquered. Luke is not so nervous about political overtones as most modern readers are and will even speak of Jesus' enemies in quite political terms (see 19:14, 27; Acts 4:25-27). On the other hand, God's way of ruling will prove to operate by very different rules than the politics of the world (see 22:24-27), and this exalted Messiah will be eager for repentance and slow to judge.

Jesus' adversaries are probably also overhearing his question, and it should make them think. This is not merely a display of Jesus' scholastic skill. In Luke's narrative, it is a prophetic warning that the Messiah and Son of David will be raised up as David's Lord to exercise dominion. The Sadducees' question about the resurrection has been exposed as foolish and lacking in scriptural understanding. Later they will be confronted with Jesus' witnesses proclaiming "the hope of the resurrection" (Acts 23:6). The resurrection of the Messiah will prove to be God's way of confirming David's son to be David's Lord, and those who plot against his life must be warned of the divine justice which is to come. As with the parable of the tenants in the vineyard (20:9-18), Jesus' response to devious and deceitful questions contains a warning that the reign of God is not mocked.

Beware of the Scribes! (20:45—21:4).   Luke uses these words of Jesus as a conclusion to the larger section of conflicts with the leaders of Israel in the temple (20:1—21:4). The first episode of conflict in this section (20:1-8) led into Jesus' harsh parable of the tenants and the vineyard (20:9-19). And "the scribes and chief priests" perceived this parable as told "against them"

(20:19). Now Jesus dispenses his criticism directly. Even his observation of the widow giving **all the living that she had** into the temple **treasury** becomes a further indictment of a perverted religious institution and its leadership. The gap between Jesus and his adversaries is becoming unbridgeable. Soon Jesus will prophesy the destruction of the temple itself within his declaration of the days which are to come (21:5-38).

45-47—Luke again distinguishes **the people** and **his disciples** carefully as the audience for this warning about the scribes (see Mark 12:37b). This attack on **the scribes** is comparable to the woes against the Pharisees and the lawyers in 11:37-52. Matthew 23 repeatedly clusters the "scribes and Pharisees, hypocrites" together in Jesus' words of woe (see Matt. 23:13, 23, 25, 27, 29), but Luke is speaking specifically in this passage about the **scribes,** and the context seems to imply that these "scribes" are connected with the chief priests (20:19), but apparently stand apart from the Sadducees (20:27, 39). In Mark 12:28-34, Jesus even commends a scribe's wisdom and notes, "You are not far from the kingdom of God." In Luke, however, the compliment of these scribes to Jesus (20:39) does not indicate any fundamental agreement. Instead, Jesus moves immediately into warning his disciples about the scribes, and the people overhear the instruction. The Messiah-teacher is exposing the scribes before the people as he had denounced the Pharisees and the lawyers earlier.

The content of the attack is a warning against hypocrisy. The standard foibles of religious leaders of every generation are laid bare. The specifics could relate to a scribal class in Israel, perhaps connected with the rituals of the temple (on the Pharisees and lawyers see 11:37-52). But **long robes,** public recognition, cathedral seating, and clergy status at banquets have long been accoutrements of religious professions. Jesus does not denounce all such practices, but he decries the love of such trappings as an evil hypocrisy. Once again, the externals have become a bill of particulars in the indictment. Jesus is charging these scribes with **liking** and **loving** all of these benefits, **devouring widows'** estates to preserve them and indulging in pretentious **prayers** to keep the system profitable.

It is not clear exactly how they took advantage of the widows, but the offense seems to lie with cheating them out of their meager estates. Perhaps these widows were at the mercy of the scribes as trust officers, or perhaps they were simply deceived by religious pretenses. In either case, the offenders were contending with God, who is partisan to the widow and the orphan (see the comments on 18:1-8). Modern religious hucksters are not the first to put on a good religious show or to plunder the poor and the widows with pretense. But **the greater condemnation** is reserved for people who prey on the poor in the name of religion.

21:1-4—These verses are usually treated as an example story which praises the generosity of the widow, and similar stories were known from Greek traditions which praised such virtue. In this context, however, the scene may be a further indictment of the religious practices of the temple **treasury** and its priests. It stands between Jesus' condemnation of the hypocrisy of the scribes who **devour widows' houses** and his oracles of the destruction of the temple. The **widow** may be virtuous. Certainly she is not criticized. But as she gives **out of her poverty** and contributes **all the living that she had,** she is also a victim of a system which was intended to benefit her.

It is not clear exactly which **treasury** or fund was involved. Some have argued that this was a building treasury, since Herod's temple was still not finished or fully underwritten. This could also be a general treasury for the operating costs and support of the priesthood. Jesus is not completely alienated from the temple. He has been teaching there for some time. But he has also driven out the sellers, confounded the chief priests and scribes, and criticized the money-hungry clergy. It is unlikely that he is now simply commending the woman for her temple piety.

Certainly her sacrifice far outstrips the mere generosity of **the rich,** and the contrast between **their abundance** and **her poverty** is restated three times. But in this context, Jesus is more lamenting the injustice which the scene reveals than commending the virtue of generosity. This is a continuation of his lament and an anticipation of his oracle of the coming destruction of the temple. In Acts 6–7, Stephen, who was appointed to care for the distribution to the widows, will speak again about Israel's misunderstanding of the house of God. Jesus may ask his disciples to abandon their wealth and possessions to serve God rather than mammon (see 16:1-31), but he does not endorse any religious system which supports wealthy institutions or clergy at the expense of poor widows. Such a system stands under the condemnation of God (20:47; 21:5-9).

The ancient prophetic spirit of Micah and Amos pervades this passage, revealing the Spirit of God to be opposed to religiosity which is not tempered with justice. Now Jesus will condemn the temple itself, in all of its splendor. The feasts, solemn assemblies, the offering of the people of God, and the house of God itself will be judged by the standard of God's righteousness (see Amos 5:21-24; Jer. 7:1-15).

Jesus and the Future (21:5-38)

Jesus' arrival in Jerusalem brought him into the temple. The temple was the goal of his journey which began in 9:51, and it was the site of his most intense conflicts with the leaders of Israel. Now it is the location of his final extended discourse. In Luke's presentation, this discourse rivals the Sermon on the Plain (6:20-49) for length and significance. It gathers up themes from Jesus' earlier prophetic discourses about readiness for the coming day of the Son of man (12:35-59; 17:20-37; see also 18:8). It also pronounces Jesus' verdict on the temple and city as divine judgment which fulfills prophetic warnings (see comments on v. 24). But, above all, this discourse distinguishes the destruction of Jerusalem from the subsequent times when there will be distress among nations and cosmic disturbances. Jesus' prophetic words concerning the temple and Jerusalem (vv. 5-24) precede his apocalyptic predictions of how God will bring about the "redemption" of the faithful (v. 28), the reign of God (v. 31), and the judgment of the Son of man (v. 36).

In order to understand Luke's presentation of Jesus' discourse, it is necessary to keep track of his use of Mark 13, his attention to other scriptural and traditional materials, and his larger picture of the economy of God's reign. Luke does not simply "change"

Mark because the end of the world did not occur in immediate connection with the destruction of Jerusalem. But Luke's usage of Mark appears to be supplemented from other traditional words, phrases, and concepts. Some of these may come from the Scriptures or other Christian literary sources. Others may be derived from the oral tradition. Luke is clearly taking an active role in a lively Christian discussion about what Jesus prophesied and how God's promises will be fulfilled.

It is important to observe that Mark's account (13:14) depicts the "desolating sacrilege" as a fulfillment of the apocalyptic vision of Daniel (9:27; 11:31; 12:11), while Luke's version speaks more historically of the **desolation** of the city (v. 20). Furthermore, Luke relates neither Jesus' prediction of the coming "tribulation" (Mark 13:19) nor his declaration that no one but the Father knows the "day or hour," "not even the angels in heaven, nor the Son" (Mark 13:32, see the comments at 21:33 below). Some interpreters have suggested that Luke's account is thus "less apocalyptic" than Mark's; it would be more accurate to say that Luke has been selective in using apocalyptic traditions to interpret "the present time" (see 12:56) within the economy of God's will and reign.

In 17:25, Jesus' death was incorporated into the sequence of the eschatological drama ("but first he must suffer"), and now the destruction of the city, wars and tumults, and persecutions are assigned their places (see v. 9, **this must first take place,** and v. 12, **before all this**). Luke recites Jesus' prophecies so that his readers who have already experienced these things are now in the midst of a thoroughly apocalyptic scene. In vv. 25-36, therefore, they are alerted to look up, watch, see, and pray as the rest of the drama unfolds. The coming **redemption** (v. 28), **kingdom of God** (v. 31), and "day of the Son of man" (12:40; 17:30; 18:8; 21:27,36) are all future events, but they are already indicated in the sign of the destruction (21:7), which probably has taken place when Luke writes.

Luke also depicts Peter in Acts 2 as projecting the dramatic displays of Pentecost against the backdrop of the apocalyptic prophecy of Joel 2:28-32 so that the fulfillment which has already happened may be distinguished from the cosmic signs still to occur. Thus in Luke 21:5-36, Jesus' discourse assures the reader that the calamities, persecutions, and days of vengeance (vv. 5-24) connected with the fate of Jerusalem lie within God's saving purpose for Israel and the nations. By sorting out the phases of the eschatological drama, Luke is not second guessing the "time or the hour" of the end. In Acts 1:6-8, the resurrected Jesus explicitly forbids such speculation, much as Jesus does in Mark 13:32. Luke's version of Jesus' discourse reveals to the readers that the present time may not yet be the moment of the great "tribulation" (see Mark 13:19, 24; Rev. 1:9; 7:14), but it is the period of tribulations through which believers will enter the kingdom of God (see Acts 14:22). Jesus' apocalyptic discourse is now primarily a word of assurance, identifying the limit of "the days of vengeance" and encouraging endurance for the future.

The discourse falls into two major sections: vv. 6-24 and vv. 25-28. Verse 5 is the introduction, and vv. 37-38 are the conclusion of the discourse.

Verses 6-24 recast traditional words of Jesus so that they now offer prophetic interpretation of the times before the end time. Three kinds of signs are revealed in that era, all of them roughly concurrent:

(1) the days of wars and tumults leading to the destruction of the temple, vv. 8-11;

(2) the time for testimony and persecution of the faithful, vv. 12-19;

(3) the days of vengeance and the siege of Jerusalem by the Gentiles, vv. 20-24.

Verses 25-38 envision the end times, and three images provide the complex medium for speaking of this future. All of them are drawn from traditional apocalyptic imagery, but they are filled with particular meaning in Luke's narrative.

(1) the signs in the heavens and on earth which precede the "drawing near" of "redemption," vv. 25-28;

(2) the coming of "the kingdom of God," vv. 29-32;

(3) the sudden appearance of the day of the Son of man, vv. 34-36.

The Coming Destruction 21:5-11

The first oracle is a complex word of judgment on the temple which is distinguished carefully from the last judgment. Luke has followed Mark's content, but he has taken more independence than usual in rephrasing Jesus' words. Commentators have observed that Luke's discourse answers the disciples' question about the temple more directly than Mark's version, because in Mark Jesus moves immediately to a revelation of the end.

5-6—The temple setting is crucial in Luke's telling, and the abuse of the poor widow is the occasion for Jesus' oracle of destruction. The contrast between her poverty and the splendor of the ornamenation of the temple must not be missed. Josephus also remembered the opulent splendor of Herod's temple with its marble stones, gold adornments, and splendid robes for a thousand priests (*Ant.* 15.388-423; *War* 5.184-226). But Luke's Jesus insists that the cosmetic adornment of **noble stones and offerings** could not legitimize or save the temple.

Luke presents Jesus standing in the temple as he declares its doom, and his words recall Jeremiah's oracles concerning the first temple, delivered in the same location (Jer. 7:1-15; 23:11). Even the phrase **the days will come** is a Lukan imitation (see also 5:35; 19:43; 23:29) of those scriptural prophecies. But Jesus is the Messiah-prophet whose very presence is the "visitation" of God, confronting Israel with God's reign to be rejected at their peril. Among the several oracles concerning Jerusalem's dire future (13:1-9, 34-35; 19:27-28, 41-44; 20:9-18; 23:28-31), only here does Jesus speak directly of the fate of the temple.

7-9—This is not a private instruction about the end, as in Mark 13:3-8, but Jesus is speaking in public. The **this** (Gk: "these things") which will happen and the **this** (Gk: "these things") for which a sign is sought for when it **is about to take place** (v. 7) is the destruction, and **this must first take place** (Gk: "these things," v. 9). It is an event of eschatological significance, since it belongs within the divine plan for the end. But **the end will not be at once.** Thus those who lead people astray appear to be false prophets and messiahs who declare the destruction itself to be the apocalypse, the sign of the imminent end. Mark 13:3-8 also indicates that "the end is not yet" when the false prophets arise and the distress begins on earth, but Luke explictly puts the end beyond the destruction of the temple.

In Josephus's accounts of the conquest of Jerusalem by the Romans, he tells many stories of visions, oracles, and prophets. The scenes of the carnage which he paints are already apocalyptic in scale:

> The roar of the flames streaming far and wide mingled with the groans of the falling victims; and, owing to the height of the hill and the mass of the burning pile, one would have thought that the whole city was ablaze. . . . With the cries on the hill were blended those of the multitude in the city below; and now many who were emaciated and tongue-tied from starvation, when they beheld the sanctuary on fire, gathered strength once more for lamentations and wailing. . . . Yet more awful than the uproar were the sufferings.
>
> (*War* 6.271-275)

In this setting Josephus tells of a "false prophet" who promised "signs of deliverance" to those who would come to the temple court and of numerous other "prophets" and "frauds" who played on desperate hopes of release from the terrors. But Josephus declares that all of the signs pointed only to divine wrath and abandonment of Jerusalem (*War* 6.285-315). "Neither its antiquity, nor its ample wealth, nor its people spread over the whole habitable world, nor yet the great glory of its religious rites, could aught avail to avert its ruin" (*War* 6.442). God had joined the Roman cause against Israel.

Jesus' verdict on these frightening realities is also a theological interpretation. **This must first take place** refers to the "necessity" (Gk: *dei*) of God's will, but even this is a word of assurance, **Do not be terrified.** God's judgment will accomplish its effects in history, but God is not yet done. Destruction is not the end or the goal (Gk: *telos*) of God's will.

10-11—Luke introduces these powerful images of judgment with a clear transition, **Then he said** (see also 5:31; 6:39; 21:29). This breaks the apocalyptic images which follow from Jesus' previous words, although they are closely linked in Mark 13. The RSV even begins a new paragraph at v. 10, but these verses should probably be read as an expansion on the theme of the fearful realities already mentioned in v. 9. The Christian Gospels were not the first to revive such ancient apocalyptic visions to interpret the dire fate of Jerusalem—nor was Jesus. These images of cosmic struggle, distress in the heavens, and political warfare are filled with theological content in the heritage of scriptural and intertestamental apocalyptic (see Isa. 19:2; Jer. 4:13-22; 14:12; 21:6-7; Ezek. 14:21). God executes severe judgment by means of wars and turmoil, earthquakes, famines, pestilences, and terrors on the day of divine judgment (see also Isa. 13:6-16; Hag. 2:6-7; Zech. 14:4; Rev. 6:12). Their force is not diminished here (see also Revelation 6). This is a picture of coming destruction, and it is drafted in apocalyptic scale. The terror is only abated by the assurance of v. 9.

A Time for Testing (21:12-19)

Luke's restatement of Mark is again significant for understanding the force of these sayings. He is still following Mark's content; but apart from v. 17, these words about coming persecution have been heavily rephrased. The possibility that Luke has used another literary or oral source cannot be excluded, but it is more probable that Luke has continued a strong initiative in his retelling. These are matters in which the coherence of his whole narrative and his assurance to the reader are at stake. The "things which have been fulfilled among us" (see Luke 1:1-4) and the interpretation of the present time (12:56) must be sorted out with care. In this passage, the persecution and sufferings of Jesus' followers are presented as the fulfillment of Jesus' prophecy. They are meaningful because they are to be expected in a world where God's reign is contested, but they are not proof of the immediate end.

12-15—These verses are a close parallel to Jesus' words in 12:11-12. In Mark 13:9, Jesus is speaking of "the first of the sufferings," and the phrase places the persecutions in the context of "the birth pangs of the Messiah (see also Revelation 12). Even the necessity that "the gospel must first be preached to all nations" is an apocalyptic reality in Mark (13:10). But Luke sets the persecutions back in a preliminary phase, **before all this,** that is, before all the tumult in heaven and earth of vv. 10-11. The question is not what the persecutions reveal about the end, but what they mean in the present.

They mean that Jesus' prophetic words here and in 12:11-12 are coming to fulfillment. The betrayals and trials to synagogues and prisons, kings and governors are an expanded vision of the public character of the opposition to Christ and his kingdom. It is for his "name's sake" that they will suffer, which in Luke-Acts is a strong image for the authority and power of Jesus' reign which the disciples exercise (see also 21:17; Acts 4:17-18; 5:28, 40-41; 9:15-16; 21:13; and see Luke 18:29; Acts 15:26). This is a conflict with principalities and powers, which should be no surprise to Jesus' followers.

Such conflict will provide the occasion for testimony. The future and impersonal verb does not indicate who is orchestrating these occasions (RSV: **This will be a time for you,** Gk: "It will turn out for you"). For the faithful, even their persecution proves to be a divine vocation. The word **testimony** or "witness" (Gk: *martyrion*) would eventually mean "martyrdom" or "death," and the martyr was the "faithful witness" even unto death (see Acts 22:20; Rev. 17:6). In Luke-Acts, the disciples are commissioned to be the "witnesses" to the resurrected and exalted Lord Jesus (Gk: *martyres,* 24:48; Acts 1:8, 2:32; 3:15; 5:32; 10:39, 41; 13:31; 22:15; 26:16). They bear witness repeatedly in scenes of trial and conflict. This is reminiscent of God's call to Israel in Isaiah 43-44 to be witnesses to God's righteous rule before the nations (see the discussion at 24:48). Thus **testimony** or "witness" is the proper activity for Jesus' followers, which gives meaning to the present struggles within God's economy. This testimony is to be the focus of concern, not speculations about the "times or seasons" (see Acts 1:6-8).

The promise of the Holy Spirit's instruction in times of testimony (Luke 12:11-12) now becomes Jesus' own promise. This is a remarkable illustration of how the words of Jesus are later remembered as the counsel of the risen Lord. Acts also affirms the unity of purpose between the Holy Spirit and the Spirit of Jesus (see Acts 16:6-7). **Mouth and wisdom** connote eloquence and understanding, and the note of assurance is again primary. Even the poor speakers and unlearned have nothing to fear, as Acts will amply demonstrate. Who but the most obstinate could withstand the **wisdom** of God (see Acts 4:13-14)?

16-19—If all of the adversaries were public officials and rulers, the testimony would still be difficult. But the profound character of the opposition is also measured in very personal terms. The list of betrayers differs slightly from Mark, but the intimate bonds of friends and family become perils. These words are recalled by Luke as predictions which were proved in bitter experience and which gave meaning to such experience. In such a light, Jesus' earlier words about the need to break bonds with family (see 8:20-21; 9:59-60; 14:26) are not so extreme. The extravagance of saying they will be **hated by all** may be set alongside of Acts 2:47, where the apostles at Pentecost found favor with "all the people." Nevertheless, Jesus' words reveal that massive animosity and hatred will be directed toward his followers, and this hatred will be linked directly with his **name** and the authority they exercise in it. **Some** will be killed, as he was.

The assurances in vv. 18-19 are, therefore, not denials of the reality of persecution and death. The assurance about even "the hair on your head" is a traditional proverb (see 1 Sam. 14:45; 2 Sam. 14:11; 1 Kings 1:52; Acts 27:34), but in this instance it offers an assurance of life beyond death. Similarly Luke's understanding of **endurance** (Gk: *hypomonē*) does not mean mere marathon determination, but faithful reliance on the word of God (see 8:15). The **life** that is **gained,** therefore, is not an assurance of surviving the persecutions while others die. Nor is it merely a "spiritual" truth. It is a promise of life and salvation which transcends the need to preserve this life (9:24). Death is physically real, and so are the adversaries (see 12:4-5). But the hope of the resurrection is grounded in God's righteousness, against which all who kill the body cannot stand. This is the eschatological hope which exposes the deceit of those who intimidate the faithful and deny the reality of the kingdom by persecution and murder (see also 17:33).

The Days of Vengeance (21:20-24)

These verses are the heart of Luke's dramatic restatement of Mark 13. In place of the Danielic "abomination of desolation" (Mark 13:14//Matt. 24:15; Dan. 9:27), Luke's Jesus speaks of the

desolation of **Jerusalem.** This is no longer an apocalyptic revelation which treats the desecration of the temple as a sign of the
imminent end. Now Jesus utters a prohetic oracle of judgment,
announcing the calamities of the Roman conquest to be fulfillments of scriptural warnings of the **desolation** (v. 20), **days of
vengeance** (v. 22), **great distress** (v. 23), and **the times of the
Gentiles** (v. 24). These words of judgment carry forward earlier
oracles of warning (13:34-35; 19:41-44) and anticipate Jesus' dire
words concerning Jerusalem as he goes to his death (23:28-31).

This is an excellent example of the evangelist as interpreter.
It is possible that Luke had another source which recalled Jesus'
oracles differently than Mark, but it appears more likely that it
is the evangelist who has recast the Markan account to "interpret
the present times" (12:56) and to demonstrate the fulfillment of
the Scriptures (21:22, see the discussion at 24:27,32,44). The
substance and many of the words of the Jesus tradition are still
preserved, but Luke depicts Jesus first as a prophetic interpreter
of history. Jesus' words both recall the scriptural traditions concerning the first destruction of Jerusalem and remind the reader
of the harsh realities of the Roman conquest. Only after Jesus
diagnoses the meaning of the desolation of Jerusalem does he
also resume his revelation of the still future events of the day of
the Son of man (vv. 25-28).

20—Only Luke mentions Jerusalem under siege. Jesus may
well have predicted such an event. Like other first-century Jews
he may also have prophesied that Israel was about to repeat her
earlier history of apostasy which led to Jerusalem's siege and destruction by Nebuchadnezzar. Certainly Luke saw the destruction
in that light. The terminology which is used in Luke to speak of
this calamity is thoroughly scriptural, ringing with the phrases
from the LXX of Jeremiah, Deuteronomy, and Hosea (see also
19:41-44). Other late first-century Jewish sources, such as 2 Baruch, 4 Ezra, and Josephus (see *War* 6.437) also interpret the
Roman destruction in terms of the Babylonian siege and conquest. Thus Luke is recalling and rephrasing the prophecies of
Jesus in order to give a Christian reading of this calamity out of
the prophetic tradition. This is a real issue for Christians too,

whether they are Jewish or Gentile. How can Jesus be the Messiah who brings the kingdom if Jerusalem has been destroyed? Have the promises failed?

21-22—Mark's version of Jesus' warning to those in Judea to flee to the mountains is expanded with counsel to those in the city to depart and those in the country to stay out. So far that is only an elaboration of Mark focused again more closely on the city. But the interpretation comes with the identification of **these days of vengeance to fulfill all that is written.** Even without the allusion to the written Scriptures, the technical term **days of vengeance** stands out. It recalls the verbatim expression in the LXX version of Hos. 9:7 and "the day of vengeance" in Deut. 32:35 (LXX, see also Jer. 26:10; 27:31 LXX; 46:10; 50:31 MT). These are times of divine judgment on Israel. The same Greek word (*ekdikēsis*) that here means **vengeance** means "vindication" in Luke 18:7, and both usages are visions of the "righteousness" or "justice" of God. Thus God's righteous judgment on Jerusalem is a fulfillment of the scriptural promise and threat of divine justice, exactly in line with Moses' prophetic words in Deut. 32:34-36. In these **days of vengeance,** divine justice means **wrath** (v. 23).

23-24—Luke begins again with the woe for pregnant and nursing women, drawing directly from Mark with no changes. But his emphasis on the Jerusalem siege has already provided a poignant setting, and Jesus' later oracle concerning the blessed state of barren women in "the days that are coming" (23:28-31) further intensifies the tradition. As Josephus's gruesome account of the starvation and brutality of the siege indicates, the horror of nursing mothers devouring their children was no stranger to Israel (see *War* 6.201-211, see also the ancient siege of Samaria in 2 Kings 6:24-31). But Luke further interprets these realities as the **great distress** (Gk: *anankē*) on the earth and **wrath** (Gk: *orgē*) on **this people.** This is not merely a prediction that people will suffer. This is a theological interpretation, probably drawn from the awesome description of the judgment on Jerusalem of the "great day of the Lord in Zeph. 1:15: "A day of wrath (*orgē*) is that day, a day of tribulation (Gk: *thlipsis*) and distress (Gk: *anankē*)." John the Baptist's warning of the "wrath which is to come" (3:7) rings with the same prophetic timbre.

The further details of death by **the sword, captivity,** and **Gentile** conquest are also filled with scriptural precedents. These are things that happened both in the first destruction and the second, but they are also symbolic pictures (e.g., "mouth of the sword") filled with meaning. Jerusalem is not merely going to be conquered, but she will be **trodden down** (Gk: *patoumenē*) **by the Gentiles** or "the nations" (Gk: *ethnē*). In the LXX version of Zech. 12:3, the oracle of the Lord concerning the coming siege against Jerusalem states, "I will make Jerusalem to be a stone trodden down [Gk: *katapatoumenon*] by all the Gentiles [Gk: *ethnē;* see also Rev. 11:2]." The **Gentiles** or the "nations" wreak God's severe judgment against Jerusalem, although their superiority will not endure forever (see also Deut. 32:26-27; Isa. 45-47; 2 Bar. 82:3; 83:4-6).

Luke's Jesus renders the same prophetic verdict, mentioning **the Gentiles** three times in v. 24. They are the instruments of divine judgment. There is no allusion here to a "Gentile mission," because the subject is the conquest of the land and the people by the pagan nations. This is a theodicy, a revelation of divine justice, exercised in wrath. Only the last line provides relief, for **the times of the Gentiles,** the times of judgment, will have their limit. More precisely, they will have their "fulfillment." Again it is the prophetic, Deuteronomistic conviction that God's justice is not finally fulfilled in wrath. God is not done with Israel.

The Day of the Son of Man (21:25-28)

Luke now shifts into an apocalyptic vision. This scene not only lies in the future in Jesus' era. It is still future for Luke. A similar shift into pictures of cosmic distress occurs in Acts 2:19, when Peter's citation of Joel 2 moves beyond events which have already been experienced. The change in tone and imagery is noticeable, and Jesus' words are no longer prophetic interpretations of past or current historical events. But the contrast with apocalyptic should not be too rigidly drawn because Luke does not indulge in speculative predictions simply to know the future. The past, present, and future are caught up in God's unfolding plan, and even the apocalyptic images are fundamental assurances that God's reign will not fail.

It is important to recognize that Luke's narrative does not yet know how God will finally fulfill the promises to Israel. Luke does emphasize that the resurrected Jesus commissions his disciples to proclaim "repentance and forgiveness of sins to all nations, beginning from Jerusalem" (24:47; see Acts 1:8), and they begin at Pentecost with that very message (Acts 2). But Acts also displays a divided Israel, and a mixed response of thousands who believe and many who reject that proclamation. In the wake of the prophetic oracles of Jerusalem's destruction as an act of divine wrath, the question of *what* God will do when "the times of the Gentiles are fulfilled" (v. 24) remains unresolved. Shall the hopes of the prophetess Anna for "the redemption of Jerusalem" (1:38) or the hope of the travelers to Emmaus for Jesus "to redeem Israel" be unfulfilled? Perhaps this passage provides the needed assurance when Jesus declares the coming of the Son of man to be the **drawing near** of **your redemption** (v. 28). It may not be clear *how* God will accomplish this **redemption,** but it is inconceivable *that* God would not do so.

25-26—Luke again follows the flow of Mark 13, but this is not a picture of what happens "after the tribulation." This is a vision of the unraveling of the fabric of the universe with heavenly and earthly manifestations. These pictures are filled with scriptural precedents from Isa. 17:12 and 24:18-20. Perhaps Luke drew these allusions from oral or written tradition, but it is not impossible that he was reading Isaiah directly. In any case, it is interesting that only Luke includes another reference to the "nations" or **the Gentiles** (Gk: *ethnē*). It is they who are confounded, when they had just triumphed and trodden down Jerusalem in their times (v. 24). Now the whole world is coming unglued.

27-28—**And then,** says Jesus, exactly as he says in Mark 13. The sequence itself is now crucial as it has been consistently in Mark. This is not merely a sign to be recognized by the faithful (see v. 20), but a prediction of a public disclosure which even **they, the Gentiles,** will see. The picture is not original with Luke or Jesus, but it is the Danielic vision of "one like a son of man"

coming "with the clouds of heaven" (Dan. 7:13). Yet every detail
is profoundly significant. The rich discussion in Jewish and Jew-
ish-Christian circles of the interpretation of Daniel 7 can still be
overheard. This is not merely "one like a son of man." This is **the
Son of man.** This is the fulfillment of "the day when the Son of
man is revealed," which was so carefully distinguished from "the
days of the Son of man" in 17:22-37. Even the singular **cloud** as
distinguished from the "clouds" of Dan. 7:13 and Mark 13:26 is
probably important. Luke does not regard the **cloud** as a mere
heavenly conveyance. It is a symbol of divine presence recalling
the cloud which enfolds God's descent in Exod. 34:5 (see also
Luke 9:34, 35; Acts 1:9; and see Exod. 19:16; 24:16; Num. 11:25).
And while many in the first century debated the identity of this
Son of man, Luke explicitly identifies him as the exalted Lord
Jesus (Acts 7:55-56). The glory and power are the marks of Jesus'
royal authority over heaven and earth in God's court.

Verse 28, therefore, supplies Luke's further commentary on
the passage from Daniel. This is a word of assurance for all those
who have longed to see even "one of the days of the Son of man"
(17:22), for "you" will look up and see **your redemption drawing
near.** Luke is fond of the concept of "the kingdom coming near"
(10:9, 11; see also 21:31), Jesus "coming near" to his goal (7:12;
18:35; 19:29, 37, 41), and the "drawing near" of the time (21:8, 20).
It is an expression for immediacy and present reality. In this case,
the "you" who are addressed are no longer "the Gentiles" who
will then be confounded. This is a vision beyond the time of
"vengeance," "distress," "wrath," and "Jerusalem trodden down."
It is a word to the faithful who listen to the prophetic word of
Jesus, assuring "you" that God's redemption will come with the
final disclosure of Jesus' reign as Son of man. God will not fail to
fulfill the promises, but the question is whether Jesus' followers
will remain faithful as they await his revelation as Son of man
(see 18:8; 21:36).

Watch and Pray (21:29-38)

Luke's version of Jesus' temple discourse remains close to the
Markan sequence but reaches a distinctive conclusion in these

verses. The parable of **the fig tree** (vv. 29-33) is taken from Mark with a few crucial alterations. But Luke's admonition to **watch** and **pray** (vv. 34-36) is dramatically different from Mark's call for watchfulness (Mark 13:32-37), and Luke's summary conclusion (vv. 37-38) is strictly his own composition. It marks the end of the discourse as well as the conclusion of the larger narrative of the Messiah's visitation of the temple (19:28—21:38).

Jesus' concluding words are an elaboration of his prophecy of the coming of the Son of man (v. 27) and the drawing near of "your redemption" (v. 28). But now it is the **kingdom of God** which is near (v. 31), and the sudden appearance of the "day" of the "Son of man" requires readiness. The coming revelation of God's righteous reign is already an assurance to the faithful and a peril to those who are opposed or indifferent to God's rule.

29-31—This "parable" is more an allegory or analogy from nature. The point is similar to 12:54-56, emphasizing that people do know how to observe and interpret the present in terms of what is about to happen. Luke expands the analogy to include **all the trees,** and some commentators suggest that he was avoiding or missing the traditional identification of Judah of Jerusalem as God's unproductive **fig tree** (see Jer. 8:13; Mic. 7:1). But this saying is not a word of judgment, and Luke does not relate any story of Jesus cursing a fig tree (see Mark 11:12-14//Matt. 21:18-22). Perhaps the expanded analogy implies only that Jesus is not saying anything mysterious about fig trees. He is merely appealing to common experience. Then Jesus' expanded word emphasizes that "you yourselves" know all about this. Certainly you do not need a prophet or guru to tell you that summer is coming, because the evidence is public and obvious. So also, **when you see these things** you will not need secret instructions or people who declare themselves to be the revealers of the end (see vv. 8-9).

These things are the same "these things" mentioned in v. 28, and they are the dramatic signs in heaven and on earth described in vv. 25-26, leading to the coming of the Son of man (v. 27). That "coming" and the "drawing near" of "your redemption" (v. 28) are the same event as the coming **near** of **the kingdom of God** (v. 31). Luke has also emphasized the present reality of the kingdom in the person of Jesus and in the proclamation of his reign (see 4:43; 8:1; 9:2, 60; 10:9, 11; 11:20; 16:16; and see the discussion at 17:20-21). But **the kingdom of God** also remains as a future event in its full public disclosure of God's judgment and blessing (see 6:20-26; 9:27; 11:2; 13:28-29). In this passage, therefore, the coming kingdom is a revelation of God's judgment. It will be the redemption (v. 28) of the elect and divine righteousness of the day of the Son of man over **all who dwell upon the face of the whole earth** (v. 35). As in Dan. 7:13-14, where the Son of man is given "dominion and glory and kingdom," Luke envisions the full public disclosure of reign of the exalted Jesus.

32-33—These traditional words are difficult to understand in all of the Synoptics; the central issue is how they understood the term **this generation.** It may be helpful to note that in the apocalyptic discussion at Qumran, the exact identity of "the final generation" or "the final age" was already a concern (see 1 QpHab. 2.7; 7.2, 7). Even in Luke 9:27, where Jesus declared that "some who are standing here will not taste death before they see the kingdom of God," both "tasting death" and "seeing" the kingdom are open to metaphorical interpretations. So also in this passage, **this generation** could be a literal reference to the people who are alive at Jesus' time or those living in Luke's. But it seems more likely that this is a reference to the whole human generation which falls under Jesus' extended indictment in 11:29-33 and 11:50-51. These are the "sons of this world" who are more shrewd "in their own generation" than the sons of light (16:8). Even more critically, these are "this generation" which rejected Jesus the Son of man (17:25).

In Luke's account, therefore, these words of Jesus offer indirect comfort for the faithful. God will not delay long (18:7). More immediately they are words of warning to a faithless generation that they will not escape judgment. In a paraphrase of the traditional word about the endurance of God's Law (see 16:17), Jesus alerts the world to mark his words. That is, his words of the coming judgment will confront this generation and will outlast even the shaking of the orders of creation described in vv. 25–26. God will have the last word, and Jesus will deliver it as the Son of man.

34-36—Luke, therefore, moves immediately into a word to the faithful to watchfulness. Following the same logic as 18:7-8, the assurance of the coming of God's rule leads directly into counsel for those who trust it. The public character of this revelation and judgment is again affirmed in v. 35. The faithful need no longer worry about that or wonder if God's righteousness will prevail. Even to speculate too long on when or whether this could take place would be misguided. Mark 13:32 cuts such speculation short with the strong word that neither the angels in heaven nor even the Son know when that day or hour will come. Luke omits this word from Mark, perhaps because a similar denial is stated forcefully in Acts 1:6-8.

Luke's account drives more to the point of instructing the disciples about what their proper concern should be. Much as in Acts 1:6-8, the counsel is that God has indeed "fixed the times and seasons" by "his own authority," and Jesus' words will endure to their fulfillment. But in the meantime, Jesus has a word for his disciples. The question is, "When the Son of man comes, will he find faith on earth?" (18:8), and the command of Jesus departing on the cloud to heaven is, "You shall be my witnesses to the end of the earth!" (Acts 1:8-9). So also in Luke 21, Jesus redirects the attention of the faithful to attend to the present. In words that resound with the apocalyptic oracle of Isa. 24:16-20 and the Christian apocalyptic tradition of 1 Thess. 5:1-11, Jesus counsels sobriety, watchfulness, and prayer, now. These are protections against temptation (see 8:13-15; 22:40, 46), lest the faithful fall away from their forthright witness to Jesus' reign (see 12:9; 21:12-19). For **you** will also **stand** before the judgment of **the Son of man.**

37-38—These verses conclude the entire discourse (21:6-36) as well as marking the end of Jesus' public teaching in the temple (19:45—21:36). Luke is emphatic that Jesus taught the people openly in the temple, even in the face of serious opposition (see 19:47-48; 20:1; 22:53). The mention of his lodging on Mount **Olivet** is the first glimpse that Luke provides of Jesus outside the temple since 19:44. A crucial phase of his entire ministry has just concluded. Much of his teaching has been dominated by hostile questioners and leading questions, but the Messiah has also spoken publicly about the state of affairs in the temple. Now he has also concluded his authoritative disclosure of the future which God has in store for Israel and the faithful.

The last line provides a reminder of the plot and characters which were identified so carefully in 19:47-48: **All the people come to him in the temple to hear him.** The Messiah has taught in the temple, and the people have been eager to hear (see also 19:47; 20:1, 6, 19, 26, 45). Now what will the chief priests, the scribes, and the captains do (see 19:47; 20:1, 19, 26, 39-40, 45-47; 21:1-4; 22:2, 4, 52, 66)?

The End: Transcending the Tragedy
(Chapters 22–24)

■ The Tragic Fulfillment of the Will of God
(22:1—23:56)

> He released the man who had been thrown into prison for insur-
> rection and murder, whom they asked for; but Jesus he delivered
> up to their will.
>
> (Luke 23:25)

This sixth major section of Luke's narrative is filled with confrontation, passion, and tragedy. The determined will of God is
exercised by the Messiah, but human willfulness has turned into
an active conspiracy with the forces of Satan for the execution of
the Righteous One. The Messiah himself, who has wept and
prophesied against Jerusalem, now suffers **as it has been determined** (22:22) of the Son of man, and his passion is real. But he
is not naive or tragically ignorant. The tragedy and the blindness
lie with Israel. It is the salvation of those who surround the cross
which hangs in the balance, not the fate of the Messiah. Shall
God's reign and will prove to be the salvation or merely the
destruction of those who willed Jesus' death?

Luke's account of Jesus' death has been subject to a great deal
of theological discussion as well as exegetical interpretation. The
element of the "expiatory" character of Jesus' death is notably
absent. Mark's clear testimony that the Son of man gave his life
"as a ransom for many" (10:45) simply does not stand at the heart
of Luke's understanding of Jesus' death. Luke does not argue with
the view that Jesus' death was a sacrifice for sin (see also Rom.
3:25). He even quotes Paul in Acts 20:28 as speaking of the church
as having been "obtained with his own blood" (see also discussion
of 22:20). But this is a subordinate theme in Luke-Acts. Even
when often alluding or referring to Isaiah 53 (see Luke 11:22;
22:37; 23:34; 24:25; Acts 3:13; 8:32-33), Luke appears to neglect
the expiatory features of Isaiah's presentation of the servant who

suffers. Some interpreters have complained that Luke has eliminated the atoning significance of Jesus' death or reduced it to a
pious martyrdom.

Instead of judging Luke for what the presentation does not do,
it is more profitable to note that it does place Jesus' death at the
very center of God's relationship with Israel and the nations. A
reading of the speeches in Acts (see especially Acts 2:36-40; 3:13-
26; 4:10-12; 7:52; 10:39-43; 13:26-43; 26:23) demonstrates that
Jesus' death and Israel's fate are intimately connected. The mystery of the story lies not in the satisfaction for sin which Jesus'
blood effects, but in the profound question of whose will is being
accomplished in the course of this narrative. The story of the
passion is first a tragic story, because it is the display of the
apparent triumph of the will of sinful humanity which finally
accomplishes self-destruction. The plot builds until Pilate delivers Jesus "to their will" and Jesus declares, "Daughters of Jerusalem, do not weep for me, but weep for yourselves and for
your children" (23:25, 28). Then the blindness and the seeing of
those who surround the dying Jesus is filled with poignant irony.

To speak of this as a tragic fulfillment of the will of God, however, requires two further comments. (1) This is not a Greek
tragedy in the sense of a hero or king who dies blindly, after
having committed a grievous sin. Jesus is not a tragic figure. He
dies in obedience to God's will, knowing and seeing what is happening. Nor are his adversaries tragic. They are so adamant in
their hostility (i.e., the Jewish leaders and Judas) or so indifferent
to God's will (i.e., Pilate and Herod) that they lack the character
of tragic figures. They will never "see" or "hear," even if they
themselves utter the truth about Jesus as the Messiah and Chosen
One of God. But the disciples and the people are caught in a
web of intrigue far beyond their understanding or vision. It is
those who weep for Jesus and stand by the cross "watching" for
whom the reader also feels great compassion and a sense of tragedy.

(2) Luke's use of some of the conventions of tragedy does not
mean that he has read Sophocles. But he has read the Scriptures
of Israel where God's will has long struggled with human defiance,
and he is aware of the conventions of contemporary Hellenistic

historiography (see the comments on 1:1-4). The Greco-Roman historians and their Jewish counterparts, such as the author of 4 Maccabees and Josephus, often interpreted the ancient stories of their several traditions in a "tragic mode" so that the pathos and emotion of human suffering were woven into the story. Literary devices such as oracles from bystanders, sarcastic accusations which are ironically true, and the interpretation of the "people" or chorus were well known. In Luke's narrative, the tragedy of Israel's dire history becomes the backdrop, disclosing human sin, but the resurrection and exaltation of Jesus will attest the ultimacy of God's salvation. The larger narrative will transcend the tragic note of the passion narrative.

Luke's restatement of Mark's account is so thorough that many interpreters have looked for evidence of other sources or perhaps even an alternative passion narrative into which Luke has inserted some Markan materials. The quest for a "proto-Luke" passion story (see the introduction to this commentary) has produced elaborate theories of Luke's special sources in specific passages, especially in Luke's account of the "last supper." No doubt Luke does know other traditions beyond Mark's account, since traditions about the passion figured so prominently in early Christian preaching. Paul's letters—which tell no Jesus stories—are filled with references to the meal, betrayal, crucifixion, and burial of Jesus. But it is not necessary to reconstruct additional literary accounts of the passion story to understand Luke's version. The Markan episodes which are absent (see Mark 14:3-9, 27-28, 50-51; 15:16-20), the new elements (see the comments at Luke 22:15-18, 21-38, 49; 23:6-12, 13-16, 27-32), and the frequent differences in phrasing still imply or display Mark's sequence. Luke's narrative is an original narrative or interpretation of Jesus' death which has used Mark's passion narrative as its literary framework and source.

The Passover Plot (22:1-65)

Luke is emphatic in placing the preparations (vv. 1-13), the meal (vv. 14-38), and the arrest (vv. 39-65) in the context of the feast of Passover. All of this elaborate detail appears to describe a very brief period preceding Passover (vv. 1-6), with most of the action clearly limited to the day and night of the feast (vv. 7-65). While the Fourth Gospel suggests a calendar where Jesus dies at the time the Passover lamb would be sacrificed (see John 1:29, 36; 13:1; 18:28; 19:14, 31-37), Luke and Matthew follow Mark in placing the meal and arrest on Passover eve. It is crucial to note that Luke's Jesus is fully aware of the confrontation which is about to take place and even stages several details. But the plot which is developing on his life lies in the hands of his adversaries. The irony is that on Passover night, Jesus will declare as he is arrested, "This is your hour, and the power of darkness" (22:53).

The Preparations (22:1-13)

Luke's literary skill is evident in these verses, not least in their simplicity. The scene is quickly set (vv. 1-2) with two sentences which are largely derived from Mark (14:1-2). But then, without Mark's intervening account of the anointing at Bethany (Mark 14:3-9, see the comments at Luke 7:36-50), Luke moves directly into a depiction of Judas's initiative to make arrangements to betray Jesus (vv. 3-6) and Jesus' initiative to send his trusted apostles Peter and John to arrange for the Passover (vv. 7-13). The tension between these two kinds of preparations is the motive force of the narrative. The reader is already aware that these two story lines represent conflicting wills and purposes.

1-2—Luke equates the **feast of Unleavened Bread** with **the Passover** (see also 22:7 and Mark 14:1; on Passover see Exod. 12:1-20; Deut. 16:1-8; Lev. 23:5-6; on the feast of Unleavened Bread see Exod. 23:15; 34:18). The feasts are linked together in the Scriptures and frequently identified in Jewish tradition (see Josephus, *War* 2.10; *Ant.* 3.249; 17.213). This is not only a historical detail which causes serious debate about the chronology of Passover week (see comments on John above), but in Luke the Passover will provide a crucial clue to Herod and Pilate's presence in the city (23:1-12) and a symbolic setting for the arrest in the dark of the night (22:53). Having merely reported the detail in this introduction, Luke follows Mark in identifying the high

priests and **the scribes** as Jesus' adversaries. Their intent is only malevolent. Jesus is no longer teaching at the temple, but it is still their **fear** of **the people** which motivates their eagerness to kill Jesus (see the discussion at 21:37-38). Luke's turn of phrase is poignant: "They were seeking 'the how' [Gk: *to pōs*] to kill him because. . . ." There is no longer any question *whether* Jesus should die. Only the question of *means* to that end is discussed.

3-6—Having omitted the story of the anointing in Bethany (Mark 14:3-9), Luke presses to identify the other adversaries in the unholy alliance which is developing. **Satan** or "the devil" (4:1-13) had been unable to entrap or overcome Jesus at the beginning of his ministry, and he had departed "until an opportune time" (4:13). Jesus has been contending with the forces of Satan all along (see especially 10:18), but now Satan takes an initiative with one **of the number of the twelve.** The Twelve are Jesus' closest circle of disciples who are also his "apostles" (see comments at 6:13), and the number is crucial to their authority in Israel (22:29-30). **Judas's** betrayal will mean that this one who "was numbered among us" (Acts 1:17, see comments at Luke 22:21) will need to be replaced.

Judas takes an active initiative in this betrayal. He **conferred with** Jesus' frustrated adversaries on "the how" (Gk: *to pōs*) he might betray; he **agreed** (Gk: *exōmologēsen*) with them, and he **sought an opportunity** (Gk: *eukairia*) **to betray.** This is a kind of opportunism or Machiavellian discussion of "the how," in which Satan finds the "opportune time" (4:13). None of these adversaries could overcome Jesus alone, and even now this plot must be pursued **in the absence of the multitude** because "the people" are Jesus' protectors. The culpability of the actors who initiate this conspiracy is extremely high.

7-13—Now Jesus takes the initiative. The Passover setting is not merely a fact. It is a significant time when "it was necessary" to perform the sacrifice. Jesus' family was described in Luke 2:41 as observing the Passover "every year" in Jerusalem. Perhaps the "necessity" is that of prescribed ritual observance or the fulfillment of the Scriptures, but in either case, Jesus **sends** (Gk: *apostellein*) two of his "apostles" (v. 14) to arrange for the feast. Peter and John have been singled out for special mention on other occasions (8:51; 9:28; Acts 3:1-2). In this story it may be that the other 10 do not know where the feast will be held. Furthermore, Jesus' special instructions about the man they will meet may imply a prearrangement which only Jesus knows. This person does know that "the teacher" is coming (see "the Lord" in 19:31). Or this prediction may imply Jesus' prophetic insight into what they will find when they enter (see also 19:29-34). In either case, Jesus is aware in advance how this feast will be arranged, and the apostles find things just as Jesus had said. With v. 14, Luke will sharpen the focus on the significance of the time and Jesus' purpose in the feast.

The Meal (22:14-38)

These verses all are set in the context of Jesus' Passover meal with his **apostles.** As v. 14 sets the scene, this is **the hour** in which Jesus speaks his final words to his followers. It is followed by Jesus in prayer with the Father concerning God's will (vv. 39-46), and then the scene of the arrest is the "hour" of the adversaries and "the power of darkness" (vv. 47-53).

Several interpreters have observed that Luke has developed this scene into a farewell discourse by Jesus. It has been profitably compared with Greco-Roman traditions of banquet speeches. Such formal observations also invite comparisons with the farewell discourses of Moses (see Deut. 1:1-5; 32:45—33:1; see also Josephus, *Ant.* 4.176-322, 179: "souls when on the verge of death speak with perfect integrity") and Paul (Acts 20:18-38; see also Tobit 4:3-20; 14:3-11, Testaments of the Twelve Patriarchs, and Jesus in John 14–16). The traditional description of this meal as "the last supper" captures some of this sense of Jesus' "final" or "farewell" discourse. Furthermore, the meal is full of symbolic associations with Israel's practice of the Passover, early Christian practice of the meal, and Luke's vision of the eschatological significance of meal fellowship. The meal is the setting for Jesus' discourse, but the farewell speech also interprets the meal.

Throughout these verses, Luke keeps the tension of his narrative alive as Jesus anticipates the ultimate triumph of the kingdom (vv. 16, 18, 28-30), predicts his imminent betrayal and denial

(vv. 21-22, 32-34), and prepares for his arrest (vv. 35-38). But Luke also must be credited with addressing matters which were probably immediate concerns of the community. The meaning of the ritual meal (vv. 14-20), the shame of betrayal and denial by Jesus' inner circle (vv. 21-23, 31-34), the character of Christian authority (vv. 24-30), and the limits of violence (vv. 35-38) are all at stake in these stories. His restatement of these episodes is often so extensive that the possibility of other sources cannot be excluded but, as they stand, these stories are Luke's testimony on crucial topics as well as episodes in the larger story.

Fellowship and Betrayal (22:14-23). Verse 14 is Luke's transition, both concluding his account of the preparations (vv. 1-13) and setting the scene of the meal (vv. 15-23). Meals are highly symbolic rituals throughout Luke (see 5:27-39; 7:36-50; 11:37-54; 14:1-24), and this feast is only for the inside circle. Like Mark, Luke's story includes both the element of intimate fellowship and that of betrayal, but in Luke Jesus does not immediately disrupt the intimacy of the feast. Jesus first declares what he is doing in this Passover (vv. 15-18) and interprets what this meal means in terms of his impending death (vv. 19-20). Only then does he reveal that he is aware of the presence of the betrayer (21-23; contrast the sequence and effect in Mark 14:17-25). The reader knows all along that Judas has plotted Jesus' arrest, but only after Jesus has divulged the mystery of the significance of this Passover is it clear that Jesus also knows about Judas.

This passage is especially full of complex problems and enticing possibilities. The issue of whether vv. 19b-20 were part of Luke's original narrative has occupied lifetimes of scholarship on its own. But larger historical, literary, and theological issues are at hand. What were the rituals, traditions, and meanings of Passover in various first-century Jewish traditions? Was it primarily a family ritual of instruction in the past or did it include the expectation of Elijah and hopes for the reign of God? What kind of meal did Jesus actually have with his followers? Was it a fellowship supper which simply concluded in a Passover observance? Did Jesus himself transform the Passover into a ritual by which his followers could later recall and understand his death as God's saving act?

And how did the early Christians shape the memory of this meal
into the central ritual of Christ's presence? How did Paul, the
other evangelists, and Luke understand this meal and communicate their distinctive sense for its signficance?

Each of these questions requires some attention even to grasp
Luke's testimony. After all, the evangelist is depicting a highly
symbolic enactment of a Passover ritual which was already full of
symbolic meanings. Myth and history are always wed in ritual,
and the Christian ritual of the supper was already well established
in Luke's day. But finally this evangelist's telling of the story must
be the focus of attention of a commentary on Luke.

In Luke's telling, Jesus' observation of the Passover marks and
anticipates the fulfillment of its hope for the kingdom of God.
Within the story, this ritual of remembrance of the exodus and
deliverance anticipated the exodus which Jesus was about to fulfill
in Jerusalem (see the comments at 9:31, 51; and 12:50) by means
of his death. Luke therefore invited the Christian community to
celebrate its accomplished and anticipated deliverance in its continuing observance of the meal.

15-18—The section is structured around two statements to the
disciples (vv. 15 and 17), each followed by a forceful word of
exposition (**for I tell you,** vv. 16, 18). In both cases, Jesus' rather
mundane act acquires eschatological significance. Eating the Passover probably means sharing the lamb that has been sacrificed,
and the cup which is passed appears to be one of the four cups
which the participants would drink in the Passover ritual. The
Greek probably means "I will not eat it again" and **from now on
I shall not drink** (Gk: *apo tou nun*); see 1:48; 5:10; 12:52; 22:69),
although it could be read to say that Jesus wanted to eat the
Passover but was constrained from eating or drinking. Within the
passage, however, Jesus' pledge not to eat may mark the important shift that occurs at v. 19 when he institutes a new phase of
Passover with the bread and cup of his body and blood. These
he gave to them, but he did not eat or drink.

The two statements offer a parallel in which the **fulfillment** of
the Passover **in the kingdom of God** is understood to happen
when **the kingdom of God comes.** As is clear from 13:22-30, such
a messianic banquet is a picture of salvation, and that banquet

will be surprisingly inclusive with no guarantee for those who "ate and drank" in Jesus' presence (13:26). These statements, which are unique to Luke, however, are not oracles of warning to Judas, but they are assurances that the meal which Jesus observed with his apostles was a foretaste of the feast to come.

Jesus' **earnest desire** to eat the Passover is a sign of the importance of this observance in the will and plan of God (see the discussion of Jesus' will in 13:31-35). This is more than a personal "last wish." It is a symbolic act which anticipates and interprets Jesus' death, which is again predicted (see 9:22, 44; 12:50; 13:32-33; 17:25; 18:32-33; and 22:37). His strong statements may even be oath formulas: **"I tell you I shall not eat . . . I tell you I shall not drink."** At least they are pledges which confirm the reality of the coming banquet. Speaking of the wine as **the fruit of the vine** may also be an allusion to a traditional blessing over the cup at Passover: "Blessed be thou, Lord our God, King of the world, who has created the fruit of the vine" (see also Isa. 32:12).

19-20—Luke now recites his version of the "words of institution," and the first task of the interpreter is to evaluate their authenticity. Form-critical studies of the historical development of the Jesus tradition will be most concerned to determine their "authenticity" as words of the historical Jesus or the earliest Christian communities. Even some who doubt that Luke included the words of vv. 19b-20 in his original narrative have argued that their similarity to Paul's tradition of Jesus' words commends them as historically more authentic than Mark's or Matthew's. That is, they may preserve a more primitive version of early Christian memory and practice whether Luke or some later copyist placed them in this context. It would be very problematic, however, to prove that Luke's version is to be preferred as more historically accurate with regard to what Jesus himself said. But it is interesting to note that these words are very similar to those in 1 Cor. 11:23-35 without displaying literary dependence. These words are "authentically early" in the Christian tradition.

It is more crucial to understanding Luke that these words were authentic to his narrative, wherever he got them. The matter is of immediate signficance to readers of the English Bible, because from the time of Wescott and Hort (late 19th century) to the RSV,

vv. 19b-20 have been relegated to the notes. Following the shorter reading of some ancient manuscripts, vv. 19b-20 have been regarded as scribal additions to Luke's text on the grounds that these verses (a) result in a longer reading, (b) are too much like Paul's phrasing, and (c) are too little like Luke's wording. But the volume and quality of the manuscript evidence clearly favors the textual authenticity of vv. 19b-20, and the non-Lukan character of the words probably reflects the oral tradition. Oral traditions which arise from rituals are are likely to appear unchanged in more than one source. Thus these words are not original to Luke or Paul, but are traditional and textually authentic. Luke used them here.

The traditional words now offer Jesus' reinterpretation of the Passover. This is a new **bread** and **cup** which is shared in **remembrance** of Jesus' passion, just as the Passover was a feast to be observed in "remembrance" of the first exodus (Gk: *anamnēsis* v. 19; Exod. 12:14, *mnēmysunon*). In Luke, **do this** means "observe this ritual as a remembrance of me." In Paul, it means "whenever you do observe this ritual, remember me" (1 Cor. 11:25, 26). The modern word "ritual" may, however, miss the performative power of this "action of remembrance." Debates about whether Jesus is speaking about a "symbolic" or "real" presence when he says, **"This is my body . . . the new covenant in my blood"** generally miss the power of such speech to name and enact. Of course the ancients understood that such speech could be fakery, but such declarations were always powerful whether in blasphemy or truth. Such speech could never be "merely symbolic" or "simply ritual." And if the word of God (or the Messiah) authorized these declarations, nothing could be more "real."

The language of **"my body which is given** on behalf of **you"** (Gk: *hyper*, see 1 Cor. 11:24) and **"the new covenant in my blood** [see 1 Cor. 11:25] . . . **poured out** on behalf of **you"** (Gk: *hyper*, see Mark 14:24, "poured out on behalf of many") is vocabulary of sacrifice or vicarious death (see John 11:50, "one man should die for the people and the whole nation should not perish"). To pour out or to shed blood means to die or to kill (see Gen. 9:6; Ezek. 18:10; Isa. 59:7; Luke 11:50), and blood is sacred to God because it is life (Gen. 9:4; Deut. 12:23). This is why blood has atoning power (Lev. 17:11). In other contexts Luke steers away from traditions which interpret Jesus' death as a sacrifice, but neither Luke nor Paul challenged this formulation.

The language of "thanksgiving" (v. 19, Gk: *eucharistein*) and **new covenant** (v. 20, Gk: *kainē diathēkē*) is also filled with traditional associations which the church will explore for meanings throughout the centuries. The element of "thanksgiving" (vv. 17, 19; 1 Cor. 11:24) is a reminiscence of the many prayers of blessing in the Passover liturgy (see also Mark 14:22). Mark's phrasing of "my blood of the covenant" is already an allusion to "the blood of the covenant which the Lord has made with you" of Exod. 24:8. In Luke (v. 20) and Paul (1 Cor. 11:25), **the new covenant in my blood** probably also includes an allusion to Jer. 31:31.

Like Paul, Luke recites this tradition with no overt commentary (see Paul's direct reliance on tradition in 1 Cor. 11:23, "For I received from the Lord what I also delivered to you"). Only the elaborate introduction in vv. 15-18 sets a unique context so that the meal which Jesus institutes for his followers in vv. 19-20 follows or completes the Passover which they shared with a new definition of the deliverance which the observance anticipated. The apparent problem of the "two cups" (vv. 17, 20) in the supper turns out to be the clue that the eschatological conclusion of the Passover meal (with its several cups) has been transformed into a "remembrance" of the "new covenant" established through Jesus' death. For Luke, this is the "exodus" or "deliverance" which Jesus is about to fulfill in Jerusalem (9:31).

21-23—The abrupt mention of the betrayer follows directly on the traditional word about "my blood poured out for you." Luke's narrative moves from the general Passover setting (vv. 14-18), to Jesus' interpretation and institution of a new feast of remembrance of his death (vv. 19-20), to the specifics of how the death will occur (vv. 21-23). Verse 22 is another passion prediction continuing the theme of the necessity of the suffering of the Son of man (see 9:22, 44; 18:31; 22:48; 24:7). In this context Mark 14:21 speaks of the betrayal as a fulfillment of the Scriptures, while Luke says "as it was determined of him to go." Both of Luke's words, **determined** (Gk: *hōrismenon*, see Acts 2:23; 10:42; 11:29; 17:26,31) and "to go" (Gk: *poreuesthai*, see the discussion at 9:51) fit within Luke's way of speaking of the providence or plan of God which directs Jesus' way.

The point is clear that Judas is not "fated" to this role, although in Acts 1:16 the Lukan Peter will declare that the Holy Spirit had spoken beforehand about Judas. The tradition seems to know an allusion to Ps. 41:9-10 about the one "who ate of my bread" becoming the enemy. But Judas is an active conspirator (see the comments at 22:1-6, 48). If anyone is the "controlled" or "determined" in this story it is the Son of man who is obedient.

The questioning among the disciples is not as poignant as Mark's (14:19) "Is it I?" and Luke reveals nothing of Matthew's (26:25) account of Jesus' answer when Judas asks that question, "You have said so!" The tension is unresolved, and Judas does not appear again in the story until the arrest scene (vv. 47-53). The reader does not know when Judas steals away, but the following verses are filled with the ignorance of the disciples and the agonizing knowledge of Jesus.

True Greatness (22:24-30).   Only Luke depicts Jesus as delivering an extended discourse on the occasion of the Passover meal, and the theme moves from his dramatic reinterpretation of the meal (vv. 14-20) to discipleship when Jesus announces the presence of the betrayer (vv. 21-22). The consternation of the "apostles" over who this betrayer might be (v. 23) and an ensuing dispute about which of them was **the greatest** combine to provide the setting for the rest of his discourse on discipleship (vv. 25-34). Verses 35-38 will then conclude the banquet with preparations for the fateful encounter on the Mount of Olives (vv. 39-53).

Verses 24-30 confound all attempts to identify Luke's literary sources, probably because Luke has composed this section of Jesus' discourse out of many traditions. In the first verses (vv. 24-27), Luke appears to follow the thoughts and sequence of Mark 10:41-45 where Jesus also warned his disciples not to exercise authority like the rulers of the Gentiles but in service, as he did. It is noteworthy that Luke omitted Mark 10:35-45 at the point in the narrative where it would have been expected (see the discussion at Luke 18:35-43). The concluding verses of the present passage (vv. 28-30) also bear enough similarity to Matt. 19:28 to suggest that both Matthew and Luke are again drawing upon "Q." Clearly, Luke did not simply dream up these sayings of Jesus. But even the use of Mark displays dramatic alterations. Luke has woven these materials from both sources so thoroughly into the fabric of Jesus' discourse that the narrative context is clearly the most decisive for interpreting the meaning of Jesus' words.

24—As noted above, the announcement of the betrayer first produces consternation among the apostles (v. 23), but this quickly degenerates into a dispute about greatness. This contentiousness (Gk: *philoneikia*) is one of the first clues in the passion narrative of the ignorance the apostles will continue to display about what is happening (see comments on the passion predictions at 9:44 and 18:34). This passage occurs between the revelation of the betrayer and the warning of Peter of his impending denial. Luke is generally credited with a more kindly picture of the disciples than Mark, but this is the second occasion in Luke where they disputed which of them is **the greatest** (see also 9:46 and Mark 9:34). The irony of this passage is compounded by the fact that one of them, the betrayer, is clearly "the worst" but they can only quarrel over who is "the greatest." Jesus' discourse addresses this mentality, and it is not impossible that Luke is hoping the leaders in his own community are overhearing.

25-27—The subject is the character of Christian authority, not only as an address to the apostles, but generalized to speak to anyone who is "the greatest" or "the leader among you." Jesus' words are also a fundamental insight into the character of God's reign in the world. The whole statement is a kind of argument in which the last line is the crucial assumption. It is because Jesus is "among you as one who serves" that his declarations about authority are compelling and realistic. The argument also depends upon a direct contrast with the way authority and power are normally exercised by kings, rulers, and benefactors. This passage is an ethical policy statement which is grounded in the Christology of Jesus as **one who serves,** which in this context probably refers to the role he has just played in the meal as host and server (see also Phil. 2:1-11).

The language of v. 25 is rich with political connotations. The "benefactors" are especially important, since this was an honorific title bestowed on rulers, generals, and wealthy community leaders who contributed some great gift or accomplished a rescue. It was a title used in close connection with "Savior" (see 2:8-20). Jesus' point is that such "benefactors" and "saviors" generally prove to be dominating in their authority. Neither authoritarianism nor entitled positions should characterize Christian authority. Even privileges of age are disclaimed, and true leadership is exercised in service. Thus Jesus' rhetorical questions in v. 27 simply underscore "the way it is" in the world, but his final word discloses "the way it is" in his reign.

28-30—These words on the kingdom further illumine Jesus' declarations to his twelve "apostles." It is crucial to recognize that Jesus does not suddenly overturn all that he has just said about Christian authority. Yes, he is the Messiah—and, as such, has genuine authority—and they are his official representatives. He does not deny the realities of power and authority, but he redefines them.

The word **trials** (Gk: *peirasmos*) may be a direct allusion to Jesus' "trials" or "temptations" by the devil in 4:1-13, where the character of his authority was the central issue. Being personally "tempted" was not the issue for Jesus, and the disciples have proved faithful to him as he has been severely tested by opponents to his reign. But Jesus has now demonstrated how he will exercise the authority with which God has invested him, and their allegiance will soon be tested (see 22:40, 46). And looking beyond the passion, Jesus speaks of their authority as a delegation of the reign of God. The peculiar sovereignty of service will extend through their service, including their eschatological role as the judges of Israel.

This is one of the most direct glimpses of the eschatological kingdom in Luke, ranking along with the royal banquet scene of 13:29. The thrones are clear images of sovereign power, drawn from such images of the heavenly court as Dan. 7:9 (see Rev. 20:4). In Enoch 62, the judgment of the kings and the mighty and the exalted by the one who sits on "the throne of his glory" precedes the great banquet, and the participation of the "saints" or "the righteous" in this judgment is variously expected (see 1 Cor. 6:2). It is possible that Luke also understands the role of the Twelve as a revival of the charismatic judges of ancient **Israel** back in the time when only God was the king. Here the emphasis on the **twelve** (see also Matt. 19:28) is an explicit signal that God is not done with Israel, and this number will need to be replenished when Judas is gone (see Acts 1:17, and see Luke 9:1; 22:3).

But the context also qualifies the kind of judgment which this authority entails. Jesus' dominion will not be mocked, but neither must it then be exercised as merely the vindictive wrath which would characterize the authority of the kings of the earth. It is still Jesus the servant who is speaking. The next stories will demonstrate that Jesus will both pray for the one who denies him and refuse to resort to violence to accomplish his will.

The Warning of Peter (22:31-34).   Jesus' words to **Simon** begin abruptly. In Mark (14:26-31), the supper is over and the group has moved to the Mount of Olives before Jesus predicts that the disciples will fall away and that Peter will deny him. But Luke follows the promise of a "kingdom" for the Twelve with warnings (vv. 31-34) and further preparations for his departure (vv. 35-38) before Jesus' banquet discourse is ended. Luke's modification of Mark's story continues to be so extensive that it is much more than a redaction. It is a composition in which other sources may have been used. The effect of Luke's telling is to compel the reader to understand the magnitude of the opposition of more than human forces (vv. 31-34) and to recognize that Jesus and his followers are contending with formidable human adversaries as well (vv. 35-38). Their faithfulness will be severely tested, and the way that they conduct themselves will reveal the character of Jesus' kingdom.

31—**Satan's** power is never underestimated in Luke's account. Even when Jesus put the devil at bay at the conclusion of his temptations, the devil departed "until an opportune time" (4:13). And when Jesus "saw Satan fall like lightning from heaven" (10:17), the struggle was still with more than "flesh and blood,

but against the principalities, against the powers, against the
world rulers of this present darkness, against the spiritual hosts
of wickedness in the heavenly places," to borrow the language of
Eph. 6:12. So also in the passion narrative, **Satan** has emerged
as an active antagonist (22:3), and the "hour" of "the power of
darkness" is at hand (22:53). Now all the disciples are warned,
just as their "kingdoms" and "thrones" have been promised.
Jesus' word to Simon uses the plural form of **you,** indicating that
Satan is about to shake them like grain in a sieve (see God's testing
of Israel in Amos 9:9). That is, they will be "tested" and "proved"
(see 22:40, "temptation," Gk: *peirasmos*).

32—Jesus' next word is directed to Simon individually, as indicated by the threefold repetition of the singular pronoun, "you"/
"your." Verses 31-32 are both unique to Luke, providing a clear
comparison with 22:3 where (only in Luke) Satan entered Judas.
The reader knows how great the risk is for Peter, as does Jesus.
Jesus' word to Peter is filled with assurance, since prayer is the
only hope against the kind of testing Peter will undergo (see 11:4
and 22:40). In this case, it is Peter's **faith** (Gk: *pistis*) as "faithfulness" or "allegiance" to Jesus which is at stake (see also 18:8;
Acts 14:22; 16:5). Certainly Jesus' prayer offers hope, even if Peter
does not realize that he needs it. But the last sentence begins
with the revelation that Peter will not be simply loyal: "**And when
you have turned again.**" Peter's role as leader of the apostles will
be a major theme of Acts, but that role will lie on the other side
of his denial, tears of remorse, and renewal of hope. Jesus already
sees that repentance or conversion must precede Peter's role as
witness who strengthens the church (see also Paul in Acts 18:23).

33-34—All of the Gospels relate that Jesus predicted Peter's
denial, linking it with the cockcrow (Matt. 26:34; Mark 14:30;
John 13:38). Only Mark intensifies Peter's warning with two cock-
crows (14:30, [68], 72), and only Luke depicts Peter's promise to
go (Gk: *poreuesthai*, see the discussion at 9:51) with Jesus in terms
of "prison and death." Acts will demonstrate repeatedly that faithfulness and denial were not only spiritual states, and here Peter
correctly recognizes the political and physical peril involved in
allegiance to Jesus. Luke's Jesus also specifies that Peter will **three
times deny** that he **knows** Jesus, which locks the prediction all

the more closely with its fulfillment, at least in two cases (see 22:57, 60).

In all the Gospels, Jesus' prediction highlights the dynamic character of the story, but none of them suggests a wooden fatalism. The tradition that Jesus did predict Peter's denial is remembered as an assurance that Jesus could see what was coming for him and for the disciples, especially in Luke where Jesus also sees beyond the denial to Peter's restoration. But this episode is also a clue to the differentiation between levels of culpability which Luke consistently weaves into the narrative. Satan has triumphed with Judas, having found a willing conspirator. Peter is not an active betrayer, but Jesus and the reader know that he is ignorant of the trial that lies ahead. He also will fail to be faithful to Jesus or to his own declarations, but his denial will be tragic because it will be a willful act against his will. The cockcrow will be the signal.

The Two Swords (22:35-38).   Only Luke relates this word of Jesus, and it is clearly linked back to 10:4 and perhaps to 9:3 where the disciples were sent on their mission without all the trappings of traveling philosophers and teachers. Jesus first reminds his disciples that then they did not lack anything, **but now** (v. 36) they must be equipped differently. When they report that they have two swords, he declares, **"It is enough"** (v. 38). Many commentators regard the entire exchange as filled with irony, since the disciples take Jesus literally; but he is only reaffirming what he said before, until finally he must tell them, "Enough of this!" But by then they have the wrong idea, and later he must rectify their use of the **sword** with a healing (vv. 49-51).

The idea that Jesus disavowed all use of the sword (see Matt. 26:52) is certainly closer to Luke's view than the later Christian usage of this passage to support the **two swords** of church and state. But the translation and narrative of Luke must be strained to support the suggestion that the disciples simply misunderstand what Jesus has said. Jesus is taking the initiative here. He is emphasizing the contrast with the former times, and he is stressing the necessity of the fulfillment of the Scriptures. Two swords are **enough,** therefore, for Jesus to proceed with the drama that follows. Only when it has gone "as far as this," when the sword is used against the slave of the high priest (v. 51) will Jesus intervene and remedy the violence with healing.

This story appears to be told to understand two crucial factors in the passion narrative. (1) Jesus' disciples did draw a sword in the darkness against the high priest's troops. This was probably cited against Jesus and his followers as the action of "lawless" insurgents (see also Acts 5:36-37; 21:38, where the Christians are confused with revolutionaries). It is not unlikely that such action of self-defense was even part of the charge of sedition against Jesus (see Luke 23:5, 14; see 23:19, 25). The Roman order and its client rulers would have been as quick as any other such power to accuse reform movements of guerrilla "lawlessness."

(2) The evangelists agree that Jesus knew what was about to happen in this fateful encounter before it happened. Luke insists that he also knew what would be used against them. So here Jesus tells them to be equipped for an alien task, one which will be out of character and leave them vulnerable to false charges. He certainly does not endorse the use of the sword, and perhaps Luke thinks that the disciples do not grasp Jesus' meaning in this ambiguous word.

Jesus is not equipping his troops for revolt any more than he was mounting a charge on the temple when he arranged for the colt (19:30-34). But he is orchestrating the symbolic action in which the Scriptures are the script. In this case it is the fulfillment of Isa. 53:12, which is explicitly mentioned as **fulfilled** or "completed" (Gk: *telesthēnai,* see 13:32; 18:31), and this scripture will have its "end" or "goal" (Gk: *telos*) in Jesus.

Thus, although Jesus appears to be playing into the hands of "the power of darkness" by allowing for swords when he was clearly not serious about a revolt, the result is not a surprise. Nor was this a futile effort to provoke the heavenly armies like the War Scroll at Qumran (see Matt. 26:53). But this is the completion of his preparations to meet the adversaries whose preparations are also underway (see the comments on 22:1-6). His word is a final passion prediction about the necessity of the divine plan. Jesus needs no more than two swords to walk into the trap which has been laid for him because this is God's mission to defeat "the power of darkness" in its own strength.

The Arrest (22:39-65)

With the conclusion of Jesus' farewell discourse and its warnings to the apostles at the last supper (vv. 14-38), Luke's narrative moves to the Mount of Olives (vv. 39-53) and the courtyard of the high priest's house (vv. 54-65). These are all scenes in the dark of the night (v. 53), filled with tension, intimidation, and fear. Such a setting has been identified as crucial to Jesus' adversaries, since they must arrest him by stealth "in the absence of the multitude" (v. 6). Luke testifies that God's will is being done by Jesus in the midst of such darkness (v. 42). These scenes, however, appear to portray the triumph of the adversaries.

Jesus on the Mount of Olives (22:39-46).   This scene of Jesus at prayer precedes the arrest in all four Gospels (Matt. 26:36-46; Mark 14:32-42; and John 17:1—18:1). Matthew and Mark identify the place as "Gethsemane," but Luke and John are interested in its being a place where Jesus often went. John adds, "Judas, who betrayed him, also knew the place" (18:2), and Luke has stressed Jesus' habit of staying on **the Mount of Olives** (21:37). The place is important as the site of his arrest (see v. 53), and Jesus is fully aware of what lies ahead. The reader also knows that a confrontation is building, but the apostles who follow him faithfully (v. 39) do not appear to understand.

The scene is framed with Jesus' two warnings to them to **"Pray that you may not enter into temptation"** (vv. 40, 46). In the meanwhile, Jesus moves away from them to pray (v. 41) and then rises from prayer to find them asleep (v. 45). Verse 42 conveys the substance of his prayer, identifying God's will as the crucial force at work in the story. Verses 43-44, which are textually questionable, elaborate Jesus' prayer as an **agony** or "struggle" with God's will. The whole episode is a kind of "last temptation" of the Messiah in which he is revealed once again to be fully obedient to the will of the Father (see 4:3, 9).

39-41—Jesus is depicted as conducting himself "as usual" or in accord with his practice (see 1:9; 2:42). Such practices would

have been known to a close associate like Judas, but their nor-
malcy is altered by Jesus' sense of the critical moment. His warning to his followers may sound more urgent to them in the light
of his words to Simon of Satan's purposes this night (vv. 31,34).
This would be the time for them to practice the prayer he taught
for the kingdom and against temptation (11:2-4; Gk: *peirasmos*,
22:40, 46). He does not go off three times nor does he take the
inner circle of disciples with him, as in Mark 14. But he separates
himself, and his **kneeling** may indicate the intensity of his prayer.

42—His prayer is the heart of the passsage, and it represents
a further play on the words for "will" (Gk: *boulein* and *thelēma*,
see Mark 14:36: "Not what I will, but what you will."). As has
frequently been emphasized in this commentary, Luke's narrative
revolves around a conflict of wills (see especially 2:34; 13:31-34).
When Jesus addresses God as **"Father"** in prayer (see also 10:21;
11:2; [23:34;] 23:46) or speaks of the gracious gifts of the "Father's
good pleasure" (10:21; 11:13; 12:30-32; 22:29; 24:49), he is speaking of God's will, and particularly of God's will to save. But here
it is clear that God's will leads Jesus into an impending conflict
with the adversaries of God's reign. His lordship will be accomplished in suffering. He must drink the **cup,** but this is a frequent
scriptural image for God's wrath which must be drunk by God's
foes (Isa. 51:17, 22; Jer. 25:15, 17, 28; 49:12; Pss. 11:6; 75:8; Ezek.
23:31-33; Hab. 2:16). Jesus is depicted as struggling, as being
tested in his obedience far beyond the tests of the devil (4:1-13).
This is one of the central glimpses in the narrative of how God's
will and reign are at work in Jesus' mission, but understanding
is difficult even for Jesus.

43-44—These verses are heavily disputed because of the divided manuscript witnesses. Either they were omitted by a large
portion of the scribal tradition, perhaps because they gave such
a human picture of Jesus' struggle (see also Heb. 5:7-8), or they
were added to dramatize the pathos of his suffering, perhaps in
direct imitation of the stories of suffering martyrs. The devil
promised helping angels (2:10; see also Dan. 10:13, 15-18), and
now one appears to Jesus. His **sweat like drops of blood** is probably an image of its profusion, but later this would be developed

into a complex idea of atoning suffering. Both the external evidence of manuscripts and the internal evidence of the reading can be used as arguments either for the inclusion or the exclusion of vv. 43-44. It may be best to regard these as a very early elaboration, noting that Luke's narrative does not require them.

45-46—Now Jesus returns to the disciples, and the intense glimpse into Jesus' relationship with God is over. The evangelist makes no effort to explain how anyone knew what happened while Jesus prayed. In fact, the disciples were **sleeping** (see also 9:32), but Luke adds, out of **sorrow.** It is also not clear how they knew to be sorrowful, since they do not seem to grasp what is happening. But this note is kinder to the disciples than Mark 14:38, where their sleep is due to the weakness of flesh. This conclusion is a preparation for the impending conflict in which wakefulness and readiness will be crucial (see also 12:37; Acts 20:31).

The Betrayal (22:47-53). The confrontation which has been building since 22:1-6 now takes place, and Luke isolates the antagonist **Judas** and the protagonist **Jesus** even more than Matthew (26:47-56) or Mark (14:43-52), where the presence of the **crowd** is more prominent. John's version (18:1-11) stresses Jesus' foreknowledge and control so strongly that Jesus initiates the action and the arresting officers "drew back and fell to the ground" (18:6) when he declares his identity. Luke's version is restrained by the Markan tradition, but this is still a critical episode which has been thoroughly composed to fit within Luke's plot. The power of the antagonists is imposing in Luke, and Judas clearly intends to take the initiative. The violence of Jesus' defenders also threatens to dominate the scene. While Jesus is subject to such willful acts, he is never subjected or mastered by the betrayer, his defenders, or the leaders who had come out against him. The power they have is the authority he yields to them in order that the will of God may be accomplished.

47-48—Luke stresses the sudden appearance of the crowd in the midst of Jesus' call to his disciples to watchfulness and prayer, "Behold a crowd!" This **crowd** is not immediately identified (see v. 52) as in Mark, but Judas stands out briefly in the lead. He is again identified as **one of the twelve** (see 22:3, 30; Acts 1:17), which is probably Luke's clue that he would have known where to find Jesus (see comments at v. 39) as well as a poignant reminder that this was a betrayal from the inner circle. He moves to kiss Jesus, which the tradition identified as the sign of betrayal prearranged by Judas (see Mark 14:44//Matt. 26:48). But Luke's Jesus does not allow Judas to control the scene, perhaps even stopping him before he delivers the kiss. It is Jesus whose question reveals that this is the means of betrayal. In a direct echo of earlier passion predictions, Jesus identifies himself as the Son of man who is now "betrayed" or "delivered" by this kiss (Gk: *paradidōmi*, see 9:44; 18:31-32; 22:22; 24:7). Jesus declares the meaning of what is really happening within God's will and plan even as it happens, and Judas recedes from view.

Luke does not develop Judas' portrait any further, except to interpret his death as divine judgment in Acts 1:18-20. Judas's motivation is never explained (see Matt. 26:6-16; John 12:1-8; 13:27-29), nor does he show any sign of repentance (see Matt. 27:3-10). Modern preoccupation with Judas as a tragic figure or victim of the divine plan receives no support from Luke. It is Jesus, if anyone, whose way is determined (22:22). Jesus' knowledge of God's will means that he is not merely a blind or tragic victim either, but his prayer on the Mount of Olives (vv. 39-46) provides insight into his human struggle with obedience (with or without vv. 43-44).

49-51—Seeing the impending arrest, Jesus' followers appear to ask whether they should strike with the sword. Only Luke includes this strange question, but it is more an expression of uncertainty expressed as a deliberative question. They do not wait for an answer. Neither does Jesus give them permission to strike the slave of the high priest. Luke adds that it was his right ear (see Mark 14:47) and John (18:10) names him as Malchus, and only Luke indicates that Jesus healed him. As noted above in the preparations for this scene (vv. 35-38), the sword is necessary for what is to be fulfilled here. Jesus' word in v. 51 is ambiguous. It could mean, "No more of this!" as the RSV translates it, but it could also be, "That will do it!" or "Let that be enough!" Jesus has not authorized this violence, except in allowing for two swords (v. 38: "It is enough!"), but neither has he prevented it when they appeared to ask. Now this ritual has proceeded far enough so that he and his disciples are thoroughly implicated as "lawless" (see the comments on v. 37 above). Thus he intervenes to limit the violence and even to remedy its effects.

52-53—Jesus is still in charge as he confronts the **chief priests and** "captains" **of the temple and elders.** This "crowd" (Gk: *ochlos*, v. 47) is clearly distinct from the "crowd" (Gk: *ochlos*, v. 6) which "the chief priests and captains" were trying to avoid in their plot (v. 6). These are the temple leaders, people associated with the operation, security, and legislative functions of the temple. The list is much like Mark's (14:43), except that the "captains" (see also Acts 4:1; 5:24, 26) have replaced the "scribes." This is a high-powered security force, hardly the group which would normally arrest **a robber** armed with **swords and clubs.** Even if Jesus is referring to the "robber-revolutionaries" (Gk: *lēstēs*: see Josephus, *War* 2.253-254, see Jesus' word against the "den of robbers" in 19:46, Gk: *lēstēs*), he is pointing out the foolishness of their action.

Obviously, more is at stake here than a legal arrest, since he could have been taken any time in the temple. They know it. Jesus knows it and confronts them with the truth. And the reader knows that this is an elaborate ruse to avoid the people who protected Jesus so long in the temple (see also the captain and officers who arrest Peter and John without violence, out of fear of the people, in Acts 5:26). Jesus' last word is a theological interpretation, which further exposes their devious scheme. Their **hour** is a limited time of the triumph of evil (contrast 22:14), and their "authority" (Gk: *exousia*) or **power** (RSV) is that of the dominion **of darkness.** Jesus has been confronted before with the devil's claims to "authority" and "glory" (Gk: *exousia*, 4:6), and he will soon confront Herod's "authority" or "jurisdiction" (Gk: *exousia*, 23:7). Thus Jesus has identified their midnight plot as a collusion with the dominion of Satan (see also 22:3) in which darkness reigns instead of light (see also 1:79; Acts 26:18).

The Denial (22:54-62).   Historical studies of Jesus' arrest and trials have long been confounded by Luke's account, and heroic efforts have been made to establish independent sources behind Luke. The problem is that according to Mark and Matthew Jesus was taken directly from the Mount of Olives to the Sanhedrin, which was led by the high priest (identifed as Caiaphas by Matthew) with the chief priests, elders, and scribes (Matt. 26:57-59//Mark 14:53-55). John says that they first took him to the high priest Annas, Caiaphas's father-in-law (18:12), and that Jesus was then taken to Caiaphas while it was still night (18:24; see v. 27) and to Pilate in the early morning (18:28-29). The account of Peter's denial is woven through all three of these versions of Jesus' trial by the Jewish authorities. Thus it is clear that they commonly understood Jesus' trial by the Sanhedrin to be held in the dark of the night, probably in violation of Jewish custom and certainly filled with the taint of clandestine judicial procedures.

Luke, however, presents the trial as commencing in the morning (22:66), when the night scenes of Peter's denial (vv. 54-62) and the reviling of Jesus (vv. 63-65) are completed. Luke's version still holds the temple authorities, among many others, accountable for Jesus' death, but the setting is not so irregular. Nor is Jesus physically abused in the presence of the religious leaders (see Mark 14:65//Matt. 26:67-68; John 18:22-23). Nor are false witnesses employed (see Mark 14:55-56//Matt. 26:59-60). Many interpreters have concluded that either Luke has drawn upon an alternative account of Jesus' arrest and trial or his narrative offers a striking restatement of the tradition. Common opinion that Luke is a "Gentile Gospel" which is generally intent on blaming the Jews has reinforced the search for a pre-Lukan origin of these differences from Mark.

It is beyond the purposes of this commentary on Luke to pursue the question of historical accuracy. But even the meticulous efforts to reconstruct pre-Lukan sources may be misguided by assumptions about Luke's purposes. Instead of explaining away these differences by assigning them to a source, a commentary on Luke must allow such distinctive elements to be understood within Luke's narrative. Even assuming that Luke possessed other oral and perhaps written sources, the story must be understood in its differences from the source Luke is known to possess: Mark.

On the most obvious level, Luke has rearranged the episodes so that the night scenes are clearly distinguished from the accounts of the trials which begin in the morning. Thus vv. 54-71 are no longer one narrative unit as the the parallel materials are in Mark and Matthew. The stories of Peter's denial (vv. 54-62) and the mockery by Jesus' captors (vv. 63-65) are developed by Luke as distinct scenes which have been specifically anticipated in Jesus' predictions. Luke's omission of details which further incriminate the Jewish leadership in Matthew and Mark can only be noted, since arguments from silence are notoriously facile. But these alterations at least require that old assumptions about Luke's anti-Jewish bias not be read too quickly into the story. The critical passages of the trial lie ahead.

54-55—Jesus is brought under arrest into **the house** of the **high priest.** It is not clear in Luke whether that means he was locked up inside and later looked out at Peter through a window (v. 61) or he was simply under guard at some distance from the group of servants gathered around the fire (see Mark 14:66, 72 and Matt. 26:69, 75 where Jesus and Peter are clearly separated). Luke has not followed Mark's report that "all forsook him and fled" or that a young man ran away naked (Mark 14:50-52). But Luke quotes Mark in saying that **Peter followed at a distance,** which recalls Peter's more explicit promise in Luke to "go with you" (Gk: *poreuesthai*) "to prison and to death" (v. 33). Thus, while none of the evangelists tell what Peter had in mind in following Jesus into this dangerous location, Luke's picture implies real courage and allegiance as a disciple (see "faith" in v. 32). Was this a rescue effort in which Peter would be expected to hide his identity? A few fibs about his identity would hardly seem disloyal, at least not by the rules of a conventional story. And when he sat "in the midst of them," he was certainly not joining them, as had Judas.

56-57—At this point, Mark and Matthew have recounted Jesus' trial inside the house, but Luke stays with the firelight scene. It is also a trial scene, but Peter comes under accusation. The servant girl does not speak to Peter, as in Mark 14:67, "You were with Jesus of Nazareth," but to the assembly, **"This man also was with him."** Peter's response is a direct fulfillment of Jesus' prediction (v. 34), stated in emphatic tones of denial (Gk: *arneisthai*), **"Woman, I do not know him."**

58-60a—The next two denials are thoroughly rephrased but substantially the same as Mark's version. The two accusers are now different men (contrast Mark 14:69), and the first speaks directly to Peter and the other speaks to the group after about an hour. The length of time between the second and third denials carries the story forward toward the hour of cockcrow. The third accuser speaks with an oath formula, "Upon the truth, this fellow with with him!" (contrast Mark and Matthew, "truly"). And Peter's answers follow the same pattern as his word to the **woman: "Man, I am not. Man, I do not know what you are saying."** Peter has successively denied (1) **knowing** Jesus (v. 34), (2) being a follower of Jesus (v. 58), and (3) being one of the **Galileans** who were with Jesus (v. 59). Matthew 26:73 indicates that Peter's dialect gave him away, but none of the Gospels suggests that the **Galilean** association meant they were revolutionaries (see the discussion of "Galilee" at 23:5-6). These are simply three forms of the question of Peter's allegiance to Jesus, now stated as accusations. These are the "tests" of the accuser in the power of darkness (v. 53), and Peter has fallen through Satan's sieve (v. 31).

60b-62—The pathos of the resolution of this scene is compounded by the fact that the reader knows that Peter has been warned, and Peter remembers after the fact. This is the stuff of tragedy in which the prophetic oracle proves true, even when Peter has shown courage to be in the courtyard at all. Certainly there was not much he could do for Jesus, especially if he were taken captive too. The cockcrow is not only the sign of the end of that dark night, but also the sign of the fulfillment of Jesus' oracle. Everything that is happening on the plane of human history in this story is also caught up in the arena of divine drama and contention with the power of darkness.

Only Luke adds that **the Lord turned and looked at Peter.** This will be a powerful touch in Christian piety, where Jesus was regularly called "the Lord" (see also 7:13 and Acts 11:16). It also drives home the point that Jesus knew what was happening to Peter even while Peter did not. The insight of retrospect is the cause of bitter tears. Peter's repentance or "turning again" (see 32) has already begun (see also the people in 23:48).

The Mockery Begins (22:63-65). This scene is remarkably different from Mark 14:65, upon which it is based, and the context marks the most important difference. This abuse of Jesus is not part of an official trial setting in Luke (contrast Herod in 23:11 and Pilate in 23:15, 22). All of the important people appear only in the morning (v. 66). These people who are **holding Jesus** are not even identified officially as "guards" (Mark 14:65). Mark's version alludes to Isa. 50:6, but this connection is weaker in Luke, where neither "spitting" nor Jesus' "face" is mentioned. The word which Luke uses for **mocking** (Gk: *empaizein*) also corresponds less well to Isa. 50:6 ("spitting," Gk: *emptyein*, Mark 14:65), but it links this scene back to Jesus' prediction of his being mocked in 18:32 (see also 14:29; 23:11, 36).

The command to **"Prophesy!"** is just the first of many ironic mockeries in which Jesus' prophetic word is being fulfilled for the reader exactly when his accusers ridicule him. They are "reviling him" (v. 65: Gk: *blasphēmein;* see also 12:10; 23:39), who is the prophet par excellence in Luke (see 7:16). The last line is Luke's phrasing about **many other words** rounding off the story without adding new details (see 3:18; 8:3; Acts 15:35).

The Trials of the Messiah (22:66—23:25)

Most of Chap. 22 was devoted to events specifically identified with the day of Unleavened Bread, on which (1) preparations were made (7-13), (2) the Passover was eaten "when the hour came" (vv. 14-38), and (3) the arrest of Jesus and denial of Peter took place in the "hour and dominion of darkness" (vv. 39-65). In 22:66, "when day came," it was the day of all the events of Jesus' trials (22:66—23:25), execution (23:26-49), and burial (23:50-56). As noted above, Luke's account has separated Jesus' trial before the Sanhedrin from the events of the previous night. Consequently Luke's narrative depicts a series of trial scenes in close parallel one with another: (1) the Sanhedrin trial, 22:66-71; (2) arraignment before Pilate, 23:1-5; (3) accusation before Herod, 23:6-12; and (4) examination and sentence by Pilate, 23:13-25.

Throughout these trials, the story is filled with irony for the Christian reader, and Luke often enhances this discrepancy between the way things appear and the way things really are. Jesus will be tried as Messiah, Son of God, Son of man, and King of the Jews; but of course he is guilty of such charges. That is, he is innocent because he is truly the Messiah, Son of God, Son of man, and King of the Jews. Thus, is it he who is on trial or are his judges already judged before the tribunal of God? The tragic element in the story is that all who participate in denouncing and executing Jesus are implicating themselves. Some participate as active antagonists of Jesus, but others seem to be carried along unknowing, or even against their will. The trial scenes are particularly important for determining exactly whose will is being accomplished in the story.

The Sanhedrin Trial (22:66-71)

As noted above (see the comments on 22:54-62), Luke's version has the Sanhedrin trial in the daylight and does not involve false witnesses or physical abuse. It also includes no charges of Jesus speaking against the temple (Mark 14:58//Matt. 26:61), and the high priest is not mentioned, to say nothing of his leading the accusations (Mark 14:63//Matt. 26:65). Jesus is not charged with blasphemy (Mark 14:64//Matt. 26:65), and he is not judged as "deserving death" (Mark 14:64//Matt. 26:66). The only verdict is the ambiguous confirmation that **"We have heard it ourselves from his own lips,"** with the result that they move on to Pilate's court.

The source problem is again difficult. Verse 66 is paralleled by Mark 14:53 and 15:1, since Luke only needs to introduce one trial scene before the chief priests, scribes, and elders. The rest of the passage follows Mark's sequence, but vv. 67b-68, 70, and 71b are non-Markan. Certainly much of the detail in this scene had been transmitted in oral recitations and preaching, whether or not Luke had access to an independent written account. Verse 70 is the most likely to be derived from a source, because it is a formal element of interrogation connected with the title "Son of God." Mark 14:61 has an approximate version in which Jesus' identity as "Christ" is linked to being "Son of the Blessed," and Matt. 26:63 makes this "Son of God."

Perhaps Luke possessed a source in which two questions were asked, but it again seems more credible to suggest that v. 70 is Luke's work, breaking the interrogators' question into two. Thus the question about Jesus as **Christ** is elaborated with a scriptural allusion (vv. 67b-68) before the answer about **the Son of man.** The second question about **Son of God** is itself a testimony in Luke heard (ironically) from their mouths (see v. 71b).

66—The Sanhedrin is composed of the **chief priests,** the **scribes,** and **the elders,** normally presided over by the high priest. The list of participants varies somewhat in other texts (see 9:22; 20:1; Acts 4:5-6, rulers; 6:12; 22:5), but Luke's picture corresponds generally with Mark (14:53, 55; 15:1) and Matthew (26:57, 59; 27:1). Luke has condensed Mark's references, written the transition (see also 4:42; 6:13; Acts 12:18; 23:12; 27:39), and carefully noted that this was **their** council. That is, although this group includes **the elders of the people,** it still does not include "the people." The arrest has been arranged to avoid "the people" (see the comments at 22:1) or "the multitude" (see 22:6), and all of these leadership groups have been intent on "destroying" Jesus since he cleansed the temple (19:45-48). Luke is not painting a picture of class struggle, but here he is depicting the particular culpability of the "rulers" as a group (see 23:13, 35; 24:20; see also Acts 3:17; 4:5, 8, 26; 5:27-30; 13:27; 14:5; 23:5).

67-69—Jesus first refuses to answer the question about "the Messiah" directly. It is not clear what this title implied for the questioners, but certainly their accountability to the Roman order would have made it inflammatory. Jesus' words are a paraphrase of Jeremiah's answer to the king in a life-threatening situation when he was instructed to "hide nothing from me!" (see Jer. 38:15, LXX 45:15; see also Paul in Acts 13:40-41). This is a scene filled with intimidation and the subtle nuances of interrogation. Jesus' encounters with the rulers in the temple (20:1—21:4) have already demonstrated that they neither believe his answers nor answer his questions, and now they appear to have complete control.

His answer is introduced with a Lukan phrase marking a new moment, **from now on** (see 1:48; 5:10). This is a picture of the future Son of man, but not an apocalyptic revelation of heavenly splendor which they will see (Mark 14:62, following Dan. 7:13). The answer in Mark is reduced by Luke so that Jesus only declares that the **Son of man** will be **seated** in royal authority at God's **right hand** (see Ps. 110:1). Luke is entering a complex early Christian discussion of the interpretation of Psalm 110, and Peter's declaration in Acts 2:32-36 will demonstrate that Jesus is predicting his resurrection as an exaltation to rule (as "Son of God," see especially Acts 13:33, "my Son"). This is how Jesus will be "made Lord and Christ" or confirmed by God as Messiah (Acts 2:36). Thus if Jesus' answer about the "Son of man" first seems to have evaded the question about "the Christ," it has only demonstrated that Jesus knows that God's answer exceeds their question. Yes, he is "the Messiah," and he will be confirmed as such by fulfilling the "exodus" (9:31) as the suffering Son of man (see especially 9:20-22, "Christ" and "Son of man"; see also 9:44; 18:31-32; 22:22, 48; 24:7). The motif of Jesus as the suffering and royal Messiah will be fundamental to Luke's passion narrative (see 23:2, 35, 39; 24:26, 46).

70—"**All** of them" then pose a leading question, which is a declaration in the form of a question: "So then, you are the Son of God! Are you?" The nuance is crucial and may best be captured by attending to the word the RSV translates **then** (Gk: *oun*). Although this question has been separated from the question (v. 67) of "the Christ," Luke would agree that Jesus' identity as "Messiah" constitutes his being **Son of God** as well (see especially 3:21-22; 4:41). As noted in the baptism and temptation stories (3:21-22; 4:1-13), **Son of God** refers primarily to Jesus' divine authority to rule. "All of them," therefore, are exactly correct in understanding that the scriptural fulfillment he has mentioned means that Jesus is the Messiah and Son of God. Jesus does not need to answer "I am!" in the powerful word of self-revelation of Mark 14:62. He may merely confirm, "**You are saying that I am.**"

The irony is that they are confirming the truth of who he is, but they think they are denying it. Their declarative question was hypothetical, "If that's true, then you are the Son of God, right?" It was also hypocritical. But it was correct. Even as the truth is now cited as **testimony** against him **from his own lips,** it comes rather from their mouths. The tragic irony, moreover, is that "all of them" are indicting themselves and willfully asserting themselves against the Messiah and Son of God. As Peter states in Acts 13:27-28, "those who live in Jerusalem and their rulers, because they did not recognize him nor understand the utterances of the prophets which are read every sabbath, fulfilled these by condemning him. Though they could charge him with nothing deserving death, yet they asked Pilate to have him killed." Thus, although no verdict is reached by the council in Luke's account, 23:1 reports the tacit decision when **the whole company of them** took Jesus to Pilate.

Arraignment before Pilate (23:1-5)

Jesus' trial before Pilate is one of Luke's masterpieces of depiction. Each of the scenes is filled with the subtle power of the encounter of politics and religion and the nuances of the variety of roles played out in the face of the power of Rome and the judgment of God. Modern interpretations are often so eager to deny any "political" claims on Jesus' part that they miss the fact that every disturbance, no matter how spiritual, was a potential threat to the Roman order. The temple leadership was charged with keeping the peace, especially during festivals such as Passover. If they told the Roman procurator that they had captured an insurrectionist, it is unlikely that Pilate would have argued with them. On the other hand, Pilate was responsible for maintaining the semblance of the Roman juridical system, and he was known for his disdain for the traditions of the Jews. The plot is thick indeed.

The narrative is, therefore, historically credible as a scene of a Roman official demonstrating his control within the strangely oriental world of Judean religion and politics. It is filled with the irony and sarcasm of the posturing and insults which such power struggles entail. Here it is the Jewish leaders who want one of their own eliminated. They recite four charges against him in a few verses, and the reader knows how deceptive these charges are. Their charges even indict the people who would defend Jesus. Pilate seems content to let them remain uncomfortable and angry even after a very ambiguous interrogation of the accused. He even sends Jesus off to the tetrarch of Galilee for whom he has no affection. All along, the reader knows that Jesus is doomed in this court. He says almost nothing. But the words and acts of all those around him reveal their complicity in this hideous act of executing the one who is truly **Christ** and **king**, as charged.

The scenes through v. 16 are thoroughly Lukan. It is possible that Luke followed a non-Markan source in these verses, but the introduction (v. 1), the summary of the charges (v. 5), the depiction of Herod's interest in Jesus (v. 8), and the fascination with their grim friendship (vv. 12, 15) are best understood as Lukan. The whole scene may well be read as Luke's amplification of Peter's sermon on Psalm 2 in Acts 4:23-31, i.e., Herod and Pilate are the kings and rulers gathered against the Lord and his Anointed. Since only Luke tells of the trial before Herod, some commentators have suggested that Luke even created the episode. But such speculation is not necessary or helpful for the purposes of this commentary except as it illumines the evangelist's method and purpose. In all of the historical and political intricacies of these scenes, the struggle remains a contest of the wills of the power brokers with the Lord God and his Christ. Their lack of integrity is also nakedly exposed in Jesus' presence, just as Simeon had prophesied (2:34-35).

1—The **whole company of them** which led Jesus to **Pilate** in Luke is still the "assembly of the elders of the people" including "the chief priests and scribes" (22:66). The early morning hearing before the Sanhedrin has resulted in this change of venue. No verdict of a crime worthy of death has yet been given in Luke (contrast Mark 14:64//Matt. 26:66), but delivering a fellow Jew to the Romans was ominous. Luke has also indicated that for some time the goal of the chief priests and scribes has been Jesus' death (19:47; 22:2).

Modern interpreters may need to be reminded that the high priesthood was a complex political and religious office in first-century Palestine, and the Romans controlled it as much as possible. Since the era of Herod the Great, who killed the last of the Hasmonean priests, the Romans appointed the high priests and at times controlled the rituals by holding the priestly vestments. For many years a new high priest was appointed annually by the procurator, but Caiaphas was reappointed for 18 years, including 10 by Pilate. He knew how to get along with the Romans.

Whether a deft negotiator who could handle the procurators or a servile collaborator, he was still the high priest. The Judeans had no higher religious or political office. For those who identified closely with the temple and the priestly families associated with it, the integrity of the high preisthood meant its faithfulness in continuing the practices. If the safety of Israel depended on the temple and its holy observances, then anyone who appeared to threaten the "holy place" was a danger to the nation (John 11:47-53).

Others were very alienated from the high priests, regarding them as illegitimate or "wicked priests" (i.e., the community at Qumran). Luke's differentiation of this priestly party from the Pharisees and the people is not merely a literary device. It is a judgment that the adversaries who occupied the temple offices were guilty of rejecting the reign of the Messiah because they sought to keep the peace by protecting their own positions (see 19:42). Their insistence on Jesus' death rings of desperation, and even Pilate seems to toy with them.

2—They open with three charges against Jesus. The first is the most Jewish concern, since **perverting our nation** or "misleading the people" is a charge of false prophecy or even a charge against rulers who deserve divine judgment (Gk: *diastrephein;* see 1 Kings 18:17-18; Acts 13:8,10; 20:30). The second is a blaming indictment that Jesus **forbade** or "prevented" **us** from paying tribute to Caesar. The scene is an intriguing display of "us" Jews and "you" Romans, but the reader knows that it is a deception. Jesus did not prevent "us," unless "we" chose to interpret his saying about tribute in radical terms (see discusison at 20:20-26). That scene was already a ruse "to deliver him up to the authority and jurisdiction of the governor" (20:20) and they did not abandon the ploy even when it failed. The third is a summary of the Sanhedrin hearing in terms which Pilate could understand. He (or they, see 22:70-71) said, **"He is Christ, a king,"** or "he is an anointed king."

Some commentators have argued that Luke has confused the story with a combination of titles in 22:66—23:2 (Christ, Son of man, Son of God, King). But the series is necessary to emphasize the divine legitimacy of Jesus' authority and rule. The title "Christ" or "Anointed One" (see Acts 4:26; Psalm 2) is a crucial royal title for Luke (see the discussion at 3:21-22), but Pilate would best understand the title "king." It is the only charge picked up by Pilate for the moment (see 23:13).

3-5—Pilate's question contains a world of meaning, and it is cited verbatim along with almost identical answers in all the Gospels. Jesus' identity as **"King of the Jews"** will not appear again in Luke's account of Pilate's trial, but it will be the stated charge under which he is crucified (23:38). It is important to realize that Herod the Great was the first who had the title "King of the Jews," since it was a Roman designation for the one they appointed to rule their province of Judea. This is the title which Matthew's Gospel (2:2) suggests caused Herod the Great such consternation when applied to the infant Jesus. None of Herod's sons received this title, although they sought it eagerly. The Romans finally removed Herod Archelaus from being ethnarch of Judea, replacing him with the procurators. The irony and intimidation of a procurator asking an accused man if he is **the King of the Jews** would not have been lost on first-century readers.

"You have said so" could mean, "If you say so!" or "You tell me!" or "You are saying so by means of this very trial!" Pilate does not appear to derive much from the answer, perhaps writing Jesus off as deluded or perhaps satisfied that Jesus acknowledged the Roman authority to declare who is **the King of the Jews.** It is not possible to tell if Pilate is sincere in declaring that **no crime** has been committed, even when that refrain is repeated in vv. 14 and 22. In John 18, the encounter is expanded so that both Pilate's and Jesus' words are much clearer, but when John (18:37) confirms the tradition that Pilate said Jesus was a king, the matter remains quite ambiguous. The Christian reader understands with Jesus that Pilate is saying far more than he discerns. No matter what he thinks, Pilate is fulfilling the Scriptures and confirming

Jesus as the Anointed One without knowing it (see Acts 4:26-28; 13:27).

The urgency or intensity of Jesus' accusers drives the narrative forward. If Pilate was baiting them because they needed him to pronounce a sentence of death, he now hears the previous charges summarized in overt terms of insurrection. This is not merely a matter of misleading teaching, which would be serious enough for the Jews (see Deut. 18:20), nor of alleged tax protests. Nor is it that Jesus has delusions of kingship. One who **stirs up the people** throughout the land is a threat to the Roman order. This sentence is a Lukan creation which offers a geographic summary of Jesus' whole ministry, just as Acts 1:8 summarizes the geographic progression of the book of Acts. Everything has come into Jerusalem and will proceed from it (see also the geographic summary of Acts 10:37). But Jesus' long journey is cited against him and against **the people** at the same time. Clearly this crowd is the priestly party whose "fear of the people" has been a motive force since Jesus arrived in Jerusalem (see 19:47-48; 20:6, 19, 26, 45-46; 21:38; 22:2, 6), but now they have found a means for counting the loyalty of the people as evidence against Jesus. **The people** would also find it dangerous to object.

Accusation before Herod (23:6-12)

The mention of **Galilee** provides the transition to Jesus' hearing before **Herod** Antipas, the tetrarch of Galilee and Perea. This son of Herod the Great always wanted to be named "the King of the Jews," and later was deposed after a futile appeal to Gaius Caligula to reclaim the title from Herod Agrippa I (Josephus, *Ant.*, 18.240-255). This **Herod,** Herod Antipas, is the tetrarch who executed John the Baptist (3:18-20; 9:9), who heard about Jesus and wanted to see him (9:7-9), and who was "that fox" reputed to be seeking Jesus' life (13:31-32). He was probably in Jerusalem to accompany the Galilean pilgrims, whether or not he intended any observance of Passover himself. Luke certainly has no pretense of respect for Herod Antipas.

6-10— Pilate's dispatch of Jesus to **Antipas** may have been a professional courtesy or an attempt to pass a problem to an adversary. Herod's "great joy" at seeing Jesus is a bitter touch (see

2:10), since all Herod has in mind is the hope of Jesus performing a **sign.** No theological seriousness is attributed to Herod's notion of a "sign," and Jesus' silence before his wordy interrogation (Gk: *en logois hikanois*) is a display of the ancient aphorism: "There is one who by keeping silent is found wise, while another is detested for being too talkative" (Sir. 20:5).

Jesus' accusers are, nevertheless, compelled to follow along to the court of this Idumean ruler and press their charges. They are also humiliated by the absurdity of the scene. Some commentators suggest that Herod is introduced as a "second witness" to Jesus' innocence or as a Jewish court alongside a Roman judgment (see Paul before Festus who consulted Agrippa II in Acts 25–26). But Herod Antipas renders no verdict except to send Jesus back to Pilate (v. 15), and there is no hint of moral or judicial seriousness.

11-12—The "royal mockery" which follows belongs with the "mockery" of those who arrested Jesus (22:63-65) and the soldiers at the crucifixion (23:36), fulfilling Jesus' own prophecy (18:32). Thus something very serious is transpiring for those who can see the fulfillment. But for the soldiers and Herod this is sadistic brutality, and the **gorgeous apparel** is more cruel nonsense. Herod goes along with Pilate's little joke, and the two of them become friends. They may put on serious faces for the crowd (v. 15), but this scene is sardonic. Luke is explicitly aware of the enmity which existed between the Roman procurator who ruled Judea and the Herodian tetrarch who wanted to be "King of the Jews." The only basis for their ensuing **friendship** was their participation in this mockery of justice. But all of it is now exposed to the Christian reader who knows that the power and name of the Lord Jesus have been vindicated by God (Acts 4:26-30). Or, as Paul put it, "none of the rulers of this age understood this; for if they had, they would not have crucified the Lord of glory" (1 Cor. 2:8).

Examination and Sentence by Pilate (23:13-25)

Christian interpretation of Jesus' death has long struggled with the profound questions of why it was "necessary" that he die and who was (or is) responsible for his death. Simplistic answers have regularly proved to be theologically misleading and humanly dangerous. After many centuries in which Gentile Christians blamed "the Jews" and often conducted persecutions on Good Friday, historical studies of the trial of Jesus have demonstrated that this was a verdict of the Roman procurator, and the execution was administered according to Roman standards. Any fair assessment of the objective "facts" must conclude that Jesus' death was deemed to be "necessary" by those charged with keeping the peace in Jerusalem and the Roman court adminstered by Pilate was responsible for the execution.

But the Gospel accounts of Jesus' trial are preoccupied with a deeper question of why his death was "necessary" in the will and reign of God, and the question of human responsibility is more than a matter of legal culpability. The story is about God's relationship with the people of God, and the indictment of Israel is a diagnosis of willful defiance of God's reign. The language and actions of these episodes are often extravagant in the intensity of their charges against the Judeans. In Matt. 27:24-25, Pilate declares his innocence of Jesus' blood, "and all the people answered, 'His blood be on us and on our children.' " In John 19:11, Jesus announces to Pilate, "He who delivered me to you has the greater sin." In later generations, these words would fuel anti-Semitic hatreds, but in the Gospels they are prophetic indictments and calls to repentance, Jews speaking to Jews. Even such terrifying words belong within the severe traditions of incrimination on the part of the scriptural prophets. History is more than facts. It is a call to repentance in which heaven and earth are witnesses against a rebellious and stubborn people (see Deut. 31-34; Isaiah 5–6, Jeremiah 22–23).

Luke's account of Jesus' trial has generally been read as an attempt to exculpate Pilate and incriminate the Jews, but it would be more accurate to say that Luke holds everyone responsible for Jesus' death—from Judas to Peter and from the religious leaders to Herod and Pilate and even to the people who have been Jesus' defenders for so long. Peter's threefold denial is not simply equated with Judas's betrayal, but both are culpable. So also the people's threefold denunciation of Jesus (vv. 18, 21, 23) is not the same as the murderous scheming of the religious leaders. The sequence of events is such that the people reappear on the scene just in time to be implicated by the charges against Jesus. Like Peter they are suddenly unable to defend Jesus, but they are all party to his death.

Pilate is also implicated. Even if Acts 4:26-27 did not confirm that he and Herod were "gathered together against the Lord and against his Anointed," Pilate's conduct of the trial is a shameful betrayal of Roman law. In 23:4, he declares that he finds no crime, almost as if to mock the vehement accusers from the chief priests. After the absurd scenes in Herod's court, Pilate declares Jesus innocent three more times and declares plans to **release** him (vv. 14, 20, 22). This is already quadruple jeopardy. What would the Roman jurists think of such disregard of procedures (see Acts 22:29; 25:11-12; 26:32) and indulgence of the will of the mob (see Acts 21:30-36; 22:22; 23:12-25)? Finally, this Roman procurator who "wills" to release Jesus (v. 20) delivers him up **to their will** (v. 25), releasing someone charged with **insurrection and murder.** The will is apparently theirs, but the verdict is his. The execution is Roman, and even if it is true that he was now unable to stop the mob, what kind of excuse would that be to his superiors? What would happen to "the Roman order" in such a case? And if Pilate is finally exposed as unable to do his duty, whose will is actually being done in the story?

13-16—Pilate is the one who summons **the chief priests and the rulers and the people.** This is the first time that **the people** have been on the scene since they were listening to Jesus teach in the temple (21:38). They have not even been mentioned, since the chief priests and the scribes devised the betrayal in their absence (see 22:2, 6). But now in Pilate's court, Jesus' accusers have less to fear from **the people.** The chief priests and their crowds have even implicated "the people" for being "stirred up" by Jesus (23:5), and Pilate opens with a restatement of that charge. The people would be in a poor position to defend Jesus against the **charges** their own leaders brought without confirming thereby that some kind of insurrection against authority was developing.

First-century Jewish sources remember Pilate as one who baited the religious leadership and lost control more than once when his taunt went too far. Philo of Alexandria described him as "naturally inflexible, a blend of self-will and relentlessness" who put the peace at risk by bringing a statue of the emperor into Jerusalem, "not so much to honour Tiberius as to annoy the multitude." Finally he backed down out of fear that they would "expose the rest of his conduct as governor by stating in full the briberies, the insults, the robberies, the outrages and wanton injuries, the executions without trial constantly repeated, the ceaseless and supremely grievious cruelty" (*Embassy to Gaius* 299-304). Josephus confirms this reputation with two stories in which Pilate insulted and violated Jewish religious traditions, one resulting in a successful popular demonstration against him and another concluding with his soldiers beating the people into submission (*War* 2.172-177).

Luke joins this chorus of criticism of Pilate as one who taunts the leaders and insults the people. Here he depicts Pilate baiting Jesus' accusers one more time, even appealing to Herod, whose mockery is now cited as justice. In Mark 15:8-10 Pilate was explicitly teasing them for their "envy." But if Luke agrees that Pilate was only posturing to make them squirm, then his summons of the people with the accusers is a further sarcastic touch which catches the people off guard. The people have been emphatically Jesus' defenders against the high priests (see the discussion at 19:47-48), but now Pilate is taunting them and the leaders who have implicated them. Or perhaps Luke's Pilate was actually moving to assert his authority by letting Jesus off with a beating (see also Acts 16:22-23; 22:24). But then the irony is that he has lost control already.

18-25—Before the Roman court, all the Judeans stand **together,** but their strange unity is expressed in rejection of Jesus. Luke does not explain why they would call for Pilate to **release Barabbas** instead of Jesus (see Mark 15:6), although the scribes that copied Luke's text apparently added v. 17 to correct this omission. The scene is strange in part because Barabbas was already in prison for an **insurrection** which had occurred **in the city and for murder.** He was an established threat, not merely accused of possibly causing trouble. In Mark (15:11, 15), the chief priests "stirred up the people" to demand Barabbas, and Pilate wanted "to satisfy the crowd." But in Luke, this has become a naked struggle of wills over whom Pilate will **release** (Gk: *apolyein*, vv. 16, 18, 20, 22), and whose "will" (vv. 20, 25), **demand** (vv. 23, 24), or **voice** (v. 23) will prevail.

As in John's Gospel (18:29-31, 38; 19:8; 19:16), Pilate declares him not guilty three times and then capitulates to the crowd. Luke identifies the **third time** (v. 22) explicitly and indicates that at least by the second time Pilate did **desire** (Gk: *thelein*, see the discussion on 13:31-35) to release Jesus. His first verdict in 23:4 is not added to the number, and it was part of his taunting of them anyway. But the point is clear that he could not maintain control, and finally he did not get his "will." This pattern fits well with the accounts of Philo and Josephus of his cruelty and ineffectiveness.

But was this the **will** of "the people" who joined the high priests in fighting Pilate? Like Peter in 22:54-61, they are depicted as crying out with increasing vehemence in threefold denial. Luke's fondness for repeating a word of direct address underscores this intensity, **"Crucify, crucify him!"** (see also 10:41; 13:34; 22:31). But the tragic element is also apparent to the reader who knows that "the people" have been Jesus' allies since he entered Jerusalem (19:47-48). Their lamenting is about to begin (23:27) as they realize what they have done and its possible consequences (27:28-30). For the moment, therefore, the only will which seems to be accomplished is that of Jesus' adversaries. To say that Pilate **delivered** Jesus **to their will** is a verdict on the scene parallel to Jesus' word at the arrest, "This is your hour, and the power of darkness" (22:53).

The Execution of the Righteous Christ of God (23:26-56)

As soon as Pilate capitulates to the "will" of the crowd, Jesus is **led away** to be crucified. There is no Roman scourging of the prisoner or mockery of him as "the King of the Jews" (Mark 15:16-20). The Roman soldiers are surely the executioners who control the details (vv. 26, 36, 47, 52), and Pilate's sarcasm is evident once again in the charge posted over Jesus' head, **"This is the King of the Jews"** (v. 38). But the drama of the story of Jesus' death is invested in the interplay between Jesus and the variety of people who surround him as he dies.

Several commentators have complained that Luke has only imitated the conventions of martyrdoms. Such an assessment at least helps the reader recognize that the story is told more to instruct than simply to inform about "the facts," and it demonstrates again that Luke does not invest Jesus' death with meanings of "sacrifice" or "expiation for sin." But the instruction is not mere moral warning or an invitation to imitation. It is rather a lesson in "seeing and hearing," discerning the tragic blindness and deafness of those who ridicule Jesus in words too true, observing the remorse, stunned silence, and repentance of the people who are now party to this death, and beholding the regal authority and declarations of the Christ of God and Chosen One in the midst of the apparent triumph of chaos.

The relationships among the various groups, therefore, are critical to the dynamic of the narrative. Jesus' words punctuate the story with constant clarity as to what is truly "happening" in God's will and plan, while the words of his adversaries are a foil, ironically filled with truth. And "the people" who have just joined in calling three times for Jesus' crucifixion (vv. 13-25) now come to a new realization of the tragedy, first **lamenting** with the **women** (v. 27), then standing by **watching** while he is derided (v. 35), and finally **returning** in remorse **when they saw what had taken place** (v. 48). The centurion's verdict on Jesus as **innocent** or "righteous" (v. 47) is the decisive disclosure for the people and the reader. It confirms both Jesus' true identity in the midst of all the accusations and the profound tragedy of his death for Israel.

If there is a tradition of martyrdom behind Luke's telling, the torture and murder of "the righteous one" in Wisdom 2–5 could well be the paradigm. But Luke does not merely tell a moralistic example story. This is a "theodicy," a testing of the righteous one who "professes to have knowledge of God and calls himself a child of the Lord" (Wis. 2:13) and a trial of God: "Let us see if his words are true and let us test what will happen at the end of his life; for if the righteous man is God's son, he will help him, and will deliver him from the hand of his adversaries. . . . Let us test him with insult and torture. . . . Let us condemn him to a shameful death" (Wis. 2:17-20).

"They will see, and will have contempt for him, but the Lord will laugh them to scorn. After this they will become dishonored corpses . . . because he will dash them speechless to the ground. . . . They will speak to one another in repentance. . . . So it was we who strayed from the way of truth" (Wis. 4:18-19; 5:3, 6).

In Luke's telling, the death of Jesus is a tragedy for Israel because it is a blind and willful challenge to the reign and righteousness of God.

Jesus' Oracle of the Coming Judgment (23:26-31)

Luke begins and ends this pericope with details also found in Mark, the mention of **Simon of Cyrene** (Mark 15:21) and the two criminals (Mark 15:27; see also Luke 23:39-43). But these are merely context for Jesus' prophetic oracle to the **great multitude of the people and of women.** In parallel with Jesus' oracle of lament on his arrival in Jerusalem (19:41-44), only Luke relates this oracle, and it offers a decisive perspective on all that follows. The fate of Jerusalem is at stake in the "visitation" of the Messiah, and now his impending death is a dire omen for the **daughters of Jerusalem** and their **children.**

26—This verse is adapted from Mark 15:20b-21. In Mark, "they" who lead him out to crucifixion are the Roman soldiers who have been scourging and mocking Jesus. In Luke, **they** would at first seem to be the people to whom Pilate delivered Jesus to "their will" (v. 25). Speculations about why Luke did not mention the scourging or mocking by the soldiers (but see vv. 34-38) have often become quite fanciful, but Luke clearly focuses upon Jesus in relationship to the people and leadership of Israel. The Roman soldiers certainly were in charge, but they recede into the background of Luke's story.

Simon of Cyrene is so well known in the tradition that Mark (15:21) supplies the names of his sons. Acts (6:9) also knows of a synagogue of the Cyrenians, apparently in Jerusalem. Thus Simon provides a glimpse of the presence and participation of diaspora North African Jews in the affairs of Roman Palestine. He is also probably regarded as one who fulfilled the call to discipleship to take up the cross and follow (see 9:23; 14:27).

27—The **women** who followed Jesus clearly belong at this point in the story because Jesus is about to address them as **Daughters of Jerusalem** in his traditional oracle. But Luke also refers to the **great multitude of the people** who **followed him,** and it is not clear what kind of "following" this could be. Later, in vv. 35 and 48-49, "the people," "all the multitudes," "all his acquaintances," and "the women who had followed him from Galilee are "watchers" of his death. When they "see," their remorse will be all the more intense. So far, however, it is not clear that this **great multitude of the people** has realized the consequence of their participation in Jesus' sentence to die. Thus they appear to "overhear" Jesus' words to the lamenting women, and his oracle is a severe prophetic diagnosis of what all of this complex process means before God and for them.

28-31—The structure of the oracle is the same as 19:41-44, a declaration of "not this, but this" (19:42; 23:28), followed by a series of predictions of consequences (**For . . . the days are coming when,** 19:43-44a; 23:29-30), and concluded with an indictment showing that the calamities arise from their (your) error (19:44b; 23:31). The oracle is also filled with scriptural allusions and prophetic pathos. This is memory material which could well go back to Jesus or to very early Christian interpretation of Jesus in scriptural terms. In Luke's narrative, the meaning of the oracle is its profound declaration that Jesus' death is more a tragedy for Israel than for the Messiah himself. Jesus has already wept for Jerusalem and her children (19:41-44; 13:34-35), and now he knows that his prophetic warnings will reach their dire consequences.

The language is again thoroughly scriptural (see 19:41-44). **Daughters of Jerusalem** is more than an apt phrase for these women (see Song of Sol. 1:5; 2:7; 5:16; 8:4; and especially Jer. 9:17-22, "Hear, O women, the word of the Lord . . . teach to your daughters a lament," and 2 Sam. 1:24, "Ye daughters of Israel, weep over Saul"). The phrasing **do not weep . . . but weep** recalls Jesus' earlier word to his disciples, "Do not rejoice . . . but rejoice" (10:20). The ominous announcement that **the days are coming** is also a prophetic refrain (see Jer. 7:32; 16:14; 38:31,

LXX [MT 31:31]; and see Luke 5:35; 19:43; 21:23). The blessed state of the barren means that they are those who have no children to suffer or die, and this is a common theme in Greek accounts of human suffering. In Israel, however, it is also a direct counterpoint to the assurances to the barren one in Isa. 54:1-10 that she will yet bear children. The cry **to the mountains** and **the hills** "**Cover us**," "**Fall on us**" is drawn from another ancient prophetic oracle, Hos. 10:8 (see also Rev. 6:16; 9:6).

The concluding statement about the **green wood** and the **dry** (see also Ezek. 17:24) is filled with ambiguity. Many commentators regard this as a statement of God's righteousness, as in Prov. 11:31, "If the righteous is requited on earth, how much more the wicked and the sinner!" Or, to paraphrase, "If God allows this to happen to the Messiah, what would God do to such transgressors?" Such a sentiment is consistent with the peril of divine wrath which is mounting in the story. But it seems better to follow the parallel structure of 19:41-44 as outlined above and to regard the "they" as the same impersonal "they" who are leading Jesus to his death. Then the contrast is between the present time when "they" perform such an atrocity in an era of relative prosperity ("the green tree") and the harsh future days ("the dry") of the Roman destruction of Jerusalem. The sense of the phrase is, "Since they do this now, the terrible consequences of the coming days of the Jerusalem siege will surely come upon them."

32—The mention of the **criminals** moves the story forward to the crucifixion site. It ties the narrative back to the scriptural fulfillment mentioned in 22:37 ("he was reckoned with transgressors") and anticipates the elaboration of the scene in vv. 39-43. The concrete realities of Jesus' impending death are the crucial context for his oracles of judgment (see also 13:31-35; 19:41-44; 21:1-38).

The Crucifixion of the Messiah of God (23:33-38)

Luke's account of the crucifixion generally follows Mark's sequence (except v. 36), but it is so thoroughly retold that many commentators argue for an independent source. Luke's account also omits such interesting details of Mark as the "blaspheming" of those who shook their heads and said, "Aha! You who would destroy the temple and build it in three days!" (Mark 15:29). But attempts to reconstruct an alternative source have generally obscured Luke's distinctive emphases in this story. Wherever Luke may have derived the particular details of this account, they contribute to the third evangelist's witness to the meaning of Jesus' life and death within Israel's history, and the roles of the various groups surrounding the cross continue to enact the drama of divided Israel which Luke has been tracing throughout the narrative. This section, therefore, confirms and illumines Jesus' death to be a tragedy for Israel and also the means of God's salvation.

The interpretation of this passage depends on such double vision, observing the terrible miscarriage of justice in the blind vengeance of Jesus' adversaries and noting the faith of Jesus in God. The story means completely different things if interpreted by the bitter sarcasm of Jesus' accusers than if seen through the eyes of the Messiah who knows that God's will and plan of salvation are at work. Between those perspectives stand the people, "watching" and slowly coming to the realization of their own terrible deed. Their second sight is the reader's clue to observing the details for signs that things are not as they appear.

32-34—Since v. 25, Luke has been referring to **them** (see also vv. 26, 29, 30, 31) which is probably "all of them" who cried out for his death (v. 18) to whom Pilate responded (vv. 20, 21, 22, 23, 24, 25). This group seems to include all the religious leaders and the people to the point that it almost sounds as if it is they who also **cast lots** for his **garments.** Mark's intervening description of the mockery by the Roman soldiers (15:16-20) identifies the group that casts lots more credibly as the Romans. But Luke's emphasis is that "they" whose will was served (v. 25) now **crucified him** (v. 33) and **cast lots to divide his garments** while Jesus prayed for them (v. 34). Their "will" is being carried to its grim conclusion, while Jesus' word to the women (vv. 28-31) and his prayer (v. 34) alert the reader to the dire consequences of their unholy alliance.

Verse 34 requires special textual comment because it is not well supported in the manuscript tradition. In several venerable and diverse manuscripts, this saying of Jesus is absent from the narrative. It is present, however, in other manuscripts. The external evidence suggests that this was a traditional word of Jesus which was inserted into this context after Luke wrote the narrative.

This word of Jesus, however, must be defended as authentic to the narrative. Its manuscript support is significant, but the argument rests more on internal grounds. The theme of the "ignorance" of those who are executing Jesus is unusual by the standard of the other accounts. But this concept will prove crucial to Luke (see also Acts 3:17; 13:27; 17:30; and 7:60). It is more probable that early scribes would have dropped this plea for forgiveness of Israel than that so deft a word of commentary would have been added by a copyist. The anti-Jewish tendencies of the scribes, especially in the "Western" tradition of manuscripts of Luke-Acts, have been documented in other passages. Of course, the interpretation of Luke's account as a whole cannot rest on the less stable ground of this verse. Jesus' prayer to the Father (23:46) for those who "do not know" is a revelation of his regal authority and of his prophetic insight in the presence of Israel's tragic ignorance. These are all central concerns for Luke.

The scriptural allusions in these verses are also crucial to the "meaning" of an act which is apparently absurd. Crucifixion was a severe form of execution, generally reserved for slaves and insurrectionists. The soldiers probably did gamble for the victim's last effects as part of the humiliation, but this was memorable to the Christians because it also fulfilled Ps. 22:18. Mark's account alludes to this psalm even more explicitly with Jesus' cry of dereliction (Mark 15:34; Ps. 22:1). Luke also has described the **mockery** and the **watching** of those who stand by in the terms of v. 7 of the psalm (21:8, LXX). Similarly, the mention of the two **criminals** is probably another fulfillment of Jesus' earlier reference (22:37) to Isa. 53:12, "he was numbered with transgressors." These are more than the "facts" of history; this is the enactment of prophecy, even if people do not know it.

Ignorance is not innocence (see the discussion at 9:45). When Peter in Acts 3:17 notes that "you acted in ignorance, as did also

your rulers," he still calls for repentance. Israel is held accountable. They have fulfilled the Scriptures by condemning Jesus
because they did not understand them (Acts 13:27). Luke's narrative instructs the reader about not repeating the "times of ignorance" which are thoroughly exposed in the light of Jesus' resurrection (see Acts 17:30), and the speeches in Acts will stress
that God will "forgive" or "overlook" such sin (Acts 2:38; 3:19;
13:38; 17:30). But this ignorance is genuinely tragic, filled with
pathos and remorse. The people are just now at the point of
realizing what they have done, as Peter was after his third denial
when the cock crowed and the Lord looked at him (22:60-61).

35-38—From v. 35 forward, it is again clear that those who
stand at the foot of the cross are playing different roles in the
human tragedy of this execution. The people are **watching.** This
watching (Gk: *theōrein*) is like that at a spectacle, an observing
which is distinguished from the adamant derision of the rulers
(contrast Ps. 22:7 as read by Mark 15:29). What are the people
"seeing" (see the discussion at 23:48-49)?

The "rulers" who scoff speak with the ignorance of blind vengeance (see 23:13; 24:20, Acts 3:17; 4:26; 13:27), posed in the
language of logic, **"Let him save himself, if he is the Christ!"**
Such attacks are also an enactment of scriptural roles. The traditions of Wisdom 2–5 cited at the beginning of this section furnish the commentary: "Let us test what will happen at the end
of his life; for if the righteous man is God's son he will help him.
. . . Thus they reasoned, but they were led astray, for their
wickedness blinded them, and they did not know the secret purposes of God" (Wis. 2:17-22). Their logic also gives them away
because they grant that **he saved others.** They also state the minor
premise as a real condition, "Since he is the Messiah of God, the
elect one." Much as the devil in 4:1-13 granted the reality of
Jesus' being the Son of God, these accusers are testing that reality.
Of course, their test implies a sarcastic statement of the reality,
as the devil's implied a deceptive acknowledgment. But they miss
the point that it is because he is the Savior and the Chosen
Messiah of God that Jesus cannot save himself and still be faithful
to the will and plan of God according to the Scriptures.

Luke certainly agrees that **"He saved others"** (see 7:50; 8:48, 50; 17:19; 18:42). Furthermore, the title **Christ of God** or "Anointed One of God" or "Messiah of God" is central to Luke's identification of Jesus (see 9:20). God designated Jesus as Christ before his birth and anointed him with such authority for his work (see the discussion at 2:11; 3:21-22; 4:1-13). Jesus the Messiah is the Savior (2:11) and the Son of God (4:41). Only in Luke does the voice from heaven at the transfiguration also confirm, "This is my Son, my Chosen!" (9:35). But for Luke, the Chosen One is preeminently the Servant of Isa. 42:1 who will suffer (see the discussion at 9:35, and see Acts 3:13, 26; 4:27, 30; 8:30-35; and Luke 22:37). The rulers have summed up Luke's whole understanding of the identity of Jesus and stated it as reality, but without understanding or believing their own words. Jesus is executed on the same grounds as the Christian confession of who he is.

The mockery of **the soldiers** picks up Pilate's first inquiry (see the discussion at 23:3), and the **vinegar** drink is another cruelty which fulfills a scriptural detail from Ps. 69:21. The charge above his head again states the reality, **"This is the King of the Jews."** The demonstrative pronoun "This one!" is probably Luke's only addition to Pilate's **inscription** (see 9:35). The sarcasm of "the rulers of this age" who unknowingly "crucified the Lord of glory" (1 Cor. 2:8) does not obscure the truth for the Christian reader, but it raises the intensity of the theodicy. This is a challenge to the justice of God. Jesus is truly the anointed Davidic king of God's own choosing. What will God do to those who kill him?

The Royal Clemency of Jesus (23:39-43)

While Jesus hangs dying, the fate of the world that surrounds him hangs in the balance of divine justice. Only Luke tells the story of the conversation between the three who were crucified, and it is a revelation of how this "Christ of God" and "King of the Jews" exercises God's reign of justice and mercy. It is also a turning point in the passion narrative, because it is the first direct indication of faith in this dying Messiah. After the first **criminal** has repeated the mockery (v. 39), the second rebukes him, declares Jesus innocent, and pleads for his blessing. Jesus' authority as Savior and his "kingly power" are thus revealed intact while the rulers rail at him and the people watch.

39—The **criminals** are called "the robbers" in Matt. 27:44, which is a term that Josephus uses for brigands or insurrectionists. But none of the Gospels indicates the charges against them. Only Luke reports this exchange, and it begins exactly where the rulers ended with a taunt to Jesus to **save** himself as the Messiah. The criminal only adds, **"and us!"** His question both assumes and challenges Jesus' identity as the Messiah. The bitter irony is that he repeats the mockery of the executioners. He is right that Jesus can save them, if not himself, but he does not speak in faith.

40-41—The second criminal **rebukes** such sarcasm as a dangerous taunt of God's justice. He is a condemned prisoner who repents and accepts the verdict of their execution as "righteous" (Gk: *dikaios*) because it is a worthy recompense for their deeds. He no longer has no cause for flattery, but he can see that Jesus is innocent, having done nothing "wrong" or "out of place" (Gk: *atopos*).

42-43—His plea to Jesus is **"Remember me when you come into your kingdom."** It is an insight of faith, quite contrary to apparent reality. In form, it is the petition of someone who sees a friend rise to high office and looks for benefits. The point of the execution is to quash this king and his kingdom, yet this second criminal is not only confident of Jesus' innocence but of God's justice. He is not speaking of Jesus' "coming with power" as at the last judgment, but of his "entering into a reign" as in an exaltation to rule (19:12). This vision is fully in accord with Luke's conviction that the resurrection and assumption of Jesus' into heaven was God's vindication of Jesus and exaltation to rule (see Acts 2:31-33).

Jesus' also confirms this with the word of promise to the criminal. He is one whose ministry is salvation **"today!"** (see especially 19:5, 9; and see 2:11; 4:21; 5:26; 13:32-33; 22:34, 61). This time reference should not be pressed too rigidly into a full-blown picture of how those who are dead "in Christ" may already be "with Christ" (see Rom. 6:5-11). But Luke does present this as a scene of final judgment in which the faith of the criminal is saving faith, and the Christian piety of this story is apparent. This is a salvation for heaven announced on earth (see 15:7, 10), because Jesus' reign is about to be established in heaven as well as on earth (Acts 1:8-10; 3:21; 7:55). The word which is used in this passage is **Paradise**, referring to a royal garden of bliss (see 2 Chron. 33:20, LXX; 2 Cor. 12:3; Rev. 2:7, the Garden of Eden restored), and Jesus already possesses the authority to open heaven's gate to those who see and trust God's reign at work in him. His word of clemency is itself an act of the kingdom of God, **today.**

Much has been written about the saving significance of Jesus' death in Mark's Gospel, and Luke's account has often been criticized for its lack of language of sacrifice. Luke does not describe Jesus' death as "saving" on the grounds that his *life* was given "as a ransom for many" (cf. Mark 10:45). But Jesus' faith in God is unshaken throughout this passion story, and those who have faith in the faithful Jesus receive the saving benefits of his reign, even as he dies.

The Death of the Righteous One (23:44-49)

Jesus' death is a saving event in Luke because he dies as the "righteous one" whose trust in God's promises is saving faith. God is the one who will raise Jesus from the dead, and faith in the faithful Jesus is faith in God's righteousness, i.e., trust in God's promises. Paul testifies that "the righteousness of God has been manifested apart from law, although the Law and the prophets bear witness to it, the righteousness of God through faith in Jesus Christ for all who believe" (Rom. 3:21-22). This "faith in Jesus Christ" is also the "faith of Jesus Christ" because God's righteousness and faithfulness are revealed in Jesus' death and resurrection.

Paul enters this Christian conversation from the point of view of God's act, paying special attention to God's freedom from the Law of Moses, but granting the concurrence of the Law and the Prophets. Luke focuses upon Jesus' display of faithfulness and emphasizes the fulfillment of the law, prophets, and psalms (24:44). Both Luke and Paul respect early Christian traditions which speak of Jesus' death as "expiatory sacrifice" for sin (Rom.

3:25, Acts 20:28), but their faith in God's salvation is grounded in Jesus' resurrection to life (Rom. 4:25; 5:10).

Luke probably had not read Paul, but both of them were party to a complex discussion of the Scriptures. Luke's scriptural resources for interpreting Jesus' death are Psalm 31 in this passage and Psalm 16 in Acts 2 and 13, and the discussion of the death of the righteous in Wis. 2:12—3:10 is at least a parallel interpretation of the psalms, if not a direct source for Luke. The larger context of these passages is significant for understanding Luke's usage of specific verses, which also demonstrates that the early Christians were not simply searching for "proof texts."

In all of these scriptures, the faithfulness of God is trusted by the righteous in the face of death. In Peter's sermons in Acts, "David's" confidence that God will not "let thy Holy One see corruption" (2:27; 13:35; Ps. 16:10; LXX, 15:10; see Wis. 2:22) proves to be a prophetic declaration of the resurrection of Jesus. Jesus' proclamation of clemency to the trusting criminal (v. 43) and his final word of resignation to God (v. 46) display his faith in such promises of God. But the broader testimonies of Psalm 31 and Wisdom 2–3 also support Luke's interpretation of this execution of the Righteous One who trusts God as a test of God by Jesus' adversaries.

Mark is again Luke's literary source, but in Mark 15:34, Jesus' cry of dereliction is a citation of Ps. 22:2, another lament which still expects divine vindication. Mark links this with the confusion of whether Jesus called for Elijah and accompanies his death with a wordless shout. Some commentators have speculated that Luke was shocked by this intensity and replaced it with a pious martyrdom. But Jesus' unswerving confidence is more than a moral example because Jesus' death is now a story both about his faith and about the human tragedy of faithlessness which surrounds him.

44-45—The **darkness** of broad daylight and the rending of the **temple curtain** are traditional portents associated with Jesus' death. This is not a normal solar eclipse—it is the season of the full moon of Passover—and explanations about local storms of wind and dust which darken the sky and could tear curtains miss the point. Luke also does not explain whether the rending of the veil meant the impending destruction of the temple or new access to the sanctuary for worship (see Heb. 9:6-28). The ancients regarded such cosmic signs to be divine, but often ambiguous. Josephus's reports of many portents preceding the destruction of the temple included "a star, resembling a sword" and a comet, both of which were present over the city for a year, the impossible event of a huge gate in the temple opening "of its own accord," and a voice from a clamorous host announcing, "We are departing hence!" (*War* 6.288-300). People disagreed about the meaning of such signs, but they were generally ominous. So also, the signs of divine displeasure are clear if the sun is darkened or if the temple veil is rent, whether before the holy of holies (Exod. 26:31-35; Lev. 21:23) or "the holy place" (Exod. 26:37; 38:18; Num. 3:26).

46—Jesus' last word is a prayer drawn from Ps. 31:5 (LXX: 30:6) of the prayer book of Israel. The address of God as **Father** is not in the psalm, but it has characterized Jesus' prayers throughout the Gospel (11:2; 22:42; 23:34; see the comments at 10:21). It also fits with Wis. 2:16, where the adversaries charge that the righteous one "boasts that God is his father." The psalm (31:5), however, attests the "faithful God" (see also Deut. 32:5), and this confidence is central to the whole question of the justice of God in the death of Jesus. The adversaries challenge God's righteousness by killing the righteous one, and Jesus proves to be righteous by trusting in God's promise of salvation.

The word **spirit** (Gk: *pneuma*) is in the psalm verse, and the word "expire" (Gk: *ekpneuein*) is in Mark 15:37, but only Luke captures the wordplay by combining these sources. The result is that Jesus' death is even more explicitly a relinquishing of **spirit.** Luke has stressed the power and presence of the Holy Spirit in the anointing of Jesus and the empowering of his ministry (3:21; Acts 10:38; Luke 4:1, 14, 18; 10:21). Even his **loud voice** may be a mark of inspired speech (see 1:42). This is Jesus' "exodus," which he is fulfilling in Jerusalem because he is "the righteous one" whose "departure" (9:31, Gk: *exodus*) proves to be God's means of fulfilling the promise of resurrection. Wisdom 3:1-4 articulates the same conviction in the language of immortality, lacking only the reality of Jesus' death:

> But the souls of the righteous are in the hand of God, and no torment will ever touch them. In the eyes of the foolish they seem to have died, and their departure was thought to be an affliction, and their going from us to be their destruction; but they are at peace. For though in the sight of men they were punished, their hope is full of immortality.

47—The centurion's confession in Mark is the central Christological revelation of Jesus as the "Son of God," even if the Roman soldier may not have understood the implications of his own words. The same is true for Luke, but now the centurion declares, **"Certainly this man was innocent**/righteous." The Greek word *dikaios* could mean merely that Jesus had been wrongfully executed, which would be small comfort now. Certainly it would not be a credible defense of Roman innocence. But Luke supplies further clues that the reader is to understand this as a full-blown revelation, no matter what the centurion thought.

First, following the tradition of Mark, this centurion spoke "when he had seen" what had taken place. Thus far only God and the readers of Luke's tragic tale have been privileged to see and hear what is "truly" happening, while the people have been "watching" (v. 35) from the side. But this "seeing" immediately follows Jesus "expiring" (Gk: *exepneusen. idōn* . . . ; literally: "he expired. Seeing this, the centurion . . ."). Perhaps someone is finally able to "see" beyond the way things appear.

Second, Luke states that the centurion **praised God.** This is most remarkable, since nothing is known about this soldier, his religion, or his view of the God of Israel. The statement, however, commends whatever he will say next as a word of doxology for what God has now done (see 5:26; 7:16). His emphatic word **certainly** (Gk: *ontōs;* Mark 15:39: *alēthōs;* see Luke 4:23, 24, 25: "doubtless," "truly," "in truth") further underscores the truth of what he is about to say for those who can hear it (see Wis. 3:9).

Third, the demonstrative pronoun **this** (Gk: *houtos*) has been used by Luke on the lips of Jesus' accusers to declare his titles: "this is the Messiah of God, the Chosen One!" (23:35) and "this is the King of the Jews!" (23:38). The centurion is not merely saying that Jesus is innocent, but at least: "This man was righteous!" Luke elsewhere understands "the Righteous One" as a Christological title which is explicitly connected with Jesus' execution (Acts 3:14; 7:52; 22:14). The identification would be even more explicit here if the centurion said "the Righteous One," but neither does he say "the Son of God" in Mark. In both cases, the centurion may still be announcing a title without using a definite article. Perhaps both evangelists do not wish to overstate what the centurion actually said or thought he said. But both agree that his word was an oracle of God for those who could hear through its slight ambiguity.

48-49—The crowds who have gathered to "watch" (v. 35) now have "watched" or "observed" both Jesus' death and the centurion's testimony. Luke's play on the words for "seeing" continues, and the only clue that they have truly "observed" or "seen" something is that they **return beating their breasts.** The text does not say **returned home** (RSV), but simply **returned,** which could be an image of "turning around" or "repenting" (Gk: *hypostrephein*), and their **beating their breasts** at least means remorse. Full repentance of the people of Judea and Jerusalem will be evident at Pentecost, preceded by their being "cut to the heart" (Acts 2:37-38), but these "crowds" at least seem to have a new level of tragic insight. Like Peter who went out and "wept bitterly" (22:62), which was part of his "turning again" (22:32, Gk: *epistrephein*), the people who have three times joined the rulers calling for Jesus' death (23:18, 21, 23) have now followed the wailing women (v. 27), stood silently watching his mockery, and observed this confession by the centurion. Their remorse is not empty.

Only Luke includes Jesus' **acquaintances** with the **women from Galilee** who **followed** him faithfully. They stand together **at a distance.** But they not only "watched what happened" like the crowds, they **saw these things** (RSV) or, more literally, "they stood in order to see these things" (Gk: *horōsai*). It is not clear exactly what they did yet see, but they were there to see. This word play on "seeing" will continue with abandon in Luke 24 when "their eyes were opened and they recognized him" (e.g., 24:31).

Perhaps only the Christian reader who knows how the story ends can see through the gloomy darkness of tragedy, blindness, and ignorance which marks Jesus' death.

The Burial (23:50-56)

This is a quiet interlude in the intense drama of Jesus' death and resurrection. The details deserve comment, but Jesus is dead. Nothing appears to be happening except routine human responsibilities, and even faithful Joseph and the women may no longer be expecting more than the completion of a proper burial. The tragic irony which has pervaded the narrative thus far, however, is about to take a new turn. The irony begins to veil and disclose hope. The ignorance and blindness of the adversaries in the narrative no longer fuels the mockery of accusers. They are gone. Their "hour and the power of darkness" (22:53) has reached its end. Now the story explores the sadness and disappointment of the faithful. But, gratefully, appearances still deceive. The story will not end in tragedy.

50-53—Joseph of Arimathea's credentials are as lofty as those of Zechariah and Elizabeth (1:6) or Simeon and Anna (2:25-27, 36-39). A **good and righteous** person is found in Israel in its darkest hour, and he is explicitly from a "Judean city" or a "city of the Jews." Although the passion narrative has indicted everyone with various levels of culpability, the point has not been to document Israel's absolute depravity. Joseph is not merely someone who was removed from the action. The **Council** in which he is a member is apparently the Sanhedrin (see 22:66; Mark 15:1, 43), indicating that even the group of Jesus' accusers were not all of one mind or type. But within Israel there have always been "the righteous" or "the faithful" (see Noah in Gen. 6:5-8; Abraham in Gen. 18:22—19:29; Elijah in 1 Kings 19:18 and Rom. 11:4). In this case, Joseph's **righteousness** is demonstrated both by his not consenting to **their purpose and deed** (see 23:25) and his faithful expectation of **the kingdom of God.** Like the righteous Israelites in Luke 1–2, Joseph trusts God's promises.

Luke trims Mark's version of the request of Pilate to a few words (contrast Mark 15:43-45). Perhaps Joseph's high standing gave him access to the procurator, but Luke offers no explanation and no comment on Pilate's response. The burial in a newly hewn tomb probably reflects his economic status (Mark 15:43 calls him "respected" or "noble"). At any rate, once an executed person is dead, the body must be taken down and buried before sunset, lest the land be defiled (Deut. 21:22-23).

54-56—Luke follows Mark in noting that **the women** observed or watched the tomb and how the body was laid, but the women are not named until Easter (24:10). In Mark 15:47—16:1, the lists of names can even be compared. But the point is still clear that these women have observed **the tomb** and **the body** so that their "perplexity" at Easter (24:3-4) did not arise from misinformation.

Luke draws attention to the Jewish festivals and rituals and rounds off the whole section with an affirmation of their careful observance of the Sabbath **commandment.** Like the "righteous" worthies in Luke 1–2, these people are all fully observant of the commandments and ordinances (see 1:6, 23; 2:22, 24, 27, 39, 41, and see 4:16). The reference to **the day of Preparation** was explained in Mark 15:42 as "the day before the Sabbath," but Luke sharpens this by saying **the Sabbath was** "shining forth." This is probably an allusion to the lighting of the candles at sunset on the evening of the Sabbath.

Perhaps the whole scene is intended to be merely a detailed account of the events, but the details of the **day of Preparation** and the "dawning of Sabbath" and the faithful observance of the commandments of God invite a more poetic sense. Luke's dramatic description of the early dawn of Easter with all the dazzling appearances (24:1-11) will soon demonstrate that God has also been at work in the day of Preparation. On the other side of this sad Sabbath rest, the faithful who have observed the commandments in expectation of God's kingdom will not be disappointed.

■ The Vindication and Exaltation of the Messiah (24:1-53)

"Thus it is written that the Christ should suffer and on the third day rise from the dead, and that repentance and forgiveness of sins should be preached in his name to all nations, beginning from Jerusalem. You are witnesses of these things."

(Luke 24:46-48)

The four Gospel narratives converge in their details and sequence of the story of the death of Jesus. They also begin their accounts of the resurrection of Jesus with relatively similar stories of the women and disciples at the empty tomb (Matt. 28:1-8; Mark 16:1-8; Luke 24:1-12; John 20:1-13). The empty tomb was probably the end of the story in Mark. From that point forward, however, the Gospels are virtually independent (see the comments at Luke 24:36, 40), just as they were in their accounts of Jesus' childhood or origins at the beginning. The stories of the resurrection offer each of the three evangelists a unique opportunity to summarize the major concerns of the narrative and to underscore the gospel message with the words of the risen Christ. For Luke, the empty tomb is only the beginning of a rich exposition of the resurrection in Luke 24 and in the speeches in Acts.

This material resists ancient and modern methods of historical verification. None of the New Testament writers merely tells of a revivification of Jesus or of a resuscitation of his corpse (see the comments on 7:11-17). Nor do they presume to depict the event of the resurrection itself (see the apocryphal Gospel of Peter 35-42). They understood that Jesus' resurrection was an event of another order. It was the single eschatological occurrence which verified that God would indeed raise the dead, anticipating the last judgment when all things would be transformed (1 Cor. 15:52).

Such distinctions were important in a Jewish and early Christian setting in which people asked, "How are the dead raised? With what kind of body do they come?" (1 Cor. 15:35). And the answers could not be simplistic, "You foolish man! What you sow does not come to life unless it dies. And what you sow is not the body which is to be . . . but God gives it a body as he has chosen" (1 Cor. 15:36-38). All the Gospel accounts display both a profound sense of confidence that Jesus has been raised and an awareness of the mystery of a unique act of God.

This uniqueness limits the usefulness of modern descriptive categories and methods of historical inquiry which are all based on analogies from verified experience. All that the modern historian can establish by the canons of the trade is that Jesus' followers reported their experience of his living, bodily presence.

Luke, however, is intent on testifying to the truth about God, a much larger task than verifying the facts. The whole of Luke 24 may be read as a exposition of the truth of Jesus' resurrection. The story of the empty tomb (vv. 1-12) is retold with some freedom to stress the central themes of Luke's story, and the subsequent episodes on the road to Emmaus (vv. 13-35) and in the commission and departure among the eleven (vv. 36-53) elaborate that truth. All these episodes are reported as occurring on one long day (vv. 1, 13, 33, 36, 44, 50-51).

The truth of the resurrection is that the tragedy of Jesus' death has been transformed into the victory of God's reign in the resurrection. Human willfulness, ignorance, and sin have now been encountered by God's will and power in both judgment and mercy. The decisive clue to the truth lies in **the law of Moses and the prophets and the psalms** (v. 44). There God's "definite plan and foreknowledge" (Acts 2:23) awaited fulfillment and disclosure until the resurrected Jesus **opened their minds to understand the scriptures** (v. 45). What was hidden is now revealed. **Remembering** (vv. 6, 8), **interpreting the Scriptures** (vv. 27, 32, 45), **breaking bread** and **eating fish** (vv. 35, 41-43), **opening the Scriptures** and **their minds** (vv. 31, 32, 45) are all means of revelation, of "seeing and hearing" the truth. And those to whom the truth has been revealed are commissioned as witnesses to all nations of this Messiah's reign (vv. 47-49).

The Empty Tomb (24:1-12)

This wondrous story is foundational for all the Gospels and for subsequent Christian telling. It is an epiphany story in which heavenly messengers confront mere mortals, reveal Jesus to have been raised in accord with his words, and send the witnesses to tell. The details are gripping, lending human interest to the experience, and the angels' message is another recitation of the central Lukan confession of the necessity of Jesus' death. For those who **remember,** this story already begins to make sense out of all that has happened, because God has been at work accomplishing a saving purpose while humanity has tragically been resisting the reign of God's Messiah. Once again the reader shares the knowledge of heaven, seeing and hearing the true meaning of these things while the mere mortals in the story are filled with perplexity, fear, and disbelief.

1-3—The first line is tied directly to 23:56b by a Greek syntactical construction (Gk: *men . . . de;* "first they rested . . . , and then on the first day . . .") so that the women provide a continuous focus of attention from Jesus' death to Easter morning (23:54—24:1). While Mark indicates that "the sun had risen" (16:2), Luke depicts the scene "at the crack of dawn," leaving an impression of a much less clear setting for "seeing" (see 9:32, 34). The women have come to complete a proper burial as Jewish law or "commandment" prescribes (see the comments on "law" at 2:22-24). They do not discuss the obstacle of the circular stone which blocked tombs like a massive wheel in a track (see Mark 16:3), but the absence of the body is the focus. It is "**the body of the Lord Jesus**" which is missing, although one manuscript and some English versions read only **the body.** Luke will further emphasize the bodily character of the resurrection (vv. 37-43), and Jesus' identity as "Lord" reflects the evangelist's Christian faith (see 7:13; 22:61; Acts 1:21; 4:33; 8:16; see also John 20:13).

4-7—The **two men in dazzling apparel** will soon be identified as "angels" (v. 23), but they are also reminiscent of the "two men," Moses and Elijah, who stood with Jesus in his dazzling raiment on the mount of transfiguration (9:29-30; see also Acts 1:10). The "perplexity" of the women is not mere confusion, but being "at a loss," which quickly becomes an occasion for an epiphany (see discussion of Old Testament precedents at 5:1-11). The women's **fear** and **bowing their faces to the ground** indicates immediately that they know they are standing in the presence of divine messengers (see Dan. 7:28; 10:9, 15).

The message is first a reproof, while in Mark 16:6 and Matt. 28:5 the women are reassured. Luke heightens the sense that even as they do the proper things to tend to a burial, they should have known better. They had actually been **seeking** the dead **among the dead.** The irony of the question exposes their ignorance, but now the contrast between appearance and reality is filled with hope. This element of reproof will prove to be thematic to the chapter (see vv. 25, 38, 44, 46). They should have known, because Jesus' words and the Scriptures testify to what God had in mind all along.

The declaration, "He is not here, he has been raised!" should be included in Luke's text although it was omitted from one manuscript and some modern translations. It is a traditional phrase from Mark 16:6, but in Luke it underscores the reproof. They were at a loss in trying to find the body. They did not understand, expect, or believe that Jesus would be alive. Even the passive voice of the verb, "He has been raised!" is crucial because God is the one who has acted.

Now the angelic messengers simply recall Jesus' earlier words to them. Their declaration is the central message of the text. The verification of the truth of the resurrection does not come from detailed evidence of how God did all of this. The command is **"Remember!"** and the content lies in Jesus' passion predictions concerning his suffering as **the Son of man.** Luke's phrasing of these prophecies again underscores their fulfillment. The prediction in 9:22 is especially similar. While 24:7 speaks of Jesus "rising" on the third day (24:7), the earlier passage states more specifically that he will "be raised." Clearly God is the active agent, the one who raised Jesus from the dead (Acts 3:15; 4:10; 10:40; 13:33, etc.). The theme of the necessity of this sequence of events also becomes more clearly the revelation of the determined will of God in the face of human ignorance and opposition (see also 9:43-45; 18:31-34; Acts 13:32-33). Jesus is not merely springing back to life. The death and resurrection of Jesus is an encounter between the reign of God and sinful humans, and God is not mocked.

8-11—These women **remembered his words,** and they returned and told **the eleven** and the others. Although Luke tells the story of Judas's end only in Acts 1:17-18, the number of the "twelve apostles" is already depleted (see the comments at 6:13 and 9:1). Luke identifies the women at the end of the episode (see Mark 16:1). **Mary Magdalene and Joanna** are also mentioned in 8:2, and the second **Mary "of James"** was mentioned in Mark. They did not see the risen Messiah, but their remembrance of his words becomes a moment of revelation. The angelic messengers have not added anything except the crucial reminder that if they remembered and believed what Jesus said, they would not be looking for a corpse. The "seeing" and "remembering" in this scene is all about "believing," and even when the women have "remembered/believed" and "told" the apostles and the others, they are not "believed." Such "disbelief" both heightens the sense of the divine wonder (see also v. 41) and exposes the hardness of the human heart to believe even when a resurrection has taken place (see 16:31; Acts 17:18, 32).

12—This verse also is omitted by one manuscript and some modern English versions, but the textual evidence is overwhelmingly in favor of its inclusion. It extends Luke's ironic theme about the **idle tale** the women have told with Peter's inconclusive visit to the tomb. This picture of Peter running to the tomb is one of the many tantalizing clues that Luke probably knew the traditions or version also used by John, but this is not a literary dependence on John. Both Gospels appear to agree that Peter did not yet believe. Luke notes that he "wondered," leaving the narrative suspenseful for the reader. John 20:8-9 suggests that "the other disciple" who ran ahead saw the burial cloths and "believed; for as yet they did not know the scripture, that he must rise from the dead." In differing ways both Luke and John attest that further appearances (v. 35) and instruction in the Scriptures will be needed for the apostles to believe what the women already accept on the basis of the angels' reminder of Jesus' words.

On the Road to Emmaus (24:13-35)

Luke's literary craft reaches a new height in this story, which is equaled in beauty only in the birth narrative (2:1-20) or in length by the story of Peter and Cornelius (Acts 10–11). The story brims with Christian piety which discerns the risen Lord's presence in the breaking of bread and the opening of the Scriptures. The theme of "seeing" and "not seeing" is woven into the whole episode, but now to the delight of the reader who knows the joyful truth. This is no longer the tragic blindness which incriminates all those who stand at the foot of the cross berating Jesus for being the Christ of God, Chosen One, King of the Jews, and Righteous One (23:35, 37-38, 47). The reader observes the sadness of the faithful who fail to see the wondrous thing that God has done until the risen Messiah makes it known. They are even chided as **foolish** and **slow of heart to believe** (24:25), but this reproof further underscores the wonder of the resurrection.

Luke presents the resurrection of Jesus as the fulfillment of God's scriptural promises in the face of their apparent failure. This story is especially emphatic in its kerygmatic recitation which leads first to the indictment of the people of God and the rulers for complicity in Jesus' death (vv. 19-20). Luke's interpretation of the resurrection is focused on the incomprehensible wonder of God's reign. God even stages the story, first preventing the disciples from seeing (v. 16) and then opening their eyes (v. 31). God is doing "a deed in your days" which "you will never believe, if one declares it to you" (see Acts 13:41; Hab. 1:5). God is not confronting the obdurate unbelief of Jesus' adversaries, but disclosing the disbelief of the disappointed. No one could have anticipated God's deed, even if the Scriptures were clear, because the resurrected Messiah himself must teach the faithful how to read and understand God's scriptural will and plan. Only after the fact of the resurrection will it be possible to grasp God's constancy to the promises made to Israel. God's reign and will are sure. Jesus and his followers are vindicated.

It is futile to attempt to identify Luke's source(s) for this account or to separate the verses into possible pre-Lukan documents. The reference in verse 34 to Jesus' appearance to Simon is intriguing in view of the fact that Luke does not tell such a story. He only narrates Peter's marveling at the empty tomb (see the discussion of textual problem at v. 12). Nothing in the Emmaus narrative would suggest that Cleopas's companion was Peter. Thus Luke has merely shown that he is aware of other stories of resurrection appearances which he does not tell (see 1:1), and this narrative is filled with more dramatic effect and less new information than generally characterizes the Synoptic tradition. This story is a literary whole and not evidently a compilation of sources.

13-17—These verses are unusually repetitive, emphasizing the walking (vv. 13, 15, 17) and talking (vv. 14, 15, 17) as they "go" (Gk: *poreuesthai*, see the discussion at 9:51). The repetitions are not forced. They draw the reader into an extended conversation.

The imperfect tense of the Greek verbs underscores the continuing process. The mention of **Emmaus** is important only in that they must walk "sixty stadia" or **about seven miles** (some manuscripts read 160 stadia). Geographers disagree over which site in Judea Luke had in mind, but Luke's point at the beginning and end of the story is that this was an extended "walk" "on the road," yet close enough so that the disciples could return quickly to Jerusalem (see vv. 13, 33, 35). The conversation is generally about **these things that had happened,** which v. 19 will identify as Jesus' ministry and death and the report of the empty tomb. That is, everything in the story to this point is generally recalled.

Jesus' identity is immediately revealed to the reader, but **their eyes were kept from recognizing him.** The imperfect tense and passive voice of the verb again indicates some duration and probably implies God to be the actor who prevents their seeing, but only for a time (see the discussion of Luke 8:9-10, based on Isa. 6:10). Their blindness is not the work of the devil, preventing salvation (see 8:12), but it is the occasion for an extended instruction to the benefit of the reader who overhears the dialog. Jesus prompts them to repeat the substance of their conversation, and they pause, **looking sad.** It is a favorite Lukan method to add gravity to the narrative by leading questions, signs of emotional intensity, and naming the speaker (see Acts 2:12; 4:7; 8:30-31; 10:1-33; 15:7-11).

18-19a—The introduction to the disciples' testimony continues with more leading questions. So far the reader does not know what they were discussing, and **Cleopas's** question implies that it would be obvious to anyone who knew anything what any two people would be discussing on this extended walk. His assumption makes sense in the story since the only things that **have happened** (vv. 14, 18) in the world of the narrative are Jesus' death and resurrection. Luke may also intend that all Jerusalem also knew how momentous these events were, but the larger portion of his narrative suggests that tragically they did not know what they were doing (23:34). Only the disciples of Jesus who "stood at a distance and saw these things" (23:49) appeared to grasp that something signficant had happened. Thus, like the crowds at Pentecost or the Ethopian eunuch (Acts 2:12; 8:31),

Cleopas's question presses the connection between events and interpretation, between what has happened and what it means.

19b-24—This speech is given by both disciples, although Cleopas appears to be the leader (see Peter and John in Acts 3:1, 4, 11, 12; 4:1, 13, 19). It is almost a mission proclamation like the speeches in Acts, since it recounts the events of Jesus' ministry, execution, and even the report that he is alive. This is a testimony of "witnesses" (see 24:48; Acts 1:8), even two witnesses (see 10:1), but only Jesus and the reader know the truth which these recounted events reveal. Jesus' identity as **a prophet** is a lofty role, fully worthy of him (see the discussion at 7:11-17), and his power in **word and deed** has demonstrated for those who can "see and hear" that he is truly God's prophet fulfilling the scriptural promises (7:16, 39; 9:8, 19, see the discussion at 7:22). Indeed he is "the prophet like Moses" raised up by God (see Acts 3:22, and see discusison at 9:51), and his mission has been conducted in the presence of God and the people (see 1:6; 20:26; see also 22:53). There is no shortage of public data. Only the truth is lacking, because they now see Jesus' ministry as a failed mission.

Our chief priests and rulers are held most accountable for Jesus' death (see the discussions at 9:22; 22:2, 4), but the disciples are implicated along with **our** leaders (see the discussion of Peter in 22:54-62). The key sentence in v. 21, therefore, is both a lament of **our** failed hopes for **Israel's redemption** and a confession of faithlessness. This **redemption** is not a naked nationalism, but it is the profound faith of the righteous (see the discussions at 2:25, 38; 23:51). In Acts 26:6-7, 23, Paul's faith in God's promises to Israel rests on the resurrection of Jesus (see also Acts 24:21). God's will and ability to fulfill the promises of redemption and renewal of Israel's vocation as light to the nations (Acts 1:6-8; 13:47; 26:18) have been tested by a contrary and disbelieving humanity.

The report of the **women** of the empty **tomb** and the **vision of angels** links this story back to 24:1-12, but the disbelief of 24:11 is still dominant. The irony, however, is now more poignant as these two "witnesses" report to Jesus, whom they do not recognize, that the women "did not see" Jesus (also Peter in 24:12).

Amazement, wonder, and disbelief are not the same as mockery and unbelief, but they are filled with their own pathos. The tension is high in the narrative, because Jesus and the reader can see and understand.

25-27—Jesus' reproof of their disbelief still does not correct their eyesight. His rhetorical question is a restatement of the passion predictions concerning the necessity of the suffering of the Son of man (9:22, 44; 17:25; 18:31) or the suffering prophet (13:31-35), but now Jesus has been crucified as the "Messiah of God, his Chosen One," the "King of the Jews" and "righteous One" (23:2-3, 35, 38, 39, 47). The risen Jesus' few words in this passage encompass an extensive exposition of **all that the prophets have spoken** and **the things concerning himself in all the scriptures.**

It is tempting to guess which passages of the Scriptures are implied, but the lack of a specific allusion or citation (see also vv. 32 and 45) appears to be intentional. Many interpreters have suggested that Luke knew that there was no specific scriptural passage which spoke of a suffering Messiah or Christ, but Luke does not seem to be groping for a "proof text." In Acts 4 Luke declares the fulfillment of Psalm 2, identifying the adversaries of the servant-Messiah. This could have been a major resource if Luke felt pressed for a passage about a suffering Messiah. But the evangelist does not cite that passage here. In Acts 8, Isaiah 53 is clearly fulfilled in Jesus' death, although no title is given (see also Acts 3:22-23 on the rejection of Jesus as prophet of Deut. 18:15). The "glory" of the Messiah into which Jesus has now entered will be further confirmed upon him in his exaltation as ruler of heaven and earth, as Christ and Lord (Acts 2:36).

The point here is that the risen Messiah undertakes a reinterpretation of **all the scriptures.** This moment is marked as the beginning of a kind of "messianic exegesis," or post-Easter reading of the Scriptures. In Luke's story, Jesus' passion predictions anticipated such reinterpretation, but this revelation was "concealed from them" until Jesus opened their eyes (see 9:45; 24:16, 31). When confessed by Peter as "Messiah of God," Jesus spoke immediately of the necessary suffering of the Son of man

(9:20-22), and Luke clearly emphasized Jesus' dying as "the Messiah of God" (22:67; 23:2,35,39; see also Acts 4:26-27; 10:36-38). A major theme in Acts will be the dispute among the people of Israel on how to understand the Scriptures, and Luke's maintains that because the people have not understood God's will and plan they have fulfilled the Scriptures by condemning Jesus (see Acts 13:27).

28-29—Luke's narrative interest continues, and the drama is heightened as the disciples—still unaware—urge their hospitality on this stranger who is Jesus (see Gen. 19:1-3 and Heb. 13:2). They are the faithful of Israel, and they are about to be blessed.

30-32—The revelation of Jesus' presence occurs with the "taking" and "breaking" of **bread,** in clear reminiscence of the last supper (22:19). This is not a complete Christian observance of the feast which Jesus instituted, but this meal fellowship with the risen Messiah is an event of great symbolic significance for the Christian evangelist. Luke does not explain how Jesus became the host of the feast, but he is in charge and the passive voice **(their eyes were opened)** again testifies to divine activity (see 2 Kings 6:17, "The Lord opened the eyes of the young man, and he saw"). Jesus' disappearance from their sight is further demonstration of divine activity in the presence of humans (see 2 Macc. 3:34). Luke does not speculate on where Jesus went, because the point is that he was given to them to see and then to recognize. Then they recall how their **hearts** were affected by the scriptural teaching he had been doing (v. 27). The **heart** is once more the seat of belief or doubt and of pondering the truth (see 1:51,66; 2:19,35,51; 3:15; 5:22; 9:47; 24:25). Luke's narrative testifies that it is in the light of Easter that the disciples begin to understand anew how all of **the Scriptures** bear witness to Jesus and how Jesus' teaching is the definitive interpretation.

33-35—These verses summarize the story at the same time that they bring the focus back to Jerusalem. The mention of **the eleven** indicates the absence of Judas (see Acts 1:17, 26) and demonstrates that neither Cleopas nor his companion was one of the "twelve apostles" (see 9:1,10; Acts 2:14). The appearance to Simon was an event which was a crucial aspect of the earliest recitations of resurrection appearances (1 Cor. 15:5), although Luke only mentions it without telling the story. The report of the women of the empty tomb was not believed (v. 11), but now this story is related to the eleven along with the appearance to Simon. Will it be believed? Will it be understood? Luke moves quickly into the final appearance story (vv. 36-53).

The Messiah's Final Appearance, Commission of the Witnesses, and Departure (24:36-53)

These 18 verses are virtually one story, although the text is usually divided at v. 44. The length of the chapter may disguise the fact that Luke has narrated only three appearance stories, all occurring on one long day. The three stories repeat the themes of the disbelief of the disciples (vv. 11, 25, 41) and the fulfillment of Jesus' words and the Scriptures (vv. 6-9, 27 and 32, 44-47). They repeatedly depict the emotions of fear, sadness, and joy (vv. 5, 17, 37, and 41). Luke's literary hand is also evident in the structure or form of each episode as an epiphany or, more precisely, an angelophany and two Christophany stories. The themes of "seeing" the risen Christ and "hearing" him interpret the Scriptures resolve the tension in Luke's larger narrative over human blindness and deafness to the will of God.

In the birth stories (Chaps. 1–2), Luke constructed a parallel between the stories of John and Jesus which emphasized God's consistent fulfillment of scriptural patterns and promises. In the story of Cornelius in Acts 10–11 and 15, he will underscore the theme of divine initiative by means of a threefold rehearsal of the details of Peter's encounter. Luke is fond of repetitions. Here he tells two stories in parallel where (a) Jesus' appearance is either unrecognized (24:15-24) or the cause of consternation (vv. 36-37); (b) Jesus presses the disciples with a leading question and declaration (vv. 25-26, 38-41); (c) he verifies his words and presence by an appeal to the Scriptures (vv. 27, 44-45); (d) he participates in a meal with his disciples (vv. 30 and 35, 42-43); and (e) his dramatic departure leads to testimony by the disciples (vv. 31 and 35, 49-53). Luke's consistent conviction is that "God has brought to Israel a Savior, as he promised" (Acts 13:23), and the resurrection is emphatically God's act which transforms human blindness and unbelief into the restoration of Israel's mission to be witnesses to God's gracious reign.

The discussion of Chaps. 1–2 suggested that they are the overture to the narrative and the speeches in Acts are the reprise. Jesus' words in Luke 24 also require the reader to understand the resurrection of Jesus as God's explication of all that the Law, Prophets, and Psalms of Israel's Scriptures have attested. Luke's presentation of the resurrection, therefore, marks a fulfillment of Israel's Scriptures which will be explicated more directly in the speeches in Acts. Above all, it is a testimony to "the good news that what God promised to the fathers, this he has fulfilled to us their children by raising Jesus" (Acts 13:32-33). The "Savior" born in the city of David, Christ the Lord, is indeed "the consolation of Israel" and "the redemption of Jerusalem" for which the faithful have yearned.

Luke declared to his own times that God has not abandoned the promises made to the people of Israel. If it is correct that by Luke's times the dire oracles of Jerusalem's destruction have already been fulfilled (see the discussion of 19:41-44; 21:20-24), this testimony to the constancy of "the promise of my Father" (v. 49) is a profound assurance connecting the resurrection with the restored presence of the Holy Spirit with Israel. This is not a simple plot, even for God, but the resurrection is God's decisive act. In raising Jesus, God has demonstrated righteousness in the face of rejection of God's reign (v. 46), given repentance to sinful humanity (v. 47), restored Israel's election to be "witnesses to the nations" (vv. 47-50), and revealed the definitive character of the kingdom in the exaltation of Jesus (vv. 50-52).

In this extended episode, Luke brings this narrative to its conclusion and lays the foundation for his story of the early Christian mission in Acts. He demonstrates the reality of the resurrection of the Messiah Jesus (vv. 36-43) which is central to the preaching of Acts. He emphasizes that the resurrection of Jesus marks the restoration of Israel's calling to bear witness to God's reign among the nations (vv. 44-49), and he reports Jesus' departure (vv. 50-53) which he will elaborate in the narrative of Acts and explicate as Jesus' exaltation in the speeches of Acts.

36-43—These verses include several details which are paralleled in the resurrection appearances of John 20:19-29. The possibility of literary dependence cannot be excluded, but it appears more likely that both Luke and John are reporting details of the common tradition which emphasize that the resurrected Jesus was embodied although his body was also altered. He could be touched, and he ate with his disciples. This is a story of the resurrection of the body and not an apparition or a mere spiritual presence which could be sensed. In Acts 1:3-4, Luke spoke of Jesus "presenting himself alive . . . with many proofs" and "staying with" his disciples for "forty days," which some early versions understood to say "eating with his disciples" (see also Acts 10:41). Luke's point is that Jesus' resurrected body was palpably present on that first day (Luke 24) and for 40 days (Acts 1) when Jesus chose to make himself manifest.

The consternation and fear of the disciples (v. 37) are appropriate to epiphany stories, but Jesus interprets them as unbelief, or at least as misunderstanding. They are the occasion for his instruction in the **flesh and bones** character of the resurrected body (v. 39). This emphasis is consistent with Pharisaic understanding of resurrection of the body (see the discussion at 20:27-45 and see Acts 23:6-9; 24:15-21; Dan. 12:2). For Luke, preaching "Jesus and the resurrection" is fundamental to proclaiming that Jesus is the Messiah (see Acts 2:36; 3:26; 9:22; 17:18). Jesus did not survive his execution. His physical presence is the fulfillment of the hope of the resurrection of the righteous, which is a hope in God's justice. The "proofs" of resurrection would be especially crucial to those in Israel who understood resurrection as a theodicy, a vindication of God's justice in history as well as beyond it. Those who perpetrate violence and murder do not have the last word, and the reign of Jesus is established as the kingdom of God.

Jesus' self-presentation, **"It is I,"** is an identification formula generally reserved for God or divine agents (see John 6:20, 35, 48, 51, etc.). This is also a testimony that the risen Christ is the Jesus who suffered. Although Luke does not mention the marks of crucifixion on Jesus' hands and feet as in John 20:40, which is omitted in some manuscripts and modern versions, it should be included. In v. 40 Jesus' display of his hands and feet implies his wounds. Their "disbelief for joy" is still unbelief, but it is the incredulity of those who believe that "nothing is impossible for God," as Mary did at the beginning of the narrative (1:34-38). The line between "unbelief" and "disbelief" even among the faithful had been carefully discerned in the angel's responses to Zechariah (1:20) and Mary (1:38). In this appearance, the risen Christ evokes joy and faith.

44-49—These verses are a summary of the whole narrative which drives forward to the mission of the early church in Acts. On the lips of the risen Christ, the declarations of vv. 44 and 46-49 offer a retrospect on the story Luke has just told. Jesus is testifying again (see also v. 27) how the preceding story is to be interpreted as a fulfillment of God's scriptural promises and why the narrative of Acts must follow. In Acts 1:1-5, Luke speaks for himself on the coherence of the whole story until he slips into a quote of Jesus in 1:4b-5. Jesus' last words in the Gospel narrative, therefore, are more easily understood as Luke's declaration of how to read the story in the light of the resurrection.

These words in v. 44 are a reference to "all that Jesus began to do and teach" in this "first book" (see Acts 1:1). Jesus is not anticipating what he is about to say, and certainly the preceding verses are emphatic that he was bodily **still with you** as he spoke. The risen Messiah is again testifying that in order to understand "the things concerning himself" in Luke's narrative, the faithful must read the Scriptures (see v. 27). There was no fixed "canon" in the first century, and certainly no "Bible" or one-volume codex. But the books of Moses (the Torah), the collected prophetic writings (with or without Daniel), and the broader collection of "writings" had attained considerable stability as **the scriptures.** Luke's collection itemizes **the law, the prophets,** and **the psalms,** offering one of the earliest identifications of **the scriptures** as taken together.

Luke's Jesus declares that all the sacred books bore witness to the death and resurrection of the Messiah as God's way of fulfilling the promises. The way of suffering, death, and vindication is the way of God's kingdom and king. This is more a messianic theology of the Scriptures than an argument from a particular passage or collection of passages. Luke does not appeal to a specific passage as testifying that the anointed one must suffer (see the comments above on 24:25-27). The argument is more formal, declaring Jesus' death and resurrection to be the key to understanding God's will in all the Scriptures. The speeches in Acts will develop specific scriptural arguments concerning the "definite plan and fore-knowledge of God" (Acts 2:23), but the strangeness of God's ruling through a crucified Messiah must not be missed (see 1 Cor. 1:21-25). The crucifixion and resurrection can only be understood within God's will and plan by reading the Scriptures, and the Scriptures acquire new meaning for the reader when it is seen how they testify to this remarkable strategy of the kingdom.

Verse 47 indicates the consequence of the crucifixion and resurrection of Jesus, and God's reign displays astounding grace. It is not difficult to believe that God's judgment or vengeance would follow such a heinous act (see the discussion at vv. 48-49), but the righteousness of God's reign has been fulfilled in mercy, not destruction (see 23:34). The policy of God's kingdom of **forgiveness** must now be promulgated. The passive voice in this case means that **you witnesses** are to be the agents of this proclamation, but the urgency and authority come from God's Messiah. When the RSV says **preached,** the English word may be too limited to churchly settings. This is the language of public declaration to all nations. Of course this is exactly what Peter "preaches" in Acts, leading the Jewish crowd to be "cut to the heart" (Acts 2:37). Thus Christian "preaching" is public declaration in the sight of all the nations.

The "witness" terminology derives from Isaiah and will be thematic to the book of Acts. It is one of the richest examples of Luke's scriptural theology in which Jesus' commission to his disciples becomes the restoration of Israel's mission. The crucial passages are in Isaiah 40–55, especially 41:21—44:8 where the nations of the world are called as witnesses in the court of the Lord and the people of Israel are God's witnesses in the court of world opinion. In Isaiah 49:6, God's call of the witnesses becomes Israel's greatest blessing, exceeding even the restoration of the return from exile. This commission to be the "light to the nations, that my salvation may reach to the end of the earth" will provide the basis for Jesus' last words on earth in Acts 1:8. Matthew 28:18-20 identifies the mission to the nations and the promise of divine power with discipleship and John 20:21-23 links the gift of the Holy Spirit with the forgiveness of sins. Luke develops these same convictions in terms of Isaiah's testimony that the height of Israel's restoration is the renewal of her call as God's witnesses.

In Isaiah's theology (see 40:2), even the "forgiveness of sins" is a thoroughly public event by which God restores the future of Israel. So also, Peter's sermon in Acts is a hopeful call to "all the house of Israel" to repentance. Jesus' death does not mean that God has withdrawn the Holy Spirit, effecting Israel's desolation. By raising Jesus as Messiah and Lord, God has restored the promise "to you and to your children and to all that are far off" (Acts 2:38-39). The witnesses to the resurrection are witnesses to God's will and reign of justice and mercy (see Acts 1:8, 22; 2:32; 3:15; 4:33; 5:32; 10:37-43; 13:31; 22:15, 20; 26:16), and they are often required to bear their testimony in public courts, equipped only with the testimony which the Spirit gives them (21:12-19, and see the trials in Acts).

These verses thus anticipate the whole book of Acts in which the Holy Spirit is sent to authorize the "twelve" as a nucleus of faithful Israel restored in witness. The mission begins "from Jerusalem" and moves to the nations and "the end of the earth" after passing through Judea and Samaria (Acts 1:8). Here the risen Christ anticipates those events, indicating that the authorization of the Holy Spirit which will follow is exactly the continuing policy of the kingdom of God and of God's Messiah.

"The promise of my Father" is the fulfillment of the hopes of the faithful for "the consolation of Israel" (2:25), the "redemption of Jerusalem" (2:38), "the kingdom of God" (23:51), and the "redeeming of Israel" (24:21). This will not be accomplished for these disciples until Jesus has been exalted and the Holy Spirit has been sent to authorize the renewal of Israel's vocation. The "promise of my Father" or "the promise of the Father" (Acts 1:4) is a scriptural promise of the pouring out of the Spirit on Israel (see Joel 2:28-29; Isa. 32:15; 44:3; Ezek. 39:29). It will be fulfilled quite specifically at Pentecost (see Acts 2:16).

50-53—Jesus' departure with his blessing appears to be a kind of priestly benediction (see Sir. 50:20-21; Lev. 9:22), but the whole story stresses his role as Messiah, prophet, and ruler rather than priest. The sacral character of the moment is Luke's concern, especially with his depiction of a sudden disappearance (see the comments on v. 31) while he is "carried into heaven" accompanied by the worship of the faithful (following the best manuscript readings of vv. 51 and 52). This story is a complete exaltation or assumption story, which may be compared with Acts 1:1-11. Many intepreters regard Acts 1 as a retelling of this story with more detail and a different timetable. But preoccupations with reconciling the accounts may miss that Jesus also disappeared—whether to heaven or not—in v. 31. This version appears to be only partial fulfillment of the "departure" or "exodus" which Moses and Elijah anticipated in 9:31 and which Jesus undertook in his journey to his passion (see discussion at 9:51).

Perhaps it is again best to regard Jesus' Easter evening **parting,** even his being **carried up into heaven,** as a foreshadowing of Pentecost. Luke's narrative has reached the end of "the first book," and the faithful **return** to worship **in the temple,** as at the beginning. **The temple** will continue to be a central location for encounters with God and conflicts with the religious leaders (see Acts 2:46; 3:1; 5:42; 21:27). But the story is only at an interlude. Jesus will continue to appear to them "during forty days speaking of the kingdom of God" (Acts 1:3) until he is exalted on a cloud into heaven to dominion (Acts 1:9-10; 2:36). That exaltation will belong more properly to the story of Acts. It will be the first step in the next phase of God's mission of righteousness and mercy in the restoration of Israel and the giving of repentance to the nations.

The promises of God have not failed. The reign of God has been renewed through the exaltation of the Messiah, and the commission of his apostles has been restored in terms of Israel's ancient calling: to be witnesses to this Messiah and his righteous reign to the ends of the earth.

SELECTED BIBLIOGRAPHY

Research Reports and Bibliographies

Bovon, François. *Luc le théologien: Vingt-cinq ans de recherches (1950—1975)*. Neuchatel/Paris: Delachaux et Niestlé, 1978.

Kodell, Jerome. "The Theology of Luke in Recent Study." *BTB* 1 (1971): 115-144.

Kuemmel, W. G. "Current Theological Accusations against Luke." *ANQ* 16 (1975): 131-145. Translated by William C. Robinson Jr.

Marshall, I. H. "Recent Study of the Gospel according to St. Luke. *ET* 80 (1968/1969): 4-8.

Talbert, Charles H. "Shifting Sands: The Recent Study of the Gospel of Luke." *Interp.* 30 (1976): 381-395.

Commentaries

Caird, G. B. *The Gospel of St. Luke*. Pelican Bible Commentaries. Baltimore: Penguin, 1963.

Creed, J. M. *The Gospel according to St. Luke*. London: Macmillan, 1930.

Danker, Frederick W. *Jesus and the New Age*. St. Louis: Clayton Publishing House, 1972.

Ellis, E. Earle. *The Gospel of Luke New Century Bible*. Greenwood, S.C.: Attic Press, 1974.

Fitzmyer, Joseph A. *The Gospel according to Luke I–IX*. Garden City, N.Y.: Doubleday, 1981. *The Gospel according to Luke X–XXIV*. 1985. The Anchor Bible, volumes 28 and 28a.

Grundmann, Walter. *Das Evangelium nach Lukas*. 6th ed. Berlin: Evangelische Verlaganstalt, 1971.

Karris, Robert J. *Invitation to Luke: A Commentary on the Gospel of Luke with Complete Text from the Jerusalem Bible*. Garden City, N.Y.: Doubleday, 1977.

Marshall, I. Howard. *The Gospel of Luke: A Commentary on the Greek Text*. Grand Rapids: Eerdmans, 1978.

Schuermann, Heinz. *Das Lukasevangelium. Erster Teil, Kommentar zu Kap. 1:1—9:50*. Herders Theologischer Kommentar zum NT 3. Freiburg: Herder, 1969.

Schweizer, Eduard. *The Good News according to Luke*. Translated by David Green. Atlanta: John Knox, 1984.

Talbert, Charles H. *Reading Luke: A Literary and Theological Commentary on the Third Gospel*. New York: Crossroad, 1982.

Tannehill, Robert C. *The Narrative Unity of Luke-Acts: A Literary Interpretation*. Vol. 1, *Luke*. Philadelphia: Fortress, 1986.

Studies

Achtemeier, Paul J. "The Lucan Perspective on the Miracles of Jesus." *JBL* 94 (1975): 547-562.

Ballard, P. H. "Reasons for Refusing the Great Supper." *JThS* 23 (1972): 341-350.

Baltzer, Klaus. "The Meaning of the Temple in the Lukan Writings." *HTR* 58 (1965): 263-277.

Bammel, E., editor. *The Trial of Jesus*. Cambridge Studies in Honour of C.F.D. Moule. SBT 2/13. London: SCM; Naperville, IL: Allenson, 1970.

Barraclough, R. "A Re-Assessment of Luke's Political Perspective." *RTR* (1979): 10-18.

Barrett, C. K. *Luke the Historian in Recent Study*. Facet Books, Biblical Series 24. Philadelphia: Fortress, 1970.

Braumann, Georg. "Die lukanishce Interpretation der Zerstoerung Jerusalems." *NovTest* 6 (1963): 120-127.

Brodie, T. L. "A New Temple and a New Law: The Unity and Chronicler-Based Nature of Luke 1:1—4:22a." *JSNT* 5 (1979): 21-25.

Selected Bibliography

Brown, Schuyler. *Apostasy and Perseverance in the Theology of Luke*. Analecta Biblica 36. Rome: Pontifical Biblical Institute, 1969.

Cadbury, Henry J. *The Making of Luke Acts*. London: SPCK, 1961; first published, 1927.

Cadbury, Henry J. *The Style and Literary Method of Luke*. Harvard Theological Studies 6. Cambridge: Harvard University, 1920.

Cassidy, Richard J. *Jesus, Politics and Society: A Study of Luke's Gospel*. Maryknoll, N.Y.: Orbis, 1978.

Conzelmann, Hans. *The Theology of St. Luke*. Translated by Geoffrey Buswell. London: Farber and Farber, 1960.

Cosgrove, Charles H. "The Divine 'dei' in Luke-Acts." *NovTest* 26 (1984): 168-190.

Crockett, Larrimore C. *The Old Testament in the Gospel of Luke*. Brown University Doctoral Dissertation. Ann Arbor, Mich.: University Microfilms, 1966.

Danker, Frederick W. *Luke*. 2nd ed. Proclamation Commentaries, Gerhard Krodel, editor. Philadelphia: Fortress, 1987.

Davies, J. H. "The Prefigurement of the Ascension in the Third Gospel." *JThS* ns. 6 (1985): 229-233.

Dibelius, Martin. *Studies in the Acts of the Apostles*. Translated by Mary Ling. Edited by Heinrich Greeven. London: SCM, 1956.

Dodd, C. H. *The Parables of the Kingdom*. New York: Scribner's, 1961.

Edwards, O. C. *Luke's Story of Jesus*. Philadelphia: Fortress, 1981.

Ellis, E. Earle. *Eschatology in Luke*. Facet Book, Biblical Series 30. Philadelphia: Fortress, 1972.

Francis, F. O. "Eschatology and History in Luke-Acts." *JAAR* 37 (1969): 49-63.

Franklin, Eric. "The Ascension and the Eschatology of Luke-Acts." *SJTh* 23 (1970): 191-200.

Franklin, Eric. *Christ the Lord: A Study in the Purpose and Theology of Luke-Acts*. Philadelphia: Westminster, 1975.

Gaston, Lloyd. *No Stone on Another: Studies in the Significance of the Fall of Jerusalem in the Synoptic Gospels*. Suppl. to *NovTest* 23. Leiden: E. J. Brill, 1970.

George, Augustin. "Israel dans l'oeuvre de Luc," *RB* 75 (1968): 481-525.

Haenchen, Ernst. *The Acts of the Aposltes.* Translation revised by R. McL. Wilson. Philadelphia: Westminster, 1971.

Hiers, R. "The Problem of the Delay of the Parousia in Luke-Acts." *NTS* 20 (1974): 145-155.

Hooker, Morna D. *Jesus and the Servant.* Cambridge: At the University Press, 1959.

Hultgren, Arland J. "Interpreting the Gospel of Luke." *Interp.* 30 (1976): 353-365.

_____. *Jesus and His Adversaries.* Minneapolis: Augsburg, 1979.

Jervell, Jacob. *Luke and the People of God.* Minneapolis: Augsburg, 1972.

_____. "The Mighty Minority." In *The Unknown Paul,* pp.26-51. Minneapolis: Augsburg, 1984.

Johnson, Luke T. *The Literary Function of Possessions in Luke-Acts.* SBLDS 39. Missoula, Mont.: Scholars Press, 1977.

Jones, Donald L. "The Title 'Christos' in Luke-Acts." *CBQ* 32 (1970): 69-76.

Juel, Donald. *Luke-Acts: The Promise of History.* Atlanta: John Knox, 1983.

_____. "The Image of the Servant-Christ in the New Testament." *SWJT* 21 (1979): 7-22.

Karris, Robert J. "Missionary Communities: A New Paradigm for the Study of Luke-Acts." *CBQ* 41 (1979): 80-97.

Keck, Leander E. "The Poor among the Saints in the New Testament." *ZNW* 56 (1965): 100-129.

Keck, Leander E. and J. Louis Martyn, editors. *Studies in Luke-Acts: Essays Presented in Honor of Paul Schubert.* Nashville: Abingdon, 1966.

Krodel, Gerhard A. *Acts.* Augsburg Commentary on the New Testament. Minneapolis: Augsburg, 1986.

Kurz, William S. "Hellenistic Rhetoric in the Christological Proof of Luke-Acts." *CBQ* 42 (1980): 171-195.

Lampe, G. W. H. "The Holy Spirit in the Writings of St. Luke." In *Studies in the Gospels: Essays in Memory of R. H. Lightfoot,*

Selected Bibliography

pp. 159-200. Edited by D. E. Nineham. Oxford: Blackwell, 1955.

Lindars, Barnabas. *Jesus Son of Man*. Grand Rapids: Eerdmans, 1984.

_____. *New Testament Apologetic: The Doctrinal Significance of the Old Testament Quotations*. Philadelphia: Westminster, 1961.

Lohfink, G. *Die Sammlung Israels: Eine Untersuchung zur lukanischen Ecclesiologie*. StANT 39. Muenchen: Koesel-Verlag, 1975.

Manek, Jindrich. "The New Exodus in the Book of Luke." *NovTest* 2 (1957): 8-23.

Marshall, I. H. *Luke: Historian and Theologian*. Grand Rapids: Zondervan, 1970.

Mattill, A. J., Jr. "The Jesus-Paul Parallels and the Purpose of Luke-Acts: H. H. Evans Reconsidered." *NovTest* 17 (1975): 15-46.

Minear, Paul S. "Jesus' Audiences, according to Luke." *NovTest* 16 (1974): 81-109.

_____. *To Heal and to Reveal: The Prophetic Vocation according to Luke*. New York: Seabury, 1976.

Moessner, David P. " 'The Christ Must Suffer': New Light on the Jesus–Peter, Stephen, Paul Parallels in Luke-Acts." *NovTest* 28 (1986): 220-256.

Moule, C. F. D. "The Christology of Acts." In *Studies in Luke-Acts.*, pp. 159-185. Edited by Leander E. Keck and J. Louis Martyn. Nashville: Abingdon, 1966.

MacRae, George W. " 'Whom Heaven Must Receive until the Time': Reflections on the Christology of Acts." *Interp.* 27 (1973): 151-165.

Nickelsburg, George. "Riches, The Rich and God's Judgment in I Enoch 92–105 and the Gospel according to Luke." *NTS* 25 (1978–1979): 324-344.

Reicke, Bo. "Synoptic Prophecies on the Destruction of Jerusalem." In *Studies in New Testament and Early Christian Literature*. Essays in Honor of Allen Wikgren. Edited by D. Aune. Leiden: E. J. Brill, 1972.

Sanders, Jack T. "The Pharisees in Luke-Acts." In *The Living Text: Essays in Honor of Ernest W. Saunders*, pp. 141-188. Edited by Dennis E. Groh and Robert Jewett. New York: University Press of America: 1985.

Sanders, Jack T. "The Prophetic Use of the Scriptures in Luke-Acts." In *Early Jewish and Christian Exegesis: Studies in Memory of William Hugh Brownlee*, pp. 191-198. Edited by C. A. Evans and W. J. Stinespring. Atlanta: Scholars Press, 1987.

Smalley, S. S. "Spirit, Kingdom and Prayer in Luke-Acts," *NovTest* 15 (1973): 59-71.

Swartley, Willard M. "Politics and Peace *(Eirēnē)* in Luke's Gospel." In *Political Issues in Luke-Acts*, pp. 18-37. Edited by Richard J. Cassidy and Philip J. Scharper. Maryknoll: Orbis, 1983.

Tannehill, Robert C. "Israel in Luke-Acts: A Tragic Story." *JBL* 104 (1985): 69-85.

Tiede, David L. *Prophecy and History in Luke-Acts.* Philadelphia: Fortress, 1980.

Wainwright, Arthur W. "Luke and the Restoration of the Kingdom to Israel." *ET* 89 (1977): 76-79.

Walaskay, Paul W. 'And So We Came to Rome!' *The Political Perspective of St. Luke.* Cambridge: At the University Press, 1983.

Wilson, S. G. *The Gentiles and the Gentile Mission in Luke-Acts.* SNTSMS 23. Cambridge: At the University Press, 1973.

————. *Luke and the Law.* SNTSMS 50. Cambridge: At the University Press, 1983.

Zehnle, Richard. "The Salvific Character of Jesus' Death in Lucan Soteriology." *ThSt* 30 (1969): 420-444.

Ziesler, J. A. "Luke and the Pharisees." *NTS* 25 (1978–1979): 146-157.

Bibliographical Additions by Major Sections

Introduction

Beck, B. E. "The Common Authorship of Luke and Acts," *NTS* 23 (1976–1977): 346-352.

Cadbury, Henry J. "The Greek and Jewish Traditions of Writing History." In *The Beginnings of Christianity, Part I: The Acts*

Selected Bibliography

of the Apostles, pp. 7-29. Edited by F. J. Foakes-Jackson and Kirsopp Lake. 1922. Grand Rapids: Baker, 1979.

Dahl, Nils Alstrup. "The Purpose of Luke-Acts." In *Jesus in the Memory of the Early Church,* pp. 87-98. Minneapolis: Augsburg, 1976.

Harnack, Adolf. *Luke the Physician.* New York: G. P. Putnam's Sons, 1908.

Hobart, W. K. *The Medical Language of St. Luke.* Dublin: Hodges, Figgis; London: Longmans, Green, 1882.

Mattill, A. J. Jr. "The Date and Purpose of Luke-Acts: Rackham Reconsidered." *CBQ* 40 (1978): 335-350.

Richard, Earl. "The Old Testament in Acts: Wilcox's Semitisms in Retrospect." *CBQ* 42 (1980): 330-341.

Stagg, Frank. "Establishing a Text for Luke-Acts." In *Society of Biblical Literature Seminar Papers,* pp. 45-58. Missoula: Scholars Press, 1977.

Talbert, Charles H. *Literary Patterns, Theological Themes and the Genre of Luke-Acts.* SBLMS 20. Missoula: Scholars Press, 1975.

Taylor, Vincent. *Behind the Third Gospel: A Study of the Proto-Luke Hypothesis.* Oxford: Clarendon, 1926.

Vööbus, Arthur. "A New Approach to the Problem of the Shorter and Longer Text in Luke." *NTS* 15 (1969): 457-463.

1:1—2:52

Brown, Raymond E. *The Birth of the Messiah: A Commentary on the Infancy Narrative in Matthew and Luke.* Garden City, N.Y.: Doubleday, 1977.

Cadbury, Henry J. "The Purpose Expressed in Luke's Preface." *The Expositor,* Series 8, 11 (1921): 437-441.

Dillon, Richard J. "Previewing Luke's Project from His Prologue (Luke 1:1-4)." *CBQ* 43 (1981): 221-222.

Luther, Martin. *The Magnificat.* Translated by A. T. W. Steinhaeuser. *Luther's Works* 21, pp. 295-358. St. Louis: Concordia, 1956.

Minear, Paul S. "Luke's Use of the Birth Stories." In *Studies in Luke-Acts,* pp. 111-130. Edited by Leander E. Keck and J. Louis Martyn. Nashville: Abingdon, 1960.

Oliver, H. H. "The Lucan Birth Stories and the Purpose of Luke-Acts." *NTS* 10 (1964): 202-226.

Pilgrim, Walter E. *Good News to the Poor: Wealth and Poverty in Luke-Acts.* Minneapolis: Augsburg, 1981.

Pluemacher, Eckhard. *Lukas als hellenistischer Schriftsteller.* Studien zur Umwelt des Neuen Testaments 9. Göttingen: Vandenhoeck & Ruprecht, 1972.

Rese, Martin. *Alttestamentliche Motive in der Christologie des Lukas.* Studien zum Neuen Testament 1. Gutersloh: Gerd Mohn, 1969.

Talbert, Charles H. "Prophecies of Future Greatness: The Contribution of Greco-Roman Biographies to an Understanding of Luke 1:5—4:15." In *The Divine Helmsman: Studies on God's Control of Human Events, Presented to Lou H. Silberman,* pp. 129-141. Edited by James L. Crenshaw and Samuel Sandmel. New York: KTAV, 1980.

Tatum, W. B. "The Epoch of Israel: Luke 1-2 and the Theological Plan of Luke-Acts." *NTS* 13 (1967): 184-195.

3:1—9:50

Anderson, Hugh. "Broadening Horizons; the Rejection at Nazareth Pericope of Luke 4:16-30 in Light of Recent Critical Trends." *Interp.* 18 (1964): 259-275.

Brodie, T. L. "Towards Unraveling Luke's Use of the Old Testament: Luke 7:11-17 as an *Imitatio* of 1 Kings 17:17-24." *NTS* 32 (1986): 247-267.

————. "Luke 7:36-50 as an Internalization of 2 Kings 4:1-37: A Study in Luke's Use of Rhetorical Imitation." *Biblica* 64 (1983): 457-485.

Crockett, Larrimore C. "Luke 4:16-30 and the Jewish Lectionary Cycle: A Word of Caution." *JJS* 17 (1966): 13-46.

————. "Luke 4:25-27 and Jewish–Gentile Relations in Luke-Acts." *JBL* 88 (1969): 177-183.

Kurz, William S. "Luke 3:23-38 and Greco-Roman and Biblical Genealogies." In *Luke-Acts: New Perspectives from the Society of Biblical Literature,* pp. 169-187. Edited by Charles H. Talbert. New York: Crossroad, 1984.

Selected Bibliography

Sanders, James A. "From Isaiah 61 to Luke 4." In *Christianity, Judaism, and Other Greco-Roman Cults: Studies for Morton Smith at Sixty*. Part One, New Testament, pp. 75-106. Edited by Jacob Neusner. Leiden: E. J. Brill, 1975.

Tannehill, Robert C. "The Mission of Jesus according to Luke 4:16-30." In *Jesus in Nazareth*, pp. 51-75. Edited by Walter Eltester. Beiheft zur ZNW. Berlin: de Gruyter, 1972.

9:51—19:27

Betz, Hans Dieter. "The Cleansing of the Ten Lepers (Lk 17:11-19)." *JBL* 90 (1971): 314-328.

Davies, J. H. "The Purpose of the Central Secion of St. Luke's Gospel." *Studia Evangelica* 2 (=TU87) (1964): 164-169.

Evans, C. F. "The Central Section of St. Luke's Gospel." In *Studies in the Gospels: Studies in Memory of R. H. Lightfoot*, pp. 37-53. Edited by D. E. Nineham. Oxford: Blackwell, 1955.

Evans, Craig A. "Luke's Use of the Elijah/Elisha Narratives." *JBL* 106 (1987): 75-83.

Gill, David. "Observations on the Lukan Travel Narrative and Some Related Passages." *HTR* 63 (1970): 199-221.

Moessner, David P. "Luke 9:1-50: Luke's Preview of the Journey of the Prophet Like Moses of Deuteronomy." *JBL* 102 (1983): 575-605.

Ogg, G. "The Central Section of the Gospel according to St. Luke." *NTS* 18 (1971): 39-53.

Reicke, Bo. "Instruction and Discussion in the Travel Narrative." *Studia Evangelica* 1 (=TU 73) (1959): 206-216.

Robinson, William C. "The Way of the Lord: A Study of History and Eschatology in the Gospel of Luke." Dissertation, Basel, 1962.

Sanders, James A. "The Ethic of Election in Luke's Great Banquet Parable." In *Essays in Old Testament Ethics: J. Philip Hyatt, In Memoriam*, pp. 245-271. Edited by James L. Crenshaw and John T. Willis. New York: KTAV, 1974.

Tiede, David L. "The Gospel for the Duration: The Lukan Gospel Lessons for the Pentecost Season." *Lutheran Quarterly* 26 (1974): 225-231.

19:28—21:38

Dodd, C. H. "The Fall of Jerusalem and the 'Abomination of Desolation.' " *Journal of Roman Studies* 37 (1947): 47-54. Reprinted in *More New Testament Studies,* pp. 69-83. Manchester: University Press, 1968.

Flucklinger, F. "Luke 21:20-24 und die Zerstorung Jerusalems." *Theologische Zeitschrift* 28 (1972): 385-390.

Kodell, Jerome. "Luke's Use of *laos,* 'people,' especially in the Jerusalem Narrative (Lk 19:28-24:53)." *CBQ* 31 (1969): 327-343.

Nicol, W. "Tradition and Redaction in Luke 21." *Neotestamentica* 7 (1973): 61-71.

22:1—23:56

Derrett, J. D. M. "Midrash in the New Testament: The Origin of Luke 22:67-68." *StTh* 29 (1975): 147-156.

Karris, Robert J. *Luke: Artist and Theologian: Luke's Passion Account as Literature.* New York: Paulist, 1985.

Kurz, William S. "Luke 22:14-38 and Greco-Roman and Biblical Farewell Addresses." *JBL* 104 (1985): 251-268.

Larkin, William J. "The Old Testament Background of Luke 22:43-44." *NTS* 25 (1979): 250-254.

Neyrey, Jerome. *The Passion according to Luke: A Redaction Study of Luke's Soterilogy.* New York: Paulist, 1985.

Taylor, Vincent. *The Passion Narrative of St. Luke: A Critical and Historical Investigation.* Edited by O. E. Evans. SNTSMS 19. Cambridge: At the University Press, 1972.

Tyson, Joseph B. *The Death of Jesus in Luke-Acts.* Columbia, S.C.: University of South Carolina Press, 1986.

Walaskay, Paul W. "The Trial and Death of Jesus in the Gospel of Luke." *JBL* 94 (1975): 81-93.

24:1-53

Dillon, R. J. *From Eye-Witnesses to Minsters of the Word: Tradition and Composition in Luke 24.* Analecta Biblica 82. Rome: Biblical Institute, 1978.

Kingsbury, Jack Dean. "Luke 24:44-49." *Interp.* 35 (1981): 170-174.

Schubert, Paul. "The Structure and Significance of Luke 24." *Neutestamentliche Studien für Rudolf Bultmann*, pp. 165-186. ZNW Beiheft 21. Berlin: Toepelmann, 1954.

ABOUT THE AUTHOR

Dr. David L. Tiede has been a professor of New Testament at Luther Northwestern Theological Seminary since 1971 and became president of that institution in 1987. He is a graduate of St. Olaf College (B.A., 1962), Luther Theological Seminary (B.D., 1966), and Harvard University (Ph.D., 1971). He has also studied at Princeton Theological Seminary (1962–1963) and taught at Scripps College and Claremont Graduate School (1970–1971). He has been a Rockefeller Fellow (1962–1963), a Danforth Fellow (1962–1970), Society of Biblical Literature Research Fellow at the Institute for Antiquity and Christianity (1978–1979), and a Visiting Professor of New Testament at Yale Divinity School (1986–1987). He served as a pastor (1972–1975), participated in the Lutheran–Methodist dialogues in the USA and between the World Methodist Council and the Lutheran World Federation (1979–1984). He has served on various editorial councils and published several articles and books on Luke-Acts.